ASTRA AND LUNA

Astra and Luna

**WENDY
EASTMAN**

Weastman Books

No part of this book shall be reproduced or transmitted in any form or
by any means, electronic, mechanical, magnetic,
photographic (including photocopying), recording, or any information
storage or retrieval system without prior written permission of the
author. Any resemblance to persons living or dead is coincidental.
Wendy Eastman
All rights reserved.
Revised Edition
ISBN: 9798218023959
Copyright ©April 2022

DEDICATION

This book is dedicated to anyone who has loved someone labeled "different" because your compassion shows us how to be wonderful human beings.

Special thanks to all the composers and musicians.

Your music inspires me.

Sergei Rachmaninoff, Ludwig von Beethoven, Enya, The Piano Guys, 2 Cellos, Thomas Newman, Claud Debussy, Alexandre Desplat, James Horner, and many others.

FOREWARD

Much of the unknown remains within our brains and in the universe. We can map the earth, but the vastness of the universe is impossible to plot with accuracy. It is ever-changing.

Our brains hold the same enigmatic maps; for centuries, it operates beyond our understanding. We're gaining more insight, but with insight comes more questions. What makes someone a savant and someone else marginal? What is the Island of Genius?

While I have researched this story's historical time, it is a work of fiction. I'm not an expert, or this will make a boring medical journal. My late father and I used to play the game of jeopardy; he told me, "Wendy, you're a jack-of-all-trades and a master of none." Then he'd laugh. I'd win more times than he did, yet, he didn't have much confidence in my academics; I was a marginal student, not cut out to be a teacher, a nurse, or a secretary. Thanks to my mom, I got a fine arts college degree.

This story occurs in Great Britain during the 1960s when social norms were being overthrown and data on mental illness was compiled. It could have happened anywhere during those years of self-discovery, peace, and love.

In the 1960s and 70s, I was a teenager and moving into young adulthood in America. Changes were the only certainty in life. Like Lenora McConnell and so many other women, we were questioning everything; our roles as women, exploring careers different from a teacher, nurse, or secretary, and our bodies we claimed for our own. As Bob Dylan sang, the times were changing.

Wendy Eastman

"Moonlight drowns out all but the brightest stars." J.R.R. Tolkien

EDITORIAL REVIEW

Sarah Watkins, Ph.D.
Editorial Review, *Astra and Luna*

Astra and Luna is a love story. Set over the course of the second half of the twentieth century in England, it follows the enmeshed lives of Astrid and Lenora, the titular Astra and Luna. Astrid, an autistic savant whose gifts for playing the piano present both staggering opportunities and monumental challenges, struggles to find a home in a world that values her gifts but is also harsh and daunting to her differences. Lenora, an inquisitive and energetic outcast, is immediately drawn to Astrid when they are both in primary school. Lenora's unwavering dedication to Astrid, and Astrid's attachment to Lenora, create a bond that transcends their childhood friendship, opening up a world of intimacy and hope that provides both with a safe harbor from the unpredictable and often traumatic changes in the world around them.

Astra and Luna follows the girls' journey into womanhood. All but abandoned by her family, Astrid is taken in by Lenora's mother and grandfather, who recognize Astrid's unique gifts and neurodivergence and seek out support for her in a time in which autism was even less understood and accepted than it is now. Lenora loved and prized by her family, sometimes struggles with jealousy at their attention to Astrid, but ultimately understands that Astrid needs their love and protection, especially as demands grow for her to share her amazing talent. Through boarding school, university, marriage, and a rapidly changing environment of social and sexual mores, Astrid and Lenora's love for one another ties them together, creating a lifelong bond of trust and commitment.

This story is wide-ranging in its subject matter, ranging from family and loss to the lack of systemic mental health support over the course of the twentieth century. The novel delves deeply into the uncertainty provoked by shifting social expectations, new opportunities for liberation for both women and neurodiverse people, and the pain of growing too quickly or not quickly enough for those around you. Of particular note is the three-dimensional way in which Astrid is portrayed. With compassion and sensitivity, Astrid is not simply an avatar of savantism, but a complicated young woman with frustrations, desires, and imperfect responses to a world around her that can be both breathtakingly beautiful and unbelievably harsh. For her part, Lenora goes beyond the sacrificial caretaker stereotype. She struggles through the tensions between love and commitment on one hand, and the desire for a liberated and truly unique existence on the other. These tensions create the meat of the story, which is never predictable.

This novel will appeal strongly to those readers who enjoy stories about love, friendship, and resilience. It will also attract those who seek out new and creative historical fiction that challenges them to think about less common experiences of those who lived in the past. Beyond this, it is an excellent read for anyone who wants to come away with a renewed curiosity about the mysteries of friendship and hope that we can all find places where we can be fully and unrestrainedly ourselves.

CONTENTS

Dedication v
Foreward vii
Editorial Review viii

1	The New Girl	1
2	The Invitation and The Piano	13
3	She's Different	31
4	London	44
5	Art and Harrod's	49
6	A Flourish of Notes	66
7	Transitions	72
8	The Special Doctor	79

9	Out of the Flames	83
10	Out of the Flames	89
11	Forty-four, Castle Street	101
12	The Sky Above Us	116
13	Be Specific	139
14	I Will, but ...	148
15	And This is Astrid	157
16	The Competition	171
17	June Bride	179
18	The Best Laid Plans	186
19	Shambles	190
20	Number Seven Mayfair Place	197
21	Pink Roses and Boyfriends	201

22	The Symphony	207
23	The Escape	218
24	He Would!	227
25	The Wedding	238
26	My First Guests	243
27	The Challenges of Marriage	250
28	The Shift	254
29	Failure	260

PART II

30	The 1980s	270
31	Lyndon	274
32	Help	281
33	Hannah with the Green Eyes	301

34	Literal, please	304
35	"Is Hannah Coming Back?"	318
36	NASA?	324
37	"Is She Staying?"	330
38	Hannah and the Snowman	341
39	A Hole in the Hat	351
40	In a Dither	365
41	The Heat in Florida	373
42	What Was and What Is	393
43	The Truth	402
44	Forever Together	408

Epilogue   415
About the Author   417

| 1 |

The New Girl

"And after school, I punched that bully Ethan in the stomach. He made fun of me in class and kicked my chair." I stood before my grandfather, ashamed. "I got caught daydreaming by my teacher. The class laughed at me."

Over the top of his wire-rimmed glasses, Grandfather scowled, "He bullied you before, but you never hit him. What made you do this now?" I'd disappointed him. He sighed as I continued; the words came out like a fast-moving train.

"He made fun of my friend, too. She started school in March. Her name is Astrid, and she's…" I shrugged my shoulders. "She's different like me. I talked with her today for the first time."

My mother called, "Come to the kitchen, Luv. The scones are getting cold, and strawberry jam is on the table." I whispered for him not to tell Mother.

The aroma of my mother's fresh-baked scones led me to the kitchen every day after school. We three sat at the table. Grandfather eyeballed me from his half-eaten one, brushed the crumb out of his bushy white beard, and said, "Your daughter beat up a boy in school today." I kicked him under the table; he winced. Grandfather ratted me out!

"Lenora! You did what?" My mother's eyes were as big as saucers; she was appalled.

Glaring at Grandfather, I said, "It was after school, and I only punched him once in the stomach. He made fun of me and my new friend, Astrid."

"Blimey, you have a new friend?" A light bulb must have turned on in her head; Mother didn't care that I hit someone. She couldn't contain her excitement, giddy at the prospect of a new friend. "What's her name?"

"Astrid Innis."

Mother put her elbows on the table! Dreamy, she asked, "What is she like?" She sounded like I'd never had a friend before. She was right, I suppose. I didn't make friends easily.

"She's..." I thought for a moment, trying to put her existence into words, "very musical."

This bit of information excited my mother and Grandfather. When I was five, my father wanted me to play the piano. He bought an upright for me. My kindergartener self didn't have the patience to sit still and play "Twinkle, Twinkle, Little Star." I later regretted it. At one time, my mother sang in the church choir. Grandfather loved the symphony. He teased me, saying the radio was the only thing he played now. My piano had become just an object for me to dust. It stood as a painful reminder of my father's death.

"So, she's musical," Grandfather said with a twinkle in his eye. "What instrument does she play?"

Now, I knew I would sound like I'd gone off my rocker. My words came out like a deflating inner tube, "Astrid doesn't play anything." Grandfather's jaw dropped; a dollop of preserves fell onto his plate. He squinted at me over the top of his glasses.

"Then how do you know she's musical?"

An interrogation, gosh! I threw up my hands. "Okay, this is going to sound crazy. Astrid keeps a notebook full of compositions she's written. She's always writing."

They shot each other an astonishing glance. I could tell they were ready to send me to the booby hatch. I'm not sure Mother believed Astrid even existed.

With my arms crossed over my chest, in a voice full of bluster, "I'm *not* making this up! She says she can hear music in her head. And she lives down the other side of the fork in the road." A place my classmates called Shanty Town. Everyone knew poor people lived there.

Offering a deep sigh, Mother said, "What a shame. Tell me, poppet, what's she like?"

All I knew about Astrid fit on the head of a pin, "She has brothers and an older sister; I'm not sure what her parents do. And I know she's Catholic because she prays over lunch and then crosses herself. Her older sister plays the piano and won't let Astrid near it. We're alike; Astrid has no friends. She's a misfit, like me."

My First Meeting with Astrid

In March this year, Astrid Innis joined my class at the St. Andrew's Community School in Brighton Beach, England. I clearly remembered her arrival; cruel gossip centered around Astrid. There was something odd about her; no one spoke to her. I felt sorry for her. The other kids made fun of me, too. If I sat at the lunch table, they moved away from me. All the way to the end of our class lunch table, she sat alone.

Astrid's family wasn't well off. She wore a tattered brown hand-me-down coat with a long, red, raveling knitted scarf. Her clothes once belonged to someone else. Her dress never fit properly. Every day I watched Astrid sit alone on the same playground bench, her head down, her long, reddish-blonde mane covering her face. Worn gloves covered her hands and the tip of her index finger poked through as she wrote in a battered brown leather notebook. I wanted to talk with her; Astrid was like me, with no friends to speak of and no one to confide in. The others called me names; they'd run by me, bumping my shoulder and knocking my books to the ground. I had nice clothes, but the other girls said I was frumpy. For Astrid, it was worse, but she didn't seem to care. Her attention was focused on writing in an old book.

Astrid was oddly pretty, with skin white as a daisy, high cheekbones, and bright green eyes, the color of lime lollipops. She stood lanky, taller than me. I was more healthy-looking, my face rounder, my hair a wavy dark brown. My hazel eyes couldn't make up their mind; hazel is somewhere between green and brown. My looks were unremarkable.

Before the school bell rang the next day, I waved at her and said hello. A sliver of a smile and a nod of her head acknowledged my presence. Astrid sat in the row to my left. When the teacher passed out graded papers, I could see Astrid's paper always showed red marks. Soon the school year would come to an end. I wasn't sure she could pass her exams.

During free time girls continued gossiping about Astrid's hand-me-down clothes, boyfriends, and latest fashions; the boys made paper airplanes, talked about kissing girls, and made fun of Astrid. Astrid continued to write, sometimes erasing furiously. I never cared for frivolous gossip; I sat alone reading books about the stars and Greek mythology. But I wondered what was in the all-consuming, scuffed-up, brown leather notebook.

The spring day was bright and breezy, filled with blooming flowers and sunshine. I summoned all my courage at recess, sidling up to Astrid as she sat on the bench. "Is this seat taken?" I inquired politely.

Disappointed by her lack of attention, Astrid never looked at me. "You want to sit by me?"

My first thought was, no, I want to stand here and recite Shakespeare. "Why do you think I asked if I didn't want to sit with you?"

"You're Lenora?"

Has she been under a rock? My tone was irritated: "Of course I am, silly. I've been in school with you since you came here in March. I sit the row next to you."

Face to the ground, she said, "I'm sorry. My mother says I'm socially awkward. I guess I am."

"No one in our class likes me because I'm smart. It could be different if I were pretty."

"I don't think so. You have nice eyes." The monotone way she talked didn't match what she said. How did she know? Astrid never held her chin up for anything except when the teacher wrote on the blackboard.

I saw the notebook in her lap. *Egyptian hieroglyphs?* "What are you writing about, Astrid? It must be a secret code in a great adventure."

She shrugged, "No, it's music."

Stunned, I questioned, "What do you play?"

I saw some emotion light in her familiar deadpan for the first time. Astrid recounted what transpired in her home. "I want to play the piano, but I'm not allowed. My older sister plays and hates it. I sat on the piano bench once." She put the book down to demonstrate, "I placed my fingers on the keys for C major. My sister got her knickers in a knot and tried to smash my fingers with the lid." Her hand returned to the pencil and book, "My mother scolded me. She said I did a bad thing."

I heard the sadness in Astrid's voice. In shock, I said, "I'm so sorry, but how can you write music if you've never played?"

"I sit in the other room listening to my sister. She can't see me. I memorize the chord sounds then get the music books when she's gone. I can hear the notes in my head."

Astrid pushed her hair behind her ear and opened the notebook to the first page. *For the Meadowlark* was written above the homemade sheet of music. She said, "It's my first composition," then smiled, staring ahead. I almost fell off the bench. It was the first smile I'd seen from her, ever.

My fingernails were chewed to bloody nubs in class as I pondered how Astrid wrote music without playing it. It would sound disjointed and strange. Of this, I was sure.

"Lenora!" I jumped at the teacher's harsh tone. "Stop daydreaming or I'll have you stay after school. And stop biting your nails."

"Gosh, I'm sorry, Mrs. McGee!" I sat there embarrassed to death. My classmates snickered; some pointed at me.

"The question, Lenora, was, what is Jupiter's largest moon?"

It wasn't like me to drift off when we studied the planets.

"Europa followed by Ganymede and…"

She cut me off. "Enough, Lenora. I only asked for one."

Behind me, Ethan kicked my chair; audible heckling came from half the sixth-level class. Mrs. McGee told everyone to pipe down.

Humiliated, I slid down my chair for the rest of the day. I probably knew more about astronomy than Mrs. McGee. I'd never gotten into trouble before; I wanted this day to end. When the bell finally sounded, the teacher reminded us of testing tomorrow—spelling and the planets.

Astrid waited for me at the bottom of the red brick stairs. Her eyes down cased, clutching her books, shuffling her feet, "I'm sorry for you. The teacher shouldn't have been so harsh."

I shrugged my shoulders. Then I heard sing-songy insults from some of the bully boys. "Haha, the brainiac daydreamed in class! Stop chewing your nails, Lenora-bora. Hey, daft cow, did you dream about your boyfriend? Wait! You're too big and ugly." The three bully boys began to cackle.

"Shut up, Patrick. You don't have a brain cell between your ears!"

Fat-faced Ethan chimed in. "Two retards! Here they are. An ugly one and a stupid one." Ethan made a heart sign with his fingers. "True love," he crooned. The boys laughed, punching each other in the arm. I'd endured enough; I balled up my fist, walloping Ethan in the stomach. He doubled over in pain and fell to the ground. Dumbfounded, the other boys glanced at each other.

"Run, Astrid, hurry! When he gets up, I'll get a beating!"

I grabbed her sweater, pulling her along like a rag doll. We ran into the woods.

Her face frozen in fear, Astrid cried, "Where are you taking me? I need to go home!"

"My safe place; it isn't far."

We dodged the trees, running through the woods, stopping at a group of tall, unkempt hedges with a tiny opening. I pulled Astrid inside, putting my finger to my lips, "Shh." I strained to listen; we were safe. Inside the small clearing stood two worn old chairs and an old coffee table I'd found in the shed. Astrid's fingers closed tight around her spelling book and precious leather notebook. She gawked at a patch of blue sky peeking between the canopy of trees. With a whisper of wide-eyed wonder, she uttered, "How did you find this place?"

I twittered, "I fell into it." Astrid's forehead wrinkled; she didn't understand.

"I felt sure someone followed me; I ran through the woods, tripped, and fell into the bushes. All scratched and bruised, I brushed myself off." With a sweeping bow, I said, "And here we are. Now we're friends. It can be your safe place, too."

Astrid seemed disoriented in her silence.

"Are you alright? Do I give you the heebie-jeebies?" I asked.

Quickly she answered, "Oh, no! It's … it's wonderful," she paused, looking at the ground, "I'm not sure how to be a friend."

Her response caught me off guard, "Of course you do; you're my friend. We're the isolationists! You know, we stay away from everyone, and everyone stays away from us. Except when I hit someone, I guess. Plus, you know my hiding place. Now you have to be my friend."

"Okay, b-b-but I have to get home," she stuttered. "My mother will be cross with me."

I wanted her to stay longer, but she got fidgety, shuffling her feet. I peeked through the bushes and motioned for her to follow. I walked her to the main road. At the fork, I turned left; Astrid turned right.

She spun around to me, talking in that monotone voice, "You live near the ocean."

"Yes, the beach isn't far from my house."

"I see," was all she said.

I called after her, "See you tomorrow." Clutching her books tightly to her chest, she waved at me.

And now, here I sat, listening to my mother. "You are not a misfit, young lady!" bellowed my mother. "You are smart and clever."

"All thanks to you and Grandfather." I meant it to be a compliment, but I'd hurt his feelings. "I didn't mean to sound disrespectful, Grandfather. You've taught me things I'd have never learned in school." I wrapped my arms around his broad shoulders and hugged him tightly, "And I love you to the moon and back."

"What kind of moon do we have tonight?" he quizzed.

"A waxing gibbous moon," I said with confidence.

"That's my girl."

"Your girl needs to study," Mother said as he put his dish in the sink.

"Spelling," I grunted, "but also astronomy!"

Grandfather laughed on the way living room, wagging his finger, "You'll have no trouble in that one."

Loudly, I proclaimed, "My Very Eager Mother Just Served Us Nine Pickles." The planets in order. Mother laughed and said it was imaginative. She grilled me on my spelling words. I wasn't so smart on this subject. Always ten words, and there's often one I'd miss. I'd have liked to get them all right.

"Spell 'necessary,'" she said. I hated the word: too many s's!

"N-e-s-s-i-s-a-r-y."

"No, darling, not correct." She handed me a pencil and a piece of paper. I knew what came next.

"Ten times."

"Oh, gosh!"

"That will be fifteen for the attitude." My mother meant business.

After dinner, dishes were washed and put away; I took time for myself on the terrace, in the big wooden chair, watching the sunset over the ocean. As the stars began to show themselves, the constellations became clear. When I was younger, my Grandfather let me sit on his lap in the evening. The first constellation I learned was Virgo, my birth month of September. The waxing gibbous moon resembled a bright egg in its oval shape.

I wondered what Astrid knew about the stars. After all, her name sounded like *astra*, Latin for a star.

On my way to school, I felt nervous. I prayed all my words would be correct. I hated spelling; however, it was *n-e-c-e-s-s-a-r-y*. Gosh, I hoped it would be right. In the distance, I could see the graveled patch of the playground filled with younger children, some jumping rope, boys kicking a soccer ball, and Astrid on the bench erasing something in the brown leather book. I realized how little I knew about her.

We exchanged greetings. Astrid kept writing in her book. "Can you stop long enough to talk?" I asked. I thought it was bad manners when she didn't look up.

"We have a few minutes. I wanted to finish something."

Irritated, I said, "I'm sorry I interrupted. But I'm curious, how many brothers and sisters do you have?"

Never stopping, she answered, "Six counting me. I'm second from the end, with four brothers and one sister. Judith is second to the oldest and the meanest." Astrid stopped writing, keeping her eyes on the pages; she asked, "How many brothers and sisters do you have?"

"I'm an only child."

Astrid looked puzzled. "It must get lonely."

"Not really. My Grandfather keeps me company. My mother teaches me how to sew and do household things. I go for walks on the beach." The school bell called everyone to class. "We can talk later," I said. Astrid said nothing.

The school day seemed like any other, except for recess. Trouble followed me; Ethan and his hooligans hounded me with jeers and threats. Astrid glanced at me in horror. I left her on the bench, not wanting to involve her. The playground monitors were supposed to be watching. They were more interested in daily gossip.

Then came a sharp pain in my back as I lurched forward. My body was falling; I couldn't catch myself. Both knees hit the ground, the palms of my hands slid across the gravel; my chin hit, mashing my tongue.

Ethan snarled, "That's what you get!" The laughing boys quickly dispersed as I rolled over with a groan. Astrid took my elbow to help me.

"They'll threaten me forever."

A monitor grabbed a wad of tissues from her pocket, "Hold this under your chin. You, girl," she said, pointing at Astrid, "take her to the nurse's office."

In her starched white uniform, Nurse Parker jumped up from her desk, "Blimey, child, what happened to you?"

I lied, of course. "I was running and fell over my own feet. Clumsy me." Astrid stood in the doorway, hands folded in front of her, head down.

"Scoot up on the table. What a mess!" In disgust, Nurse Parker told Astrid to return to class as she began to pick the gravel out of the underside of my chin. I gritted my teeth. It was the worst pain I had ever experienced. I could feel blood running down my neck. At the edge of the table, my legs swung to the rhythm of my heartbeat pulsating in my head.

"Hold this gauze on your chin and hold still," she commanded. A warm trickle of blood rolled down my leg.

"That's a nasty cut. Your chin might need stitching."

I let out a firm "No!" Nurse Parker said she was obligated to call my mother.

Alarmed, I said, "No! Please, let me tell her. My grandfather might come and make a scene. I don't want to go home."

"It's policy," she said as I begged her to let me tell Mother. The stodgy Nurse Parker made no promise. She wiped the blood from my neck and legs, and bandages covered my knees. "What bloke did this to you?" she spouted off.

My silence betrayed me, yet I wasn't about to snitch on those boys.

"Tell me!" she demanded.

I said again, "I fell, that's all."

She huffed, cleaning my wounded palms with stinging alcohol. A crisscrossed bandage between my thumb and wrist would keep blood off my paper. With hands on her hips, she asked, "Can you write with that skinned-up hand? Stick out your tongue. Will you be able to eat?"

My tongue didn't hurt that bad. I said yes; Nurse Parker sent me back to the classroom with a huge gauze bandage taped under my chin. I prayed she didn't call my mother.

As I slinked into the classroom to snickering, Ethan sneered at me. I glanced toward Astrid for comfort. She just stared at her reading book. I was absolutely gutted. Astrid didn't have an ounce of sympathy for me.

"Are you okay to finish the day, Miss McConnell?" asked Mrs. McGee.

"Yes, ma'am." It hurt to talk. I didn't realize how much my chin moved when I spoke. The teacher probably thought my silence a blessing.

The clock above the teacher's desk crawled, tick, tick, tick. I wanted this day to be over. Not yet; time for the dread spelling test, a Thursday ritual. My penmanship was terrible; holding my pencil hurt. I don't remember much about the day other than the scar I'd wear for the rest of my life. And Astrid's silence. Alone, I made my way down the path home when a voice hollered, "Wait."

Astrid ran to meet me. Then she stopped, her eyes cast down. She rocked side to side like a pendulum, "I'm sorry this happened. It's partly my fault." Then a pause. Emotionless words came, "I let you down, Lenora. I'm sorry."

"I'm miffed. Why didn't you look at me when I returned to the room?"

"I felt embarrassed," her voice quivered, "I told you, I don't know how to be a friend."

"Yes, you do. You came to apologize; that's what friends do."

Astrid peered down at her ill-fitting shoes. I dropped my books and hugged her. Poor Astrid didn't know what to do. Her body tightened, stiff as a board. I could tell she didn't experience much affection. Her behavior pained me; Astrid needed to see the love in my family. I decided I'd ask my mother if Astrid could spend the night on Saturday.

The rest of the way, we walked together. When we came to the fork in the road she said robotically, "I feel something bad is following us, Lenora."

"Oh, Astrid, no one will follow us. If my grandfather heard me holler, he'd come, and he'd beat the hell out of those lads."

Astrid flipped her lid when I said the word *hell*. Her face could've stopped a clock. Heaving breaths came out, "Don't be cheeky, and don't say that word anymore, or you'll go there! I'll pray for your forgiveness. I'll pray for you." I thought she'd pass out.

"Okay, no more curse words, promise. I'll stay here and watch until you go down the hill to be sure no one follows you." *Sometimes she's just odd*, I told myself; *besides, I can take care of myself.* If Astrid thought to pray for me, she'd need a lot of words.

I opened the front door to my mother's shock.

"You look bloody awful; what happened to you? Why didn't the nurse call me?"

"I fell arse over teacup, just some scraps."

"Watch your tongue, young lady!"

When the bandage on my chin came off, she was horrified. My Grandfather came downstairs from his room, "What's all this commotion?" Seeing my skinned up my chin, he pounded a fist in the palm of his hand, "Those hooligans did this, didn't they?"

Lying to the nurse was one thing; lying to my grandfather was out of the question. "Yes." I didn't want to say more.

"They need a good paddling! I suppose you didn't tell anyone, did you? Well, I'm going to call the principal!"

"No," I said in shame, "They'll just call me a snitch and try it again."

"Balderdash! Snitch or no snitch, they deserve to be punished."

I pleaded, "Please, Grandfather, don't do anything. I'm afraid for my friend Astrid. She could never defend herself against them."

He stroked his white beard in contemplation, "If you feel that strongly, alright. In any case, I'm going to teach you how to fight back."

My mother put her foot down! "You'll do no such thing, John Michael McConnell! No fisticuffs; she should fight back with words."

He reassured Mother it was not what he meant. I didn't believe what he said. Behind her back, he winked at me. At supper, I questioned Mother if Astrid might spend the night Saturday. Happy that I made a friend, she smiled, saying, "I'll write a note. Astrid can deliver it. Just don't be too disappointed if her mother says no."

"Yes, ma'am."

On the outside, my appearance stayed solid; inside, I wanted to jump up and down with joy. I prayed to the god of the universe that Astrid's mum would say yes.

| 2 |

The Invitation and The Piano

Since my dust-up, Astrid waited at the fork in the road on the way to school. Excited, I said, "Do you suppose your mum will let you spend the night at my house?"

Astrid's forehead wrinkled, her eyes stared past me, "You want me to spend the night with you?"

"Does sleeping at my house frighten you?"

A quick shower of *no*'s rolled out of her.

"My mother wrote a note asking permission from your mum. I'll give it to you later."

Astrid acted strangely; she squealed with delight but changed with the first step on the grassy lawn of the schoolyard. Astrid turned gloomy. We distanced ourselves from one another for protection. If they messed with Astrid, I'd bloody well fight again.

As I passed Ethan, I whispered, "My Grandfather will find you if you hurt me again and beat you to a bloody pulp. So you better not try any shenanigans." Then I emphasized, "Ever."

Although Grandfather was older, he stood tall and strong as an ox. He still chopped his own wood, and they knew it. He may have seemed like Father Christmas, but if I got hurt again, they would feel the wrath of the Almighty Zeus.

At the last bell, we poured out the door like ants on fire. I waited for Astrid, who always seemed last. Handing her the invitation, she stuck it in her notebook. Astrid clutched it to her breast, watching the clouds, saying, "Please, Mary, Mother of God, grant me favor in your holy heart." Then she crossed herself. I didn't know what to think, so I said an awkward, "Amen."

"Have your mum ring my mother. Okay?"

"I couldn't; we don't have a telephone."

There was shame in her voice, "Gosh, okay, plan B." I needed a plan B. "If your mum says yes, meet me at the fork in the road at eleven o'clock. If you're not there by noon, I'll know you couldn't come."

"Say a prayer for me. I've never been away from home. I have Saturday chores, but I can get them done real fast."

"I will!"

The Visit

At ten a.m., I paced the floor looking at the clock, irritating my mother, who sent me out of the house at ten-thirty. On the fifteen-minute walk, I examined rocks and identified tree leaves as I watched for Astrid at the fork. I assume it took her longer. It's funny; I never thought of a reason to travel down that part of the road. The Crum Crunchers at school said the houses were run down, the streets were dirt. Sitting under the tree near our meeting place, I hoped Astrid would show up, or my mother might wonder if I was mad as a hatter. Under the tree, I drew pictures in the dirt with a stick. There was no need for a watch; my grandfather taught me about sundials. Shadows disappear with the noonday sun, so I poked the stick in the dirt and waited.

I pictured Astrid's face when she saw my never-played piano. I thought it was a test of sorts. Could she play the melodies she wrote? I remembered the expression on Grandfather's face. His skepticism was not unfounded; I worried the same. The timid Astrid might be too scared to try.

I knew it was past time for Astrid to come; the shadows disappeared. Standing up, I brushed the leaves and dirt from my dungarees. Making my way to the hilltop, I saw the empty road. She wasn't coming. Halfway home, I heard her yelling at me. Thank God! Now my mother wouldn't think I'm bonkers.

Astrid carried a small suitcase, the kind you put doll clothes in. Strands of hair stuck to her red face, tiny beads of sweat dotting her forehead. Out of breath, she apologized, "I'm sorry for being late. My mum kept finding things for me to do. When I finished, I ran halfway here. I'm sorry."

"I'm just happy you made it. I almost gave up." Astrid wore a faded blue summer dress, the cotton fabric worn thin. There was a swollen red knot peeking out above her fringe.

"Are you okay? That's a nasty bump."

Her worried green eyes darted from side to side, "I hit my head, that's all." Truthfully, I wondered how it really happened. Astrid licked her hand, smoothing her fringe over the lump. When we came inside, my grandfather and mother waited for us with a cold glass of lemonade. I swear Astrid drank the entire glass in one gulp.

In her flat tone, she asked, "Could I have another, please? It was a long walk. I ran all the way."

Mother smiled, "You may have another, dear."

"I'm sorry, Mother, Grandfather. This is my friend, Astrid Innis. Astrid, my family is my mother, Mary McConnell, and my grandfather, Mr. John Michael McConnell."

Grandfather smiled, trying to make eye contact with Astrid. He probably thought she was shy. She eyed the floor, making circles with the toe of her shoe. "I'm very pleased to meet you. Thank you for letting me visit." She must have carefully rehearsed her response.

My Grandfather turned to me and winked, "Why don't you show your friend the rest of the house?" I knew what he meant: the piano. I ushered Astrid into the living room. The upright piano was to the immediate right when anyone walked into the room. Two steps in, Astrid dropped her suitcase. Both her hands covered her mouth like a peacock's tail.

Overwhelmed, she asked, "Why didn't you tell me you owned a piano?" Astrid drifted into a dreamlike state.

"Partly because we've only known each other for a week and partly because I didn't want you like me only because I have a piano."

Astrid's shoulders slumped; her feelings were hurt. "I liked you without knowing."

Grandfather came around the corner; Astrid wasn't one to look up, yet she must have thought he looked like Santa Claus because she peeked at him. "This is better than Christmas. I mean if…" her voice trailed off, "I'm allowed to play."

Enthusiastically, Grandfather opened the lid and said, "I'd love to hear you play."

My stomach quivered. What if Astrid couldn't play? The infamous brown leather notebook sat closed on the bench beside her. What was she up to?

I stood holding my breath in the doorway as her fingers made a perfect arch. My face knotted, telegraphing my uncertainty. Then it happened; music flowed from her like a mountain stream. Grandfather's eyebrows were raised to the roof. Taken back, he sat straight up in his chair. My mother came from the kitchen, drying her hand on her apron, "Beautiful," she whispered. Astrid froze with the last chord sounding, never lifting her head.

Grandfather called out, "Smashing! What is the title of the song? Who composed it?"

"'For the Meadowlark.'" She appeared to be frightened. "I wrote it."

With side glances, my mother and I were equally gobsmacked. She asked Astrid where she learned to play so expertly.

"I dunno. It just comes out of me," Astrid's innocence was astounding. There was no doubt she was telling the truth.

My Grandfather pointed his finger at her, "You, young lady, have a gift."

Astrid bowed her head and said, a meek, "Thank you."

"Look at me, child," his voice was loving, the way he always talked to me. She peeked through her fringe. He continued, "I will talk with your parents. You can come every day to play in my house."

Sheer terror came over her, "No, no, please, don't!" She dropped her head, "They won't let me come anymore."

Puzzled by her reaction, my mother inquired why Astrid thought this. "My mum says I'm peculiar. I was surprised they let me come today. If you invite me for one night, it's fine only if I make it home Sunday before eleven o'clock Mass. I must go to Mass. I heard them talking about next year. I have to be good…" her voice was barely audible. "They're sending me away."

"Oh, horrors!" I gasped. Astrid was my only friend; they couldn't send her away.

My mother sat on the piano bench, putting her arm gently around Astrid's shoulders. She stiffened as Mother spoke. "We'll make sure you're back in time for Mass, dear. While you're here, put those thoughts out of your mind and have fun with Lenora."

"Yes, ma'am."

Grandfather made a promise to say nothing, as she wished.

In my room, we sat on the bed together. I held Astrid's hand, "How could they send you away?"

Astrid gazed straight ahead, "I heard them talking. They don't know what to do with me." Astrid hung her head, "I heard them say I'm not the same as my sister and brothers. They talked about a Catholic convent school where girls are novices."

"Novices? What does that mean?" I asked.

"It means I'm going to learn to be a nun."

"Oh, how awful!" I blurted out. Astrid began to hum, low with pain. With my arm over her shoulders, I said, "I'm sorry, Astrid; we'll figure something out. My Grandfather is a powerful man who knows loads of people in London. We'll find a way to keep this from happening. I promise." She buried her face into my shoulder. Feeling a bit awkward, I stroked her long strawberry blond hair. I held out hope Grandfather knew what to do.

I ran cold water over the washcloth in the bathroom, wringing it out for Astrid's face. Her long hair needed brushing; I asked her permission to make a ponytail. Reluctantly, she let me.

Saturday lunch was a big meal for us. Not being religious, we watched Astrid fold her hands and pray while we sat, uncomfortable, glancing at each other; then she crossed herself. Mother began sending around bowls of food. Astrid's family must be poor; she took one potato, a carrot, and a small piece of roast, staring at her plate. She seemed afraid, so I put more food on her plate. Frozen in her seat, I nudged Astrid. Mother's eyes met mine; she nodded with approval. Astrid shoveled her food in like a starving orphan. She thanked my mother for the food and then strangely patted her stomach. After lunch, I asked Astrid if she wanted to walk on the beach.

"Yes, but I only went once when I was little."

Caught off guard, I couldn't imagine living so close to the sea and only going there once.

"Let's go for a walk. The beach is just beyond the house down the grassy bank."

I asked my mother if we could go. She took off her watch, "You can stay until five, not a minute more. My watch doesn't fit your wrist yet, Lenora. Put it in your pocket. Don't get it wet, and don't lose it."

"Yes, ma'am." I stuck the watch carefully in the pocket of my dungarees. Astrid focused on her shoes, furiously clapping her hands; she acted oddly.

May brought light breezes to the pleasant early afternoon. Sunny skies and laughing gulls accompanied us on our walk; Astrid shielded her eyes from a swarm of gulls.

"They're looking for food," I chuckled, "Once, a greedy gull grabbed half a sandwich from my hand!"

I laughed. Astrid stopped, "Really?" She sounded scared.

"Don't worry. When the flying rats figure out there's no food, and they go away."

"They're birds, not rats."

"I know that, silly. Is it okay if I call you Astie?" Her name sounded rigid; however, I didn't want to offend her.

She shrugged, "Okay. I guess I like it." Astrid trudged along in the sand, "Have you lived here all your life?"

"We used to live in Dublin until my father," I chose my words carefully, "my father died."

"Is Dublin across the water?"

She didn't know where Dublin was, blimey. "Yes, my great-grandparents were merchants here in Brighton. Grandfather said when he was young, they moved to Ireland to start a woolen mill." Proudly, I said, "Grandfather attended Trinity College in Dublin; he's very smart."

"Oh, okay." By her response, I could see she wasn't interested.

The tide rolled back into the sea, exposing rigid ripples in the sand, clumps of seaweed, rocks, and mostly broken shells. We wandered along the beach, our beach; an older couple strolled past us, a man and his dog ran by. Large boulders jutted from the rocky shoreline, creating a perfect place to sit and watch sailboats go by. Astrid's blank stare made me curious. I couldn't stop wondering what was going on in her head. "What are you thinking about?"

"I hear music in the waves." Her voice got very low, "Sounding like a bass drum rolling with the tide"; in a higher pitch, "the birds sing staccato songs, and the breeze is a smooth melody." Astrid's fingers floated from side to side as she played an imaginary piano. What staccato meant, I had no clue. I jumped up, running to the water's edge twirling in circles, my arms outstretched, sun on my face.

Astrid shouted at me in a panic, "Stop! You'll get dizzy and fall. Stop!" That didn't stop me. "You'll get wet, and your mum will spank you!"

I stopped immediately; her voice sounded fearful. Astrid's face contorted with terror; my heart fell. I took both her hands; she wouldn't hold her head up. "No, she won't. She has never spanked me." I could tell she didn't believe me. For a moment, we stood looking at each other, holding hands, as if we were connected by an invisible string. Breaking this magic spell, I pointed down the shore, "Hey, I see some shells washed up on the sand. Let's go!" I pulled her along; I giggled, but she did not. We came to an abrupt halt; I began to remove my shoes and socks. I commanded, "Take off your shoes and socks!"

"Why?"

Did she have to ask why? Astounded, I said, "You'll get your shoes wet!"

Reluctantly, Astrid removed her shoes. Her socks were thin with a hole in the toe. We laid them on a boulder near the tide line. "Come on," I motioned for her. The cold water washed over our toes, sending a shiver.

"It's cold. I'm sinking in the sandy water!" Astrid lamented, "Am I going to get swallowed up and die?"

Those little thoughts from her, the innocent questions, baffled me. How could someone our age not know the sensation of standing in sandy surf?

I used a simple voice void of judgment, "No, you're not going to die, geez. Yes, it's supposed to feel that way, Astrid."

"Okay."

Astrid bent down, examining a large, unbroken scallop shell rinsing it in the surf. She stepped from the water's edge, entranced, examining the shell.

I said, "If I find pretty ones, I save them. That one looks like a fan."

"It's white! May I take it?"

"Yes, you can. I'll put it in my pocket."

I took my mother's watch out to see the time. Four-forty-five; we needed to hurry back. I flipped over the watch, reading the engraved words, "To my darling wife, Love, Danny." My father was Danny. I closed my fingers around it and kissed it.

"Why did you do that? Why did you kiss a watch?"

"It was a special anniversary present from my father." Astrid asked why my father didn't live with us. Calmly, I said, "he lives in heaven." She nodded and did her crossing her heart thing again.

We walked back to the house; I told Astrid about my family, more for me than her. It's a story I'd never shared before.

"After my grandfather's parents were killed in an accident, he sold their wool mills to an Irish family. He worked in Dublin, then started banks in the countryside. I didn't know my granny. She died young. My father, Danny, earned an accounting degree to work in one of my grandfather's country banks; my mother deposited money from her family's sheep farms every Friday. It was true love. They got married and had me." I left out some parts on purpose.

When we walked back inside, I handed Mother the watch; she slipped it on her wrist with a pleasant smile. Cold milk and cheese sandwiches awaited us. I dug in my pocket and gave Astrid the shell.

"I have an idea!" I ran to get an ink pen from my grandfather's desk. On the smooth side of the shell, I wrote my name, then handed the pen to Astrid. She just sat there.

"Go on, write your name." She carefully printed her name, her fingers folded around the shell. "Keep it," I said, "it will always be your good luck charm. The ink will smear, so don't get it wet." Astrid wandered to the bedroom. I saw her fold the shell in a handkerchief for safekeeping.

"The sun is going down. Let's go outside." Astrid followed me down the steps to the terrace to a place Grandfather named The Observatory, with an uncluttered view of sea and sky. The two of us huddled together in one chair. Orange and pink cotton candy clouds streaked across the sapphire sky, fading into indigo. One by one, stars dotted the darkening sky. I heard soft, calming waves from the house as the incoming tide lapped the beach. The faint call of an owl hooted from the woods. Before long, the ocean shimmered with light from the half-moon. "Here is the best place to see stars. Look up. We're under a blanket of stars." I pointed to a constellation, "Virgo, the first constellation I learned from Grandfather."

"The stars have names? What's a consolation?" She spoke in childlike amazement.

"It's pronounced *constellation*, like pictures in the sky. I'll show you." I pointed to Virgo's head. "It's like a kite; you have to connect the dots and use your imagination." I took Astrid's hand, "Make a fist, then use your index finger to connect each star. Like this," I guided Astrid's hand to connect the kite-like shape, "That's her head; there are her shoulders, two arms, and two legs."

Mesmerized, Astrid whispered, "I see it. It's like magic."

"I was born in September. Virgo is my constellation. See the four stars over there? They make a small cross. Mariners called it the Southern Cross to help them find their way."

"Just down to the left of the moon, what's the bright star? Does it have a name, too?"

"Aldebaran. It's a bright orange star, the eye of the constellation of Taurus."

"Taurus?"

"Yes, Taurus is a bull, April twentieth to May twentieth."

Softly Astrid said, "May sixteenth is my birthday. Am I a bull Taurus?"

"Yes. You're going to be twelve in three weeks. Did you know your name means bright star?" I studied Astrid. "You are a bright star," I said with enthusiasm. I thought I caught a glimpse of a cheeky smile; then again, it was dark outside.

"What does your name mean, Lenora?"

"Compassionate light," I answered with pride.

A crisp breeze blew through our hair while watching the stars and listening to the waves.

Astrid gripped the arm of the chair with lightning speed and whipped her head around; slightly crazy, she said, "You are Luna, the moon, bright and full of compassion. Luna means the moon in Latin. The priest speaks Latin."

Astrid made eye contact with me for the first time. Even if her eyes bugged out, I didn't care. She paid attention to me. We sat quietly; our arms entwined with eyes scanning the sky until our necks hurt.

Still looking skyward, Astrid asked, "What will happen to us?"

"I don't know. No matter where life takes us, Astie, look at the night sky, and we'll always be together. Astra and Luna, forever together."

Her eyes fixed on the shimmering sea, she whispered, "Forever, together."

Astrid's Birthday

Astrid's birthday came with no party or fanfare just before our summer break. Her mother forbade her to spend the night with me that weekend; we were both sorely disappointed. Friday was the day of Astrid's actual birthday. I watched the slow-moving clock awaiting the dismissal bell. Bursting at the seams to give her a gift on the way home, I waited until we reached the fork.

"I have a present for you." Her head swung from side to side, "Hold out your hand and close your eyes."

"Why?" Her hands trembled.

"It's nothing yucky, I promise. Just do it!" my patience wore thin. I put the oblong box in her hand, "Okay, open your eyes!"

"What is it?"

"For gosh sakes, open it!"

I took the books from under her arm as the paper came off. My heartbeat jumped; I wanted her to like it. Opening the case, she uttered, "A pen and pencil?"

The wood grain pen and pencil set had gold trim with her name engraved on each one. Astrid ran her fingers over the letters. "They have my name on them," she said quietly. My grandfather purchased them, especially for her.

Excited, I said, "The pencil is for writing your music. It has refills under the holder." I waited for a reaction. "Well? Do you like them?"

"Yes," she thrust the box out toward me. "You keep them." She took a breath, "I couldn't take them home."

"Why not?!" The blood rushed to my ears, turning red with anger.

"It's what my mother says is too posh. She'd make me give them back anyway because your family is hodey-todey."

"What's that mean?"

"Mum says your family has too much money. That's why I couldn't take it."

How could anyone be so cruel? I couldn't believe what I was hearing. Her mum said we were hoity-toity? My mouth dropped open. Sadness filled my heart, my poor Astie! We just stood there. I exchanged the box for her books. There were no words in me for the first time in my life. Astrid turned toward home.

"Wait!" I hollered. Running to her, "Tell me, did you like them?"

"Yes." Devoid of happiness, she said, "I liked them very much."

"I can keep them with me; you can use them anytime. Okay?"

My affirmation came in the form of a headshake.

"I'll see you Monday, Astie." I wanted to hug her. I thought I shouldn't. "Happy Birthday to my shining star." She turned; I know she must be upset even if it didn't show.

I cried all the way home. Before I entered the house, I tried to regain my composure. When I told my mother and grandfather what occurred, they understood my heartbreak; they were heartbroken, too.

Summer Break

Finally, summer! No bully boys! They smelled like wet puppies; they had big mouths, dirty knees, and stained shirts. Girls had better hygiene, even if they could be mean and hateful. Most of all was my relief; Astrid passed to the seventh level.

This summer would be different, better because I had an actual friend. Grandfather visited Astrid's parents. I overheard him speaking with Mother. Her parents were skeptical about his concern for Astrid. He said they lived in a run-down farmhouse with children everywhere. Although he received a cold reception, Grandfather convinced them to allow weekday visits and overnight stays. He explained how I needed a friend since we live isolated near the beach with no one my age nearby. In truth, he wanted Astrid to have the opportunity to play the piano. It sounded like her parents were glad to be rid of their "strange child." Grandfather said Astrid's father mumbled, "One less mouth to feed."

I knew I shouldn't overthink the future; regardless, I wondered what would happen to Astrid. After next year I'd leave for St. Agnes Preparatory School for Young Ladies. Who would be around to protect her? My guts turned to mush thinking about the threats of Astie being a nun. I wished on a star last night that she could come with me. They had an outstanding music program; alas, Astrid's grades were barely passing. Perhaps she could still come here and play the piano for Grandfather when I was gone.

The Piano

When I was six, we lived in Dublin, where my father bought an upright piano. He wanted me to learn how to read music and play. It was important to him, not to me. When my father was shot through the heart by bank robbers, he died instantly. Grandfather was the bank president and owner of the bank. He telephoned my mother, distraught; he felt responsible.

Even though the policeman came, and my mother was crying, I didn't believe it. It was a lie; he wasn't dead. Someone got the facts mixed up. Every evening, I pulled the lace curtain back from the living room window, watching for him. I watched out the window, waiting for him to jump off the trolley and wave his newspaper at me to say hello. That day the sunset, and he never came home. When the bank robbers shot and killed him, I just couldn't play that piano anymore. I wondered if he watched from heaven, ashamed of me.

People came to the house in black clothes. I hid, putting my hands over my ears. If I couldn't hear people talk, it wasn't true. But it was. I prayed to God, asking him not to make me go to the wake. I was obligated to go, for Mother's sake. In silence, Mother dressed me in a black dress, a sweater, and woolen leggings. Mother gave me shiny black shoes. Her graceful hands brushed my long brown hair; she tied it back with a black ribbon, then helped me with my black coat.

The undertaker took my father's body to Granny's house. She was my mother's mum. Unlike my mother, Granny wasn't very affectionate. Her house always felt cold, even in summer. I didn't want to see my father's dead body; I tried to hide. When you skin your knees, it hurts. You don't want to see the blood running down your leg. No matter how hard you try, you look, and the pain worsens. My pain was bound to get worse.

The awful wailing sounds hurt my ears. I sat in the living room with strange people. My head followed the conversation; people on the left said words like poor girl, she'll lack a father's guidance. People on my right told each other how my mother should be pitied for raising a child alone.

For the first time in two days, I did feel like crying. I peeked around the corner to see my father lying on the table in the dimly lit dining room; I will never eat there again. Between the neatly dressed men in black suits and women in long black dresses, I wove my way around to see my father. He wore new black shoes, his navy and gold pin-striped suit, and a white dress shirt; his arms were folded across his chest. My mother gave him the black onyx cuff links for Christmas. I snuck around a fat lady in a black skirt to see his face; coins were over his eyes. Mother sat in a chair next to him, wiping her eyes. I didn't understand until later the reason for the coins. His face was bluish. I watched his chest hoping for a rising sign of life; it didn't move. This scared me so badly that I ran outside, threw up all over my black wool coat, and spattered my new shoes. It was cold out; I used my coat to wipe off my shoes, pitched it in the rubbish bin, and ran inside. All I thought was my mother should be upset with me. Scared, I hurried to my granny's closet and hid among the long coats and dresses. I figured with all the wailing, no one missed me.

Mother called for me; I heard her go from room to room. She found me in the closet. My tears made my eyes sting.

"Where's your coat, Lenora?"

"I don't know." I didn't usually lie. Rummaging through Granny's closet, my mother found a woolen wrap.

"Keep this around you to keep out the cold. We'll talk about your coat later."

The wind blew right through me, to my bones. I heard the minister say,

"… is survived by his wife of ten years, Mary Catherine McConnell., née O'Malley, and his daughter Lenora Irene McConnell."

"Survived by." I didn't feel I survived. I felt nothing except dead inside. I wanted to crawl in the coffin with my father before the men put the dirt on him. I didn't care if I got dirty. I didn't care about anyone but him. Selfish, I didn't think about anyone, only my pain. Surely my blood turned black, and I was going to hell.

In the evening, it was just the two of us at home. The darkness made the house feel empty; I turned on the kitchen light above the table. Mother filled the tea kettle.

"Mother, why were coins on my father's eyes?"

She lit the stove. I wasn't sure if she heard me, I didn't ask again. Her thin frame stooped with grief moved in slow motion.

She sat by me, gazed into my eyes, took my hand, and said, "People believe the coins are to pay a boatman ferrying souls to heaven. He is paid not to stop at the gates of Hades but go straight to Heaven. The real answer to your question isn't pleasant. They put coins on the eyes of the dead to keep their eyes shut."

I cocked my head, puzzled, my forehead wrinkled, "Dead people can open their eyes?"

"Yes, it's true, dear."

Terror gripped me, "Can they see?"

"No, Luv." She stroked my hair, "They can't see." I scanned her eyes with unfallen tears. The tea kettle's whistle broke our moment of silence. She asked if I wanted some tea, something she had not done before. I stammered, "Y-yes." I took the milk from the refrigerator.

Outside the window, the moon illuminated clouds hanging heavy in the sky. My tears stayed deep within me. Although questions still filled my mind, I needed to be strong for my mother. Not wanting to upset her, I could ask Grandfather.

Bedtime came; my mother held me tight. She brushed my hair back, and her hand slipped under my chin. Looking into my eyes, she said, "I don't want you to worry, Lenora. He's in heaven now. We're going to be alright. Your father made sure of it."

"The bad guys…" I was scared they'd find us.

She pulled me closer. Her chin rested on my head, "They are in jail forever." Mother kissed my forehead, "It's been a very long day for us. Go on to bed, my darling."

On my way to my bedroom, I turned to see her slumped silhouette against the bedroom door frame; tightly crossed arms held her body, her fist rested under her chin. I pulled the covers over my head; my pillow muffled my sorrows. My tears weren't for me; they were for my mother's broken heart.

The next afternoon the doorbell rang. The shadow on the other side of the door's frosted glass was Grandfather. My grandfather was a widower. No one told me what happened to my other granny, only that she died young. Whatever it was, the cause remained unspoken. I only remember them saying it was the C-word, whatever that meant.

I ran to open the heavy beveled glass door; Grandfather, dressed in his black tweed coat and matching cap, asked how I was feeling. My soft voice quivered with despair. "I had nightmares, father's eyes popping open, and he was buried alive; they scared me."

Grandfather squatted down to my level, leaning on his cane; he said, "Lenora, I promise he wasn't buried alive. I promise, and I don't make promises unless they are true."

"I know," I said, shaking my head.

Grandfather McConnell came to check on us. His cane tapped on the black and white tiled foyer as he moved to the kitchen to speak with my mother. I'd gotten in trouble for eavesdropping before. This time I couldn't help myself. I sat on the stairs, listening to talk of moving in with him at the beachside house in Brighton, England, where he grew up. Overjoyed, I squealed.

"Lenora Irene!" my mother called sternly. I just knew I was a goner. She told me to come down from the stairs and sit. She pointed to the kitchen chair, "I know how you love the sea and the stars. Your grandfather asked if we could move in with him at the big house by the sea in England."

"Dublin City is no place to discover the beauty of the world." He was wise, and I loved him.

"What about your banks?" I asked.

"I'm selling them. It's a dangerous business. I've lost your father, my only son," his voice quivered.

My mother interrupted him, "John Michael McConnell, what happened was not your fault."

"It weighs heavy on me, Mary. You and Lenora are all the family I have left. We could take care of each other."

He saw disapproval on my mother's face, "I've checked the local school in Brighton. They are superior to others in the area. It's a charming town. The shops aren't far," he stopped. With his warm eyes, he said, "She will have many advantages, and with her personality, she will make new friends, and so will you, Mary. There are organizations for women there; book clubs, sewing circles."

I kept my mouth closed, not wanting to jinx the plan; our city house appeared like all the others in this part of Dublin, a row house. The thought of living in the big white house, walking on the beach, collecting shells, the sound of the sea all excited me.

My mother said, "I agree it's a beautiful place to live; having said that, where will I put everything?" She watched me, knowing I hung on every word, "Go to the living room while we talk." I dutifully obeyed.

She and her grandfather discussed the details. I retreated to the living room, staring out the window. Pushing the lace curtains aside, a small white horse pulled an old wagon loaded with vegetables to the farmer's market. Lots of cars filled the streets. It always smelled of exhaust. People honked their horns and shouted at each other over the place to park. A newsboy stood on the corner, yelling out the headlines. I thought of my father. Did I wonder if I'd miss all of this? Not really, yet I wondered if the quiet could be just as unnerving.

"Lenora!" Grandfather thundered. "You and your mother will live with me at the beach house in Brighton."

"Yippee!" I couldn't control my excitement. My long brown curls bounced on my shoulders as I danced down the hallway. A new adventure was about to begin.

Four years ago, we moved here. The adventure I'd anticipated wasn't what I imagined. My mother seemed content, but I wondered if she got lonely. Once, she told Grandfather she'd never marry again. He didn't argue. Some days, she sat by the window overlooking the sea, knitting sweaters or blankets for the hospital.

Last year, Grandfather finally convinced Mother to volunteer at the hospital once a week, probably, so he could play chess at a local pub. She met some ladies who invited her to a book club.

Everything was lovely, except school. Second-level classmates were not very friendly. My teachers liked me; I outshined most of my classmates with my flashes of brilliance. Things changed in the fifth grade; I got tired of being picked on and the name-calling; brainiac, daft cow, and posh brat. I stopped trying to be popular. The beach became my escape where no one bothered me. Grandfather was my best friend, teaching me about Greek mythology, sea creatures, and most of all, the stars. Mother worried about my friendless situation. When I met Astrid, I had the friend I longed for. Being a new student so late in the school year was hard for Astie. Being alone is even harder, something I knew a lot about.

| 3 |

She's Different

Astrid spent most of the summer with me, and her parents stopped talking about the convent school. My grandfather drove her to Saint Mary of the Woods Catholic Church on Sundays. He didn't mind waiting. At a car park near the church, he read the Sunday newspaper.

For the summer, Mother bought Astrid two pairs of Bermuda shorts, flowery cotton blouses, and a pair of sandals. Astrid slumped; her hands clasped behind her back. She rolled up on her toes and back down again, staring at the clothes laid out on the bed.

"Aren't you happy to get new clothes?" I asked. I turned to Mother with a shrug.

Her voice sounded wobbly, "They're nice, very nice, but my mom won't let me keep them." Mother put her hand on Astrid's shoulder; she froze. To see her like that made me sad.

"It's alright, dear. We can keep your clothes here in Lenora's closet." In a voice of promise, she said, "You can wear them when you visit."

"Okay." Later, Astrid told me she had never worn new clothes before.

In June, Mother's book club met at a friend's house on Tuesdays; she did her Thursday volunteer work at the hospital. On those days, Grandfather drove Astrid and me to the library. The magazine racks were full of teen magazines with music groups, the latest fads, and fashion.

"Astrid, they have fashion magazines." I was in heaven. She waved me off and proceeded to the albums of classical music. A room with a record player and headphones excited Astrid more. She was no fun.

On Thursdays, Grandfather took us for ice cream. I assume he took us there for a banana split, but he flirted with the widow lady who owned the shop. I saw the way he eyed her; my laugh stayed inside.

One day after the library trip, Astrid sat down at the piano. "Listen," she said.

Astrid began to work her magic on those eighty-eight keys. I'd never heard this music before; it was definitely a complicated classical piece.

Grandfather's jaw dropped. "Sergei Rachmaninoff, Piano Concerto, No. 3. Where did you learn that piece of music?"

"In the library," she responded in her flat monotone. "It's just the piano part."

Astrid said she listened to the album, memorized it, then played it. What Astrid played was extraordinary. We were used to her compositions; this was different. Grandfather joined Mother in the kitchen. In hushed voices, I heard him say he knew who to call, a friend from his college days who worked in London. I didn't tell Astrid what I overheard.

Every week Astrid listened to the BBC broadcast of the London Symphony. After hearing Beethoven, she played his music repeatedly. Sometimes I just had to go outside. I preferred more modern music like Brian Hyland and Brenda Lee or Etta James' song, "At Last."

We slept in the same bed and got scolded for talking after the lights were off. Astrid rarely laughed. If I laughed out loud, sometimes she cringed and covered her ears.

One night she rolled over and asked, "Do you like to read, Lenora?"

"When do I not have a book in my hand?" The way I answered must have confused her. She glared at me with a scrunched-up face.

"Yes, I do. Don't you like to read?"

Astrid pursed her lips, shook her head, and said, "You can read out loud if you want; I won't mind."

For a second, I thought about what she said. Maybe she wanted me to read to her. "I have a book you might like. It's a great adventure."

Astrid withdrew from my excitement.

"I'm sorry. I get carried away sometimes. I can read to you all summer."

"What's the book called?"

"*The Chronicles of Narnia*, by C.S. Lewis. They are seven books. The first book is *The Lion, The Witch, and The Wardrobe*. Doesn't that sound exciting?"

"A witch. Witches are evil and scary," she stammered.

I held my head, "Oh, Astrid, it's not that kind of scary. I promise there's nothing to be scared about."

A glum "Okay" came out.

I read to her with a theatrical flair. For me, it was fun, but she often fell asleep.

We opened all the windows to let the salty sea air fill the house when the weather turned hot. Some days, Grandfather turned on the lawn sprinkler. At first, Astrid just stood there watching me run in and out. "Come run with me, Astie. It will cool you down."

Getting her to move was a hard job, so I sprayed her. The steadfast soldier stood dripping in a puddle. Her face turned red, her nostrils flared; Astrid was mad at me. I did it this time.

"Why did you do that? It was a bad thing what you did."

"Aww, come on, Astrid! I don't want to play by myself. You came to have fun with me." Now I wasn't sure of myself. "Didn't you?"

Her eyes were fixed on the ground as she shuffled onto the lawn. "Okay." Spraying myself in the face, I undid the sprinkler to hand her the hoses. Astrid didn't smile.

"Here, squirt me. Put your finger over the hole." Poor Astie couldn't make it work; she flung the hose around like a wet noodle. I followed her around just to get wet.

The summer was filled with our trips to the library, stories I'd read to Astrid, her music, and the chores. I'd often watch my patient, loving mother teach Astrid to wash clothes or make cookies. I loved my mother and wanted to be like her.

In the summer's heat, Astrid fell asleep. Mother sat in the kitchen. "Mother, I'm glad Astrid's been here for the summer; on the other hand, I'm sad. She'll be going home soon."

"I know you'll be lonely."

"It's not that. When Astrid returns to her family, I worry that they won't want her anymore. She's not the same, you know."

Mother nodded, "I understand, poppet. Sometimes I worry, too. Lenora, we can't dwell on what might be, only on what is. You still have two weeks left before school starts. Let's make it Astrid's best summer." I hugged her around her neck and kissed her cheek.

As she folded up her summer clothes, I watched Astrid's blank face, void of emotion.

"Are you sad?" I asked.

Her head bobbed up and down without a tear shed. It hurt me to see her go; I couldn't cry in front of her.

"I'm sad, too. It's only a week before we see each other again. Mother says we should think about now instead of what will be in the future. It's hard to do."

"I think about what will happen; I'm scared of going home because they won't like me anymore, and I can't play the piano anymore."

"Remember when we gazed at the night sky? I am the moon; you are my star. We'll always be together. The moon and the stars are forever, just like us."

"Sometimes, the moon is gone."

"No, sometimes we just can't see it. I promise it's still there watching over us. So, even if you can't see me, I'm still here," I gently touched Astie's chest. "Okay?"

"Okay."

Back to School

I was a terrible eavesdropper. Before school started, I overheard a conversation with Grandfather telling my mother he spoke to his friend at some conservatory. Grandfather said Astrid should first finish this school year. I didn't know the reason, but I stayed hopeful everything would be better.

On the first day back to school, waiting for Astrid at the fork in the road, I worried she might not come back or if her parents had mistreated her. My heart raced when I saw her head pop up over the hill. She clutched her book then raised her hand with a slow wave.

Astrid told me her sister now worked as a nanny for a family in Leeds. She said with Judith gone, her chores were twice as hard; her brothers called her Miss High and Mighty. And Astrid's father forced the boys to work, except the youngest one was still in nappies.

Anxious, I asked, "Are you okay?"

"Over the summer, my dad sold the piano. I couldn't find my other music books." I would have lost my mind, yet she didn't seem upset.

"Oh, Astie, why?" My heart was breaking.

"I dunno. I searched for my other music books; I couldn't find them."

Our pace quickened, "Did you search everywhere? Maybe your sister hid them before she left."

She shrugged her shoulders. I wanted to beat someone up for being so cruel. It wasn't a great way to start the first day of school.

Our new teacher was Mr. Smyth. When he gave us our new books, Astrid held her head. All hope disappeared. No matter what, I decided I would help her with everything.

I stayed pretty quiet at home, which is not normal for me. Grandfather asked about Astrid. "Judith left. Her father took her music books and sold the piano, Grandfather."

Downtrodden, shaking his head, "I was afraid something might happen. At any rate, this is heartless. I'm not sure what to do."

"Be careful. I don't want Astrid's family to hurt her. Perhaps she can remember the music and rewrite it."

Putting his finger to the side of his nose, then he pointed at me, "It might work. I'll see about getting a new book, you can bring it home with you every day. They would be none the wiser."

I shook my head profusely. "It's a great idea."

The next morning, I asked Astrid if she could remember all the songs she'd written. Without hesitation, she said, "Yes. They're in my head, up here in my head. Why?"

When I told her of Grandfather's idea, she didn't act excited. All she said was he is a kind man. Constantly, I wait for her to get excited about anything. Astrid never showed much emotion. I supposed I should be used to it by now.

As the year moved on, we sat alone, not always by choice. Astrid had her new music book. We never got invited to birthday parties or sleepovers. It used to bother me, but not anymore. My only friend would always be Astrid. We were now misfits of the seventh level. I wasn't sure Astrid could tell she was being teased. From the way she acted, I doubt she noticed.

Before the end of October, Astrid came to me one day during recess, all upset. We were required to pass the end-of-year written tests for promotion to the next level. At the rate she was going, I wasn't sure she'd make it. Her spelling tests were on the edge of failing. When we practiced our words during recess, she spelled the words out loud correctly but then couldn't write them. I agonized over her on the way home.

As soon as I walked in the door, my mother sensed something was amiss. "You look troubled, Lenora. Can we talk about what's wrong?"

A sigh escaped me. "It's Astrid. She has so much trouble with school now, worse than before. I'm afraid she'll be left behind. She does well in arithmetic and geography yet struggles in reading and writing. Sometimes, it's painful for her when we have to read aloud. She's teased unmercifully. I write her papers for her."

Mother gasped, "Lenora, that's cheating."

"It's not like that, I promise. Astrid tells me what she thinks about her assignments. I write it out after school when she goes home; she copies them."

"So that's why you dilly-dally on your way home. Do you correct them if she's wrong?" Mother put me on the spot. I couldn't lie.

I bit my lip, "Sometimes," I added quickly, "but not always."

Mother said nothing, then gave me a disapproving face.

Grandfather rattled his paper from the living room, "I'll see what I can do."

Later, I eavesdropped on his telephone conversation with someone. From what I could make out, the discussion centered around a type of exceptional learning. He spoke of Astrid.

The next day, I heard a familiar car drive up during the silent reading time. When I peeked out the window, Grandfather's cane tapped on the stairs as he made his way up. There was no concentrating on my book; I squirmed in my seat, raising my hand, asking to be excused. In the bathroom, I rubbed a wet paper towel over my face; in the mirror, a sad face stared back at me. When I returned, the car was gone. The headmaster called Astrid into the hall. Astrid never turned back to me. I stuck my nose in my book. The pounding of my heartbeat pulsed in my ears.

No time for talk; I'd failed Astie. I couldn't move on without her, I just couldn't! I heard our teacher ask Astrid to stay after school. The bell rang, everyone filed out of the room. I mouthed words, *I'll wait for you.*

Outside I paced in front of the steps, nervously waiting. An eternity passed, then Astrid appeared with her expressionless face.

"Well, what happened?"

In her usual monotone, she said, "Mr. Smyth told me I take oral exams instead of writing. I said my spelling words to him just now. I'm to stay after school on Wednesdays and Thursdays to pass seventh-grade exams."

"On those days, I will wait outside the door for you." I never heard of oral exams; whatever it meant, I was all for it if they moved Astrid to the next level.

In the by and by, whatever Grandfather made happen worked. I continued to help Astrid with her written work and seeing her become more relaxed did my heart good. Christmas sat just days away from winter break. At the dinner table, Grandfather announced he'd spoken to Astrid's parents.

"Yesterday, I asked if Astrid might come for the weekend. It took some convincing but she's coming on Friday after school."

"Yippee!"

"Lenora," said Mother, "Control yourself."

"Yes, ma'am." I knew my grandfather well enough to know he'd been up to something. However, he gave no hints.

"How are Astrid's studies going now?"

I think he already knew my answers. "Much better. She doesn't seem so terrified. I still help her," I sensed my mother glaring at me, "just not as much."

"Good, good," Grandfather paused, "Delicious meal, Mary. Shall we go to the fish market tomorrow? I believe Astrid eats fish on Friday."

I wonder what had gotten into him. He seemed exceptionally happy. I didn't want to think he paid them off, but I did wonder.

Friday, on the way to school, Astrid seemed more withdrawn than happy at the prospect of spending the weekend.

"Astie, are you afraid of something?"

Five minutes into our walk, she said, "Yes. My mum said this will be the last time I spend the weekend with you. She sounded mean."

"Oh," I didn't know what else to say.

At recess, we sat together, as usual. I handed Astie the new music book. Holding it to her chest, she slumped forward.

"Don't worry, Astie, we'll figure something out. Let's try to have fun this weekend. As Mother says, concentrate on today, not tomorrow."

"Okay."

During the last hour of school, fog rolled in from the ocean. It began to rain, perfect for our mood. I couldn't bear to think this would be our last weekend ever. My future included St. Agnes Preparatory School for Young Ladies near London. We were going to be separated then. I tried not to think about it as Mother said; now we stood to be separated forever after this weekend.

Grandfather came to school in his car to drive us home. On the dreary ride to the house, I saw his eyes in the rearview mirror, "My, my, you girls are awfully quiet." Astrid stared out the window. I felt helpless.

We shook the rain off before Mother handed me a towel. Mother offered us tea and a freshly baked blueberry scone to break the silence. I wanted to say something. There were no words in my mouth.

"Why so glum, girls?" asked Mother.

"This is Astrid's last weekend here. Her mother said so."

All Mother said was, "I see. I found little comfort in her response.

With Saturday's typical English weather, we moped around the house. Mother had us help with dinner. She made tea after dinner; Grandfather brought out a box of pastries. *Was this some special occasion?* I thought. Then he announced that Astrid might join me at St. Agnes Preparatory School for Young Ladies next year. Petrified, Astrid knew her parents couldn't ever allow it.

"Leave everything to me," he said. "I just have one request: keep this to yourself."

Keep it to yourself? I'd heard the best news in forever, and he wanted me to keep it a secret!

"It may take a lot of convincing to get your parents to sign off on my proposal; at any rate, I'm determined to make this happen. If you study hard this year, you will be able to join Lenora."

I thought Astrid remained calm; she trembled when we sat outside together. "What's wrong, Astie?"

"I don't know if I can do it, I don't know."

"Do what?"

"Go to that school. I'm not smart like you. I don't have nice clothes."

"They have pink plaid uniforms. You'll be fine. I'll help you like always; I promise."

"Okay." Her head rested on my shoulder.

The longer I knew her, I noticed the oddities more than before: hair twisting, clapping, stomping, repeating words as if I were deaf. There were bruises; I never said anything because I was afraid of the truth. The extra help at school made her worry less about her grades. Astrid never spoke again about her home life. Though quiet about her parents, I sensed fear. Nightmares plagued my sleep; I'd be standing in the schoolyard calling for her, but she was gone.

Seventh grade is a turning point for all students. You either moved up, or you became an apprentice in a trade. With five nervous days left in the school year, everyone waited by the bulletin board for exam postings. Uncertain if Astrid made it, my finger slid down the paper until I found her name.

"By gosh, we did it! We're going to St. Agnes!" She squealed, clapping her hands. Our classmates took a step back from us; the misfits shocked the class. We held hands until we got to the fork where Grandfather stood by the car. Puzzled, I waited for him to say something.

"Astrid, I've made arrangements with your parents. You'll be living with us now if you want to," he grinned. "Do you want to?"

My heartbeat could be heard for miles. She stood there under some magic spell, "Okay. Yes."

"I collected some of your belongings along with your pictures of Mary, Mother of God, and your Bible. Do you want to say goodbye to your family?"

She peered at the ground, shifting her weight from side to side, clutching her books, "What if they change their mind? Am I dreaming?"

His words were reassuring, "They won't, Astrid. I'm certain."

"Okay. I just want to go with Lenora."

"Then hop in the car; we'll go home."

I prayed Astrid could flow with change. Our new school required a train ride, miles from Brighton; the subjects weren't as easy. St. Agnes might prove too challenging for Astrid. My worries were not baseless;

she struggled. What often was easy-peasy for me would be difficult for her. Grandfather's good intentions could be Astrid's downfall.

Before attending St. Agnes, Grandfather announced a summer trip to London for the four of us. Astrid was family now. How my grandfather got permission from her parents baffled me, yet, it wasn't mine to question. Due to her peculiar nature, I believe they didn't want to be bothered with her. When Astrid was around, I didn't feel like an only child. Life was never boring with Astrid. And we were going to London!

Together we rummaged through my closet. Astrid was thinner and a bit taller. The blouses she brought were nice enough. I owned a black skirt that was too long for me. I hated a sundress that was a perfect fit for her, but she refused to try it on. The thin straps made her self-conscious. Last summer's clothes barely fit her after a two-inch growth spurt. Somehow, we came up with five outfits. Without hurting her feelings, I suggested we use my suitcase.

"To save room," I told her.

I don't know how she did it, but Astrid secretly saved a bit of money by helping a neighbor with chores. In the living room after dinner, I got to make an announcement that made Astrid gasp. With a grand gesture, I proclaimed, "We have tickets to the London Symphony!"

Astrid's hands covered her face, she tried to cry, but a strange wail came out. Grandfather put his arm around her, "There, there, child."

Her hands still covered her face, "I prayed to Mother Mary of God all my life for just one time to hear real music. I never thought she heard my prayers, but she did. God sent me to you. Mary, Mother of God, you heard me."

I hugged Astrid; she just stood there. Then my mother smiled and said, "It takes a blessing to be a blessing. Your music blesses us every time you play, Astrid. It's only fair you hear a real symphony."

She stood by my grandfather, watching the rain. Taking her hand, Grandfather said, "Every time I hear you play, it's delightful, Astrid. We all want you to develop your gift."

"Well," I screeched, "I'm a little jealous."

Grandfather turned to scold me, "Your turn is coming. Patience. We're going to the observatory and planetarium."

My jaw dropped, "Oh, gosh!"

My mother told us to take care of the dishes. It was the most enthusiastic dishwashing ever. Astrid pushed up her sleeves with great zeal, washed dishes, and I dried them.

Finished with the dishes, we stood side by side in the living room. The rain stopped; my mother handed me a towel. We stood before Grandfather. He ruffled his newspaper, peeking up over the top of his gold wire-rimmed glasses, "Go on," he said.

I giggled, grabbed Astie's hand, and ran outside to see the fading sunset give way to the full moon's reflection rising on the rippling waters. We squeezed into the deck chair. Astrid stared up at the sky, "We sat together in this same chair before."

A snort came out of me, "Yes, now my rear end is too big."

Her head made a short, sharp nod, "Is not," insisted Astrid, "We both grew up. We just grew up. Not all the way, yet."

"I hate being thirteen," I said with my arms crossed over my chest. "My breasts are too big."

"At least you got some," she said in her monotone. "My sister said I should stuff tissues in my bra. I won't do it. I hate growing up, too. Yes, I hate it."

I was afraid to laugh. Instead, we listened to the whoosh of waves on Brighton's beach. "We're both going off to prep school. Oh, Astrid, I can hardly believe it."

"I'm afraid to believe it." She rocked back and forth, "I'm nervous, Lenora, really scared. My mum doesn't love me anymore, Lenora."

"Oh, Astie, I'm sure she does. She wants what's best for you. That's why you're here now."

We talked about going away to school with anticipation and fear. Astrid never ventured far from home except to stay with me. Frightened by the uncertainty of new surroundings, Astrid grew quiet. I figured I was more adventurous and daring.

"I'm not smart like you," she uttered. "I'm different. I could get lost. It's a good thing you'll be with me in case I get lost."

"Grandfather says you learn differently than I do. I'll make sure you don't get lost."

My feelings were mixed. There were times when she seemed fragile and dependent on me. But, on the other hand, I cared for her and wanted to protect her. Deep inside, I worried for her, too.

"Time to come in, girls," my mother called from the kitchen window. We scrambled through the door.

"Wash up and brush your teeth. Are your suitcases packed?"

I chimed in, "We got everything in one suitcase!" I didn't want to embarrass Astrid.

"The less you'll carry on the train. Now off with you. We have a long day ahead."

"Trains! I love trains." Astrid's hands smacked together hard. I jumped. She loved trains and could tell you every type of engine in the world; I could care less, but she prattled on.

I huffed, "Blimey, I've heard enough, Astrid. Put on your nightgown." My bed would soon be too small for both of us. We pulled the covers over our heads. Astrid turned over, and I faced the wall, but our backsides touched; I giggled. "Is that giggling I hear?" Grandfather bellowed.

"Uh-oh," Astrid whispered.

"It's okay, go to sleep."

I barely slept. I'd never been to London; in fact, I never traveled outside the city of Brighton since we came here from Dublin.

| 4 |

London

We tried not to dress like country bumpkins in floral blouses and black skirts. Unfortunately, keeping up with fashion trends was impossible in our village. Arriving at night and seeing other teenagers in the train station, we'd failed miserably. Their clothes were mod, colorful; some girls wore miniskirts, others appeared like bohemians in long floral skirts. The boys wore denim jeans with tee shirts and shaggy hair. Caked with blue or green eyeshadow and false eyelashes, the girls wore frosted pink lipstick, too, like in the teen magazines. When Grandfather heard us talking about them, he grunted; under his breath, he huffed, "Trollops! They're too young for such nonsense, and the lads all need haircuts." I felt out of place and glad it was getting dark.

"Don't worry, dears, we'll buy some modern clothing," said my sympathetic mother.

"The bloody hell, you will!" Grandfather bellowed; people noticed. It was the first time I'd seen him this grumpy.

My mother pulled him aside, whispering in his ear. I strained to listen, but I thought better of it. Grandfather grumbled and hailed a taxi ride to one of London's finest hotels, the Hotel Saint Ermines. I elbowed Astrid, "Look over there! It's Buckingham Place." The lights shining on it gave an eerie glow. "I bet it's full of ghosts!" I made a woo sound—Astrid cowered. Mother chided me for such foolishness.

The hotel was grand, with crystal chandeliers and columns of marble; the floor shined like glass. The porter with bronze skin and dark eyes looked Indian. He was dressed in a crimson uniform with the hotel name embroidered on the pocket. He called my grandfather "Mr. McConnell," like he knew him. The porter took our luggage in a large elevator to our third-floor rooms. We took a different, old-fashioned elevator.

When the door to our room opened, I gasped.

"Are we living here, Lenora?"

"No, Astie," I rolled my eyes.

A luxury suite; white leather sofa and chairs, Art Deco trim, and a fireplace! Oh, and a small refrigerator held water, cola, and wine. Two bedrooms flanked the suite.

Floor-to-ceiling deep red velvet drapes and a matching bedspread were simple posh in the bedroom. Above the queen-size bed, a crown high on the wall draped with white netting touching the corners of the headboard; it served no real purpose. We felt like the bee's knees; a tufted chaise lounge in a muted pink sat by the window with two matching armchairs. The closet was as big as my bedroom at home; the bathroom held an oversized clawfoot tub with a showerhead. The large lightbulbs over the mirror were blinding; I wanted to know why they were so bright.

"They're for putting on makeup."

Huh, makeup. Something we weren't allowed to wear. Pressed powder and lip gloss with no color, hardly enough for girls our age.

"Thirteen is not too young for makeup," I rebelled. My mother did not answer. "Please, Mother, at least some blush and real lipstick?"

"We'll see."

In my head, *we'll see* was code for *probably not*. I plopped myself down in one of the chairs, defeated.

"Who's sleeping where?" I asked.

Astrid chimed in, "I can sleep on the floor. I don't mind. Or on the fainting couch." She plopped herself down. "I can sleep here. It's pink."

"The fainting couch?"

"Yes, this couch where women fainted if their corsets were too tight. My sister said so."

"Did you know that, Mother?"

"Your grandmother owned a fainting couch, but we call them chaise lounges now since we don't have corsets anymore."

"Thank God." What women went through back then was mortifying. I hated wearing a bra.

"Astrid, you will not sleep on the floor. The sofa in the other room can be made into a bed. It is where I'll sleep. It's perfect for an early riser," said Mother.

Like a pouty little girl, Astrid crossed her arms over her chest. "It hardly seems fair. I sleep on the floor at home."

Mother and I glanced at each other, shocked. Then mother explained she liked to fix morning coffee and have some quiet time. One thing Mother did insist on was a nine o'clock bedtime. Astrid sighed; I threw my hands up with defiance, "But it's a quarter till eight now. My stomach is growling. We haven't eaten supper yet."

Grandfather appeared from his room, "Dinner will be here shortly."

"In this room? Food in the room?" Astrid said in disbelief.

Grandfather nodded in affirmative, "Baked cod with mashed and green beans."

We turned our noses up with disgust. Astrid cupped her hand to my ear, "I don't eat green stuff."

He stated, "You'll eat it or go to bed hungry. It's your choice."

My eyebrow arched, timidly I said, "Grandfather, Astrid doesn't eat green beans or peas."

Grandfather cleared his throat, "Then I'll have them send carrots. Oh, by the way, a clean plate wins dessert." There was a twinkle in his eyes; he wagged his finger, "but don't inhale your food. Manners, my dears."

Room service wheeled in the dinner cart when a steward set the table; Astrid clapped her hands with glee. As we ate, Mother zipped through tomorrow's schedule. I didn't pay much attention to her; the dessert was apple strudel with vanilla ice cream.

"If it rains, we shall go to the National Gallery in Trafalgar Square. Seeing masterworks of art should be a wonderful experience for us all."

"You realize I won't be accompanying you for most of this trip?" He sounded rather pleased with himself.

Surprised, "Why not?" I asked.

"Your grandfather has many friends from the banking business here in London."

"And I don't move as fast as I used to." He punctuated, *used to,* with his ivory-handled walking stick. "I will accompany you, Lenora, to the planetarium and The Royal Observatory. Astrid, I've arranged a private tour of the Barbican Center, home of The London Symphony."

"And you're going to the Symphony with us!" Astrid decreed.

"Of course, Little Star. I won't miss it."

"Grandfather," with my face of stone, I pleaded my case, "this is exactly why we need new clothes. We couldn't go to the London Symphony like housemaids." I didn't want to make him upset, but I stood my ground.

He learned long ago never to argue with a woman. Well, I was almost a woman.

"None of the mini skirt business. I won't have you showing your behind, young lady."

He referred to me as a young lady! It tickled me, but I dared not smile. Standing in front of my mother, he said, "Take them to Harrod's sometime tomorrow." With a dismissive wave, he said, "Let them try on the whole store."

I broke out with an ear-to-ear grin. I'm sure Astrid didn't understand what Harrod's was.

"But," he added, "only choose three outfits each."

Astrid studied the floor, but I saw her smile. I kissed his cheek. "I want you to know how much this means to me, to us."

"And," Astrid added, "school shirts, for our uniforms. Please and thank you."

He smiled his all-knowing smile, "You both are welcome." He stood up gingerly, "I know you will both accomplish much when you grow up." Before he stepped into the bedroom, he turned to us, "I'm glad God gave me the privilege of being a part of your lives. And Lenora, I'm sure your father could not be prouder."

My eyes watered, and a lump stuck in my throat. I ran to Grandfather and squeezed tight, "Your father shines through you, Lenora." He straightened up, "Off to bed with you."

My mother was teary-eyed; Astrid sniffled because we were sniffling. Mother said, "Brush your teeth, wash your face; you can bathe in the morning."

While in the bathroom, I could hear Astrid pacing the floor talking to someone. My ear was glued to the door. I tried to make out what she said. Was Astrid talking to my mother Mary or Mary, Mother of Jesus? I stayed in the bathroom until she got in bed. I didn't understand why Astrid didn't just pray to Jesus himself like other people. When she finished, I got in bed. I wanted to ask her about Mary, Mother of God, but we were too tired.

| 5 |

Art and Harrod's

Mother pulled the curtain back, the rain streamed down the windows. She announced a change of plans; we were going to the art gallery, ho-hum. The prospect of exploring old paintings didn't thrill me. Astrid, on the other hand, could hardly wait. In the center room, she paced back and forth, reciting artistic works and painters that I'd never heard of before, one after another like a machine. My mouth gaped open, my hands on my hips; jealousy swept over me.

"Where did you learn about art?" I snarked.

"The Catholic Church," her response was sassy.

As my mother powdered her nose, she took Astrid's side, "I know this is true. Many great works of art are in churches."

With an eye roll, I retreated to the bedroom.

Grandfather bellowed, "Five minutes until we go down to breakfast! You best be ready, ladies."

"Yes, sir," I called from the bathroom. I wet my brush to tame my wild hair. Foggy London town had wreaked havoc with my curls.

In the old-fashioned elevator, I noticed the very ornate metalwork on the cage. Brass swans were the closing handles. Iron bars of ivy climbed from top to bottom. Every few inches were horizontal braided brass ribbons. Astrid traced the ivy with her finger. It's too bad we weren't on the seventh floor. I'd enjoy the ride even more.

After breakfast, we took a taxi to the Royal Art Museum. Unfortunately, there was little to see along the way. Fog hung over the roads making the ride long and tedious.

"Is it always this dreary?" I questioned the driver. Mother pinched my arm and shot me a look of disdain.

I saw the driver's smile in the mirror. His two front teeth were gone. He spoke with a thick Cockney accent, "I get that question a lot, Misses. The river Thames runs right through the city; the temperature shifts bring fog and rain. Wait a while; it'll change."

Mother paid the entry fees on our arrival, and we checked our macs. I didn't realize how big this place was until a uniformed man gave Mother a map.

Mother sat in the middle of us on a white marble bench, reminding us to stay behind the ropes in the galleries. My mind flashed to a picture of Astrid touching a painting, setting alarms off.

"What gallery shall we start with, girls?"

I rested my elbow on my knee, and my chin rested on my hand, "I don't care, let's just go." I was bored already. I wanted to go clothes shopping.

"Lenora Irene," I'd stuck my foot in it now as Mother stated, "stop ruminating about yourself for once."

From that point on, I decided to be quiet. Out of defiance, I only spoke when spoken to. However, I couldn't help myself at the Picasso exhibit, where I blurted out, "Picasso's early stuff is fine. But this one is like a kindergartner's temper tantrum!"

Everyone in the gallery stopped murmuring.

Mother pulled my arm, "Hush, Lenora! I don't know what has gotten into you. Art galleries and museums are places of reverence, like a library." My outburst mortified my mother.

"Sorry," I whispered. Later, behind my mother's back, Astrid cupped my ear to whisper, *"I didn't like him either; they were messed up."*

My mood matched the day, dark and gloomy. Shuffling from gallery to gallery made me want to scream until I saw a painting by Pierre Auguste Cot entitled, The Storm, with a young couple fleeing a nearing thunderstorm. It was how the young man was trying to protect a beautiful young maiden. The way he beheld her; he loved her; she trusted him. The young woman held a cloth corner; the young man grasped the other end to shield them from the oncoming storm. If only I could find such love.

"Come on, Lenora, we're almost to the end," called Astrid in a childlike voice, grabbing me by the hand. "Just the Gogan paintings!"

I didn't correct the way she said, *Gauguin*. His paintings were embarrassing with my mother present; too many images of colorful barebreasted native girls. Astrid felt self-conscious, dragging her toe on the marble floor. My mother hurried us along to the coat check.

It had stopped raining; the sun finally came out. We begged to ride on the top of the red double-decker bus. Mother asked the driver if the seats were damp. He turned his nose up, "Wouldn't be running if they were."

"Very well."

We dashed to the top; the wind blew our hair. I heard the sounds of cars and a whistle from a bobby who directed traffic at the center of the cross streets. The busy London streets were full of taxis, fancy cars, a huge marquee for a new James Bond movie, "Goldfinger." Astrid remarked how the buildings were sooty. Compared to the picture books I'd seen, the Big Ben clock didn't seem very tall to me.

All that mattered getting to Harrod's, the place of the London Look in the magazines, and everything else under the sun. I read they once brought a lion from a circus inside, a real lion! In the distance, unlike most other brick buildings, Harrod's seemed to be a bright golden color, seven stories high with many windows; the entryway sat right on the street corner. Rounded green awnings shaded the large ground-to-floor windows displaying everything from kitchen appliances to mink coats. I never imagined such a big store; it took up a whole city block. I grasped Astrid's hand, afraid of losing her, as she gawked at all the displays. We, even Mother, were amazed by the entry, a department store with marble floors and columns; two young women in navy blue uniforms greeted us and handed out a floor plan. People were everywhere. We moved out of the way to have a gander.

"Three hundred departments!" I thought my mother might faint. I thought I might faint.

"Gosh," Astrid said in awe, with her head twisting this way and that. She gripped my hand tight like a mousetrap.

"Mother, there are restaurants inside here," I pointed to the map. "We should have lunch and study the floor plan." My mother was very sensible until she saw twenty different restaurants listed. She chose a sandwich shop close to the entrance.

A sign above us read The Fresh Market Hall. I shook off Astrid's hand, gobsmacked. The smell of rotisserie chicken, bangers, chips, bananas, and fresh-brewed coffee permeated the air; the rattle of cutlery and banging dishes echoed through the Hall.

"This is no sandwich shop," I stated, "It's an open-air market inside a building."

"This way," said Mother. We followed like little ducklings to the deli counter. The glass display case sat full of delights: coleslaw, American potato salad, green gelatin with pears, slabs of meats for slicing, and a world of cheeses.

Mother whispered to us, "Keep your order simple." We waited to see what order she gave to a jolly man sporting a white puffy hat and a black handlebar mustache.

"Ham and Swiss cheese, please."

"What kind of bread, ma'am?"

We held our breath.

"Rye bread with mayo, please."

"Any crisps or salad with that?"

My mother was quiet for what seemed forever.

"Humm, I'll try the American potato salad, a small portion," she smiled.

Turning to Astrid, he said, "And you, young lady?"

Breathless and fidgeting, Astrid said, "I'll have the same."

Oh, brother, Astrid lacked imagination. When he asked for my order, I said, "I'll have the Black Forest ham with Provolone cheese on a Kaiser roll and crisps. Oh, and a dill pickle spear, please."

Surprised, he asked if I wanted butter or mayonnaise. "Butter, please."

The sandwiches were in baskets lined with parchment paper. We slid our trays down to the drink area. There were choices of water, tea, or cola. *Cola!*

Then the hammer hit. "Water for the three of us," Mother said. Astrid mimicked my disgruntled expression, then just shrugged her shoulders and gave me the *oh well*.

Mother was deep in thought. She cut her sandwich into two, holding it with her pinky up. Studying the floor plan, Mother asked, "Should we go to the junior misses department or shoes first?"

"We get to buy shoes?" I questioned, "I didn't know we could buy shoes!"

"Your grandfather is a very generous man."

Astrid interjected, "But what about you, Mrs. Mary? Don't want to want to buy a new dress? We get new clothes. You should get new clothes, too." Astrid mumbled to herself.

I piped up, "Maybe we should go to the ladies' floor first. You should try on some dresses and be our runway model." Astrid clapped her hands.

Mother shook her head, "Don't be silly, Lenora. I have no one to dress up for." At that moment, I truly felt sorry for her.

"Mother, you can buy an everyday dress. Why not something different to wear to the book club?"

"I have plenty of nice clothes."

"You haven't bought anything new since," I stopped, took a breath, and finished, "since moving to Brighton."

"That's not right; I bought a sweater and some new shoes." My mother sighed, put an arm around me, and said, "All right, I don't want to disappoint the two of you." Astrid began to do a little dance and flap her hands.

To get to the elevator, we walked through the perfume section. The endless glass shelves lit up with fancy bottles, tall, small, cut glass, colored glass, stoppers of butterflies, and figurines.

"Close your mouth, Lenora. It's not polite to stare." Ladies handed us small rectangular cards sprayed with perfume; brand names were written on the back if we wanted to buy some. Sniffing the card constantly, I told Astrid to stop it. She hung her head, sticking them in her pockets.

The elevator doors opened, and several people got on, packed in like sardines in a can. The elevator operator described the departments on each floor.

"Fourth floor: womenswear, lingerie, hosiery. Next floor, formal-wear, junior misses, women's shoes."

"This your floor!" I uttered. It was indeed Christmas in July. We stood for a minute to get our bearings while women's undergarments stared us in the face.

Astrid pointed to an arrow overhead, "This way to women's clothes."

Mannequins scare me. I walked in the middle of the wide aisle as if they were going to reach out and yell *boo*! Ahead, Mother saw the casual dress section. There was a rack of pantsuits; she didn't even pay attention to them. A saleswoman asked, "May I help you find something, madame?"

The lady, who I guessed to be in her fifties, was wearing a blue suit with gold piping, with hair pulled in a tight bun. So tight, she came across as Asian.

"I'm seeking a daytime, causal, ah, book club dress."

My cheeks flushed; I broke out in a sweat. It was the first I felt nervous for my mother. It was so unlike her; we lived in a big city until my father's death. She stammered, for God's sake; she needed to get out more. The sales lady pointed the way to casual dresses. She offered her help, but Mother declined. The woman left, thank God! Was there something wrong with my mother?

I softly asked, "Are you okay?"

She straightened her spine, "I'm fine, dear."

Astrid began sifting through the racks of casual dresses.

"Looky at this one," shouted Astrid, holding up a dark blue dress, "it has tiny white pokey-dots."

My mother's eyes brightened. How could she resist the excited Astrid? Oh, brother.

"Let me check the size." Holding it up, Mother gazed at her reflection in the three-way mirror. The corners of her mouth turned up. "It might fit."

In the meantime, Astrid and I rummaged through the racks pulling out more dresses.

"Slow down," said Mother. "Let's see what you have for me."

Mother was enjoying herself for the first time in a long while.

"Three dresses, no more. You'll wear me out!"

I picked a short-sleeved dress with pink rosettes on a black background. Finally, Astrid and I agreed on a mid-length sky blue dress with a sophisticated dark blue patten-leather belt.

"Very well, I'll try these."

In anticipation, Astrid and I sat together on a blue velveteen bench near the dressing room. Astrid flapped her hand furiously.

I gritted my teeth and said, "Stop it! People are staring." I hurt her feelings.

"Sometimes I can't stop," she whispered. I told her no clapping or flapping when Mother came out. To subdue Astrid's excitement, we'd give a thumbs up or down when she appeared.

Astrid's heels bounced on the floor, "She's been in there a while."

"You know my mother has to smooth every wrinkle."

We sat in awe when she came from the dressing room wearing the blue belted dress. My mother appeared younger and alive.

"Oh, Mother, you look…" I searched for the right words, "stunning!"

Astrid stared at her. "I wish my mum looked like you."

My sensible mother replied, "Darling, I'm sure she does her best with six children."

"Yes, ma'am. I suppose she does."

Mother shined in the three-way mirror, "I must buy this one. I don't need to see the others. It's not too fancy for the book club or shopping."

I must admit my jealousy; Mother didn't try the dress I picked for her. Astrid told me she felt bad for her mum. I suggest she buy something for her mother, maybe a scarf.

"Do you wear a scarf to Mass? I heard women put a tissue on their heads if they didn't have a scarf."

Astrid's anger came out, "Of course, we don't. We don't wear tissues. We blow noses with tissues."

When I laughed, she put on her mad face. I stood there with egg on my face. Mother came out, the dress folded neatly over her arm, "Why those awful faces?" she asked.

"Lenora thought Catholics wear tissues on their head for Mass."

"Lenora, that's just silly."

To keep myself from more humiliation, "I just meant Astrid might buy her mum a nice scarf."

Mother thought it was a nice gesture. Off to the accessories we trotted. Astrid found a black lacy scarf with a "Made in Italy" tag.

"Oh, yes, yes, my mother will love this." She gasped at the price tag, "Oh, I better put it back."

"Nonsense!" said Mother, "Your Mother was gracious enough to allow you to stay with us. I'll have it gift-wrapped."

"Oh, thank you, Mrs. Mary." Astrid quietly said, "I hope she likes it. I hope she likes the scarf."

We paid for everything then caught the next elevator. The elevator man was shorter than I. Everyone who worked there wore a uniform and a navy pillbox hat, a strap under the chin. He sounded out the contents of the fifth floor. The doors opened to a fairyland: formal dresses in blues, pinks, greens, and shimmering white for a debutante ball and weddings. We walked forever to find regular teenagers' clothes.

Mother reminded us Grandfather was paying for sensible clothes, no short skirts or low-cut dresses.

"Well," I said without thinking, "you don't have to worry about Astrid. She stuffs her bra." Her jaw dropped. I betrayed her trust. Words came out; I couldn't take them back.

I could tell my mother was cross with me. She turned to a red-faced Astrid, "Don't worry, darling, so did I."

With her eyes ahead, Astrid giggled. My mother glared at me; I felt small and terrible

"How much can we spend?" I asked.

"Don't worry about how much, but how many." Mother explained how to arrange five clothing pieces for an interchangeable ensemble.

A neon sign above the junior section flashed, "The London Look." Mannequins dressed in miniskirts, blouses with puffy sleeves, and red or white patent leather knee-high boots. One mannequin dressed in a plastic-looking Union Jack flag dress caused my mother to grab at her chest.

"Dear God! I'm glad your grandfather won't see this one!"

Astrid and I spotted a poster of a teen magazine model who painted eyelashes under her eyes; Twiggy. She was a twig! By my mother's reaction to the fashions, we lived in the Stone Age. Two teen girls going through the rack of clothes glared at us. They laughed at us and even pointed.

"Well," said my prudish mother rather loudly, "you never point at anyone or anything; it's rude. They weren't given a decent upbringing."

"No, Mother, we're country folks. Country folks don't wear go-go boots. Please don't send us to prep school like this." I pleaded, "We will fall prey to a new set of mean girls."

"You'll have uniforms to keep that from happening."

I whined, "I don't mean to be rude, but we don't have to wear our uniforms all day and on weekends."

Astrid's sad face always melted my mother's heart; some days, I resented her, but not today. That puppy dog face caused Mother to reconsider.

"I understand, darling. We'll be modern yet simple."

"No," I said, "not simple! It's a terrible word meaning stupid." *Uh oh. Careful. Don't overstep the boundaries.* "Here's what I mean." I pulled out a white blouse with a rounded collar and short puffy sleeves. "Like this, not a boyish Oxford shirt."

Astrid's eyes lit up, "I like it! I like puffy sleeves."

My mother tapped her cheeks, scrutinizing the material. "You will have to iron it."

"Yes, ma'am," I affirmed.

Astrid lilted with her head bobbing, "We can wear white and pastel pink blouses with our uniforms, Mrs. Mary." We found white and pastel pink blouses with rounded collars for school.

"One of each," Mother reminded. She gave us the run of the teen section while she chose skirts for us. Astrid and I were clueless about what size we wore; odd numbers like nine or eleven were confusing. We disappeared into the dressing rooms, arms loaded.

"You first," Astrid glared at me. I certainly wasn't as modest as her. I almost ripped off my shirt. Astrid's eyes widened. All the time we knew each other, we never saw each other in a state of undress.

"Stop staring," I balked.

"I'm sorry, but I didn't know you were big." Deadpan, she said, "I don't need a bra. My sister said I need band-aids."

A loud *ha* came out of me. I immediately covered my mouth, fearing my voice would echo around the hall.

I tried not to laugh, "I'm sorry. I'm not making fun of you, but what you said was funny."

Astrid pouted.

"Having big boobs is not that great, Astie. Boys stare at me. As you can see, button blouses fit everywhere but across my chest." In the mirror, there were gaps between the buttons.

Astrid didn't undress yet. She examined her shoes, "I'll get you a bigger one." She retrieved another.

We came out of the dressing room with the blouses and tartan plaid skirts my mother found. We scanned the area for my mother.

"Over here, dears." She discovered the clothing section from Laura Ashley, floral patterns in pastel colors, modern but not too flashy. We balked at first, but on the wall above were large pictures that positively influenced us. Astrid tried on a puffy white long-sleeved blouse and a long skirt with tiny periwinkle flowers. Astrid appeared taller; I loved it, and so did she. A saleslady commented on Astrid's beauty. Astrid cast her eyes on the worn carpet; she turned red from embarrassment.

I chose an A-line dress; it covered a multitude of sins. Mother loved the white cuffs, rounded collar, a navy-blue conservative color. I didn't want to stick out any more than possible. I'm curvy and grew up unmercifully teased.

Astrid stood five feet, seven inches, slender, and four inches taller than me. Mother said I took after my father's side; they were big-boned. My father stood tall at six feet, a large man but not fat. I knew I was doomed when Astrid shot up like a weed last year.

"You look adorable, Lenora." Mother chuckled.

Just what I wanted to hear, I was "adorable," like a fat-cheeked baby. Astrid was beautiful; I was adorable. Geez.

We returned to the hotel, each with three blouses, two plaid skirts, a floral skirt for Astrid, my dress, and black Mary Jane shoes. Mother let us buy stockings with garters without telling Grandfather.

Tossing our bags on the bed, we pulled out the clothes. My mother never let me wear new clothes until they were washed. While my mother busied herself in the bathroom getting ready for dinner, Astrid and I darted into the closet to quickly change our new tartan plaid skirts and blouses; me in blue, Astrid in red with matching knee socks. We heard my mother come from the bathroom. I struck a pose like girls in the magazines.

"Well, aren't the two of you the dog's dinner!"

"Please, can we wear them?" I pleaded.

"Well, you both have me hoodwinked. You've no time to change."

When we arrived, Grandfather sat in the dimly lit formal dining room. The dark wood paneling and the fog of cigar smoke gave me a chill. The smell of cigar smoke brought sad memories of my father, who smoked an old stogie every Friday evening.

Mother reminded us of posture and manners. Her words echoed in my head; *you weren't raised in a barn.* Back straight, hands in lap, feet crossed at the ankles, don't speak unless spoken to, and use the proper utensils.

"I see you young ladies have new clothes." He scrutinized us as we sat. Twirling his finger, "Turn around." We made a quarter turn like the models in fashion shows. "Hmm. I guess they'll do. Astrid, you look very nice."

Her hands were folded in front of her; eyes down, she said thank you. *What about me?* I thought! I wanted to say something spiteful but resisted. After all, my clothes were just like hers, just different colors. We took our place at the table. My mother chimed in, "You should have seen some of the other dresses, John. If a girl bent over, well, I think you understand."

I battled my eyelashes and added my two cents, "Grandfather, thank you, now we won't be the laughingstock of St. Agnes Preparatory School. Astrid and I want to blend in. Isn't that right, Astrid?"

She didn't hear a word I said with her nose buried in the menu. I kicked her under the table, "Isn't that right?"

Wide-eyed and oblivious to what was said, she answered, "Yes." Sometimes she infuriates me. Her mind was out in space somewhere.

She nudged me and whispered, "What is patty de foy grass?" instead of the correct pronunciation of *pâté de foie gras*. I was embarrassed for her and glad she whispered.

My grandfather heard her. In a quiet voice, he said, "So, it's French, my Sweet; I shall give you a culinary lesson. According to French cuisine, foie gras is the liver of a duck or goose. Pâté means ground, so ground goose liver. And it's delicious."

I watch the blood drain from Astrid's face. Her muted response came, "Oh, I will pass."

I ordered it just to be spiteful. I said I was fond of it, and Astrid could have some of mine. Astrid kicked me hard under the table. An audible *ouch* came from me. Just for that, I put some goose liver on her plate of Brie and bread, forcing her to take a bite of a cracker. We all watched her swallow. She wanted to gag but gulped down a full glass of water.

She gawked at me with those puppy-dog eyes, "That wasn't very nice." I wanted sweet revenge, but I anticipated a reprimand. Mother shot daggers at me.

We ordered duck with root vegetables except for Astrid. She ordered the salmon with dill sauce. Duck is somewhat difficult to eat in polite society. Pulling off the legs isn't very ladylike in a posh dining room. I struggled, and Astrid snickered. I observed my grandfather put the napkin under his beard and then pull the legs right off! Now I knew what the small bowl of water was for; he dipped his fingertips and wiped them on another napkin. I then decided to do as Grandfather did by pulling the legs and thighs loose, slippery, and greasy, but I managed not to drop it in my lap. I know I will never order it again.

In the elevator, I thought my stomach might burst. The flaming cherries jubilee was too much, but I couldn't resist, especially when the waiter singed his hair while lighting the cognac.

In her awkward way, Astrid said, "Thank you, Mr. McConnell. I'm so very grateful for all you've done for me."

"You are quite welcome, my Sweet. The best is yet to come," Grandfather said, patting her shoulders. "The day after tomorrow is the tour of the concert hall."

I could tell he was up to something.

I woke up the next morning excited. A trip to the London Planetarium today! I could scarcely contain myself. We were to meet with the director, Mr. Roger Weldon. A coppery green dome sat like a half ball in a courtyard. A tall, slender gentleman greeted us with a Sherlock Holmes pipe in his hand. I could tell he caught my mother's eye; he had movie-star good looks. He sounded like someone you could listen to for hours. His pipe seemed more of a prop for punctuating words than smoking.

"So," he smiled at me, "You are interested in the stars?" I swear his eyes twinkled.

"Yes, sir. My Grandfather taught me many constellations, and I love Greek mythology, but I want to learn so much more."

"Let's go inside." He ushered us into the sizeable dome-shaped room. The lights were on, circular rows of seats surrounded a giant machine in the shape of a barbell with rounded heads. He called the Zeiss projector; it projected the night sky onto the dome's wall. "When the lights go out, the seats recline. Sit, please, anywhere you like."

My heart thumped so hard against my chest. I thought surely everyone could hear it. Grandfather and Mother sat in the front row; I ran around to the other side with Astrid in tow. We sat in the third row.

"How about a demonstration?" he asked. I stammered, "Y-yes. Please."

"You've come at the perfect time; the public viewing is only open Tuesday through Sunday at four-thirty and again at seven-thirty. We allow school groups during the day. Today you are my special guests. Programmed into the star projector are coordinates and the narration is added; by me, of course." He gave a little twitter. "Sit back and enjoy the show."

The lights dimmed, and the chairs reclined. Astrid gasped and closed her eyes, acting scared to death. I held her hand. "It's not scary. It will be like having a special sky over our heads. Open your eyes," I encouraged. The room darkened to black, and then the music started; Astrid whispered, "'The Planets' by Gustav Holst is playing,"

The voice was Mr. Weldon's, smooth as milk chocolate. The stars began to dot the ceiling, and sunset shone against the London skyline's backdrop. I died and went to heaven: constellations, galaxies, and planets. The hour-long program was beautiful, but I wanted to know more. When the show finished, I thanked Mr. Weldon. He did an excellent job with the show, but truthfully, I knew most of what we'd seen. That's when he pointed his pipe at me and said, "I'll bet you knew most of the constellations, didn't you?"

I managed a modest *yes*.

"Your Grandfather talked of your desire to visit the Royal Observatory. It's on the Prime Meridian. The place where all time is measured." I floated on his next statement, mesmerized by this Wizard of Worlds in the sky.

"Tonight, you will be my guest at the Onion Dome to observe outer space through the Equatorial Telescope. We'll scout for nebulas."

I felt goosebumps from the top of my head to the bottom of my feet. Shocked, all I could do was breathe through my gaping mouth.

"My, my, Lenora, I've never seen you at a loss for words," Grandfather laughed.

Mr. Weldon shook my hand! "I'll see you and your grandfather at eight o'clock sharp, young lady."

"Yes, sir," life returned to my bones, "Yes!"

In the taxi, my mother made it clear that a nap was in my future. Astrid spoke up, "What about me, Mrs. Mary? I don't like naps."

"You won't be going, dear. This part of the trip is for Lenora." I sat up straight; Astrid pouted like a little girl.

"Not me, Mrs. Mary?"

"Don't worry, Astrid, your turn is next," said Grandfather.

"Did you nap, Lenora?" Grandfather asked, knowing the answer.

"No. How could I? You have made me the happiest girl on this planet!"

A jolly laugh came from him as we walked together. It took an eternity for the taxi to arrive. Against the darkening, I could see the observatory's white dome awash in yellow lights; I understood why it's called the Onion Dome.

"Grandfather, how do you know Mr. Weldon?"

"In his younger days as a journalism student, Roger Weldon interviewed me for a business publication. Poor chap didn't have a clue what he was doing. I told Roger he should go into broadcasting with a voice like his; he secured a job in radio. We stayed in touch off and on, talking of life on other planets and all the galaxies. The next thing I knew, last year, he called to say he was the new curator of the planetarium. And here we are, all visitors have gone for the day."

And now, a special privilege granted to only me would be envied by others. On the main gate, a large clock kept time for the world. A sign pointed the way to the dome. I wanted to run, but I waited impatiently on Grandfather's slow strides.

Mr. Weldon met us at an open side door marked "Employees Only." He asked me if I minded climbing stairs; a strange question, I thought. Once inside, I knew why.

"Gosh! How big is it?" I thought my eyes might pop out at the behemoth-sized telescope.

"It's seventy-four meters high. Imagine a comparison; it's taller than a three-story building. You should study Annie Maunder, a brilliant astronomer. She received little credit for her discovery of solar flares. Mrs. Maunder could only volunteer to work with her husband as his assistant. At the time, her husband got the credit. The astronomy committees didn't allow women scientists. If you aspire to be an astronomer, I recommend her books." He used his pipe to point to the sky, "I want you to consider this; we are all dust from an exploding star."

How profound, how magical! I stood bewitched in front of the telescope. Tonight, we're viewing nebulas light-years away, interstellar clouds of stardust. All matter is made of stardust, including me.

I climbed the steps to a platform where Mr. Weldon entered coordinates for these unique star groups. He gave me an eye patch; like a pirate waiting for a ship of stars, I stood in awe. The nebulas have funny but fitting names: The Crab, The Cat-Eye, and The Swan. So many galaxies; the Milky Way and Andromeda are the ones I knew of, but millions more dot the universe. I had so many questions, maybe too many. Mr. Weldon pointed out the Ring nebula; if God owned an eye, this was the nebula. God's eye, a deep blue iris, and instead of white, green surrounded it, the eyelid lined with a fiery red. God was watching me, and I beheld the eye of God until my eye hurt. I didn't *want to be* an astronomer; I *was* an astronomer. After prep school, my goal was admittance to Cambridge University with the best astronomy department in Great Britain. The sky is not the limit; it's limitless.

Mr. Weldon shot a grin at my grandfather, who winked at me, pleased as punch.

In awe, I said, "There is so much to learn. I want to know as much as my brain can hold." I wanted to lose myself in space. "I'd give anything to work in this place, discovering new stars and nebula."

Mr. Weldon sat me down, giving me in the eye with a piece of advice "Calculus and physics are not easy subjects, but they are essential to astronomy. Study hard, and learn them well. Your Grandfather mentioned your desire to go to Cambridge."

"Yes, sir."

"The Observatory is being incorporated into the curriculum there. Cambridge will add an apprentice program soon. I expect by the time you attend Cambridge, the program will be in full swing."

My heart stood still, "You mean here at the Observatory?"

Mr. Weldon nodded. The prospect of working here made my head swim.

"Understand, I don't have input over programs and grants or much influence with some of the new administrators, but somehow I don't imagine you'll need much help finding a place here."

Grandfather pointed his finger at Mr. Weldon, "I told you she was bright, as bright as a full moon."

My face showed the grin of a Cheshire Cat. I knew this required concentrating on subjects that didn't come naturally. I'd never taken a physics class: chemistry in prep school needed my full attention. And Astrid couldn't be the center of my world now.

| 6 |

A Flourish of Notes

Ricardo Vercelli led our private tour of the London Symphony facilities. I learned that he was more than a tour guide; he was the concertmaster, a place of honor. We walked to the practice rooms first, then sat in the balcony listening to the history; I was bored to tears. Try as I might, I didn't share Astrid's enthusiasm. My feet were killing me from wearing my new shoes.

Astrid fidgeted as we moved to the backstage area. As we walked onto the stage, her head tilted upward. She acted weird, flapping her hands like a baby bird. I grabbed her hand to stop her. It was like wrestling an alligator; flapping turned into short bursts of clapping.

Ricardo asked if I played an instrument. I gave a resounding no. He turned to Astrid with the same question anticipating a positive answer.

She gave a vigorous nod, "I play piano," she paused, "and write music!"

In his thick Italian accent, "You write de music?" He tried to act surprised. I knew this was a setup. He pointed to the grand piano, "How about you, ah, play something?"

Astie's eyes widened; her hands came together prayerfully. Astrid asked, "It's okay?"

"But of course."

"What should I play?"

"Do you know any of Beethoven's piano sonatas?"

Her eyes were on the keys, "Oh yes! I heard this once! It's in F Minor Opus two, yes, yes."

We all sat down in the orchestra seats. I held my breath. I could see my grandfather's bright eyes over the top of his glasses; he leaned forward on his cane. Astrid's arched fingers brought a flourish of notes, melodic and full of passion. I'd watched her play before, but not like this. She played for us all the time; today, at the grand piano, Astrid became someone else. She transported herself into another dimension, taking us with her.

I studied her movements with the music; her head bobbed with emphasis, fingers dancing across the keys. Her actions were intense, almost scary. By the last cord, her hair covered her face; she threw her head back, sweat beads sprinkling her forehead. She tucked her long, reddish-blond hair behind her ears. The tremendous applause came from two people hidden in the shadows of the balcony. Astrid jumped, startled by the applause.

Astrid caught her breath from the musical marathon; the individuals came from the balcony to the stage. The man identified himself as Sir David Roth, the symphony's musical director. The woman, Rosamunde Ryan, was a teacher and a concert pianist. Sir David gushed over Astrid, who nervously shifted her weight from side to side. Miss Ryan offered her services as Astrid's mentor and teacher. I should have been happy for her, but the hair on the back of my neck stood up. I just knew I was going to lose my best friend.

St. Agnes Preparatory School boasted one of the best music programs. Along with her studies, Astrid was to receive private lessons. Miss Ryan asked how long Astrid had studied piano.

Her eyes fixed on the keys, Astrid muttered, "I never took lessons before." Glances one to another were expressions of disbelief.

"How is it possible?" Miss Ryan scoffed.

My grandfather assured them Astrid was truthful, "Astrid possesses a gift wrapped in a different package. You see, she can hear music once and play by memory." Grandfather's chest puffed out, "Astrid's gift is unexplainable. And she composes music." He patted Astrid's shoulder.

"This is highly unusual." Miss Ryan sounded vexed.

"Well, Mr. McConnell, if your assumption is correct, we will work with her."

Indignant, Grandfather answered, "I assure you, Sir, it is."

Sir Snobbishness asked for a test if Astrid did not mind. I thought this test to be rude; poor Astie sat cluelessly. He practically pushed her off the bench. He played something I'd never heard. Pleased with himself, he smiled at Astrid. Miss Ryan stood, arms crossed over her black velvet jacket.

"Let's see what you can do." He motioned to the bench. I whispered to her, "You're better than he is."

Taking her place, she sat in silence as we waited. And waited while Roth and Ryan smiled evil smiles.

Astrid sat up straight, fingers flying.

Ryan's eyes widened; I smirked inside, *knock their knickers off, Astie.* Everyone took note of Astrid's recall expertly played.

Roth looked at Astie, "You've played this before."

"No sir," she quietly replied.

He scratched his head, dazed, "Chopin's Polonaise, number three in A major. I am flabbergasted. And you played better than me."

Astrid gripped the bench with knuckles turning white.

"My, my, child. We have classes for gifted musicians, but that can wait until next summer. Miss Ryan's technique class will hone your skills."

Astrid seemed like a frightened animal with nowhere to run. Finally, Grandfather stood behind her and put his hand on her shoulder, "This is a terrific opportunity, my Sweet. I'm sure you're feeling a little overwhelmed, but we'll help you with everything."

Making rare eye contact with my grandfather, she asked, "Will Lenora be there too?"

He didn't answer, I assumed, knowing my personal goals might not include Astrid. I sat by her and said, "I will be with you." I cupped my hand over her ear, "I am the moon, and you are my star, together forever." The corners of her mouth turned up ever so slightly.

"Okay."

Astrid's face and hands were plastered to the window of the black limo, the city streets turned into a narrow road out the outskirts of town.

"Where are we going?" I asked Grandfather as the driver made his way down the tree-lined road. Our last stop before heading home came as a surprise. At the end of the driveway stood a rod iron gate with a brass-plated sign: St. Agnes Preparatory School for Young Ladies. A three-story red brick building trimmed in white stood at the end of the circular drive, matching two-story dormitories to the left and classroom buildings on the right. Manicured lawns and stone paths led from building to building. The campus resembled a park. The normally confident me disappeared. Astrid, oblivious to where we were, gawked at the buildings.

A white-haired woman in a gray jacket and skirt met us. "John Michael McConnell, you're a sight for sore eyes," she chortled.

Grandfather laughed, "Yes, it's been a while, Martha."

Evidently, Grandfather knew this woman. She greeted my mother as well. Puzzled, I listened to their candid conversation. Blimey! Grandfather was, at one time, a trustee of the school. No wonder he got Astrid a place here. Now baffled, I waited for proper introductions while Astrid focused on the trees.

"Miss Martha Dobbins, headmistress, this is my granddaughter Lenora Irene McConnell."

"Irene? Named for your grandmother, I can guess. Your grandmother was my roommate at this very school before she married your grandfather."

Taken aback, I'd had no idea my grandmother's name was Irene; no one ever talked about her. Astrid watched the clouds.

"And this," said my grandfather, "is Astrid Innis, the gifted young lady I told you about."

I pulled on Astrid's arm to get her attention.

"This is our new school?" asked Astrid.

"Astrid," I rolled my eyes, "Yes."

Miss Dobbins's eyes darted from Astrid to my grandfather; she didn't know what to think. Miss Dobbins invited us inside for tea to discuss school rules and expectations. Astrid's head swirled from side to side, squinting at the ceiling or down at her shoes. I doubt she heard a thing. In the middle of a discussion over my curriculum, Astrid blurted out, "It's a nice place, Lenora." The conversation stopped. Mother agreed, asking Astrid to pay attention. I almost laughed; Astrid had the attention span of a firefly unless a piano was involved.

"Miss. Purdy, our house mother for younger students, lives in the O'Brien House. She'll be along shortly. Do you have any questions?"

Astrid exclaimed, "Where's my piano?" I realized the coming semester could be a long one. Miss Dobbins assured Astrid they had two pianos, to which Astrid replied that she only needed one.

Miss Purdy, undoubtedly another spinster, gave Astrid and me a tour of the dorms. The adults stayed behind. My face was on fire with embarrassment, and Miss Purdy was mortified when Astie said loudly that she needed to piss.

When we arrived at the hotel, I pulled Grandfather's sleeve, "I need to ask you something in private," I whispered.

"Mary, you and Astrid go up. Lenora and I will be along shortly."

In the lobby corner, we sat together on a plush emerald green sofa. "Grandfather, I don't mean to seem rude, but are you sure you told Miss Dobbins everything about Astrid?"

"I understand your concern, Lenora, but Astrid will be fine. I sent Miss Dobbins an in-depth report on Astrid's learning. I'm sure Astrid's needs will be met. Don't worry over Astrid too much, my little astronomer."

When I got back, the room was dark. Astrid was in bed. I gently slipped under the covers. After a few minutes, Astrid got up. I acted like I was asleep. She stood by the window and pulled the curtain back, eyes turned to the black sky. I wondered, *where are you, Astie? It must be a place where no one can go, not even me.* From the bed, I watched her lost face.

"Come to bed, Astie."

Astrid curled up beside me, a scared little rabbit; I tried to comfort her. "Astie, we're going to be all right. Life is changing; it will always change."

"I want us to be together forever. The school is big and far away. I don't want to change, Lee."

"But we'll be together, I promise. Everything will be different for a while, then everything will be regular."

"Okay."

| 7 |

Transitions

Astrid and I were "late bloomers." My mother sat us down before we left for boarding school. I already knew how a girl's body changes for motherhood. Frightened by the notion of blood down there, Astrid became contentious. With stomping, she loudly proclaimed, "No, no, no! Not me. I don't want babies! So, it's not going to happen to me!" Stomping out of the room, the bedroom door slammed.

Turning to Mother, I threw my hands up, "What I'm going to do now? God help me if she gets her period before me!"

Sympathetic to my dilemma, Mother patted my hand, "You'll do your best, darling."

I rolled my eyes, "It's easy for you to say; you won't be there." This is a responsibility I wouldn't wish on anyone; lucky me, huh?

St. Agnes Preparatory School for Young Ladies

Rooms were arranged in suites, two rooms with a shared bathroom in the middle. Our suitemates wanted little to do with us, unsurprisingly. It was a blessing when housemaids brought fresh linens and cleaned our bathroom once a week.

At supper, we were together. All the girls, one hundred and fifty, ate evening meals together in the Grand Hall. The tables had six place settings of China dinner plates, and servers brought our food. The other girls, like always, whispered unkind words about Astrid. I defended her as best I could, but she always seemed disheveled, even in our uniforms. Astrid didn't have a filter; anything she thought came out of her mouth. I knew sitting with the others couldn't last. To no one's surprise, we were put at a table by ourselves. Miss Dobbins explained sitting away from the other girls was best for everyone. Another hit to any social life I might have. Portraits of successful alumni hung throughout the room; the heavy tapestries and chandeliers were overwhelming at first. It was still unnerving to be watched by the portraits of sourpuss old ladies; their eyes followed me.

Astrid and I had two classes together: algebra and French. Even though she seemed so far away, Astrid's grades were passing (with my help, of course). This time we had different levels of literature class. Astrid was in a remedial class while I was in an advanced group. I helped her write out her essays again. All of Astrid's exams were oral, a condition my grandfather insisted on. She excelled in French. French! Astrid could recite the lesson word for word with correct inflection. She never cracked the spine of her French book. I wasn't good with the conversational lessons, but we spoke French every day for an hour in our room. The trade-off worked. I needed help speaking; she needed help with writing assignments.

Typically, Astrid came back from Miss Ryan's piano technique instructions by seven-thirty in the evening. It was dark out after eight. *Why wasn't she back?* My worry prompted me to search for her. Running down three flights of stairs like a lunatic, I came to an abrupt stop, hearing whimpers coming from under the staircase.

I found her with her knees pulled to her chest on the floor, face buried in her crossed arms. Shocked, I stood frozen, compelled to comfort her. Offering my hand, I pulled her to her feet to hug her.

Her hair hung in her eyes, "Oh, Astie, what happened?"

No answer. Astie lumbered step by step up the stairs with her hand in mine. Collapsing on the bed, I wiped her tears away. Astrid had never ever cried like this before. I cuddled up next to her and pushed her strawberry blond hair behind her ears.

"Can you tell me why you're upset?"

Nothing, she said nothing. It terrified me to think someone hurt her.

"Did someone hurt you?"

Again nothing. Nightmarish thoughts raced in my head. When Astrid was ready, she'd talk. I sat at the desk watching helplessly. Astrid sat cross-legged on her bed, rocking back and forth.

"What made you so upset?"

Astrid slammed her hands on her legs, "I'm mental, and I don't belong here. I'm stupid, stupid, stupid. I shouldn't be here."

Jumping up, I grabbed her hand. "Stop it, Astie! You're not stupid. I'll pummel anyone who says different!" My hand tipped her chin up, my eyes met hers; her pain was my pain, "I'd be lost without you."

Astie kept rubbing her arm. "Did someone hurt you?" I pushed her sweater up her arm, and my jaw dropped. Wide red marks covered her arms! Grabbing her left arm, bruises. My eyes narrowed; I felt my nostrils flare.

"I will beat the bloody hell out of whoever harmed you!" Everything got quiet; I felt like shaking an answer from her. I implored her to answer me.

There was a knock on the bathroom door. "Are you okay, Lenora?" asked Silvey, our suitemate. Silvey was kind to us. I assured her we were alright; she carefully closed the door.

She scooted back to the wall, "I did it."

"What?" My forehead wrinkled so hard it hurt, and my jaw dropped. "Why? What horrible thing happened to make you hurt yourself?"

"I'm a nothing, a stupid nothing."

Something happened; I suspected something with her lessons. I instinctively knew the problem must be Miss. Ryan. "It's Miss Ryan, isn't it? What has she done to you?"

Astrid's lower lip quivered, "I am unteachable. She couldn't teach me." She pointed to an imaginary version of herself. Astrid began to imitate Miss Ryan's high-pitched voice, "Astrid, you're not paying attention. Astrid, sit up straight! Astrid, you're unteachable."

"What?" I was incensed. "Why? I don't understand."

"That hateful lady tells me my fingers aren't arched enough; I don't sit right. Then girls here make fun of me, call me a retard, a simpleton. I can do this anymore, Luna. I'm retarded."

Her fist clenched; she began to hit herself again. I pushed her down on the bed, wrestling, her face an inch from mine. Out of breath, I said, "Stop, Astra, my shining star. You called me Luna."

She closed her eyes. "Think, Astie. I am Luna, and you are my Astra. Remember, under the stars on a special May night? The moon needs her star." I rolled off her. We sat, exhausted.

Astrid pushed her hair from her face, unclenching her fists, wiping her nose on her sleeve; she sniffled, "Okay."

"That night, you said, what will become of us? Do you remember what I said?"

"You are the moon," she moved to the window, "I am a star." Standing by her, my arm instinctively wrapped around her shoulders. Her head rested against mine.

"Nobody said accomplishments come easy. You certainly aren't retarded. You're gifted, unique." Giving up was not an option. We needed each other. "In a couple of years from now, we will remember this night, too." I kissed her head, "Don't let them win, Astie. We are different, but it means we are exceptional. We see the world in different ways. Besides, no one has your musical gift. Miss Ryan can't understand how special you are, that's all." I cradled her head on my shoulder.

In a whisper, Astrid said, "When you're here, I can make it. I know I'm different. I don't want to go home."

"Being different is hard sometimes. You're not going anywhere. Please, promise me you won't hurt yourself anymore," my plea came from desperation. How could I stop her? My heart didn't know where to turn.

"I promise," she whispered.

Astrid took a shower to calm herself. When she came out, I said, "Come here," I patted the bed. We both got under the covers, "We can figure out what to do over the weekend."

She sat up next to me, dressed in her flannel nightgown. I braided her shiny strawberry blond hair. Still a little shaky, she murmured, "You won't tell Grandfather, will you?"

"I don't think so. We'll figure out a way to deal with Miss Ryan." She didn't respond. After I tucked her in, Astrid whispered a prayer to Mother Mary again.

Through Saturday breakfast Astrid didn't talk, a typical morning. She worked on algebra homework in silence. Talking with her never started until she was ready. Keeping my mouth closed seemed impossible. Maybe because I was getting older, I noticed Astrid's differences more. Used to the clues of her frustration—mumbling repeated phrases, furious erasing, hair-twisting—they were now her signals for help.

Since sixth grade, being her only friend, I'd noticed the disconnect with others; it put her in the category of odd. Since childhood, she seldom looked anyone in the eye. Astrid daily repeated her class schedules. Astrid said people thought she was weird. No one understood Astrid like me. A couple of weeks before, I'd overheard an English teacher say to another adult that schools were meant to educate normal girls, not half-wits. Their lack of compassion cut me straight through the heart. I wanted to kick them as I walked by. Across the desk in our room, I got her attention. "Put your pencil down and get your jacket on. Let's go for a walk."

She dutifully complied. A brisk wind twirled the red and yellow leaves like mini tornados through the archway into the courtyard; our hair blew to one side. Finding a bench under the shelter of a barren lattice, we talked. With this chilly weather, the early afternoon sun warmed us.

"I need you to talk to me. Tell me exactly what's wrong with your piano lessons. Help me understand what we can do differently."

Astrid didn't comprehend what I was asking. I took a different approach. "Show me how you place your fingers on the keys."

Her hands gripped the bottom slat of the wooden bench. Clenching her jaw, Astrid tuned me out. Prying her fingers from the slat, staring ahead, she resisted.

Frustrated, I cried, "Why are you doing this? Stop it, Astrid!"

She put her hands over her ears, violently shaking her head from side to side. I was helpless and scared. All I knew to do was hold Astrid tight. I wasn't going to abandon her. Finally, with a gulp of air, she stopped. Some girl walked by us, gawking. I stared daggers back at her, saying, "You've never seen an upset friend? Oh, maybe you don't have any friends!" The girl hurried off.

Tipping Astrid's head, I forced her to see. "You're going to be all right," I said with purpose. "I'll get some lunch for us. Come on." I heard her whispering *Hail Mary, something, something*, as I helped her to her feet.

After lunch, Astrid fell asleep. Sitting at my desk, I turned to watch her breathe. Confused, I slipped out and made my way to the third-floor lounge. The only telephone on our floor was in use. One of the vicious girls giggled and talked nonstop to a boyfriend. Pacing the floor, I bothered her. With her hand over the receiver, she glared at me, "Do you mind?"

"I don't mind at all. I can wait all day." My response didn't sit well with Miss Prissy. I didn't care; it was urgent. I had to speak with my mother. She uttered something, then slammed the phone down. "Are you happy now, bitch?"

Bitch! Those were fighting words. I narrowed my eyes, glaring at her. "Very happy. Bitch."

Enraged, she stomped out. Frantic, I called Mother. She sensed the worry in my voice. Halfway through our conversation, she put Grandfather on the phone. I told him of Astrid's fit, how she hurt herself and hated Miss Ryan.

"Hmm. It's best if Astrid sees a doctor," he said in earnest.

"But I don't think she's sick, Grandfather."

"A different type of doctor, Lenora."

"You mean ... This throws a spanner in the works. I didn't know Astrid might have gone mad."

He said, "Not mad, Lenora," in his always-wise voice. "Depressed, bogged down. Remember your feelings when your father died? Well, unfortunately, Astrid isn't resilient like you. I worried school might be too much for her."

On the verge of tears, I sighed, "Oh, no. What if Astrid has to quit school? I'd be undone, Grandfather."

"I don't think that will happen. Astrid might require some extra help, that's all. On Monday, I'll take the train to London and see what I can do to help. I don't want you to worry Astrid with talk of doctors."

"Grandfather," I spoke slowly, "it's her piano teacher, too, I'm sure." I didn't want to sound like I knew all the answers. "I understand, and mum's the word."

"I'll visit with you two on Monday or Tuesday," he sighed, "It was good of you to call, Lenora. You're a good friend."

"You always know what to do. I love you, Grandfather."

"I love you, too, my Stargazer. See you soon."

Thank God, if things weren't bad enough, it happened to me first. In English class, when I felt a warm wetness between my thighs, I excused myself. The dress code had changed last year, a true blessing. We were allowed to wear black polyester slacks with our uniform jackets. Hiding in the bathroom stall, I pulled my pants down. Yes, I started my period, great. I waded up a half roll of toilet paper. I shoved it in my panties. The blood spot in my slacks wasn't visible. Class ended in ten minutes; I'd go back.

I made my way quickly across campus to the dorm. My mother sent two boxes of sanitary napkins with us. A stretchy band thing that fits around the waist with two eyelets to hold the bulky pad. Thank God there was a picture on the box. Now I could tell Astrid I wasn't dying, and she wouldn't either. They say hormones wreak havoc on girls' emotions. I wondered if this could be part of Astrid's dilemma.

| 8 |

The Special Doctor

One chilly November Tuesday, Grandfather sat on a bench outside our dormitory. Dressed in his black wool topcoat, Grandfather donned the black woolen cap covering his balding head, a red tartan scarf wrapped around his neck, and his whiskers lay neatly over the scarf. His gloved hands rested on the top of his ivory-handled cane. I loved him so very much. Running across the courtyard, I waved at him.

"Don't squeeze me too much; I might pop! Where's Astrid?"

"She's coming. Her last class ends fifteen minutes after mine. Let's go into the lounge."

Pushing himself to his feet, he asked how Astrid was doing today. "I got her out of bed and helped her dress. Once she put herself together, she seemed fine. I'm so worried about her, Grandfather; Astrid needs to stay here. Her grades have fallen over the past two weeks. Something happened; it changed her."

He patted my knee and winked, "Don't fret. Astrid's going to get her some help."

Out the window, I saw her watching her feet, shuffling through the fallen leaves, hugging her book tight. I waited at the door for her.

"We have a guest," I said gleefully. Her eyes narrowed, her expression pensive as she came into the room.

When she spied Grandfather, Astrid ran. With a panicked expression, she came to an abrupt stop. "Am I in trouble?"

"Sit down with me." He waved me off. I waited in the hall of the main floor study room. Through the window on the door, I watched in silence. Astrid stared at the carpet, showing no emotion as Grandfather spoke with her. She shook her head a few times as she wrung her hands over and over. Not once did Astrid make eye contact.

I saw him reach out to hug her; she shook her shoulders and bristled. She wasn't my Astrid. Grandfather glanced up at me. I came into the room; chills ran down my spine. I didn't want to lose her. He motioned for me to sit by Astrid.

"Astrid and I need your help." Sitting on the edge of my chair, I listened. "Astrid will not leave school; she will get a new piano teacher who understands her special gift. Her classes are limited to French, algebra, and geography." Then came the news I never expected.

"Astrid will see a special doctor twice a week. You will accompany her to appointments, making sure she gets there. His name is Dr. McLean, a very kind gentleman, very qualified." He handed me the address and two six-month bus passes. Duty-bound, I took the bus passes. The appointments were on Tuesday and Thursday at three o'clock. On those days my classes lasted until noon.

"This matter concerns only the two of you. The bus stops at the end of the road. On rainy days, Miss Dobbins will drive you to the stop. The ride is approximately thirty-five minutes. The doctor's office is near the observatory and a library. If you like, Lenora, you may go to either and return to the office a few minutes before four."

Grandfather never made demands of me; today was different. If asked, I was to say Astrid has lessons outside of school. He kindly dismissed Astrid. When she was out of sight, the corners of his turned down, his forehead wrinkled with concern.

Addressing me, he said, "I believe our Astrid is overwhelmed by the demands on her. As we've always known, Astrid has difficulties. I spoke to Miss Dobbins, and we agreed Astrid needs special attention. She wasn't willing to write her off. A pianist from the Royal Symphony,

Mr. Godfrey—an understanding soul—will meet with her Wednesday evening and Saturday afternoon.

"What can I do to help?"

Like an owl, his eyes were wise, "Continue as you've always done, Lenora. Be her friend."

My eyes welled with tears. "Will she get better?"

He patted my knee, "We can hope and believe, Lenora. I know you love her. And we refuse to stand by and watch her fade away."

Pushing himself up with his cane, he slowly stood. I was shocked to see him have trouble standing. Hooking my arm in his, I helped steady him. It was the first time I noticed he was becoming frail. I called a taxi for him, wondering if I'd see him again.

He kissed me on the cheek and said, "You're compassionate and rational. Taking care of a friend is a great attribute, Lenora. You have always made me and your mother proud."

I pulled a letter from my pocket. I'd written it when I heard Grandfather was coming. "This is for Mother." It explained how my body was changing and how much I missed her, things I couldn't call her about. Helping him into the car, I said, "Stay well, Grandfather. Christmas vacation is around the corner. I expect to see you then."

"I'll wait by the fire for you." He waved goodbye as the taxi drove out of sight.

Curious to find out what Astrid thought, I jumped every other step until I reached the third floor. Before entering the room, I brought my hands up, even with my shoulders pushing down as I slowly exhaled. Regaining my composure, I pushed open the door.

Astrid's legs swung back and forth over the edge of the bed. Writing furiously, I knew what was in the new notebook: music.

Astrid read my quizzical expression, "I'm different. I always have been. Sometimes, I'm weird. My daddy didn't want me because he treated me bad sometimes." She stopped talking, examining the ceiling, "I should feel sad, but I don't. I tuned them out, not on purpose. I don't even know I'm doing it."

Curious, I asked how she knew these things were true. She told me Grandfather asked questions. Astrid didn't understand the word "depression." Grandfather explained how people with depression feel. "I feel like depression. Grandfather made me an appointment. I'm sorry because…" Astrid rocked back and forth, "I'm sorry you must go with me. Your grandfather says it's best."

Sitting beside her, with a gentle hug, I assured her it was no bother. "I promise, Astie, I will always be here for you."

Her affect was flat as she said, "I'm the star, and you are my moon."

"Yes. And we'll make it through everything together." It was heartbreaking; she'd come to know how different she was from everyone else.

After the first visit to the psychologist, she was in the bathroom, crying. Scared, I opened the door to find her sitting on the toilet. "Am I going to die?" She showed me bloody wade of toilet paper.

"Am I dead? I started already, and I am not dead. Right?" I sat on the edge of the bathtub, belt and a sanitary napkin in hand, teaching her how to put it on; I prayed I was getting through to her. I left her to try. She came from the bathroom, asking if she fixed it right. *Oh geez, I didn't need to see that!*

"Yes, it's right. Now go put on your underwear."

Oh, my God, what more do I have to endure?

| 9 |

Out of the Flames

Before Christmas vacation, Astrid made some progress. She loved her new piano teacher, Mr. Godfrey, and passed the semester with extra help.

Back at home, a fire blazed as we decorated the Christmas tree. Mother knitted a Christmas stocking with an angel for Astrid. She wanted to sleep with it; Mother asked her to leave it on the mantle. In the evenings, Astrid played a couple of carols. Grandfather read us chapters from *A Christmas Carol* by Charles Dickens. Everything seemed perfect.

Before bed, I heard Astrid sobbing in the bathroom. I tapped on the door. "Do you want to talk?"

Mother stopped reading. She listened. Slowly Astrid opened the door, "They don't want me anymore."

"Who? Astrid, who are you talking about?"

"My family, they don't love me anymore."

My mother intervened. Lovingly, she said, "No, darling, they loved you enough to make sure you lived a better life. We, fortunately, have the means to help you."

Astrid's face was full of innocence. The ability to understand such things seemed to confuse her.

She said, "Okay."

Astrid threw herself onto the bed staring at the ceiling. Without a clue as to what set Astrid off, I joined Grandfather, expressing my concerns about Astrid. He motioned me to sit on his ottoman.

"You know Astrid is different. The psychologist met with other professionals working to understand profound mental retardation. They believe she is what is called a savant. Astrid has an extraordinary musical talent, but there's a catch. After a battery of tests, Astrid functions at a mental age of ten to eleven, Lenora. The experts believe she has a mental condition sometimes referred to as 'the island of genius,' a disorder of which little is known. Lenora, savants have often been called idiots or retarded. Progressive doctors changing those perceptions, though. Firstly, Astrid is high functioning, taking care of her hygiene, feeding herself, attending classes, et cetera."

I interjected in a whisper, "With my help." At first, I needed to make sure she wore underclothes. The doctor gave her a plan of methodically laying out her clothes in a certain order before dressing.

"Lenora, Astrid will never learn to function independently. She will need to have an aide."

I know what he meant, "Grandfather, I couldn't take care of her all the time. I want to do things on my own." In the quiet, the fire crackled. I sighed, "I can help her through school, but after … I don't know what will become of her. I love her like a sister." He nodded in acknowledgment. I counted on him for a solution. He gave me an all-knowing look but no answer.

A few days later, the postman brought a Christmas card for Astrid from her family. It made me happy for her. In the armchair, she rocked back and forth, reading the card repeatedly. Suddenly, she threw the card into the fireplace.

Jumping up, yelling, "Why did you do that? They took the time to write you."

She started smacking herself in the head, yelling, "It was all lies, lies, lies, lies."

"Stop it, Astrid!" I took hold of her hands, focusing on her eyes. She jerked away from me. "What are you talking about? What lies?"

"Your mother made them write stuff that isn't true. They don't love me anymore."

My forehead wrinkled to the point of pain. Running into the kitchen, I demanded, "Did you call Astrid's mother?"

With her back to me, Mother answered, "I did not; remember they have no phone." She turned around to face me. "However, I did visit; I said some things and may have overstepped my bounds. I tried to help them understand that Astrid loves them and how she's musically gifted." Mother motioned for me to stand by her. In hushed tones, she explained, "Her mother said Astrid was our problem now. Her mother was indifferent, almost callous, Lenora. I suggested sending a card."

"Well, they did. It's in the fireplace." I stormed out of the kitchen to find Astrid lying in bed, groaning. I laid down next to her, turning over to my side; I pulled her close, "I don't know what they wrote; I only know it upset you. Mother visited to explain how much you loved them. She meant well."

"No more crying, Lee, no more." She sat up to blow her nose, never saying another word about them.

On Saint Nicolas Day, Grandfather played the jolly man for the orphans' home in town. I tried to get Astrid to be an elf with me and hand out presents. She wanted no part of it. However, Mother enlisted her help with cookie decorating for shut-ins to get her out of the bedroom.

On the way home, Grandfather asked about Astrid, "Do you have a sense she's getting any better about school and music lessons?"

"Astrid seems to like Mr. Godfrey. She says he's a lot like her. But she tries to get out of going to her therapy appointments."

"Yes," he sounded disappointed. "Dr. McFarlane says she has trouble expressing herself. We know about that, don't we?"

"I'd like to say no. But truth be told, I do. When Astrid plays the piano, she turns into a different person, Grandfather. An unbelievable amount of emotion comes out of her when she plays."

"I'm getting older, Lenora. I don't move as well as I used to, but I still have influence. I don't worry about you. You're Irish strong, like your father, and smart as a whip. Financially, you and your mother will be sound. I don't want you to be jealous because I'm taking care of Astrid."

I shook my head, "Oh, I don't think that way, Grandfather. I care about Astrid. I might be more thankful for you than Astrid herself!" I sighed, "If I ignored her like everyone else in primary school, I'm certain she would have fallen on hard times." He nodded his head and said nothing more.

Before we returned to school, Astrid stood at the window between the newly purchased single beds. Snow fell against the moonlight.

"A million feathers are falling down; snowflakes are feathers," she said. Astrid showed no emotion. They were just words. She continued, "Your Grandfather is letting me stay at school. I will study with the London Conservatory for gifted musicians at the practice place in Cambridge."

"What? He didn't say anything to me." I felt betrayed. "Why didn't he tell me?"

In her blank stare, "I'll stay at school taking algebra and French."

I thought Astrid didn't care about me or how I felt. All I could say was, *oh*.

Grandfather was snoring in his room, and Mother went upstairs to bed. There was no one to ask for an explanation. My heart hurt; I felt left out and wanted to cry. Astrid stood at the window, totally oblivious to my upset.

I slipped into my robe and house shoes the next morning, tiptoeing to the kitchen. I followed the enticing aroma of freshly brewed coffee and a fried slab of bacon. Mother and I had our usual routine; good morning kisses and I was allowed coffee now. At the kitchen table, I held up my head with my hand.

"What's wrong, Poppet? A glum face? This isn't like you." She pulled up a chair.

"Grandfather set up a whole different course of study for Astrid and didn't tell me. It came as a shock when she told me last night."

"I see. I agree your grandfather should have informed you. However, he voiced his concerns to me. He didn't want to bother you, Lenora. Astrid's progress with Dr. McFarlane wasn't going as planned."

"Yes, I know. After a few weeks, I bribed Astrid to go to see him with the promise of ice cream or a trip to the bakery."

Mother prattled on, saying they spoke with the school's headmaster and the piano teacher. "Mr. Godfrey said she *is* a true savant. He, too, is a gifted pianist."

"Poor Astrid. I feel helpless."

"All you can do is be there for her. Mr. Godfrey has experience with children like Astrid. On Saturdays, Mr. Godfrey will take her to practice in London. He wants her to get used to playing for her recital. She will still keep her appointments with the doctor."

Grandfather overheard us. He tottered into the kitchen, "The next year of school will be decided by her progress."

"Your Grandfather has something extra planned for you."

My eyes brightened. I begged my mother to tell me, but she left the news up to Grandfather's telling. I chose my words wisely. If I showed any jealousy, his disappointment might kill me.

"I was going to sit down with you later," he said.

Mother placed his coffee and creamer on the table.

"Mary, if it isn't too much trouble, could I have my eggs scrambled today?"

I wanted to say, *hurry and tell me my news!* Mother put our toast and butter on the table. *Jesus, Mary, and Joseph get to the point!*

"What news?" I implored him.

He scolded me, "Don't be so pushy, Lenora. In due time."

He tried to teach me patience, which I failed miserably on most accounts. My chin rested hand, "Yes, sir."

Astrid stumbled in and plopped down in the chair next to me in time for breakfast. A delayed good morning came out of her. Breakfast dragged on without conversation. Not knowing my fate, I pushed my eggs around on the plate. Mother told me to sit up straight and get my elbows off the table. I rolled my eyes.

Mother clenched her jaw, "Lenora, you can clean the kitchen floor today. And I mean sweep and mop."

My grandfather finished eating and took a sip of coffee. Then, he finally spoke to me. "Lenora, do you like the Observatory?"

"Of course I do. What a silly question!" By his unsettled expression, I'd put my foot in my mouth twice in ten minutes. I pushed cold scrambled eggs around my plate, groaning. "I'm sorry."

"Well, I hope so." Clearing his throat, he continued, "I have spoken to Dr. David Gilmore, coordinator of the Observatory's Young Astronomy Society. He agreed to give you a chance to join even though you're not yet eighteen."

I was barely fifteen; I hung off every word he spoke. The YAS was an exclusive group of talented senior school students and college students.

"Your superior grades in calculus and chemistry will give you an edge on the college-level exam. Everything is contingent on a positive score, which I believe you will have no trouble passing. The group meets on Saturdays for six hours. They study everything from recent discoveries to the operation of the equatorial telescope."

Unable to contain myself, I jumped from my chair and hugged him, smothering him with kisses. I must have thanked him a million times. Astrid clapped her hands until I reached over to push her hands down.

I smiled at Astrid, "You will be a concert pianist, and I'll be an astronomer!"

With feet tapping, she blurted out, "I am the star; you are the mooooon!"

Mother and Grandfather didn't understand what she meant. But I did.

| 10 |

Out of the Flames

In our last year at St. Agnes, I excelled in my studies and helped Astrid get through her academics. I became jealous of her command of French; she showed difficulty when reading but spoke fluently. One sentence, one time, and bam, just like the music, it stayed in her head. Even the doctors were baffled.

Now taking geography, Astrid knew every country in Europe and its capital cities. I saw a blank map on her desk where she'd labeled every country with capitals perfectly matched.

An exceptional time for Astrid was approaching: her first recital. Late at night, I'd hear her pacing the floor, praying, fingers drumming on the desk, reciting note sequences or geographical information. She interfered will my sleep. After I complained to Mother about Astrid's anxiety, the doctor prescribed pills. I watched her swallow the medication before breakfast and a sleeping pill before bed; we told her these were vitamins. The evening pill for sleep was more for me than her; not as much pacing or Mother Mary and Angel talk.

A week before Astrid's recital, Grandfather fell ill. He struggled with breathing, landing in a London hospital. Yet, he remained determined to attend Astrid's big day. Astrid worried over him.

"If he dies," I said, "it will be after he sees your recital. Stop worrying."

Mother met me after class on Wednesday. We walked among the smell of lilacs and wisteria—the expression on her face stood in opposition to the beautiful day. We found an empty courtyard bench; she slumped, sad and tired.

"Lenora, your grandfather is gravely ill. His tomorrows are not promised. I want you to know this, so you won't be caught off guard. He is determined to be at Astrid's recital. If permitted, I will bring him. However, I want you and Astrid to visit him tomorrow."

Not able to control my tears, they spilled over the edges of my eyes. Mother put her arm around me. My body quaked; I lost my breath. My mother was never overly emotional but today was the exception. She cried, too.

The only seats on the crowded bus were in the back. The spring air disappeared, overpowered by diesel exhaust. This smell brought me a wave of nausea. As soon as someone left, I grabbed Astrid by the shoulder, pushing her into a seat closer to the front. The bus stopped close to the hospital. Astrid paused at a flower vendor; she picked up a pink carnation and daisy bouquet.

"It's to cheer him up. Do you think he likes flowers?" I delighted in her smiling, naïve face. She'd turned sixteen, yet she truly was the eleven-year-old I met in school. At times she talked as if nothing was amiss, but those quirky mannerisms were ever-present.

"I'm sure he'll like them," I assured her.

On the second floor, we saw Room 210, John Michael McConnell. When we signed in at the nurse's station, she told us to keep the visit short. I tapped lightly on his door.

To my surprise, he sat up; we were greeted by a jolly laugh, "My favorite girls!" He opened his arms wide, waiting for hugs.

His room was private. The blinds were open, filling the white room with sunshine. Grandfather's skin was pale, his eyes glassy and dull. I didn't want him to get older. I wanted him to live forever and was alarmed by the oxygen tube under his nose.

Astrid sat on the edge of his bed. He thanked her for the cheerful flowers. I sat in the chair, listening; he paused before each sentence.

"I will be there Saturday." He was coming to her two o'clock debut performance. How could he promise such a thing? He gave Astrid false hope. We didn't stay long; he needed his rest. We each gave him a peck on the cheek. Then, with a wink and a squeeze of my hand, he told me not to worry so much. I kissed him again.

As her big day approached, Astrid fidgeted, wringing her hands, tapping out the rhythm with her pencil.

"Stop tapping! I'm trying to study."

"I'll be in the practice room in the music hall."

"Are you through with your French paper?" She nodded.

"Give it to me. I'll make the corrections." What a mess! "Come back here."

Her head hung low. The strawberry blond hair fell over her face as if she were hiding.

"Push your hair back; let me see your eyes, Astie. I have corrected your papers many times before, but this is a mess! I couldn't fix this one."

Oh, how I disliked talking to her in a stern tone! "Sit at your desk and read what you wrote." Our desks faced each other; she sat down hard. Then she began to mouth the words. Not even two minutes into her reading, she got up. Going to the window, she stared out into the afternoon sky, mumbling something repeatedly. This was the only written exam she must finish.

"Astrid." I softened my tone. "This is your last assignment before the semester ends. I can correct the punctuation, but you only have to write a conversation between two people, only fourteen sentences. You speak perfectly; write as if you were speaking to me. Please try. I want us to graduate together. If we don't, I may never see you again." Those words motivated her. Returning to the desk to finish reading aloud—simple sentences strung together with *ands* and *buts*. I made notes on the meaning of meaningless phrases, asking her if she meant what she read. Astrid left for the practice room. An hour later, I finished writing. Tomorrow she would recopy the paper, but not tonight. Our instructor knew of Astrid's difficulties. Hopefully, Mrs. Arlen wouldn't be too harsh.

Astrid's sleeping patterns were still erratic. When I think about it, this behavior started from the first sleepover. Back then, it happened when Astrid prayed before bed, which was okay. There were times when she climbed over me in the middle of the night. Straining to listen, she talked as if someone stood before her. Her guide was Mary, the mother of Jesus and the angels. She told me they listen to her and reassure her. They help her make decisions.

When I spoke to Mother, I thought Astrid might be delusional. I can still hear my mother say, "Now Lenora, Astrid was brought up differently than you. If she's not holding a conversation with them, she's just praying. There is no harm in praying." I let it rest.

Saturday mornings, I woke up first. Worried, I watched to see if she was breathing as I rubbed the sand from my eyes. She was lying on her stomach, both hands tucked under the pillow, "I can't hold your hand forever, Astrid," I whispered.

Groggy from the sleeping pill, she rolled over, "Did you say my name? I thought I heard someone call my name."

The corners of my mouth turned up slightly.

"I wanted to make sure you were still here," I chuckled. But unfortunately, Astrid didn't get it, as usual.

She sat straight up, "I didn't go anywhere; I'm here. Today is Saturday. I have to play, and your grandfather is coming!" She clapped her hands.

I didn't want her to fall apart, "Astrid, he's very ill. Please don't be disappointed if he can't come."

"He'll be here; my angels said they're bringing him. He's coming." She remained confident, oblivious to his decline.

On weekends, breakfast was special, eggs benedict or cherry crepes. My eyes grew large when I saw Astrid's plate overflowing with crepes and bacon.

"Good God, Astrid! Are you going to eat everything on your plate?" I sat there, astonished.

"Well, of course." She scrutinized me as if I grew three heads.

"Don't make yourself sick. You have a recital today."

She fired back, "I need to eat now, not before I play! There'll be no lunch today." She put me in my place. I hoped she didn't overdo it with six crepes and six strips of bacon.

Astrid and I made a schedule of everything leading up to the performance, including braiding her hair. My curly hair made me jealous of her straight, shiny strawberry hair. Some days, she took her braids down. What a mess. I threatened never to fix her hair again when she did that.

Her dressing ritual was to lay out a nude-colored underskirt, black leggings, and shiny black Mary Jane shoes. My mother bought a special outfit for her, a black dress with a high white collar and elbow-length sleeves. When I finished her makeup, no one could doubt her beauty. I envied her high cheekbones, smooth rounded chin, and those bright green eyes.

Walking with Astrid to the concert hall, I was more nervous than her. Astrid didn't break a sweat. Playing piano, for her, was life itself. Outside of music, Astrid didn't communicate well. It saddened me. I knew her life ahead stood full of ridicule and torment. I wanted desperately to protect her.

Mother waited for us at the stage door in her blue dress with the wide belt, matching purse, and hat, straight out of the 1950s, gloves and all. She waved; Astrid ran to her, hugging her. I caught up with her in time to hear her ask about Grandfather. I cringed behind her. My mother wouldn't look at me, "He'll be along soon."

She accepted the answer. The door opened; Mr. Godfrey greeted us. He spoke to Astrid. It was our cue to find our seats. Before we left the stage, I let Astie know she was my shining star.

"Are you alright, Lenora?" Mother asked.

"It's probably just hormones," I said. "Why did you tell Astrid Grandfather was coming? Have you given her false hope?" She didn't respond to my question; she only smiled. *What if no one showed up?* We sat in the third row, center. After fifteen minutes, I turned around; a few people filtered in, mostly students required to attend. I squirmed in my seat.

A few minutes passed. My mother squeezed my arm, "Stop fidgeting."

"I'm sorry, I'm extremely nervous for her. Hardly anyone is here?"

"Turn around, Poppet."

I twisted my body around to see the concert hall. I gasped; the hall was almost full. My jaw dropped, "How?"

The lights dimmed; a spotlight shined on Mr. Godfrey.

"Good afternoon, guests and fellow musicians. When I met the young lady you're about to hear, I knew she was special. Astrid Innis can hear Beethoven's music once; she plays like a seasoned concert pianist without sheet music. I'm quite jealous." His remark garnered a chuckle. "I've never taught a student quite like her. In our program, you will be treated to Debussy's Clair de Lune and Beethoven's piano concerto number eight in C Minor, opus thirteen. Astrid has also chosen a very advanced piece, Chopin's *Berceuse* Opus 57. We will have a five-minute pause, and then breaking with tradition, Astrid will play a composition of her own, *For the Meadowlark*. And for the finale, she has chosen a most complex piece."

I elbowed my mother and whispered, "*For the Meadowlark!*" It was the first thing she played on my piano.

Calmly Mother said, "I remember."

The spotlight dimmed. The red velvet curtains parted; a hush fell over the audience. A soft, warm light illuminated the stage. I held my breath as Mr. Godfrey led her to the grand piano. Astrid took her place; with fingers arched and gentle touch, *Clair de Lune*'s soft notes were brought to life.

You could hear a pin drop. Each piece built on the other; I felt lifted off my seat. At the end of the first half, Mr. Godfrey walked Astrid to the wings accompanied by thunderous applause. The roar of the crowd disturbed her. The lights came up, and my mother excused herself. My thoughts were with Grandfather. Astrid will be so disappointed. Perhaps he sat in the shadows. Soon the lights blinked, signaling for everyone to return to their seats. Mother came back with a bouquet of roses wrapped in cellophane. She sat them on the empty seat beside her.

She whispered, "Your grandfather asked for you to give them to Astrid at the end of her program."

"Is he here?"

Mother answered with an emotionless, "No."

That same lousy feeling came back. Everyone applauded as Astrid took her place. The thrill notes I heard the first day she played brought goosebumps. Tears welled in my eyes. Mother handed me a tissue. *For the Meadowlark* was longer than I remembered the sound from childhood. Then, finally, Mr. Godfrey appeared at the corner of the stage, washed in a spotlight.

"Astrid's finale piece is very special to her. It's in honor of John Michael McConnell, Mary McConnell, and especially Astrid's very best friend, Lenora." He gestured toward my mother and me. Then, Mr. Godfrey continued, "Astrid has chosen Beethoven's *Hammerklavier*, one the most difficult pieces ever written for the piano."

He turned to the audience. "This young lady is one in a million; Astrid is an extraordinary talent at just sixteen."

There was murmuring in the rows behind us. I thought, *just wait, all doubters!* He turned to Astrid, staring at her hands placed in her lap. "Ready?"

She nodded.

My heart fell into my shoes. I had never heard this music before—powerful, then lilting soft notes, followed by solid notes building a staircase, up and down again with strong crescendos. Astrid punctuated the robust run of notes with her body moving rhythmically from side to side. I was glad I'd braided her hair

Astrid's fingers moved so fast; they were a blur. At one point, Astrid put her hands behind her—then swung up to play softly. I swear there were times when her hands were six feet apart. I closed my eyes, picturing waterfalls cascading over rocks into a stream of music. She came off the bench a couple of times then sat back down. This piece of music lasted over forty minutes. She poured herself into the music. In the end, she stood up exhausted, steadying herself on the piano.

Sensing Astrid was about to lose it, I grabbed the roses and darted to the stage. Running to meet her, I hugged her tight. She whispered, "I'm tired and scared, Luna."

I whispered in her ear, "The moon is here, next to the shining star." Backstage, Mr. Godfrey instructed her to shake a few hands and say thank you to all the right people. Then, he and I took her to a dressing room where we stayed with her until everyone left except Mother, Mr. Godfrey, and me.

"Can we go now? I want to see Grandfather," she sounded frantic.

"Sit down, girls." My mother's voice broke. I knew what came next. Mother opened her purse, handing Astrid an envelope. Her hands trembled, so I opened it for her. Grandfather's handwriting was barely legible.

Upset, she hollered, "Read it!"

To my sweet little star, Astrid,

It was a privilege to watch you grow up to fulfill your dreams. Today is just the beginning of a bright future. In my heart, I will always be there with you to watch your training and revel in your accomplishments.

Having people judge you for your uniqueness will be a part of your life. But there will always be someone you can talk with, Mary or Lenora. I know they listen if you need help. Mary is going to help manage your finances.

You are reading this because my body has died, but my spirit lives in my girls, Astrid and Lenora.

Love you very much, My Sweet,

Grandfather

Astrid said nothing; grasping the letter, she held it to her heart. A primal noise came from Astrid; this was her sound of sorrow. My mother cradled Astrid's head against her body to stop her from heaving sobs.

Astrid jerked away, "No, no, no!" she yelled, "My angels promised!"

"Even angels can't stop death, darling Astrid." My mother always knew what to say. Still holding on to Astrid, she glanced in my direction, "I have a letter for you also."

"I'll read my letter later." Astie's mental state took priority.

"I don't want to play anymore." Upset, Astrid ran the emotional gauntlet.

"Oh, darling, think how disappointed Grandfather might be if you quit." Mother tipped Astrid's face to see a grimace and eyes full of pain, "You must go on playing and composing. You were a huge success today. I'm sure he was watching from heaven. Your angels brought his spirit to hear you."

Mother's explanation seemed to soothe her. Then, finally, Mother said, "We have many things to discuss, but it can wait."

We spent the night in her hotel room. Stopping at a nearby café, even though none of us were hungry, Mother informed us of Grandfather's funeral. He would be laid to rest in Brighton the next week.

Sunday, we returned to campus. When we opened the door, a banner hung from the ceiling, "Congratulations, Astrid!" with autographs from the London Symphony musicians. Astrid covered her mouth, then squealed with delight, hands flapping.

"Oh, how wonderful!" exclaimed Mother.

"We can take it down and save it," I said. Mother concurred.

I stood on a chair to take down the banner. Exhausted and emotionally spent, I asked Astrid if she wanted a nap.

We trudged up the stairs. When Astrid settled in, I joined Mother waiting in the lounge. Grandfather's letter lay in my lap, unopened. I sighed, "What will we do without him?"

"We'll do what we've always done, live our lives. Your grandfather and I discussed many things. We decided what should happen after he was gone. I'm selling the house."

"Oh, no! The house where I grew up! The house where Astrid first played for us! My beach, my sea, our sky!" The floodgates opened, tears flowing down my face. "I will lose all those years."

"No, you won't. Those memories are right here," she touched my heart. "Lenora, remember me, not just you. I'd stay by myself in a house void of rattling newspapers, music, and laughter. I want to be closer to you and Astrid, to watch you fulfill your dream of being an astronomer, Poppet. When I was young, girls could be four things: a nurse, a teacher, a secretary, or a wife. I loved your father, so being a wife was wonderful. Being a mother is what I wanted. But you. You can be anything you choose, Lenora.

Your grandfather told me how much admiration he held for you. It wasn't just how smart you are, but how caring you always are. He called you a little scrapper, never afraid of a fight." She chuckled, "You are your father's daughter."

"Am I truly like my father?"

"You have his heart of gold."

The Last Summer

Unbeknown to me, Mother took driving lessons. Astrid and I spent the summer reminiscing about our school days, going to the library and a county fair. Our last summer in Brighton, we took full advantage of the beach sunsets and shell gathering—Astrid's notebooks held more music.

One clear evening, Astrid bent her head, eyes lost in the sky. "Do you believe in God, Lenora?"

We never talked about God. "I suppose so. I believe something greater than us made all of this." I held up my arms and stretched as far as I could reach. "There can be no other explanation in the universe."

"Do you believe he watches over us?"

"God or Grandfather?"

"Both."

"I think so," I said.

"Do you think they still love me?"

Used to Astrid's disjoined thoughts, sometimes her questions didn't make sense to me. "Who are *they*?"

"My family, do you think they still love me? When Mrs. Mary took me to Mass Sunday, they weren't there. They don't go to Mass anymore. Father John said they weren't there for a while, but he liked seeing me. But they don't go anymore. Why aren't they there? They always go to Mass."

I paused, remembering my letter from my grandfather. He knew someday this question could come. "Astrid, Grandfather kept something from you. He wrote letters to your parents giving them a progress report. I know you love them because of the feelings you keep inside. Do you want to visit them?"

"I dunno," she said. "What if they don't recognize me?"

"They would remember you, silly. You're taller, your hair is longer, but your eyes are the same. Think about it. We can call first if you like."

"We don't have a phone. Maybe they have a telephone now," Astrid said in her monotone.

"We can see tomorrow."

I spoke with my mother about visiting Astrid's parents. She shook her head sharply, "They're gone, Lenora. Over the last four months, your grandfather's letters came back. The landlord told him they left in the dark of night, leaving no forward address. Don't tell Astrid. Hopefully, she won't ask again." How sad; her parents abandoned Astrid without a word.

Summer came to an end. The three of us packed boxes of pictures and books Mother wished to keep. Astrid and I found an empty cigar box. We made a time capsule with memories, keeping pictures of Grandfather dressed as Father Christmas and a picture of Astrid playing the upright piano. I found a unique gray rock with a hole, a wishing stone, and a spiral shell. Mother handed me a photograph she'd taken; I'd never seen it before. Astrid and I were twelve, playing in the sprinkler. She put it in the cigar box. I taped it shut.

Some of the furniture sold; other pieces Mother kept for her new house near Cambridge. I begged her to keep Grandfather's chair. She did. In mid-August, we loaded up the car, gave the new owners the keys, and drove to Cambridge. Astrid stared blankly out the passenger side window.

| 11 |

Forty-four, Castle Street

Near Cambridge University stood number forty-four Castle Street, a lovely red-brick rowhouse garnished with a small garden and white wrought iron gate. A quiet corner in an upscale neighborhood with lawyers, bankers, and doctors; reminiscent of our Dublin home.

Inside stood a mid-sized kitchen. There were no dividing walls, unusual for a house like this. The view of the walled garden could be seen from the kitchen. The feature I loved most was the living room space complete with a handcrafted ebony mantel and a grand fireplace. Grandfather's chair sat to the left, just like in the beach house; I felt his comforting presence.

I claimed the third story with a smashing view of a park. Once a studio apartment, the converted attic included a water closet and two skylights. The large second-story bedroom with two windows included a standing shower for Astrid, but the ground floor was Mother's domain. The largest bedroom belonged to her, situated just beneath Astrid's room, where she could listen to footsteps in the night.

Getting "settled in," as my mother put it, should not be my priority. We didn't have time to object to Mother's decorating the apartment. Astrid and I explored a nearby park, watching people feed the ducks and ride bicycles. By three, the moving truck had vanished; the coast was clear.

As soon as we walked in the door, Astrid demanded, "Where's my piano?"

"It's coming from Italy. I purchased an electric piano with a headset. You can play forever, and we won't hear." Seeing the disappointment in Astrid's eyes, she quickly added, "Unless, of course, you want us to."

Class enrollment at Cambridge began in five days. Astrid wasn't aware her classes weren't for a degree. The university would allow her to audit a few classes with an aide. In addition, Mr. Godfrey would prepare her to play with the London Symphony, and Sir David Roth enrolled Astrid in a class for young composers.

We set appointments with our advisors. For the last seven years, I'd watched over her. I was tired of being her keeper, yet I felt responsible for her. My coursework in subjects foreign to me would require intense concentration.

Being a special needs student, Astrid was assigned a tutor to help her study, which relieved me of that responsibility. We knew this could take some adjusting. After breakfast, Astrid and I scanned the bus routes and directions to our different campus advisors. The School of Music was close to the apartment. The School of Mathematics and Science was situated across campus; we both needed practice navigating our way. We sat waiting for the correct bus number at the stop around the corner.

Onboard, I reminded Astrid, "Three stops from our home, remember three." I held up my finger. She slapped them down. Loudly she said, "I'm not retarded, Lee!"

I slid down in the seat, embarrassed on a bus full of strangers. When we got off the bus, I was fuming, "Why did you do that?"

"What did I do?"

"Astrid, God could have heard you bellow at me!"

She covered her ears and howled, "I made you mad, ohhhh, I made Lee mad!" Everyone and their grandmother stared at us. I slung the satchel strap over my head, taking hold of her hands; a flurry of *okay*s flew from my mouth.

"Astie, it's okay. I'm not mad anymore. Hold my hand; we'll cross the street."

I turned to the gathering crowd, waving them off, "She's okay, just a little misunderstanding. We're fine."

We zigzagged through the buildings as I instructed her to breathe. The Dean of Music, Dr. Richard Arnhold, knew everything about Astrid thanks to Mr. Godfrey. We were introduced to Astrid's aide and escort, Hillary Caldwell, a psychology graduate student studying abnormal behavior. Astrid played the shy flower; Hillary was in for a ride. Pleased as punch, I didn't worry over Astrid's whereabouts with Hillary at her side; I handed her the reins.

Finally, I made my way to Fremont Hall, the astronomy section of the endless building. Four floors up, the black and white sign on the wall pointed me to Dr. Lyndon Hammersmith, Dean of Astronomy, my advisor.

I stopped at the door, my tongue stuck to the roof of my mouth; water! At the end of the hall were restrooms and a water fountain. The water shot up my nose and dripped all over my crisp white blouse. *Super, this will make a great impression.* I stood in the bathroom in front of the mirror, planning my next move. With only fifteen minutes before my appointment, I spied an air dryer! I didn't give it a second thought. I balanced my folder on the sink, unbuttoned my blouse, and held it under the dryer.

"Please, God, don't let anyone come in."

The wet spots were still there, but I ran out of time. As I buttoned my shirt, a woman around thirty, I guessed, came around the corner from the bathroom. This woman scrutinized me with a raised eyebrow as she washed her hands. Thunderstruck, I snatched my folder, darting into a stall. I took a deep breath, gathering my wits before walking in the door. The receptionist asked my name.

"Lenora McConnell. I have an appointment with Dr. Lyndon Hammersmith."

"I'll tell her you're here." Her? I assumed Lyndon Hammersmith was a man.

At the end of the small hallway, the door was open. "Come in. Please sit."

Oh, my god! My cheeks flushed. The tall woman with black hair and blue eyes in the restroom sat before me. She acted like she never noticed me. "I've reviewed your files; impressive. Some of your scores are high enough to earn extra credits. You won't repeat advanced calculus or chemistry like many incoming first-year students. Introduction to Analysis plus Physics will be for you; this won't be a walk in the park, Miss McConnell. Can you handle those classes?"

Good God, I said yes, I've stepped into it this time.

"So, you're being inducted into the Young Astronomer Society at the London Observatory this fall," she paused, "if everything goes well."

"Yes, ma'am, beginning in October."

"Well, aren't you an Ace? For now, you will be taking French and Medieval British History along with Physics and Analysis classes. We'll see how you do with these."

Dr. Hammersmith's presence was quite intimidating, but I still said, "No astronomy classes?"

With a rather smug chuckle, she removed her glasses. "We'll see how this semester works out before we cross that bridge. Upper-class men have the first go at Astronomy classes."

Dr. Hammersmith smiled at me. "Lenora, it's nice to see a young woman interested in astronomy. So come back on Wednesday to pick up your schedule. Just to let you know, the water fountains here shoot up very high." A twitter of nervous laughter escaped me. Before I left, she handed me a list of the books and study materials.

While sitting at the bus stop, I studied the list and broke out in a sweat. It was too late to question my lofty goal now. I must forge ahead. Although Grandfather was gone, I couldn't disappoint him.

Along the ride home, I wondered how Astrid was doing. A tinge of guilt ran through me, but she must learn to stand up for herself.

My key turned in the door. I heard my mother talking and stopped to listen. She was talking to Astrid. Suddenly, my mother's voice rang out, "Stop eavesdropping, Lenora, and come in here."

Bollocks! Caught again!

"Did you find your way?" Mother asked. I shot a look at Astrid.

"Did you mean her or me?" I felt a scowl coming across my face.

"Well, it obviously not Astrid."

"Yes, I found my way just fine—my classes are set. Seniors and juniors get the first choice of most classes. The classes I'm assigned are going to be unbelievably challenging." I shot a glance at Astrid. "What about you? You found your way." My remarks were purposely catty.

My mother's eyes narrowed, "Lenora, stop that."

I took exception to her remark. "Did Miss Know-it-all tell you about our bus ride?" My eyes narrowed and I crossed my arms over my chest.

"This is so unlike you!"

"Astrid embarrassed me in front of everyone on the bus and the bus stop." Mother's forehead wrinkled like a prune. Then, she took Astrid's side, "Were you treating her like a child? According to Hillary, everything was just peachy."

Sarcasm was never my strong suit, but it burned in me today, "Very well, I'll make a note of that." I stormed up the stairs, pacing the floor, trying to make sense of the situation. I lay on my bed, staring at the skylight discussed.

"May I come in?"

"Yes, Mother." I wasn't getting up. Mother took a seat at the end of the bed. She didn't say anything, but I did.

I slammed my fists into the covers in frustration and unloaded, "How is it she can be helpless one moment and so enraged the next? We've been attached at the hip since sixth grade. I couldn't have a close friend or go out with anyone because she's different. Some days I love her but today isn't one of those days."

"I know, Lenora. You have sacrificed a lot for her. That's why I moved to Cambridge. I'm here to lighten your responsibilities with Astrid. She's often inappropriate, you know that."

"Yes, she has extraordinary musical abilities, blah, blah, blah, but she cannot process social cues or emotions properly. I know all of this."

"Today on the bus, did she make eye contact when she seemed angry?"

"No, she pounded her fist on her purse. She really showed out today."

"It's her mannerisms; she claps her hand or flaps repeatedly when she is happy and sometimes hits herself or pounds her fist in frustration. Sometimes she struggles to know how you feel about things?"

"Yes, to all of those things," I said quietly. "All of her struggles make sense. But what will become of her?"

Mother hit the sympathetic nail on the head, "I see." She paused. "You're worried you're losing her."

With my arm over my face, I hid my expression; she was right. Juggling balls, quickly, hand to hand, I was bound to drop one. The one with Astrid's name on it.

"You must never repeat what I'm going to tell you." Those words were enough to make me sit up. She continued, "Mr. Godfrey put me in touch with a researcher. Astrid must never know this, but Dr. Albert Dryer, a pleasant man, will be working with her, studying her. He is a neuropsychologist who works with others to unlock people's minds with this disorder. He, himself, is an accomplished musician and friend to Mr. Godfrey."

"What do you mean by study? It sounds like she is a lab rat." This concerned me. Mother assured me this wasn't the case. Instead, he'd observe her reactions to different stimuli and how she processed information.

"Today, she didn't want your help, Lenora. Astrid told me she sees a map and knows exactly where to go. It's uncanny how she can relate spatially to maps."

"Well, that explains why she recites countries and capitals for hours on end."

"In my conversation with Dr. Dryer, he explained how the music for her is like a map. It's the reason she can play a concerto just by hearing it played once. Her brain maps out notes very quickly.

My mother hugged me. "Lenora, the world around Astrid is confusing. Please remember, Astrid will always be eleven. We're getting older; she is not."

"When we were younger, it didn't matter. Now Astie is aware she's different. My heart breaks for her."

My mother invited Dr. Dryer for dinner; she intended to let Astrid develop a relationship with him. I didn't approve, but my opinion didn't matter. When introduced to Astrid, the doctor's title was left out on purpose; it made him less threatening.

The commonality between Dr. Dryer and Astrid was music. The first meeting was difficult for her. Astrid practically sat in my lap at dinner. I wasn't surprised; he was intrusive. Astrid answered his clinical questions with one syllable, yes or no. Dr. Dryer gave me the creeps. Fortyish, average looks, intelligent, but he seemed overly anxious about our lives.

Eventually, Astrid tolerated him. One afternoon, he and my mother took Astrid to practice with Mr. Godfrey. According to Mother, Godfrey and Dryer had known each other for years through the symphony and something called music therapy.

I knew little about Mr. Godfrey. Mother relayed how his slow speech development and withdrawn personality led to a false label of a savant instead of a prodigy. By age four, he took lessons, developing the ability to read music, practicing for hours, and memorizing piano concertos. By age six, he played worldwide; by age twelve, he burnt out and withdrew. A wise teacher suggested he should teach, and so he did. Mother said he treated Astrid with kindness and patience. Knighthood must lie in his future.

Astrid spoke fondly of her tutor. I must admit, Hillary made me jealous. Astrid spent more time with her than I did. However, my class load weighed heavily on me; analytics and physics might do me in. It was written in the stars; I'd burn the midnight oil and exist on coffee for the next two years. When I was overwhelmed, Astrid had a sixth sense.

A light tap on the door caught my attention. "Lee, are you in there? I want to see you."

"Astie, come in."

"Mrs. Mary said you knock, not barge in. Am I barging in, Lee?"

"No, lay on my bed and look up." I turned off the lights, "Astie, can you see the stars?" I lay next to her, "I miss spending time with you."

"Me, too, but Mrs. Mary says I need to give you space. You have lots of space in the sky. I don't know how to give you space. I couldn't reach it."

"Astie, she means I need lots of time to study. My classes are much harder at Cambridge."

"Mine is too, but Hillary helps me. Hillary is nice."

Astrid continued to work with Dr. Dryer, but my mother was never far. When I questioned her about activities with the doctor, she told me they played games.

"Like Old Maid cards and Rummy; it's matching cards. Sometimes, Mrs. Mary gives me hints. On Fridays, we go to London for practice. Mr. Godfrey says, soon, I will play with the big symphony. Can you take me sometime?"

"I'll try, Astie."

Astie's routine never varied. Mother was happy with Dr. Dryer's treatment of Astie, but I was unsettled. There's something about Albert Dryer I just didn't trust. Lately, I'd been out of the loop, what with five advanced classes. There was little time to breathe. I managed to make a couple of friends in the YAS group, but I just wasn't party material. I found myself nervous with the prospect of Dr. Hammersmith's Astrophysics class looming over me. Stories of her staunch manner and expectations of perfection put the fear of God in me.

My Junior Year

As an upperclassman, I found myself president of the Young Astronomers Society. I should have been thrilled, but what a pain. My responsibility for organizing events came with little experience in planning fundraisers. While much of the budget came from endowments, expenses for activities with the public did not. Between school and society duties, my grades were lagging.

Mother intervened. "You must learn to delegate. Form an events committee and let others have responsibilities. You don't have to do it all."

"I have a feeling I was elected because no one else wanted the job. I accepted because it bodes well on a resume. And you're right about delegating.; it's time for a change."

At the next meeting of our lovable nerds, I proposed an events committee to oversee the gala at the planetarium: a meet and greet followed by a show and Q&A from VIPs, short and sweet. The gala was always a formal affair, evening dress and black tie; after all, it was a fundraiser for our upcoming trip to Sark Island, a designated dark sky area. With Dr. Hammersmith in charge of our expedition, everything had to be spit-spot.

I'd never owned formalwear before and couldn't wait to go shopping. "The gala is two months away, Mother," I pleaded.

"That's exactly why you can wait."

"Couldn't I at least look for a dress? Besides the nerdy guys, I might be able to impress some of the guests. I've been on one date. It wasn't an actual date; there were two couples, and he was a dork."

"Lenora," she had that *come-now* expression on her face.

"It's true! My life has revolved around school and Astrid. I don't want to be an old maid all my life."

"I know, dear, it's not been easy. You've just turned nineteen. There's no reason to rush."

"Oh, Mother, dear, you were twenty when you married. Please don't hamstring me for wanting to date. I haven't one particular in mind, but the gala brings many people together. I should make a good impression as president. Will you hold me back from socializing?"

"I guess not. But, please, no older men."

"Never. Firstly, whoever is out there for me must understand my relationship with Astrid. I'd never get involved with any man who doesn't empathize with my love for Astrid."

"That's good," she replied. "I guess I'm having a hard time with the notion you would leave me soon."

"Oh, please. Don't worry about that now. I'm finishing school and possibly getting a higher degree. You know I want to work at the Observatory; that means you're stuck with me for at least another three years."

"Then go Saturday. Take Astrid with you. She seems to know what looks good on you."

"Must I?" I whined.

"She has a winter concert coming up at the end of November. You can help her."

"Gosh, Mother, she'll want to come home after an hour."

"Lenora, tell her she can get pizza for lunch. That always works." She wasn't going to take no for an answer; I wasn't old enough for that argument.

After dinner, I asked, "Tomorrow, could you come with me to go dress shopping, Astie?"

Preoccupied with a book on international flags, "What kind of dresses?"

"A recital dress for you and an evening gown for me."

Placing her finger on the last flag, she studied, "Evening gown? Like a nightgown?"

"No, like a party dress. I'm going to a gala in December."

"I don't want to go to a … gala."

"No, Astrid, you're not going, I am. So do you want to buy a new fancy dress for your recital?"

She sounded a flat, "No." I was saved!

Mother did her best to change Astrid's mind. It was too much. She threw her book across the room and then proceeded to hit herself in the head with her fist. The "Dr. Jekyll and Mr. Hyde" behaviors were rare, but when they happened, it was intense. She was too big for my mother to hold her like she used to do. I sat on the floor and put my hands on the sides of her head. She hit my hands instead of her head now.

I didn't raise my voice, "You don't have to go this time. You don't have to go. You can stay here with Mrs. Mary. Breath, Astie." A gulp of air filled her lungs; this animal-sounding wail came from her. I sat her on the sofa by me; her head rested against my shoulder as she whimpered. Astrid threw the worst tantrum I'd ever seen from her. It frightened Mother. Indignant, I warned her not to push her will on Astrid again.

Saturday, I shopped alone. Gathering my wits about me, I took the bus to Harrod's. I remembered the elevator door opening to all the beautiful ball gowns, hoping someday I'd wear one. But I was hunting for an evening gown, not a debutante ball gown. I wanted to feel, well, sexy—but not too sexy, or my mother would throw a fit as bad as Astrid.

My dress must be black, long-sleeved, and not dragging the floor. Mother put a cap on how much I could spend, which immediately sent me to the sales rack. Hideous colors and necklines opened to my navel—no, thank you. I found a couple in my size; not exactly what I'd hope for, but I'd make do. The saleslady kept trying to up-sell me, but my limitations became apparent. She gave up.

I arrived home with the dress in tow; Mother wanted to see it on me right away. Before I tried it on, I told her, "Your budget constraints left little choice. I did my best."

On my way upstairs, Astrid opened her door. "Did you get a pretty one?"

"Go downstairs and wait with Mrs. Mary. I'll come down and show you."

Dressed in the smooth velvety dress, I sucked my stomach in. Reflecting in the mirror, the V neckline wouldn't meet Mother's approval; I didn't care. The long-sleeved, floor-length black dress is what I wanted. Down the stairs, I came, met with *ooh*'s from Astrid. Mother wasn't too keen.

"The neckline is very low. I was hoping for something more conservative."

"Conservative cost more than what you allow. Besides, it's sophisticated. It would be perfect if I could borrow your pearl necklace and earrings."

Mother thought for a minute. She wasn't pleased with my choice but gave in, "Okay. The pearls will make you more presentable."

I gritted my teeth at the "presentable." "Presentable, indeed! You should have seen the other dresses. I would be mistaken for a Call-Girl."

I hiked up my dress and stormed upstairs as I heard Astrid say, "I think she's upset. What's a Call Girl?"

The Young Astronomers Society met on the third Saturday of every month; this evening meeting made me hold my breath. Our sponsor said patrons were more in the giving mood in December. Finals were one week after the gala. I wasn't happy.

Was everything ready? I called the meeting to order, asking for a full committee report. Our venue was the planetarium. Mr. Weldon put together a special presentation; the planetarium was losing attendance, and maintenance on the aging build became costly. We were guaranteed a grade-A showing. Two hundred guests received invitations, around half accepted; I'd hoped for better attendance. Silvey Ahmed arranged catering at a reduced price from a Persian restaurant owned by her sympathetic uncle. It fits with our theme of "A Hundred and One Nights." Phillip Hopper, a real knobhead, offered to DJ; all classical music, he assured me. My phone rang off the hook for two weeks; I held my breath in anticipation.

The night of the gala, I borrowed my grandmother's tortoiseshell comb with the tiny pearls matching my mother's pearl necklace and earrings. Mother kept asking if I needed help while Astrid hovered over me as I did my make-up. I made Astrid go downstairs so I could finish. Stomping down the stairs, Astrid mumbled God knows what.

I bought a particular type of bra for the plunging neckline. I also purchased a girdle and was not going to wear garters. I tried to wear my garters, but they caused bumps in the fabric, so no hose. My dress barely covered my feet; it was good. I hated pantyhose. I loved seeing myself in the mirror. My hair wasn't long enough for an updo, so I swept it to the side with the tortoiseshell comb. Pleased with myself, I carefully lilted down the stairs to await the scrutiny to come.

"The neckline is too low for someone your age," my mother gasped. "I'd be ashamed to be seen in public with that dress on."

"Well," I countered, "I'm not you." Mother huffed and continued to knit.

The pearl necklace and earrings were the perfect complements. Then she mumbled, "You should have let me fix your hair. It looks odd, swept to one side." I wasn't happy with it either.

"Can you do something better in thirty minutes? That's how much time I have." She came back with matching rhinestone combs. I'd never seen them before.

"Where did you get these?"

"Your father."

Each side was pulled back, the waves were tamed. While Mother coated my hair with hairspray, Astrid furiously clapped her and bounced up and down. "Now, Mrs. Mary's not mad; you look like a movie star!"

Mother let me use a small, beaded handbag to complete my ensemble; pleased with my appearance, I put on my long wool coat at the taxi's horn. "Be careful, Lenora, especially with men."

"I will."

I was twenty minutes late, on purpose. Deborah Hines, the coordinator, was in a tizzy. She wondered if something had happened to me. Then she noticed my dress, "Gosh, Lee, you'll catch a big fish with that dress."

Mr. Weldon came to speak with me, "My, how you've grown up." His eyes drifted to my cleavage; I rather enjoyed it, at first. "I've heard great things about you! Oh, and I'm sorry about your grandfather. He was an exceptional man."

"Thank you, Mr. Weldon. Yes, he was. I miss him every day."

"I have put together a special program tonight. I believe you'll be pleased." He made me uncomfortable. I tried to get away from him when another club member, Zora, liberated me.

"Thank God you rescued me. He kept looking down my dress."

"Well, you are well endowed."

"It can be both a blessing and a curse."

Zora chuckled, "It looks like a blessing tonight!" We laughed.

Dr. Hammersmith introduced me to her friend, Claudia Bandeaux, the Professor of Astronomy at the International Space University in France. Tall and shapely, she stood like a model. I was quite taken aback by her stunning features. She inquired about my interest in the stars; I recounted how, as a child, my grandfather taught me the constellations.

"Ever since then, I was fascinated by astronomy."

"She's one of my star pupils and president of the Young Astronomers Society."

"*Très bon*, I see; you can count on a nice donation from me."

"*Merci beaucoup*. The trip to Sark Island will be a kick. I've never been to a dark sky area."

"It's *fascinante*! And you're most welcome."

I headed for the bar, wondering about those two. Phillip Hopper stopped me. "I wanted to introduce you to my cousin, John, and his date, Emily Thurston."

The Thurstons were patrons of our group; they came also. The stunning Emily was studying ballet against her parent's wishes. John Hopper studied law; his chiseled jaw, blue eyes, and brown hair made him extremely attractive. They were a perfect couple. I should be so lucky to find a catch like him.

The lights flashed, and we moved to the planetarium. I ended up between Zora and Phillip. I found Phillip to be crass and mouthy most of the time. His cousin was much more refined and handsome, the type of young man who never gave someone like me a second take. When the lights darkened, Phillip tossed a piece of a napkin down the front of my dress.

In an angry whisper, I said, "What are you, in seventh grade?" From then on, he didn't bother me. The show didn't disappoint. Mr. Weldon used Gustav Holtz's *The Planets* as background music for the "Solar System and Beyond" presentation.

Dr. Hammersmith gave a talk about the spring trip; she thanked everyone for their support. The night was a success for everyone except me. Compliments on my attire came from people, but no dates. Before we ended, I went for a glass of wine. I wasn't aware Phillip's cousin was behind me. When I turned around, he was a breath away. His sky-blue eyes pierced me. "You have beautiful brown eyes."

Stunned, I said, "Thank you."

"My cousin is a true wanker. I apologize for his behavior."

I chuckled, "Oh, I know; he can be totally obnoxious. I secretly love it when our advisor threatens him with expulsion." John smiled at me, then excused himself to return to Emily. He was attractive but way out of my league. Mr. Weldon moved in my direction; I ducked into the ladies' room.

As the event wound down, the announcement of donations pledged came to thirty thousand fifteen pounds, more than what we needed.

"Brilliant job, Miss McConnell," Dr. Hammersmith complimented. She then said she hoped I studied as hard for my finals.

Just before midnight, I arrived home; of course, Mother sat in her chair knitting. I saw her glance at her watch.

"I'm home before midnight. I didn't lose my shoe or turn into a pumpkin. And before you ask, I did get lots of compliments, but, alas, no dates." I plopped down on the sofa and kicked my shoes off, "I don't want to be an old maid, but that might be my lot in life."

Sympathetic words came from my mother. "Oh, don't say that, Lenora. There's someone out there for you. You're only nineteen. Don't rush what you're not ready for, dear. Your time will come."

| 12 |

The Sky Above Us

Sark Island stood an ominous rock-face island, tall with no port, only a small pier. I prayed for the weather's cooperation on the boat through rough waters. Nine of us made the trip with Dr. Hammersmith. Claudia came along, too, under the guise of research.

April was cold and windy. A hearty bowl of lamb stew warmed us at the wee bed and breakfast. There were four rooms for the nine of us, three to a room. Conveniently for Dr. Hammersmith and Claudia, the main bedroom had a queen-sized bed. My suspicions were all but confirmed.

The wind died down, and we unrolled our sleeping bags at sunset to watch the changing sky. The deep purple hues of dusk turned into a sky full of glitter. Spectacular doesn't begin to describe the night sky. Remembering Grandfather, I wished we could have shared that experience. The Milky Way kept the night sky unrecognizable.

The wonder of life on other planets, exploding stars, discovering new nebulas and black holes occupied my thoughts. No one said a word: we were as quiet as church mice. Nothing made noise except a gust of wind that blew through the shrubbery. The tilting sky of the earth's revolution filled my heart with awe. We were microscopic grains of sand in this vast unknown universe.

This outing was my peace away from all problems, all doubts; nothing else mattered in this glorious moment. One by one, people began to make their back into the B and B. I wanted to stay there forever. At some point, I fell asleep. Someone called my name; Dr. Hammersmith. She said I shouldn't stay out all night because of the dew. I barely remember getting into bed. I dreamt of floating among the stars.

During the summer, I worked at the Observatory as a museum guide, which was not my cup of tea. Nevertheless, the history of the museum was important, I supposed. I'd have rather been working in the lab using a new piece of equipment: a computer.

Astrophysicist Dr. Edward Grimes took charge of the program the previous spring. His knowledge of computers caused old Mr. Graham to retire early. We could use the computer for collecting data. Alas, the senior class students had the first crack at it. I was just a museum guide with limited access to the Observatory, reading analysis of collected data.

Astrid spent more time practicing with the symphony and writing music. Dr. Dryer learned more about Astrid by observation.

"If interrupted, Astrid gets upset when questioned repeatedly about anything," Mother relayed. I shot mother a look, forcing her to remember Astrid's fits. Dr. Dryer said we must learn to be more direct in communicating with Astrid.

Astie still loved to wash dishes, but they weren't always clean. Vacuuming for her could be in one spot until she was shown to vacuum in another area. Dr. Dryer said we shouldn't get upset with Astrid because she would get stuck in a time loop doing one thing over and over again. He explained that if Astrid dressed herself thinking what she had on was perfectly fine, even when her clothes didn't match, we shouldn't correct her at home, for it didn't matter.

"All of these behaviors are characteristic of high-functioning mental retardation. Astrid is different in perfectly playing the music she hears or repeating phrases in learned French. These words get stuck in her mind, causing her to sound like a scratched record with the needle stuck in the groove. What's different with her is her ability to write music.

The neurologists are baffled by her. A brain chemistry imbalance is believed to be the culprit. Part of the puzzle is why less than 16% of all savants are women."

"Mostly, she can't understand if I'm upset or don't want to talk. Yet, other times she tries to comfort me," I told Dr. Dryer. He wanted to use a new piece of equipment coming to the neurological center this fall. It would allow a neurologist to image the brain.

"Is it invasive?" I asked.

My mother sat there, never saying a word.

"No. It's an x-ray of sorts. I'm going to a conference in two weeks to find out more." His tone sounded patronizing. "You'll be the first to know what I find out, Mary."

She thanked him. He tipped his hat and left. Clueless, Mother and I looked at each other. Astrid jumped down each stair and hollered, "I'm hungry!"

"What are we supposed to do? It's hours before supper," I stated.

"Astrid, please don't jump on the steps," Mother said in a non-threatening voice.

Astrid wrinkled her forehead, "Why not? It's wood and won't break."

"You're right, it is wood, but it makes a loud sound," Mother replied.

"I'm hungry, I'm hungry," she repeated.

Here was a textbook case: the repetitive phrases, the one-track mind. Mother and I exchanged glances; she shrugged her shoulders as if Astrid were my problem. It made me mad.

"Come to the kitchen, Astie. I'll see what we can find."

In rapid-fire, she began to repeat, "Cheese, crackers, cheese, crackers, cheese, crackers!"

Impatient, she jerked the refrigerator door open, rattling the contents.

"Wait!" I hollered at her as she dug through the shelves.

"I can find the cheeses!" She hollered back at me. A carton of milk spilled on the floor; Astrid turned to me with a block of cheddar in one hand and a piece of Swiss in the other. "Uh-oh." She closed the door and walked away.

"Astrid," I said, trying hard to keep my anger at bay, "you've spilled the milk on the floor." I wanted to say *get over there and clean it up*. But I kept a level head, "Should we wipe up the milk now?"

"No, I'll help later, after my cheese and crackers."

It infuriated me, but it was precisely what Dr. Dryer meant. She'd acted this way forever, but now I'd become aware of why. If her parents were in the picture, she'd have been locked away in a convent. I hated to think what could become of her.

Dr. Dryer was more than a researcher, becoming a frequent visitor to the house. He and my mother worked on different tasks with Astrid, simple things like jigsaw puzzles, laying out clothes, and vacuuming correctly. They worked hard to help her express her emotions, often upsetting her. And me.

Astrid developed her own unique, bohemian style; she liked the long Indian print skirts and hated sleeveless blouses. She couldn't tolerate polyester fabrics. Astrid grew taller still, another inch, standing at five foot nine. She was stunning, making my mother hypervigilant of anyone trying to make advances. Astrid gained notoriety among musical circles but didn't understand all the fuss.

Pantsuits for women were all the rage; I had several for work and school. I still wore dresses to functions. Dating was hit and miss, mostly miss. Those lads had one-track minds. By the end of my sophomore year, Dr. Hammersmith allowed the observatory classes to be part of my curriculum. It became my second home; I learned to be a night owl. From then on, astronomy wasn't a hobby anymore.

Something strange began to happen. In January, I received a bouquet of mixed flowers. The card read, *From an admirer.*

"Well, Lenora, you have a secret admirer. Any ideas on who it might be?"

"God, I hope it's not Mr. Weldon from the planetarium. Last month, he was full of innuendos at the gala, and he's much older than me." I racked my brain over who this admirer might be.

When the second bouquet arrived on February fourteenth, a dozen red roses came arranged in a cut-glass vase. An expensive vase. The message only said, "*Happy Valentine's Day,*" Accompanied by hand-drawn hearts and the word, *soon*. I showed my mother the card.

"*Soon?* I wonder what *soon* means."

"I'm as baffled as you are. The only young men I know are in the society; I doubt it's any of them. They're only interested in sex and science. No one has ever given me a second look except Phillip Hooper. I'd be gutted if it's him. I'll vomit."

"Lenora, please." She continued to knit.

"I couldn't help it. Phillip's a rich mouthy guy who thinks he can get away with murder, twice threatened with expulsion. He drives me bonkers. If I had the power, I'd have thrown him out months ago."

She put her knitting in her lap, "Young men like that shouldn't give you the time of day."

"Absolutely! I'm miffed. It wasn't a problem putting it out of my mind last month. I reasoned it was a prank and still could be until I saw the word *soon*. Now, I'll be watching over my shoulder. It's become scary."

"Oh, goodness, I didn't think of that." Alarmed, she continued, "Maybe you shouldn't go anywhere alone, at least not at night."

"My evening shift at the observatory; what am I to do?"

"I'll give you taxi fare." She returned to her knitting. And that was the end of our conversation.

February passed, but not without anxiety. On March first, another bouquet arrived. I was scared to open the card. Mother watched as I opened it; *"I finally can reveal myself to you. Meet me at 12:30 for lunch on Saturday at Limoncello on Mill Road. It's easy to find. Casual, not fancy."*

"What am I to make of this, Mother?"

"First, It's in broad daylight; a good sign. Second, you're still not going alone."

"Please, don't say you're coming with me," I begged.

"Astrid can go along. She loves pizza." At first, I balked at the idea. But then I reconsidered.

"You're right. If someone cares for me, that person must accept Astrid. And I don't think of this as a first date. With Astrid in tow, most likely, it will be my only date with this person." The challenge was explaining to Astrid we'd be meeting someone I didn't know. Of course, the questions came: what kind of restaurant, who is this person, why do I need to go, and endless more questions.

"You can order pizza. We're meeting the person who sends me flowers; I want you to meet him, too."

Her pointy finger was in my face, "I have at rehearsal, you know. I must be there at six o'clock. Six o'clock spit-spot!"

"Don't get your knickers in a knot. I promise you'll get there before six."

"No six o'clock, not before, and you can't watch!"

"Yes, six o'clock. And I promise not to watch."

"Pizza, for lunch ... on Saturday."

She repeated this phrase at least ten times. Every day, she asked, is it Saturday? Finally, I could say yes. After breakfast, Astrid came downstairs wearing a black polka dot blouse and a pink plaid skirt.

"Astrid, I know you love the plaid skirt. You can wear your pink skirt, and I'll braid your hair. You'll need your jacket, too."

"With pink ribbons? You can braid my hair with pink ribbons?"

"Yes, of course." I made her presentable. I wore a houndstooth pinafore with a white blouse and a white open cardigan, nothing flashy.

We boarded the bus and walked two streets over; I held Astrid's hand while searching for a sign. Thoughts filled my head. He must know what I look like; I have no idea about him. It could be *her*, a creepy thought. The sign, *Limoncello,* made my heart beat faster. Uncharacteristically, Astrid didn't say anything until we were close.

"Pizza, I smell pizza!"

"We're almost there, then you can have pizza."

"Pepperoni, extra cheese. Pepperoni, Lee, with extra cheese."

"Yes, Astrid, I know."

A bell rang as I opened the door; I noticed a young man get up and walk toward us. It was Phillip's cousin, the dashing John Hopper! I felt faint; I couldn't imagine he might be interested in me.

"Lenora McConnell. We met briefly at the gala. And you've brought a friend."

Two minutes with Astrid, and you knew she was different. "Yes, this is my friend, Astrid Innis. Say hello to John."

"Hello to John, hello."

I could tell he didn't know how to react to Astrid's head swaying back and forth. My excuses started; my explanation was memorized.

"I see. Well, ladies, right this way."

Astrid slid into the booth; I sat next to her. For the life of me, I couldn't read his expression. Immediately, the waiter came to the table for our drink orders; colas for Astrid and me. John ordered a beer. Now is the one time I wished I for a shot of whisky.

Astrid blurted out, "I want pizza, pepperoni, extra cheese. Extra cheese, please. Pepperoni with extra cheese."

"Yes, Astrid, he heard you." She clapped her hands until I took ahold of one.

From the corner of my eyes, I watched John, who was staring at Astrid. The waiter was stunned by Astrid's demeanor. John cleared his throat and said, "Are you ready to order? You haven't even peeked at the menu." I asked the waiter if the chef made the ravioli in-house.

"Yes, today is ricotta cheese, spinach, and chives."

"I'll have that," I said with certainty. I could tell John was flustered.

"I'll have the same." I could tell this was the beginning of the end; I'd never see him again.

John spoke, "I owe you an apology for all the mystery. But you see, ending my relationship with Emily wasn't easy; she was fonder of me than I was of her."

I was dumbfounded. Emily Thurston, a wealthy, beautiful ballerina; he threw her over for me? "I hardly know what to say except I'm flattered."

"What's your name?" Astrid asked while folding and unfolding her napkin; I didn't stop her. John needed to see her in all her glory.

He tried to engage Astrid, who didn't make eye contact. "My name is John Hopper. I'm a student at Oxford. What's your name?"

"My name is Astrid Innis. I play piano, and I'm weird, I'm weird. I'm really weird." The word *weird* came out in a contorted fashion. Now, out came the story of Astrid.

"John, Astrid has been my friend since we were eleven."

Astrid interrupted, "I'm twenty-six. Or maybe sixteen."

"You're almost twenty, Astrid." I hated speaking about her in the third person while she was here. "Astrid is gifted in many ways. Astrid, will you tell John what you like to do?" She continued to fold and unfold her napkin as I waited for a response. "Please?" I asked again.

Astrid got my attention out of the corner of my eye, whispering, "I don't know him."

In a bright tone, I said, "I just met him, too, Astie." She glared at me like I had lost my mind. She didn't understand why I lunched with someone I didn't know.

"I met him at the astronomy club party." I prayed for no tantrums.

Astrid cupped my ear, whispering what to say to him. John leaned in to hear our exchange.

"Astrid has some difficulty relating to strangers; she wants you to know she loves music."

"How wonderful!" he said with great enthusiasm. "At my home in Gloucester, we have a grand piano."

"Astrid is a concert pianist. She can read music but plays everything by hearing it once."

Needless to say, John was shocked; seeing her as someone who lacked normal behavior, he was stunned.

"Where does she play?"

Astrid jumped in with "The London Symphony. I play for Mr. Godfrey at the London Symphony. I play the piano. I'm a weirdo."

I inhaled, "Astrid, please, stop saying your weird. You are gifted."

"Yes, I'm weird."

In my frustration, I stopped trying to change her thoughts. John was very patient with her. The waiter brought our drinks; I asked if the cook could cut the pizza into squares instead of slices. He assured me they could. John cocked his head in Astrid's direction. I explained Astrid makes a mess unless it's cut into pieces.

"Oh," he said. Surely, any future dates with John were out of the question. I might as well enjoy a free lunch. I wanted to include Astrid in the narrative when trying to explain her quirkiness. It became a monologue.

"Astrid and I were the odd girls in the Brighton community school, so naturally, we became friends. Isn't that right?" No response, just napkin folding.

"She carried a leather notebook, writing non-stop. Astrid told me she wrote music, yet she had never played the piano before. I had a piano catching dust at home. When she visited, unbelievable music came from her. Can you tell John the name of your first song?"

"A song, I played a song."

Continuing my prompt, "What kind of song was it? What was the title?"

"It was a song!" she thundered as if I were an idiot.

"Okay. Astrid wrote it without ever playing any piano before. It was called..." Astrid interrupted me, "For the Meadowlark song."

Thank God the food arrived; I was sure I was boring John Hopper to death. I unfolded the napkin and said to her, "Don't make a mess, please."

In a droll voice, "Mind my manners, mind my manners, I know." She sat with her hands folded in her lap, waiting for me to say something.

"You may start," The waiter brought a pile of extra paper napkins in anticipation. Astrid crossed herself and mumbled something, then began to eat.

I apologized and informed him I could understand if this was our first and last meeting.

"Nonsense," he said, "as long as we could have some dates with just us."

I stuttered, "You, ah, want to see me again?"

"Of course I do. I want to find out more about you, Lenora. What I've found so far is you're very caring and compassionate. People might cast Astrid aside. That's very admirable of you to care for her."

What planet did he fall from? For the first time in my life, I felt flattered. I gave him a most sincere thank you.

"We both know my cousin Phillip is a jerk. Truthfully, he admires your smarts. In fact, he says you're the smartest female he's ever known."

"Somehow, I bet there were a few negatives, or he wouldn't be Phillip."

"Yes, but there are always a few. Phillip's sarcasm is to cover his lack of intellect."

Wow, that caught me off guard. "Well, you know more about me than I know about you. What are you studying?"

"Law. I'm graduating this year from Oxford and will begin my vocational training this summer. I want to work as a barrister in chancery law."

"Pardon my ignorance; what is chancery law?"

"I will be working on behalf of estates and trusts. It sounds boring, but I find it intriguing. You gain a true insight into people's lives and history."

"Novels are made from stories like these."

"That never crossed my mind, but, yes, I suppose so."

Off-putting sounds broke our exchange; Astrid licked her fingers. An eye roll was in order, "Astrid, use the napkins to wipe off your fingers."

Her plate sat littered with bits of crust; then, she belched. I wanted to slide under the table. She knew I disapproved.

Her head dropped, "Sorry, bad manners, sorry."

"Astrid," John Hopper asked, "do you like ice cream?"

Her eyes stared at her lap, "Yes." A smile came from her as she continued to stare at her lap. He spoke to the waiter as I wiped Astrid's face, which she hated.

"If you wish to have ice cream, you must wipe the sauce from your hands and face." I handed her a dampened napkin. When the waiter returned, he put a plate of ice cream in front of Astrid, vanilla in the shape of spaghetti with strawberry sauce.

"I hope you like strawberry sauce." I know he meant well, but the novelty only confused her.

"This isn't ice cream," she poked it with her finger; Astrid could not hide her disdain, "It's cold! I don't like cold spaghetti." Crossing her arms, scrunching her face, "I don't want that."

"It's alright," he said. "What kind of ice cream do you want?"

"Chocolate, with whipped cream, please. I like that kind, not cold spaghetti," Astrid glared at John. Arms folded, in a huff, Astrid spouted off, "He tried to trick me; that wasn't nice."

"I didn't mean to trick you, Astrid. I promise. I should have asked you first."

I took the spaghetti ice cream. Astrid didn't understand why I ate it. I mixed it up like strawberry ice cream, but she still didn't understand. Poor John. I explained a lesson my mother and I learned: everything is literal to Astrid. Spaghetti was spaghetti, not ice cream; he was beginning to understand what I experienced daily. When we finished, John hailed a taxi and rode with us. I told him it wasn't necessary. He countered, wanting to know where we might meet for our next date! I had no idea what had got into this man. I was no slender, graceful, beauty queen like Emily Thurston; I was just an average girl who liked the stars.

Astrid opened the car door, "John Hopper has black hair."

He chuckled, "Yes, John Hopper has black hair." He turned to me, "Can I see you again?"

I still couldn't believe this was happening. "Yes, anytime."

"Next Saturday evening? I don't have your phone number."

"My mother wants to meet you if you're okay with it. We can go in; I'll write my number down." Astrid wandered in ahead of us. I heard my mother call my name.

"Mother, come here, please." I retrieved a pen from the kitchen drawer. She came from her room. "Mother, this is John Hopper. John, this is my mother, Mary McConnell." I know I heard my mother gasp.

They exchanged pleasantries while I wrote our number down. I thanked John for lunch and for putting up with Astrid. He smiled, "I'll call you on Thursday."

I smiled at him, and he smiled back.

"Well, well, it seems you have found yourself a nice beau," said Mother.

"Don't be hasty. I'm still baffled by the whole situation. I met John Hopper briefly at the December gala. John is the cousin of Phillip Hopper, the smart mouth of YAS. John swears he's nothing like Phillip, and I see he's not. However, he was dating Emily Thurston."

"The ballerina?" Mother inquired.

"Yes, and her father is a Trustee of the Planetary Society. I have no idea what he sees in me. Let's face it; I am not Vogue magazine material. I'm a plain Jane."

"Lenora, stop judging yourself so harshly. The models in magazines at too thin, and boney. You have a beautiful face and hazel eyes."

In the background, I heard Astrid, "Her eyes aren't hazelnuts. They're eyes."

My mother rolled her eyes, "Anyway, it's a good sign, asking for your phone number." She suddenly had panic in her eyes. "What did he think about Astrid?"

"Astrid is Astrid. She was subdued, considering everything. Folding and unfolding her napkin, she didn't understand the novelty ice cream spaghetti with strawberry sauce. She couldn't figure out how anyone could eat the frozen noodles. John apologized for upsetting her."

Mother interjected, "Oh, darling, I'm sorry I made Astrid go with you."

I explained to her why I didn't mind. If John, or anyone, were to date me, they must understand Astrid was part of my life. And at some point, undoubtedly, Astrid would be in my care. Mother felt sorry for me, but I brought Astrid into our lives. The responsibility was mine, even if it meant I was to be alone.

"This scenario is why I never pursued a relationship. Mother. Now the decision lies with John Hopper. Honestly, I never expected to hear from him again."

Two weeks dragged on without a call from John; I knew he'd never call because of Astrid. Staring at the glowing embers of the last fire, I felt sorry for myself one minute, sorry for Astrid the next.

Mother came from the kitchen. Dr. Dryer had just left. "Why such a glum face, Lenora?"

"I can't imagine why you'd even ask me that question." It just upset me more.

"There'll be other young men, Lenora."

I cringed. Spinning around, "Do you actually believe that? Do you really believe someone there will love and respect me; who will also care for Astrid? Because I think not." My voice trailed off with a sniffle.

Mother knew the possibility. It was bound to happen. I was going off to bed when she stopped me with false hope. "Maybe he's involved with his studies. You did say he was entering his pupilage."

"It's a false hope. I'm not hoping anymore. It just makes me depressed, and I have exams next week." On the second landing, I peeked in on Astrid. She slept with her arm draped over an overstuffed teddy bear, a gift from the musicians. I loved her, just not the way she loved me.

My alarm popped off at six-thirty; after a restless night of sleep, I wanted to stay in bed. I never skipped class. Today I just wanted the world to go away. I saw visions of myself sitting in my mother's chair, knitting, Astrid with long gray hair playing the piano. Just the two of us, sipping tea and eating scones. I pulled the pillow over my head. My mother's voice echoed up the staircase, "Lenora, the coffee is finished. Are you up?"

"I'll be down soon." I dragged myself out of bed and stood in front of my wardrobe of sensible clothes; black slacks and a crimson crewneck sweater made expertly by my mother. Trousers, socks, and ankle boots were the same things I wore every day. I made my way downstairs. Astrid was sitting at the table with a grumpy face.

"What bug bit you?" I asked and immediately wished I hadn't.

She snarled at me, "I don't have bug bites."

"Of course you don't. Why are you grumpy?"

Mother refused to let Astrid bring her bear downstairs for breakfast. "He wasn't going to steal food from me. He just wanted to sit with me."

"He'll wait for you to come to bed," said my sensible mother. "Now eat your scones and porridge, and there's honey for you." Astrid's elbows rested on the table. I pushed her hair behind her ears.

Out of the blue, Astrid jumped up. "Where's John? Is he coming back?"

I gave a straightforward answer, "I don't know where John is, and I don't know if he's coming back."

Astrid said nothing else, but I knew she understood what I meant. To comfort me, Astie patted my arm. An emotion I'd never seen before, empathy. Even Mother noticed. Astrid took my plate and cup to the sink; her kindness touched me. I repressed my tears.

Religion in British History stood at the top of my boredom list. At nine o'clock, the class began; at nine-forty, I fought to stay awake with only five minutes to go. Silvey, a friend from my St. Agnes days caught up with me after class. "What's up with you?" It was a question of concern.

"Oh, I didn't sleep well last night. I'm alright."

"He still hasn't called?"

"No, and he won't, either."

"It was cruel of your mother to make you-know-who go with you."

"No. The thing is, Astrid and I are attached at the hip. It's the 'if you don't like her, you couldn't love me' thing. And it's true, Silvey. Sad, but true."

"I'm sorry, Lee. I wish I could do something."

"You're a good mate, but there's nothing to do. It's been two weeks, and I've given up. Last night, I heard a song on the BBC, the Beatles,

'There's a Place I Can Go.' It's a song about a place to get away from everything. I wished for an enchanted place to go."

Silvey put her arm around me, "You always have the stars. Listen, Lee; there's a 'do at Michael Embry's flat Saturday night. Why don't you come along with Pamela and me? It beats sitting at home. We can get blathered, forget our problems."

"I don't know, Silvey."

"Come on, Lee," she whined. "It will get you out of your rut. He has Elvis, Cliff Richards, The Beatles, and lots of records. God knows you deserve it, and everyone thinks you're cool."

Silvey shrugged her shoulders. "Stop feeling sorry for yourself; loosen up and live a little. Your life is just beginning. Come with us." With a sheepish grin, she added, "I'm sure there'll be some fit lads."

"Okay, I'll mull it over."

A bone-chilling wind and drizzling rain at the bus stop is the perfect way to end the afternoon. I came around the corner; my mother talked to a man with an umbrella standing on the stoop. I couldn't see his face, and my heart skipped a beat; was it John? The closer I got; my heart sank; it wasn't John. He tipped his hat and left. He was a courier with a message, Mother informed me. It was for me.

An apology! John was swamped with exams. Time got away from him. He was afraid to call and get rejected because he'd broken his word to contact me. *"If you still want to see me, I'll be waiting at Toliver's Tavern Saturday at six. They have good food, nothing fancy. Love, John"*

"Oh, John," I said out loud. My heart took flight; the corners of my mouth must have touched my ears. My mother immediately wanted to hear the details. The message changed hands; my mother put her hand to her mouth. "Oh, Lenora, I prayed he might see you again. I feel it was my fault for sending Astrid with you. I've suffered from such guilt. Now, I can breathe a sigh of relief." Mother prodded, "You are going?"

"Well, I have been invited to a party on Saturday." Mother's eyes darted in a panic for a second. "Of course, I'm going, sans Astrid," I said firmly.

"Yes, I'll keep her here. That won't be a problem."

At school, the next day, Silvey and I ate lunch. "Well, have you made up your mind? Are you coming Saturday?"

I played coy without giving away my news, "No, I can't."

"What do you mean you can't? Is it You-Know-Who? You can't bring her, is that it?"

I stopped eating my fish and chips; a shifty-eyed expression danced over my face. Silvey squealed so loud that everyone stopped. She slid down in her chair.

Eyes as wide as dinner plates, she whispered, "He called you, didn't he?"

"Not exactly." I reached into my handbag and handed her the telegram.

"A telegram, how romantic! Oh, Lee, I'm so jealous. And he was so kind."

"Promise you won't tell anyone, Silvey. I'm afraid of jinxing myself."

"Don't worry. No one thought you'd come anyway." I squinted, irritated. She continued, "I'm sorry, but face it, the only time you do anything is with your starry bunch. That's not a barrel of laughs."

I agreed with her. "But promise you won't say anything until Monday after I tell you the details."

"Mum's the word. Call me on Sunday! I can't wait until Monday," she implored. I gave in; I'd call her Sunday.

Before dinner, I must have read the telegram twenty times in my room. Mother called us down; I didn't tell Astrid. She was practicing, headphones on and eyes closed. The only way to get her attention without startling her was by flipping the lights off and on. Looking up, she pulled her headphones off, "What?"

"Dinner."

"Five more minutes." The headphones when back on; she lacked a sense of time. I flipped the lights again. She glared at me; not another tantrum, please.

"Mother will not be happy. You'll have to eat a cold dinner." She totally ignored me! *Fine*, I thought. *Cold shepherd's pie for you!*

"She's not coming, Mother. And she was cross with me. I haven't found a chance to tell her about John. You didn't, did you?"

"It's not mine to tell, Lenora. Albert and I thought we might try to take her to dinner at Angelo's. She loves their pizza, you know. Maybe you could braid her hair on Saturday. She fusses when I try."

I wanted to buy something new to wear, and all my clothes were dated. Fashion changed monthly. I saw a smart-looking dress in a boutique, a red and black block print. I didn't have to wear garters; tights and pantyhose were the trends. Whoever thought of those was a genius.

"Lenora, did you hear me?"

"Sorry, my mind was somewhere else, sorry."

"I asked what you're going to wear on Saturday. I think you should wear a dress. Slacks are alright for school but…" I interrupted her.

"There's a boutique near campus that sells sensible clothes. I'll go after class. I saw a red and black dress there. My clothes are already outdated."

"Already? I have clothes from ten years ago that look brand new!"

"You're not nineteen, Mother. And the styles have moved far away from the fifties. Even the clothes we bought for St. Agnes are outdated and don't fit well now." She didn't argue with me; she bought Astrid's clothes.

The next day I rocketed to Hattie's Boutique before they closed. I tried on a couple of dresses—a royal blue A-line that sported an oversized zipper. It might have been a bit risqué. The short-sleeved, wool-blend dress came just above my knees; squares of red and black were flattering. I didn't come across as frumpy. Thank God I'd lost weight. The short bus ride made me think about what-ifs.

Once home, I expressed my fears. "Mother, what if this is a cruel joke? A setup?"

"Honestly, Lenora, why do you suppose someone else went to all the trouble?" Pouring tea, she glanced up at me, "You don't think … Who could do such a thing?"

My face turned stony, "John's ass of a cousin, Phillip. Ever since I called him out for his shenanigans in a Society meeting, he's had it out for me."

"A woman shouldn't humiliate a man, dear. If he's done this deceitful thing, you may have brought it on yourself."

The hair on my neck stood up; she defended him! My words came booming out, "How dare you defend him! You don't know what he's capable of doing. He's dodgy, admitted to Cambridge because his family is wealthy!" Too angry to finish, I left my half-eaten crumpet, storming off to my room, leaving Mother speechless.

I heard my mother check on Astrid as I flopped on the bed in a huff. She knocked on my door with an apology and an invitation to return to the table. I rolled over to face the wall, refusing. She had the nerve to say I was just bull-headed. I wasn't going to let her win this battle, even if I was hungry.

After a silent breakfast, I rehearsed what vile words I would say to Phillip to humiliate him. But, if it truly was John Hopper, I wanted to make an impression. The door opened to Astrid full of questions. Mother never uttered a word after the fireworks of last night.

"Did you buy something for me?" asked Astrid, clapping her hands. I was in no mood for her.

"No," I said calmly. "I bought a new dress for myself." She asked why; I wasn't sure how she might react. "I have a date tonight, hopefully with John Hopper."

She stood there, frozen. I held my breath.

"He's your boyfriend. John Hopper is your boyfriend," she said in her unemotional monotone.

"Well, not yet. After seeing them once, Astrid, people don't say someone is their boyfriend."

"This is number two." She held up two fingers. "Charles is my boyfriend; he gave me Beary."

My mother jumped into the conversation, "No, Astrid, the orchestra gave you the bear. Charles is your friend."

"Oh," she said softly. "Two dates, Lee, he's *your* boyfriend now." She sounded so sad. Changing the subject, I pulled the dress from the plastic bag. Mother was pleased; *nothing flashy,* her words. Astrid gave her pronouncement, "A checkerboard."

At lunch, to my annoyance, Astrid had got in the habit of counting: our forks, spoons, and knives were one, two, three-one, two, the three- the tempo of a waltz. My mother's advice to me was to *pick my battles.*

With the last count, Astrid turned her face up, "I'm writing a song."

I wasn't sure if it was a statement to us or the angels. "It's a waltz like Mr. Strauss writes." She cocked her head, waiting for a response.

"Is it a happy or sad waltz?" I asked.

She whipped her head around, indignant. "Lee! All waltzes are happy! They're for dancing!" She twirled around in the dining room.

"Astrid! Sit down before you break something," Mother barked. "Eat your lunch."

Astrid was not happy. She plopped into the chair, elbows on the table. She grumbled, "I'm weird." I heard the eleven-year-old come out of her.

I responded, "Stop saying that, Astrid. You're, well, unique. Unique is not weird."

"What's that mean?"

"It means you're one of a kind, Astrid. There's no one like you." I got up, hugged her, and kissed her on the cheek, "That's why I love you."

She stiffened, "Yuck." My kiss disappeared with the swipe of her hand. I shouldn't have expected a return of affection by then, but I still wanted her to know how I felt.

After lunch, I lay in my bed, wondering what that night might bring. Calculating the taxi ride, I decided to be ten minutes late. John made me wait in agony and self-doubt for two weeks; ten minutes could give him some doubts. I wasn't going to throw myself at the first young man who tried to woo me.

Around four o'clock, Astrid stomped up to my room. As usual, she watched me do my makeup and hair. Our routine was like an operating room: brush, hairspray, foundation, eyeliner, mascara. With each task, Astrid handed me what I wanted in silence. I tried to flip up the bottom of my wavy hair in the latest trend. Astrid made strange, distorted faces of disapproval. I teased my hair to give it height.

Astrid glared at me in the mirror, "Your hair looks like an octopus, a big bubble with squiggly curls."

"Thanks a lot, Astrid. I'll try something else."

"Okay." Just okay, and she left back downstairs.

My hair ended up like it always did, wavy. All the girls wore long, straight hairdos or pixie bobs. In a world of Afghan hounds, I was a cocker spaniel. At least I had lovely eyes and long lashes, geez. I shimmied my dress over the satin slip and wrestled with the pantyhose.

One last look in the mirror and suddenly my mother called up the stairs, "There's a taxi out front for you!"

"What? I didn't call a taxi!" I jumped into my shoes and dashed down the stairs. Bewildered, I slipped on my wool coat.

"The driver said he was here to fetch Miss Lenora McConnell!" My mother was more excited than I was. Blimey, I wanted to make him wait!

She hugged me, "Have a good time, Lenora. You deserve it." I gave her a peck on the cheek, and she handed me my purse.

All the way, nerves jangled inside me. The ten-minute ride gave me time to gather my wits. The driver opened the door and said the fare was paid. *Gosh!* I thanked him, took a deep breath, and pushed the door open.

Inside, I stepped into a different era: a long oaken bar with a grand mirror, people seated on leather barstools; libations of various shapes, sizes, and colors reflected. Tables for two and four dotted the wooden floor, and stained-glass lamps hung from the ceiling. It was a murmuring crowd of mostly older people. Then I heard him. "Lenora."

I shook myself. "John, this place is a step into the past."

"Do you like it?" he asked tentatively. He helped me with my coat.

"Oh, yes! Absolutely. Thank you for the taxi. It was very thoughtful of you."

His blue eyes met mine, "I wanted to be sure you'd come."

A chill ran down my spine. I grinned. In the back, John had reserved a table. The place survived years as a traditional pub with traditional food. I asked, "How did you discover this place?"

"Family history." His great-grandfather had won the pub in a game of cards. He owned the pub for years, but John's great-grandmother disapproved. "To keep peace in the family, he sold it to a friend with one condition."

I was on the edge of my seat when the waiter came. We ordered fish and chips. He ordered Jameson's Irish whiskey neat, and uncharacteristically, I ordered a whiskey on the rocks. John cocked his head at me with intrigue. I was so uptight; I needed a drink.

"You like whisky?" he asked.

"Sometimes." Truthfully, I never tasted the stuff; I just knew *on the rocks* meant with ice. I pleaded for him to finish the story.

This great-grandfather's condition didn't sit well with his great-grandmother. "He told his friend the pub must be called Toliver's. His name was Thomas Oliver Hopper; hence, Toliver's Pub."

"What a cracking story!"

"Oh, that's not all. My family secretly owned the pub for another two generations until my father sold it when I was younger. It's a piece of family history."

"Why did he sell it?"

"My mother could never allow it. Besides, we moved to her family's estate in Gloucester. I love the city, though."

The waiter brought the drinks. I watched John sip his. I followed suit; the amber liquid was warm and smooth. On an empty stomach, it burned a bit; however, I liked it.

"Carry on," he leaned forward. This part wasn't light-hearted like John's story. I struggled not to be gloomy.

"What about you, Lee?"

"I'm an only child, too. I lived in Ireland when I was small; I don't remember living there. My grandfather started a chain of small-town banks. My father became a branch manager when he met my mother. My mother's family owned a woolen mill."

"A very lucrative business.

"We moved to Brighton when my grandfather sold the banks after ..." I stopped. This part of my life I found harder to explain.

"I can tell this is painful for you, Lenora."

"It is, but I want you to know. It was terrible, but everything I have now came out of tragedy. My father was killed, upsetting my grandfather greatly. My grandfather moved to Brighton, where he grew up." I never used the word murder when speaking of my father's death. When I told Astrid's story, he smiled.

I asked him about his studies. He apologized for his lack of insensitivity over the last two weeks. I learned becoming a barrister happens in three stages. John just finished his written portion.

"Lenora, it's hard, time-consuming work. I should have explained better and not promised to call so soon," he faltered.

He took a sip of whisky, leaned back, gazed at me, then said, "You're a special person, Lenora McConnell. I watched you at the gala. You're kind, smart, and self-assured." Awestruck by his comment, I listened as he continued. "The way you engaged people when you talked. Your interactions with your Astrid. And your unique hazel eyes."

I gave no response, I needed to say something, but all that came out was a blushing *thank you*. I felt like an idiot. I took the last sip of my whisky, wondering where this was going; if it was sex, he could just forget about it.

"Call me Lee. I like it better. Lenora is for functions and professors."

"Alright, Lee. I guess you can tell; I like you a lot."

"And," my speech was slightly slurred, "I like you too, John Hopper."

"I have another year to prove myself worthy. I can't promise to see you every week. But perhaps if you like, we could get to know each other."

In that split second of silence in my head, I heard Astrid say, *you have a boyfriend*. "Yes, John. I'd like that, too."

I floated up the porch steps and into the door. It was ten o'clock, and Astrid was staring at the fire. Mother jumped up, dropping her knitting ball.

"You're home early." Her voice trailed up at the end of her sentence.

"Don't panic," I guffawed. "Just because I didn't stay till midnight doesn't mean it ended badly."

Astrid sat cross-legged on the floor, in her own world, oblivious to everything around her as my mother waited with bated breath.

"He threw over Emily Thurston, a rich, beautiful ballerina, for me. I'm still having trouble wrapping my head around it all."

Mother sat and patted her hand on the sofa for me to with her. "You're intelligent, witty, and kind, Lenora. It's hard for you to accept those attributes lost in a fog of studies and," she paused, glancing at Astrid, "and the challenges you face. You must have made an impression on him, or tonight wouldn't have happened. Right?"

"Yes. John Hopper was candid with me tonight. He's studying law." When I said that, my mother gasped in awe.

"A barrister? How admirable."

"I didn't realize all the stages one must complete before practicing law. It's like climbing mountains." Anticipating the next question, I said, "And yes, I'll be seeing him again." I smirked, "And again, and again."

A smile so wide came over her, an expression I hadn't seen in a very long time. She hugged me.

"Okay, Mother. We're just dating, not getting married. John is a gentleman, not pushy or forward. His family estate is in the Gloucester countryside; I tried not to be nosy. They are well off. His father is in the import/export business. I told him of living in Brighton and Grandfather's banks; somehow, I think he already knew."

"Is John Hopper coming to our house?"

"Not anytime soon, but he'll come. He's still in college, just like you and I."

"You're in college; I'm in music school," she said emphatically. I politely agreed.

| 13 |

Be Specific

Getting more familiar with John, I found him romantic and supremely intelligent. Parties were few; John didn't care for frivolous conversation. He'd rather spend his free time away from his studies coming over for visits. One thing John found difficult was relating to Astrid. While most people didn't find clever remarks offensive, Astrid took everything literally.

Once John told Astrid her eyes were green like shamrocks. She went on a tangent—eyes are not flowers or grass; they are eyes, she told him. She did not have grass in her eyes.

After that incident, we talked about being direct and not teasing Astrid; I hated squelching his good humor.

Six months we'd been together, but it all seemed so surreal. Truthfully, I didn't know what to think about our relationship. We were affectionate and conversational in our time together, expressing our likes and dislikes. Yet, self-doubt lingered in the back of my mind. Last week, John informed me he needed to return home for a family function. He invited me to come along, but I wasn't ready to meet his family.

A positive for him, in my eyes, came from his evolving relationship with Astrid. It took a while before John understood her quirks and nuances, treating her with respect, knowing she would forever be an adolescent. It was hard for Astrid to accept my relationship with John. She tolerated him, but I saw the scowl on her face when he turned around.

Astrid expressed her concern about losing me; I allowed her to sleep with me every few weeks to appease her. From our first weekend together, magic from some cosmic entity drew us together with an unbreakable bond. Now we looked at the moon and stars through the skylight; her childlike wonder was still there. Once, she lay beside me and held my hand. "Are you still my moon, Lee?"

"Of course. Remember back when we were children?" I laughed, "When we both fit in one chair. I told you, you were the star to the left of my moon."

"Astra and Luna, I remember. But you have a boyfriend now. I don't want a boyfriend."

"Just because I have a boyfriend doesn't mean I don't love you, Astie. You will always be my star."

"Okay, I guess, okay."

Her ever-present signs of innocence warmed me. I did have a boyfriend, and Astrid had Dr. Dryer and my mother to take care of her.

John loved Sunday walks in the park and quiet dinners at upscale restaurants in out-of-the-way places. When he came to the house, Astrid always made a pronouncement.

"He has black hair. John Hopper has black hair," she blurted out in front of him. He'd smile and say, "You have strawberry blond hair."

She said, "I don't have strawberries in my hair!" He cringed, knowing that comment backfired.

Over the summer, John learned more about Astrid. We attended her performance with the university orchestra, a precursor to the London Symphony. Without being too obvious, I watched John as Astrid played; his jaw dropped, staggered by her connection to the music. My eyes focused on the stage; I waggled my shoulders and smiled.

Proud of herself, she stood up to take a bow. When the audience clapped for her, my little bird flapped her arms; she was happy. Mr. Godfrey grasped her elbow to lead her off stage when the applause and cheers grew louder. Astrid held her ears. After the concert, we drove to dinner with Dr. Dryer. Mr. Godfrey chose not to join us. Astrid held my hand underneath the table. John winked at me; he was patient with Astrid. I loved him even more. My mother began to call Dr. Dryer "Albert"; I wondered about those two.

In September, for my twenty-second birthday, John bought me an expensive telescope to upgrade my old one. We loved watching the stars, often traveling to the countryside where light pollution didn't exist. We sat on the boot of his car. I pointed out constellations. When he kissed my neck, I allowed him to touch me in places never touched. New sensations shot through my body. Before losing control, I stopped him. We packed everything and traveled home in silence.

"Did I upset you?" he asked.

"No. I've never done anything like that before. Staying a virgin is important to me."

"I understand, Lee. I don't want to push you."

John implored me to visit his family soon. To appease him, I gave in. On Saturday, during my birthday celebration, John asked my mother's permission to visit his parents in October. John gave her the telephone number. She promised to speak with John's mother in the morning. Mother didn't divulge the conversation but approved the arrangements.

On the next sky-watching trip, we brought Astrid along. I insisted she have a chance to view the sky away from the city lights. It kept John at bay. The three of us traveled outside the city, where we could see the rings of Saturn and Jupiter's moons. Astrid fell asleep in the backseat on the way home.

My virginity preoccupied my mother's thoughts. I promised her there wouldn't be any shenanigans. On his visit the week before we left, John made a point of telling her the guest room was at the other end of the house, next to his parent's room.

The morning we were to leave, the ever-eavesdropping Astrid came downstairs with her overnight bag asking what time was John coming.

My mother and I explained that she couldn't go with me on this trip. However, my mother's promise to visit the London Zoo appeased her.

We took the two-hour train ride. John fell asleep on the train after a night of studying law briefs. He had begun his pupilage, the most challenging part of his training. I studied his face as he slept.

The Hopper family chauffeur met us at the station. *Chauffeur*, I thought. *Oh my*. We weren't poor by any means, just less lavish. The country home was a sprawling mansion of six bedrooms, formal and informal living rooms, a dining hall with chandeliers, and servants' quarters. I was caught totally off guard; the extravagance gave me pause.

"I feel like a country bumpkin. Why didn't you tell me about this?"

"We both come from old money, but I wanted to make sure you loved me."

"We have our own finances, thank you very much. My grandfather was much more conservative."

"Well, there are times when all of the trappings of my family are overwhelming. It's one of the reasons I don't like coming here often. Besides, I'd rather be with you."

Taking a step back, "Really?"

A sigh escaped him, "You haven't met my mother yet." He kissed me like never before; I knew where my future was going. Yet, I'd have to win his mother over first.

His parents appeared charming and down-to-earth. John's mother, Catherine, gave me a tour of her herb garden, explaining the different flowering shrubs with their intoxicating fragrances. However, her tone had a condescending edge. His father owned an international import/export business. John often spoke of his father's pressure to take over the company; his mother's scrutiny could be off-putting. I understood why he liked staying in the city more.

Later that day, we walked along the rambling creek deep into the woods. "My father wanted me to take over the company, but it wasn't for me. He was always traveling, away from us. I resented him for being away so much. Then he sent me to boarding school." A downheartedness echoed in his voice, "I want to be involved in our..." he paused to correct himself, "in my children's lives."

For a few minutes, we didn't speak. John's intentions were clear to me; I panicked for a second. Then he continued. "I also feared not living up to my father's expectations; I chose to be a barrister in corporate law. A position respectable enough to appease him." We stopped; he leaned on a maple tree. "Did I make the right choice, Lee?"

"Are you happy with your decision to be a barrister?"

"I believe so. Yes."

"Then," I replied, "you made the right choice."

He asked me if my goal was to keep working at the Observatory as a guide. I didn't understand why he asked that question.

"Not as a planetarium guide, but the Observatory holds a lot of promise for me. And yes, and I want to move up the ladder." Puzzled by his insinuation. "I'm much more than a stargazer. They use my data to create presentations and programs for the Starball Projector at the planetarium. I also map stars and nebulas. It's all very complex."

"I just thought…."

A touch of sarcasm came out, "What? I want to stay home and pop out babies?"

The palm of his flew up, "No, no. I didn't mean it that way, Lee."

"John, being at the Observatory is important to me. It's what I love to do. You could see it as a hobby. Some women like to garden or go to book clubs. I like working at something bigger than myself, and I'm good at my job. I'm not a women's liberation proponent and won't embarrass you by burning my bra. But this work makes me feel useful. Is that justifiable?"

I'd put him on the spot. I loved John, but I wasn't ready to give up my life and have children right away. I continued, "I want to be with you. I know how to be a gracious hostess and throw dinner parties. I helped with dinner parties as a young child, but my mother accommodated my father out of love, not an obligation. Before his murder, my father was a rising star in the banking business."

Shocked, John didn't know what to say, "I knew of his death but …"

After all these years, it was still difficult to talk about what happened. My memories of my father came only through a few old photographs. But, when I told John, a knot lodged itself in my throat. "My father, Daniel McConnell, missed my growing up, all my graduations, and he won't walk me down the aisle at my wedding. Two men, now serving life in prison, stole him from me."

He reached for me and held me tight. Then, brushing my hair to the side, he kissed my forehead. "Oh, Lenora, I didn't know about the murder."

I wrapped myself around him. John made me feel safe against the warmth of his body. Then, the sun began to slide under the horizon; he held my hand and we returned to the house.

The dinner party made me a bundle of nerves. Mother taught me proper etiquette for such occasions, but I was under scrutiny from John's family members. His Aunt Marie was charming. There were side glances and whispers from John's mother, and the younger girl cousins giggled at John. Shocked to find out lovely Aunt Marie was Phillip's mother, I almost choked. Phillip's sister, Louise, eleven, and Maggie, age nine, were the two giggly girls. An absent uncle, according to John, was never mentioned. Curious but quiet, I didn't ask.

Food found its way to my mouth and not on my outdated, pink Jackie Kennedy suit, nor did I pick up the wrong utensils. I loved goose liver pâté, but it smelled terrible, but I smiled and swallowed it. Typically fatty, the Cornish hen half was slightly overcooked. With every bite, I took a sip of water. Somehow, I made it through dinner, polite conversation and all.

The topic of having a job, I avoided. The Hopper women gave teas and held galas to raise money for various charities. Lord Hopper, John's father, made a point by telling me the family estate would someday belong to John. I nodded; *how generous*, I said but thought differently knowing John's wishes.

After dinner, we moved to the drawing room. Men were in a corner with cigars and whisky while the ladies sat on satin settees drinking blackberry liqueur. John's seventy-year-old Aunt Pauline, a spinster, commented on my smart choice of clothes. Frankly, I hated the pink suit; my mother made me pack it. His mother wanted to know my family background. I spoke of my late grandfather, John Michael McConnell.

"Oh, I recognize the name; he was an investment banker?"

"Yes, ma'am, he was. He owned several banks and contributed to the arts. I loved him dearly."

Then came the question of my father. I felt conflicted and chose my words carefully. "My father died when I was eight." I tried to leave on the murder part to no avail.

"Oh, my dear, growing up without a father must have been horrors for your mother."

Left with no choice but to stand up for my mother, I detailed how Grandfather cared for us, living at the Brighton Beach house and paying for our education.

John's mother butted in, "Our? I thought John said you were an only child."

I didn't care for her accusatory tone, so I informed her of Astrid's story. "Rejected by her family because she was a peculiar child, we took her in. Astrid is a concert pianist." By the end of the depressing story, their pity was enough to make me hang myself. Our family became saints to this poor odd child. Frankly, I wanted to get out of there. I kept trying to get John's attention. On the third try, I thought I'd hit him with the fire poker if he didn't rescue me.

I yawned loudly, covering my mouth. John's mother asked in a sarcastic voice, "Are we boring you, dear?"

"Oh, no. It's been a long day. John took me for a very long walk. A day in the outdoors tends to make one a bit tired. Don't you agree?"

I put her on the spot, and I never backed down from a catty exchange. Finally, John came to rescue me from the jaws of his scornful mother. Drunk as a lord, stinking of whisky, he suggested we go outdoors.

"If it will sober you up, I'm all for it."

Outside suddenly, I was pushed against a car out of sight from others. John began to kiss me, his hand lightly squeezing my breast.

Part of me was afraid; he was aggressive. The other part of me felt aroused. His other hand found its way up my skirt. I heard how men got aroused; he pushed himself into me. I felt his lust.

Out of breath, I said, "I promised my mother I would stay a virgin until I got married. So please don't make me break my promise."

"I won't, I promise. I just want to touch you." He ran his hand over my breast. My breaths were deep as he kissed my neck; his breath was off-putting.

"You're drunk," I said.

"I don't do this very often. Drinking, I mean." He saw my face. "Or groping either. I mean."

"Stop." I laughed at his goofy face, "I believe you."

He slumped as the weight of the world was lifted off him. He then took my hand and began to say, "Will you …."

"No, don't you dare ask me anything when you're drunk, John Hopper."

He stuck out his bottom lip, "You're right, I am drunk. I want to be sober if I ask someone to marry me. Someone deserves better."

I took him by the hand, and we moved inside. I physically turned him in the direction of his room. I loved him and soon would be his wife. I wondered how Astrid might process the news. I'd be leaving her.

Sunday morning came and John's parents drove us to the train station. We said nothing until we boarded. John's father put his hand awkwardly on my shoulders.

"If you so choose, you'd be a welcomed addition to our family. Isn't that right, darling?" He waited for his wife's response.

She didn't even look at me but replied with a condescending "Yes, dear."

I was never so glad to get on the train as John's mother smothered him with kisses. When we sat down, John apologized for his mother's behavior. I understood; she was about to lose her baby. I fell asleep in the private car. I woke up to John's hand between my legs. "Excuse me!"

"Come on; we won't be in Cambridge for another hour; we have a private car."

"John Hopper, I am keeping my promise to my mother."

His hand traveled up my blouse as he kissed me hard. Overcome with desire, I let him continue, unable and not really wanting to stop him. He placed my hand on the rock-hard bulge under the zipper on his pants. I'd never seen a man's erection, only nude men in a magazine circulating through St. Agnes when I was in school.

"Dear God, we have to stop!" I shouted.

"Alright, but I promise I'll be gentle with you the first time." It gave me a lot to reflect on. I knew I was in no rush to get married.

| 14 |

I Will, but …

John dropped me off at the house that evening. As I fixed a cup of tea, Mother asked, "You're awfully quiet. Are you alright?"

"Yes, his family was very… well, his father was lovely, but his mother was snippy with me. I love his maiden aunt and his Aunt Marie. The family home is nestled in the country, a sprawling estate with many beautiful rolling hills. It's a large house, Mother, six bedrooms and two living rooms. And servants' quarters."

"What's the matter, Lenora?"

"What do you mean?"

Mother patted the cushion beside her, "Come sit by me. You haven't mentioned a word about John. What happened?"

I didn't want to tell her what transpired on the train. I just wasn't prepared to talk about it.

"Did he propose?"

"Not in a formal way. Oh, Mother, I kept my promise. I'm still a virgin, but I'm scared." A sigh escaped my lips, "I'm afraid of … sex."

"I was, too."

"Really?"

"The first time it happens, I'll tell you the truth; it's painful. And, on your wedding night, most men get too drunk to perform. When it happens, you may bleed the first time. From then on, you're able to enjoy things. Lovemaking becomes an expression of devotion."

I was biting my lower lip; it was a lot to process. I finished my tea. "Thank you for being frank with me."

"It's what a mother should do."

I retreated to my bedroom. I seriously wondered about what I wanted for my marriage and life. With one more year of school and a promising career in astronomy, where could a marriage fit? I loved John, but I didn't know what he expected of me. I was going to have to find out.

My stomach and my future turned upside down on the bus ride to John's. I'd never been to the house he shared with three others. It wasn't in the best neighborhood, but I wasn't scared. At least not of the location. On the corner, I stopped to ask myself if I was doing the right thing by putting him on the spot. Summoning my courage, I knocked on the door of John's flat. Dorian, another soon-to-be barrister, answered.

"I need to speak with John Hopper."

He showed me to the living room full of dusty shelves and half-full beer glasses with cigarette butts sticking out. The air was stale. No way I could sit down; it was filthy.

John came running down the steps in shoes with no socks. I breached the hallowed hall of the boys' club. "What are you doing here?"

"My being here, is it a problem?"

"Well, for starters, I could have cleaned up the place. But, no, it's fine. Maybe we can sit in the garden?"

"Yes, please," I said, relieved.

A breath of fresh air filled my lungs; the sun's radiance kissed my face—unlike the inside, the garden sat perfectly manicured with flowers and roses. We sat on the wooden garden bench, side by side. Unsure of where to start, John spoke first. "This must be serious for you to come here."

I nodded my head yes. "John, I need some answers. What do you see in your future?"

After years of rigorous study, John was "called to the Bar of England and Wales." Being called to the Bar meant he was successful in his academic and training to practice law. As a result, he hoped to be offered a position with a prominent group of barristers.

Then, confidently said, "I see myself being an attentive husband, and eventually, a father." His eyes were full of love.

"And what do you expect of a wife, John?

"Well, someone who understands long working hours, a woman who will stand by my side at functions. We will go to concerts. I want a woman who's smarter than other wives, one who doesn't sit around eating bonbons and gossiping."

He gave a half answer. I needed to know more. "What if a woman held a position in a philanthropic organization? What if she wanted to hold a full-time job?"

"I believe if a woman wants to work, it's fine as long as she keeps the household running properly." John's answer wasn't enough; he knew what I meant. Truthfully, I needed more.

"I see. You have no objection to marrying a working woman?"

"I suppose I don't mind."

"I see. When do you see yourself being a father?" It was a loaded question, and he knew it. For now, I didn't want to be a mother.

"Well, I won't want to wait too long." He knew the ice was thin; he winced when he said, "Maybe two years?"

My response came out indifferent. "I see."

"Sit tight. I'll be right back." I wanted to hear more; he jumped up and hurried to the house.

I waited and waited, wondering what would happen if he didn't come back; should I leave? My self-doubt aside, I found myself caught up in the beautiful smell of yellow tea roses and the lavender wisteria's overpowering sweetness. In a suit and tie, he came to the garden. I knew the time had come for the question every young lady awaits.

"It is a gorgeous day. You're what my father calls a classic beauty. You are beautiful, Lee."

My cheeks flushed bright red, a demure smile on my face.

"I spoke to your mother yesterday, so this is a perfect day." He knelt on one knee. Even though I knew what was coming, both my hands covered my mouth.

"Lenora Irene McConnell, will you do me the honor of being my wife? Lee, I couldn't imagine my life without you." He opened a black velvet box. Inside was a square-cut diamond flanked by tiny white pearls. The setting was Victorian; it was my mother's engagement ring. John's eager eyes lit up, his beautiful face filled with anticipation.

"My mother's ring." Caught off guard by the sight of her beautiful ring, "Yes, John Hopper. I love you and couldn't imagine my life without you." I honestly did love him. I loved him for carrying on intellectual conversations and for his romantic heart. I would give him every chance to prove he didn't want a stereotypical housewife.

After a year of flirtatious dates, meeting family approval, and innuendos, he'd finally asked! The easy part was over; we immediately set to planning. I worried about Astrid. Respecting my wishes, I asked John to let me talk to her alone before telling anyone; with a half-smile, he understood.

We agreed to wait until I finished school to get married. John would have a year at the firm under his belt. We'd have time to save for a townhouse in London near his law practice. He would call his parents, and I'd break the news to my mother before speaking with Astrid.

Mother sat in the garden; Astrid was at rehearsal. "I didn't hear you come in. Lenora. What have we here, the Cheshire Cat?" She knew what came next. I held out my hand.

Her hands covered her cheeks, "I knew it should fit! Oh, my baby's getting married!"

My forehead wrinkled, one eye squinted at her, "As if you didn't know."

"He called me yesterday and came by while you were in class. Lenora, John is madly in love with you. He promised me to treat you with respect and will provide a good life for you both."

Something didn't feel right. Mother knew. "Are you worried?" she asked. I nodded.

"How do I tell Astrid? She won't understand why I'll be leaving her."

"You're not getting married right away, I hope?"

"No, I wanted to wait until I graduated. By that time, John ought to be ensconced in his work. We'll have more time to plan."

Inside, Mother put the kettle on. We seemed to do our best thinking at the kitchen table. We discussed Astrid's schooling. Dr. Dryer enrolled her in a full apprenticeship with the orchestra. "Astrid's learning to write in-depth compositions."

"She's what? I knew about her writings from her notebooks; simple melodies." It was hard to believe she'd advanced this far.

"It's true. Albert and Mr. Godfrey have been working with Astrid on a symphony. He's been tapping into her ability to discern each instrument. For example, she can hear a French horn and play the same notes to bring harmony or a complement to the piano melody. He's never experienced behavior like this before." Her bright face turned somber, "There's a dark side, though."

I couldn't believe Astrid had a dark side. I wanted an explanation.

"Astrid has trouble turning the music off inside her head for a while. A few months ago, I heard her pacing the floor."

"Ever since I've known her, she's paced the floor and talked with her 'angels.' I got used to it, Mother. Some nights, Astrid only gets a few hours of sleep or practices until they turn the lights off, sending her back. It's nothing new."

Concerned, her forehead wrinkled, "Because my room is underneath hers. I was worried, so I sat on the stairs listening as she paced. She repeated sequences of notes; she'd say no, Astrid, that's not right, do it again."

"Oh, Mother, is she going mad?"

"Albert told me this could happen. She's harder on herself than before. Albert and I walk with her in the park; walking helps. She still can't express her emotions properly or tell anyone what she's feeling. Her anxiety causes her frustration; Albert prescribed medication. As usual, she assumes they're vitamins. They are stronger to quell her anxiety."

"Oh, God, how can I tell her now about the wedding?"

Mother hugged, "You don't have to yet."

Mother was right, as always. I could show her my ring and continue to say he's my special boyfriend. We can go places with her; she could get used to John. The last thing I wanted to do was upset her. My poor Astrid! I couldn't stand the thought of her losing herself.

It was monkeys out there, with cold winds and swirling snow around me, walking home from the bus stop. I finished my work early. Opening the door, I heard Dr. Dryer and my mother in an intense conversation. I hung my cloak on the hall tree, then Dr. Dryer asked me to join them. First, I wanted to know if Astrid was alright. Mother assured me Astrid was fine. She was asleep. Dr. Dryer asked if I knew whether Astrid had suffered a head injury.

"None I can remember, but I came to know her when we were almost twelve." A memory popped up, "I remember once, she did have a large red knot at her hairline just under her fringe. I questioned how it happened but never got an answer. I didn't give it a second thought. That bump was the size of a ping-pong ball; she never acted differently. But she does beat herself in the head when frustrated. Have you contacted her parents?"

"Remember, Lenora, no one seems to know where they jetted off to," said Mother. "They may have felt threatened by your grandfather's letters or my questions from years ago."

Albert's elbow rested on the arm of the chair. He emphasized his words with hand gestures, "Being a neuropsychologist, I'm trying to determine the brain's function related to her abilities. As far as scientific studies, most savants have lower intellectual abilities. While Astrid cannot pick up social cues and her comprehension of academia is subpar, she demonstrates strong spatial areas. Sadly, Astrid cannot write more than three or four sentences."

I rolled my eyes, "Tell me about it."

"Savants like her could come as a result of head trauma. That's why the question. I wanted to test her problem-solving skills."

"What are you going to do?" I asked.

"When her brain hears a piece of music, it's imprinted somewhere in the frontal lobe of her brain. I wanted to see if she interprets information differently in a clinical setting. Simple tests, like solving riddles."

It sounded like a bunch of hooey to me. In a sarcastic tone, my response flew from me, "What if Astrid can't? Have you set her up to fail?"

"Now, darling, I'm sure Albert knows what he's doing." Unfortunately, her response was far from convincing.

I snapped back, "From what you've said, doctors know little about people like Astrid. She's your experiment."

Dr. Dryer took exception to my tone. He assured me that doing this was for Astrid's benefit and the benefit of science. It would take more than his words to convince me, but I didn't have a say in the matter. My mother was compliant. Dr. Dryer prattled on about the positive aspects of her musical abilities.

"Since your mother has guardianship over Astrid, we plan on entering her in two international piano competitions. Your mother has agreed to chaperone."

My nostrils flared and my ears burned. "And how do you suppose Astrid will take rejection if she doesn't win?" My heart skipped a beat. "What if she falls apart? The wedding is in June." My teeth pressed into my bottom lip.

Dr. Dryer spoke up. "She doesn't understand what a competition involves. All she knows is a group of pianists is going play for a small audience."

"When is this taking place?" I demanded.

"Lenora McConnell, what is wrong with you?" My mother's tone came across as condescending. "We do what's best for Astrid."

"No, you don't; you're turning her into a circus act!"

There was nothing left to say; I darted upstairs. Astrid's door stood open; shadows crept across the floor, turning day into night. Peeking in, she hugged her bear, sleeping in a place where torment could not touch her. I brought her into this life of uncharted waters. Soon I would leave her. Oh, my Astie, what have I done?

Mother received an invitation for Christmas from John's parents. John reminded them again about Astrid. He said she was different, peculiar, but highly talented. We prepared Astrid for the people in John's family. Meeting strangers was something she didn't do well. I assured her we were going to a beautiful house in the country.

"Not like my old country house?" she sounded terrified.

"No, Astrid, a beautiful house with fireplaces and a baby grand piano. You can play the Christmas carols you love."

"Will people sing?" she asked.

"Does it bother you if they sing?"

She fidgeted in her seat, wiggling around. I took her hand, and she asked, "Have I met those people?"

"You know John; the people are John's mother and father. His aunts and cousins will be there."

At least ten times, she repeated, "I don't know these people."

"I promise, Mother and I will not leave your side on the train or at the house, okay?"

"Okay, I guess. Trains? Will we ride trains?"

"Yes."

The non-stop handclapping began; she was happy. Then, she said, out of the blue, "I am holding a baton."

Clueless, I asked, "What's the baton for?"

"The orchestra, silly, the orchestra."

"Oh," I was taken aback. "You're conducting the orchestra?!" I played along.

The flurry of handclapping now came with foot-tapping; I was clueless about what she said. Whatever it was, it made her happy. I pushed her hands back in her lap; she made a mad face at me. "I get it; you're very happy."

Nine o'clock was approaching; I needed to sleep. I asked Astrid to get ready for bed. Mother sat by the fire finishing her evening glass of wine.

"I'm taking Astrid's medicine up to her." I turned the tap on to fill a glass. Then I asked, "Do you know anything about a baton and orchestra?"

"Yes, darling, Albert is teaching her to conduct." She talked as if she were giving the weather report.

"When did this start?" Last fall, Astrid told me she was writing a symphony. But conducting remained a significant next step. "Piano competition, conducting an orchestra, where have I been?"

"With John and school, darling."

Her "darlings" were beginning to sound more patronizing. I took Astrid her medicine; we sat on the bed together.

"Astrid," I asked, "are you happy?" She was never quick to respond to emotional questions. "Do you feel good about working with Dr. Dryer? Is it fun?"

Head cocked like a robin listening for a worm, she pronounced, "Yes, because you are my moon, always in my sky."

I kissed her forehead, "And you are the brightest star in my sky."

Then, totally out of the blue, she squeezed my cheeks and kissed me on the forehead. Her affect was flat; leaning back, she said, "You love me."

It wasn't a question; I blinked, trying to wrap my head around what she just said. I responded, "I do. I do love you, Astie."

"Do you love John Hopper?"

"Yes, I do, but not the same way I love you."

She took medicine, jumped in bed, and said, "Turn off the light."

And I did.

| 15 |

And This is Astrid

At nine a.m., we boarded a train bound for John's family home. We could barely control Astrid's excitement. Several times she popped up and I pulled back into the seat. Every time the train stopped, she thought we were supposed to get off.

"Now can we go?"

"Not yet." Mother's patience wore thin.

When we finally reached our train stop, a chauffeur met us at the station.

"Ohhhh, a big black car. Who's that man?"

"He's taking us to John's house."

"It's a big taxi."

John met us at the door, "Hello, welcome! Astrid, how did you find your train ride?"

She hesitated; Astie's forehead wrinkled up, unsure how to respond; then, "I found it. We rode on it." Everything had to be touched, everything in the entryway.

With a shrug of his shoulders, he whispered to Mother, "Did I say something wrong?"

"Just be more direct, dear." Mother changed; everyone became dear and darling. A maid helped us with our coats. Astrid grabbed onto hers, "No! this is mine!" A terror came over her.

John stepped in, "It's alright, Anna; Astrid may keep her coat. Let me show you to your rooms."

Astrid clutched the buttons on her coat. We'd share the same room I stayed in before. John led my mother to the other end of the hall.

"You can take the coat off now. It will be safe in here," I assured Astrid.

"Take my braids out. They're too tight."

"Let's unpack first."

"Okay."

Astrid grabbed at her hair, waiting for me to unpack. I tried to redirect her, asking if she wanted to unpack her clothes. She could be so annoying.

I snapped, "Alright."

There was a knock on the door; Astrid didn't move. John stuck his head in, seeing if we were comfortable and settled. Astrid sat in a chair; he watched me in the process of unbraiding Astrid's hair.

"I wanted to let you know we're dining at seven. If you like, Astrid, I'll show you the piano."

No response. "It's a baby grand piano."

Still no response, "Well, I'll see both of you at seven. Causal dress, nothing fancy. Does your friend eat pork?"

"I can hear you," Astrid studied the hardwood floor. "Yes, she likes pork chops."

"Very well." He made a face at me. "See you at seven."

"A piano, they have a piano!" She tapped her heels on the wooden floor, "A piano, Leelee!"

"Yes, they do. Sit still. And when did my name change to 'Leelee'?"

"Just now, out loud," she said, with a voice full of bluster. I brushed Astrid's long, reddish-blond hair and handed her a headband. She didn't want it. "No, thank you."

"You will wear it to dinner," I ordered. "I will not have you droop your hair into the soup. Is that clear?"

She took it from me and shoved it on her head.

"I know, mind my manners, mind my manners, and don't embarrass Leelee."

"Right, don't embarrass Leelee or yourself. If you don't like the food, what do you say?"

"No, thank you. I say, no, thank you."

Predictably, when we left the room, her demeanor changed to pensive. The evening could be a long one.

When the staff served the food, I held my breath. Astrid didn't understand why someone removed her plate after eating. To make matters worse, his snobby mother said something to the effect of polite society's manners. Astrid became even more confused.

"Huh?" Astrid was befuddled by her pronouncement. I took her hand and said, "Excuse us." I whisked her away to another room. Astrid was upset, repeating the exact words over and over. I took her by the shoulders,

"Look at me," I said as she slumped. I slid my hand under her chin, "You've done nothing wrong. John's family has never been around a genius like you." She turned her head away from me. I hugged her tight and whispered in her ear,

"Remember, I told you it would be different here. You are just fine. Do you want to have dessert?"

"What kind?"

I knew the flapping came next. "Chocolate cake with chocolate frosting. Take my hand, and we'll go back to the table."

When we returned, John's mother asked me if she was okay. Of course, I knew what Astrid might say, and she didn't disappoint. In her staccato voice, she said, "I'm in the room. I can hear you; I'm okay."

Astrid's voice shut John's mother up. His dear grandmother winked at me. My mother cleared her throat, "She's fine."

We got on with dessert, and the repetitive behavior started, this time with the palms of her hands doing silent clapping. John understood Astrid's quirkiness. He was so sweet to her.

"I knew you liked chocolate cake. I requested the cook to make it special for you."

My mother said to Astrid, "What do you say?"

Swinging her head, she smiled, "Thank you, Johnny. Thank you."

John glanced at me. I sighed, "I'm Leelee tonight."

His smile was bright, full of love. It filled my heart with joy. I didn't care what anyone thought about Astrid. John loved her as I did; that was all that mattered.

With dinner finished, Astrid became fidgety, a distraction to polite conversation; John's grandmother, the grande dame of the Hopper family, greeted us. John informed me that her ninety-first birthday was in May.

"I want to hear this young lady play. Will you play for me, young lady?"

"My name is Astrid, and yes!"

John held out his arm, "It will be an honor to escort you, Astrid Innis."

Astrid knew to take his arm, an action practiced with Mr. Godfrey before each recital. John invited everyone to the music room. Astrid got comfortable.

"John told me you possess amazing piano skills," said John's grandmother. Astrid swayed back and forth, staring at her the ceiling.

"Yes, she does," my mother answered.

"I daresay most anyone could figure out how to play children's nursery rhymes," came from John's sour mother. Not one person agreed with her.

"We'll find out soon enough." His mother's smugness was revolting.

"Mother," John whispered, "I don't know what you have in mind, but I don't think you should embarrass yourself. It's not your strong suit. I told you, Astrid is a concert pianist. "

"We will see, John." Her condescending tone got under my skin.

John's father, with brow arched, said, "Catherine." That's all he needed to say.

"Christmas carols; don't sing," Astrid uttered.

Mother stepped in, "Astrid, remember what we talked over. One song to play, two songs to sing."

She said nothing. Everything was quiet as her fingers arched over the keys. "Sit up straight," Astrid told herself. With fingers arched over the keys, she played *What Child is This?* The room was silent.

"Silent room means *Silent Night*." She laughed at her own joke.

"May we sing?" asked Aunt Marie.

"If you know the words," Astrid popped off. Everyone held their breath, not knowing how to act.

John broke the tension, "Astrid, you are so silly. We know the words."

"Well, okay." She played a short introduction. After that, everyone joined in except John's mother.

I didn't like her, not one bit. Nothing positive ever came from her. As cordial as John was, she was the direct opposite. After three carols and several rounds of Scotch whisky, the singing waned.

"No more singing; the last song, last song." Astrid was adamant.

It wasn't a Christmas song; *Claire de Lune* was one of her favorites. The glasses stopped clinking; no one said a word. Snow fell like giant goose feathers outside the window.

After the last note, Astrid put her hands in her lap as everyone clapped; she clapped too. Then she announced it was time for bed.

The family and friends moved to the living room, where the fire burned warm and bright. Astrid wanted to go to bed. I helped her undress and tucked her into bed. Placed on the nightstand was a pitcher of water and two glasses. Astrid took her medicine, then repeatedly asked where I was going. I handed Astrid the bear. I let her know I wasn't far if she needed me. She was fine.

I joined John with the others in the living room.

"Your friend is quite a virtuoso," said Lady Hopper, John's grandmother.

John said with pride, "I told you, she's a genius. They say she's a savant, Granny. She has played three concerts while at the university."

"Astrid has an extraordinary ability to play by ear," chimed my mother. "She hears the most difficult music and plays."

Lady Hopper, a patron of the arts and matriarch of the family, chatted with Mother. She showed interest in Astrid.

John tugged at my sleeve, motioning with his head; I followed. He took me to the drawing and shut the door.

"I expect you to be a gentleman, John Hopper."

He undressed me with his eyes; my cheeks flushed. Then, he gave an unexpected apology, "I'm sorry for my mother's behavior. She can be a real a first-class bitch."

"John! Such language," I scoffed.

In the moonlight, his eyes sparkled like glimmering snow. He wrapped his arms around me, "I love you. You're nothing like Emily; she's shallow and manipulative." I feel his warm breath on my neck. Too much wine; was the room spinning? His hand pulled my blouse out of my waistband. A warm hand slid under my bra, and he grasped my breast. At that exact moment, Mother called for me.

Within seconds I tucked my shirt and called, "I'm coming." I smoothed my hair down. She met me in the hall.

"Your lipstick is smeared." Oh, God. I waited to be reprimanded. Instead, she just blew air out her nose.

"I'm going to bed. Behave, young lady. You should go to bed, too."

"Yes, Mother. I will." John pulled me into the room. I giggled.

Continuing down the hall, she said, "Now."

Catching my eye, he winked at me as I shrugged my shoulders in defeat and moved to my room.

Astrid stared out the window, crouched in bed, balancing on her knees, "I see half of you, Luna." There was melancholy in her voice. "The dark half is for me, isn't it? John has the bright half."

"Oh, Astie, you should be asleep." I sat on the bed and pulled her to me. "You are my star; you will forever be my star. What you and I have together is so special, Astie. You will forever be my star, and I will always be your moon. The moon has different phases. It's not always bright and shiny like you. I love John differently. Can you understand?"

Without emotion, she stated, "But you will go away with him. And leave me."

Trying to explain how relationships change over the years only confused her more. I lost count of the "but whys." Desperately, I searched for the right words, words she could understand.

"Astie, John, and I will buy a house. We will live there. You will still live with Mrs. Mary. You can come to visit us, even spend the night. Anytime you want to visit, you are welcome. Do you understand?"

In her innocent voice, she answered, "I guess I can." The innocent voice could be hard to decipher, but tonight it became a sign of displeasure. I tucked her bed like a mother with a child.

On Christmas morning, the sound of sleigh bells came down the hall. Astrid sat straight up in bed with joyful eyes to say, "The bells of angels getting their wings!" Feet tap-dancing while she sat on the edge, she fluttered her hands. A knock at the door caused us to freeze.

"May I come in?" It was John.

Astrid pulled the covers up to her chin. He peeked around the door with a Santa hat on, making me smile.

"Did my girls sleep well?"

Astrid shook her head. "I'm not your girl. She is," still peeking over her covers.

"Yes, Astrid, she is. Brunch is in one hour. Then we'll exchange gifts!" He came to me for a quick kiss. He started for Astrid; her hand shot up like a crossing guard.

"Okay, I'll blow you a kiss."

She pulled the cover over her head. We could hear a muffled *yuck*. We both tried not to laugh.

"See you in an hour." The door closed. Astrid peeked from underneath the covers.

"He's gone. John was hurt; you turned him away."

"I didn't hurt him!"

"No, that's not what I meant. Never mind. Let's get dressed."

"Braid my hair, just one braid."

"I don't remember hearing the word *please*."

"Please and thank you, please and thank you. Braid my hair, one braid."

"Okay, once was enough."

The puffy white shirt, red jumper, and black tights lay on the bed. No matter what Astrid wore, it was always black tights, part of her obsessive-compulsive behavior. She sat at the vanity table, waiting for me to put on my green cable-knit sweater.

"Mary made the sweater for you. I like it."

I stood behind her, seeing our eleven-year-old selves in the mirror. Now, we were twenty. Astrid handed me the brush. I braided her strawberry blond hair. The braid ran down to the middle of her back, the result of three years of growth. There was a trust issue about the cutting of hair. My mother was allowed to cut her fringe.

She watched me like a curious cat while I applied my makeup; she'd seen me do it a million times. It could be unnerving. I handed her the compact, and she dabbed her forehead and nose. I smoothed it out for her.

"Eyeliner!" she demanded. I refused. She always smeared it.

"No, not today, Astrid."

"Okay, my lipstick." I handed her a tube of the tinted pink lip gloss.

"Are you ready, my Luv?"

I took her hand, and she froze. I assured her again; these were the people she played for last night. She gave me an okay.

The banquet hall reminded me of a smaller version of St. Agnes; portraits of sour-faced ancestors, dusty tapestries and all. My mother greeted me with orders to stop holding Astrid's hand. She tried to navigate unfamiliar surroundings by herself.

"Tell her that; she's practically cutting off my circulation."

John saved us, showing us where to sit. Mother followed, "Mrs. Mary, ladies, my Aunt Marie has requested your presence at her table."

Covered with red linen cloths, five tables with six place settings adorned with gold-rimmed plates and Waterford crystal wine glasses, four Austrian glass chandeliers hung down the center, and a buffet set for a king spread out on the other side of the room. John's father tapped his water glass with a knife. "What a happy occasion, surrounded by family, friends, and the new family members of the bride-to-be. Let us pray."

Astrid crossed herself in the name of the Father, Son, and Holy Ghost. I never felt comfortable with the "Holy Ghost" part. The men first made their way to the buffet table after the "amen," a tradition I thought to be ridiculous. We were in the 1960s, not the 1690s. But I kept my mouth closed and followed along.

Astrid pointed to the ten-foot-tall, decorated Douglass fir tree. She started to clap; I handed her a plate. Trying not to help her or let her make a mess of herself, I decided this morning wasn't the time to test her independence.

Brunch went off without a hitch. I couldn't help remembering the first time I met Astrid at school. It might be my imagination, but I don't recall the hand-clapping or other quirky mannerisms. Why did I think Astrid was regressing socially and progressing musically? I tucked a large napkin under her chin with protest and explanation. Astrid ate, pretending to be me. She dropped a dollop of sauce and whispered, "uh oh." The napkin caught it with no problem.

"Hello in there!" John called me back to the moment. "We're moving to the living room for presents."

Leaning forward, Astrid said, "Presents. Am I getting a present?"

"Yes," said John, "I picked it out just for you."

We were the first ones there; Astrid began to fidget. John's father wore a Santa cap, handing out presents. Unfortunately, the festivities were going too slowly for the wiggly Astrid.

"When? When? Where is my present?"

Astrid didn't whisper in my ear. Everyone heard her. John sat next to her, "I'll see if I can find it." Then, returning with a small box, a disappointed Astrid said, "It's little."

He was sweet with her. "Good things come in small packages." Astrid rocked back and forth, trying to decipher John's words. Finally, he tapped her shoulder. "Go on, open it."

She carefully removed the wrapping, "It's a velvet box, so smooth."

"Open the box," John nudged her.

She gasped, her hand covering her o-shaped lips. "It's a little music note!" Her slender fingers traced the golden note. Oh! You gave me a musical note." She stared at it, wide-eyed and in disbelief.

John took it carefully from the box, "It's a necklace. Should I put it on you?"

A polite "Yes, please," came from Astrid.

"Do you like it?" John asked.

"Can I see it?" she asked.

John escorted her to the mirror in the hall, putting the necklace around her neck. Her eyes stayed focused on the necklace. She hurried to my mother, who sat next to Lady Hopper. Astrid could barely contain her excitement, "Look, Mrs. Mary, John gave me a musical note! He loves me!"

Mother, "Yes, he does." John winked at his grandmother. Astrid navigated the boxes and wrapping paper on the floor, plopping next to me.

"Where's your present, Leelee?"

"Astrid, you may call me Lee or Lenora, okay?"

"Okay, Leelee, where's your present?"

I shrugged my shoulders and raised my palm. "I don't know."

John disappeared but soon returned. I already possessed my beautiful engagement ring. "This is from my grandmother and me." Astrid was breathing down my neck. In an oblong velvet box laid a necklace. Pearls; not one strand, but three strands with an exquisite gold Victorian clasp, I ran my fingers over the pearls; my eyes welled with tears. Then, crossing the room to the Hopper family's grande dame, I embraced her and knelt by her chair. "Your generosity is unparalleled. I can never thank you enough."

"You, my dear, are a perfect match for my grandson. He's brought other girls home, but they couldn't hold a candle to you, Lenora. You're smart and well-mannered. I want you to have the pearls for your wedding day. Then pass them along to your daughter someday."

My lip quivered as tears ran down my cheeks. "I am honored to wear them, Lady Hopper." I stood up and everyone applauded, catching me off guard. John stood up and held out his hand. Was I transported to another century? This family's history glowed with centuries-old oil portraits and fine silver.

Lady Hopper asked Astrid if she could play the piano for her again. She nodded her head, "Okay, okay, I can play my songs."

Astrid played *I Wonder as I Wander*. When the music stopped, the dinner bell rang. The banquet hall shimmered candlelight: the chandeliers dimmed. All the tables formed one long table. White linen and lace tablecloths, gold-rimmed plates, fine silver, and holly with evergreen arrangements adorned the table. Traditional confetti crackers decorated with candy cane stripes lay on each plate. Astrid picked hers up.

Mother said, "Put it back on your plate, Astrid, please. When John's father says, we can pull them."

The servers filled our glasses with champagne. He filled Astrid's glass halfway. Her forehead wrinkled; she raised an eyebrow. I interrupted her. "It will tickle your nose. Wait for the toast."

"Why are we having toast?"

"It's a different kind of toast." John's father made a speech on the prosperity of the passing year. He addressed my mother, thanking her for joining the family. Next, he congratulated John on our engagement. The more he spoke, the more Astrid fidgeted in her seat. Then he mentioned Astrid; she sat up straight. He finished his toast; everyone raised their glass to a flurry of "Cheers!"

I tried to stop Astrid; she emptied her glass. Covering her mouth, she let out a belch. Pops from the cracker masked her belch, thank God.

"Excuse me, can I pop this now?" She swung the popper over her head.

"Yes," John glanced at me, "you may."

It popped; Astrid jumped. Inside was a paper hat; we all put ours on. She blew the confetti from her plate and found a tiny plastic cat.

"Oh, I have a cat!" Astrid was giddy, "I always wanted a kitty." The champagne went to her head, "Meow, meow, me ..."

Mother grabbed her hand, sternly but lovingly saying, "It's enough meowing, Astrid."

Thank God for the food. Astrid's head lay on my shoulder by the time we finished the cherry tarts; John was on one side, helping steady her. I managed to get Astrid to bed.

John took my hand. The family milled about chatting in small groups; we ducked into the study. John closed the door. I stood in front of a picture window, mesmerized by the gas lamp outside, illuminating the feathery snow floating to the ground.

"It's beautiful," I whispered. John's arms wrapped around me. My head rested against his chest.

"It will all be ours someday."

I should have been thrilled, but the prospect terrified me. My mind began to question if this was what I wanted for myself. A yawn escaped me.

"Are you ready for bed, my love?"

"My body is tired, but my mind isn't."

"It's been a bit overwhelming, I'm sure."

I nodded in agreement as John nibbled on my ear. I turned away from the window; his kisses were warm and inviting. He pressed his body into mine. His hand cupped my buttocks, pulling me hard against his pelvis. Sitting me on the desk, he pushed my legs apart, rubbing his penis against me.

"Stop it! What if someone comes in?" I asked.

"I locked the door." His hand was inside my panties. I begged him to stop, "I'm not ready, John, please." I shivered. He pushed my panties down.

"We're engaged; it's okay."

I shoved him with a hard kick. "Don't get cheeky with me. You will not bully me into stealing my virginity, John Hopper." I pulled up my panties and glared at him in disappointment. "Our first time should be special. It's the greatest gift I can give. Unlock the door!"

Not a word came from him as I walked past, not even an "I'm sorry." Finally, I turned around, "All I am to you is a conquest with money."

He latched onto my arm, "That's not true, Lenora. I love you. You're smart and witty, and I'm an idiot. Forgive me."

I touched his lips then turned from him. "I'll think about it."

"Please, Lenora."

"I said, I'll think about it." The memory of punching Steven, the yard bully, came to mind. It gave me the same wicked sense of satisfaction. I'd let him ruminate over what he might lose, especially in the eyes of his family.

A housekeeper knocked gently on our door as I was about to undress. Astrid was sleeping soundly. The housekeeper sent a message to meet Lady Hopper in the formal living room.

What could she want? It made me jittery. On the golden settee sat the grande dame of the Hopper family, like Queen Victoria herself, ready for a private audience. She patted the sofa, a signal to sit beside her. She said, "Come here, child. Sit with me." Her wise expression made it hard to know what she wanted to say when I sat by her. "Tonight, I overheard the conversation in the hallway."

My face flushed; I sat embarrassed. Lady Hopper took my hand, "You were right to put my grandson in his place. Stand on principles and standards, I say! I was tempted to applaud," she chuckled. "I made sure my Henry knew I didn't put up with shenanigans before the wedding, too."

Now, I quietly chuckled along with her.

"You're a fine young woman, Lenora." She winked at me; her message was unexpected for a lady her age. "Your goals are admirable. I wish I had such freedom in my twenties. And I don't think you'll be burning your bra." We both laughed at loud.

"No, ma'am. But I do hope to be an assistant curator of the London Observatory."

"Well! Lofty goals. Does John agree with your decision?"

"He knows of my dream. He's raised no objections." I paused, "At least not yet."

"Just make sure this is clear before the marriage, my dear. You need not divulge our discussion."

"I understand."

There wasn't any doubt about her intentions. But it became abundantly clear that John wanted me to be a housewife and hostess at some point. If this was his expectation, the wedding might not happen. John and I never found time for a private conversation that weekend, but we would. I wanted him to understand this was not his mother's nor his grandmother's world anymore. In the words of Bob Dylan, "The times are a-changing."

| 16 |

The Competition

"It's only a week before Astrid's first competition," my mother reminded me. "We'll be in Paris."

I got the "talk." Having John over was forbidden. Keep all doors locked, no fire in the fireplace.

"Mother," I slammed my hands down on the counter. "I'm not a child! I will have a fire if I want to! For God's sake, it's January. I will have John over for dinner; he will leave before eight. Being a young barrister requires hours of research. Don't worry. Oh, and please call me as the competition progresses."

She walked to embrace me. "I'm sorry, darling. I know you're not a child. I will call."

"How is she?" I asked.

"She'll be just fine. She doesn't understand it's a contest. Dr. Dryer has worked with her. We're leaving on the train tomorrow for Paris and returning Sunday afternoon."

On my way upstairs, I turned my back to her. "I'll make sure John is gone by then." She couldn't see the mischievous grin on my face.

"Lenora Irene!"

"I'm just kidding!"

The light in Astrid's room was still on. The sound of mice running made me curious. It was the sound of her fingers running across her keyboard. Her headset was on; she was practicing.

She caught me watching her. She continued to play.

I sat on her bed, watching her.

"You're interrupting me." I didn't expect that comment.

"I'm sorry, your Royal Highness! There's a full moon tonight. You can come upstairs later if you like."

"Okay, later."

As the night sky swept the daylight away, the moon rose. I waited for Astrid. At ten o'clock, I gave up. She never missed an opportunity to gaze at the stars and sleep beside me. A tear trickled down my cheek as reality set in; I'd be without her. The space between us was growing.

Friday evening, John and I had just sat down for dinner when the phone rang.

"Bonjour, Lee!" Astrid sounded upbeat. I heard my mother in the background saying, "go on, tell her."

"Lee, they liked me! Out of everyone, they liked the way I played at the Store barn." Astrid, an expert in French, made me snort at her pronunciation of Sorbonne. I bit my cheeks to keep from laughing. She rattled on, "I get to play again tomorrow, tomorrow again, I get to play! Mrs. Mary bought me a black dress, a black velvet dress with white cuffs that button; pretty, sparkly buttons!"

"Oh, Astrid! I'm so happy for you. I know you will have fun." Astrid didn't say a word. I heard her sigh. "Astrid, are you alright?"

"I'm sad you're not here. Where are you? Why aren't you here?"

John waited on me impatiently. I held up two fingers; *two more minutes*. Then, in a huff, he stormed to the kitchen.

"Oh, Astrid, I have to be at school and work. You know I'd come if I didn't have school. I love you, and I know you will play like an angel. Won't you?"

"Yes, I will. For you, I will."

"That's the spirit! You can call me again tomorrow, okay? Tell my mother I said hello."

"Okay, bye-bye."

John glared at me. "Dinner is cold."

"You should have eaten without me."

"If you're going to be my wife, I will expect dinner together."

"I don't like your tone, John. Astrid is like a sister to me, a little sister. I know we're the same biological age, but she is still the eleven-year-old I met in primary school. She'll never be married or never have a child of her own. She will never have a job. Her future is to compose music and play the piano. Like it or not, when my mother dies, it will be left up to me to take care of her."

John pushed his plate back, staring at the table.

"John, you know how she is." I waited for his reaction. He gave none.

"You have caught me completely off guard." I left the table feeling sick. Turning to him, "I thought you loved her. If you truly love me, you must love Astrid as well." I paused, "It will be years before she comes to stay."

"You're sure?"

"I am."

We cleaned the dishes and built a fire. Quietly sipping brandy, John broke the overwhelming silence.

"I do care about Astrid, but I'm selfish. I just want you to keep me at the center of your life. My father asked if I wanted to be married to a modern woman. I love your drive to achieve your goals. In this respect, we are alike. You'll go to work, and I'll go to work. We will always have dinner together, go to the movies and attend Astrid's concerts. She can join us for dinner or walks through the park. But I wonder if it's what you want?"

I watched the fire, deep in thought. Then I sat in John's lap, my arm around his shoulders. To his surprise, I kissed him with passion bubbling up inside. I wanted the same, but could he truly understand when it came to the reality of Astrid?

"That is my answer. I do want some of the old standards for us. I picture you in a three-piece suit with your powdered wig and flowing rob, arguing a case."

"Uhm, this a romantic notion, Lee. However, I'm not that type of barrister. Unlike television, we aren't all criminal lawyers. Right now, I'm working with another barrister. They don't want to throw me to the wolves yet. I must work my way up the food chain."

It wasn't what I'd expected; I knew he was a legal assistant of some type, but... I asked pensively, "But you will be a full-blown barrister soon?"

Picking up on my confusion, "I am. I put in long hours, and the group is happy with my work. But, Lee, you need to understand that I'm not cut out for criminal trials; it can be perilous. I'm not willing to put us in danger. I studied contract regulations. I thought you understood."

"You probably told me, but I don't remember." I blew it off as my mistake.

"It's getting late; I should go," said John. "I must pore through volumes of case files to find judgments matching our cases. There's a lot of reading and note-taking."

Holding the wool topcoat, he slipped his arm through; I turned him towards me. Buttoning his coat made me happy. How lucky I was to have him. Turning up his collar, he braced for the wind. My beautiful diamond ring dazzled in the moonlight.

Performing my house duties, I changed the sheets on all three beds. Mother would appreciate fresh linens. I busied myself with cleaning to keep the worries about Astrid at bay.

I'd never been much for regular worship but felt so close to God in nature. My grandfather called this belief Pantheism. I bundled myself up in my coat and scarf to sit in the garden, collecting my thoughts. Oh, how I missed our home near the beach. I talked to God, thanking Him for all the beautiful places on the Earth. I also prayed for Astrid's protection. Success for Astrid was a success for those listening to the music.

Returning to the fireplace, I wondered what she'd be like if she won the Paris competition. Medals and prizes meant little to her for the time being. Startled by the phone, I hurried to answer it. The clock showed four-fifteen.

"Oh, Lee, they liked how I played three different pieces! They really like Chopin. I liked him, too. A man put a gold medal with a beautiful blue ribbon around my neck. I didn't want to shake his hand, but I bowed. Dr. Dryer said it was acceptable. And they gave me flowers! Oh, Lee, *tu me manque!*"

"I miss you too, *ma étoile* (my star.) When you get home, you can show me your medal!"

"Yes, yes, yes!"

Mother took the phone; I heard the hand clapping and stomping in the background.

"Wow, and here I thought medals and fanfare meant nothing to her."

"She almost got disqualified."

"Why?" I couldn't imagine the committee disqualifying her.

"Two judges expressed their concerns over Astrid's mental condition, claiming an unfair advantage." I heard the righteous indignation in her voice.

"Dr. Dryer met with the judges as Astrid nervously paced the floor with her hands tucked under her arms, saying her *Hail Mary*s repeatedly. It must have worked. Albert asked the judges if any of the contestants played from memory. It was a loaded question because all contestants played by memory. Therefore, there was no reason to disqualify Astrid."

I chuckled, "I love it; she put them all to shame."

"That she did. Astrid is so wound up that I may have to give her 'vitamins' early tonight. We have room service for dinner. I couldn't take her to the reception when she's like this."

"No, I agree. There's no telling what she might do. Did you take pictures?"

"Yes, I'll drop them off at the photo booth on Monday."

"Our train arrives at five tomorrow evening. We'll take a cab home."

"I'll have dinner waiting for you."

Surprised, my mother said, "How nice of you, Lenora."

"Call me before you leave the train station. I'm making Astrid's favorite: spaghetti and garlic bread."

"She'll love it. You're so thoughtful."

"I'm pretty sure I learned that from my mother."

Her voice smiled, "I love you; see you soon."

Astrid burst through the door, "Lee, *où êtes-Vous?*"

"I'm in the kitchen; you can stop speaking French now, my prize-winning pianist!"

Flat-footed, she raced into the kitchen; stopping abruptly, she hollered, "You have Mrs. Mary's apron on!"

Mother said, "I don't mind, Astrid. She's cooked supper for us."

Then Astrid told me I wasn't in trouble; I felt great relief, I assured her.

"Well? Let me see your medal."

The medal came from under her shirt, her eyes brightening, "It's big!"

"I'd say so."

She threw her arms around me so tight I could barely breathe. "I missed you, Leelee." She kissed both my cheeks. Her eyes were so big, she resembled an owl, "They kissed everyone."

"I thought you didn't like kisses!"

"I don't! They trapped me. I wiped their kiss off my cheeks." Prying her hands from my waist, I said I loved her. I asked her to set the table.

"Nope! I don't want to."

My hands were on my hips, "Excuse me? This is not a question. Set the plates and silverware at three chairs. I'll get the drink glasses."

Her head drooped, and she sounded like a foghorn, "Okay."

My mother barely contained a laugh; she whispered, "You could be a comedy team at the Palladium."

I rolled my eyes. Mother gave me the *you're-in-trouble* face. I tied a bib around Astrid's neck. She slammed her fists on the table, "I'm not a baby; I don't need a bib!"

"Listen, missy," I said, "You're wearing a white blouse. Besides, I'm going to get a bib for myself, so there!"

Mother and I gave up on teaching her to cut her spaghetti. Big slurps came from her with sauce everywhere. Astrid sucked down the saucy noodles like a vacuum cleaner. She sounded like a pig; the bigger the slurp, the louder her giggling.

Mother raised her voice, "Astrid, enough!" My mother couldn't take it anymore, "You stop with the giggling. You're not funny. Is that clear?"

With her green eyes, she waited for my support only to see my arched eyebrows. "Don't look at me. You do eat like a pig."

Astrid made a futile attempt to cut her pasta and ended up with spaghetti sauce in her hair. Frustrated, her hands covered her face. "Do you want help?" I asked. She nodded. I dabbed spaghetti sauce from her face.

In silence, we finished our dinner, which was a blessing. Next, Astrid and I washed the dishes. She let out a yawn so broad the corners of her mouth stretched.

"Can I go to bed now?" She asked my mother.

"You have sauce in your hair; you'll need to shower before bed tonight."

She grunted and stomped her foot with a face full of sour grapes. Mother turned to Astrid, glaring. "Get yourself upstairs," then a punctuated, "Now!"

While Astrid showered, I unpacked her suitcase. I held the beautiful black velvet dress. When she returned from the bathroom, I inspected her wet hair, making sure the shampoo was washed out. Astrid said in her pink pajamas, "That's my piano dress. I couldn't wash it. No, no, no, no," she told me emphatically. I hung it on a hanger, knowing it needed to go to the dry cleaners. Then, tucked in the side pocket, I found a shell, the same shell from our first childhood trip to the beach. Sitting on the bed, I clutched it tightly with a sigh.

"What's in your hand?" It was an innocent question.

Opening my hand, I wanted to cry, "You've kept it all these years."

Astrid sat down by me; her wet head rested on my shoulder, her hand closed over my hand. "You said it's my good luck charm. Remember?"

My eyes burned with tears that couldn't fall. "Oh, yes," I said, "I remember that day, Astie."

Word came slowly, "I am Astra, and you are Luna. Forever together, we will always be."

"That's right." She sat on the rug by her bed; I towel-dried her hair and combed the tangles out; she hated the untangling. I laid a fresh towel over her pillow, "Now, off to bed with you. You have a free day tomorrow."

When I closed the door, I hurried up the stairs. Laying on my bed, through the skylight, I watched the stars move, wondering what might happen to Astrid after my mother died.

| 17 |

June Bride

My quiet, early morning coffee was interrupted by a barrage of motherly questions. Graduation was two weeks away; what should we plan? John and I had finally settled on a late June wedding. Overwhelmed by the tasks of planning the wedding and college finals, I broke down and cried.

"Oh, Lee, I'm here to help you. What can I do?"

"I don't want a graduation party; a quiet dinner will do. Just our little family and John."

"May I invite Dr. Dryer?"

I knew she accompanied him on several dates. These were always disguised by concerns over Astrid.

"Of course, you can. I know the two of you are involved with more than Astrid. It's alright, Mother, you've been a widow for over twelve years. I think it's good for you."

Mother's face flushed; not a word came from her, which silently confirmed my suspicion. Finally, my mother rattled off, "Let's see; Astrid can help with the invitations. You've confirmed your catering service. We booked St. John's Church. What about the flowers?"

"I thought we might meet with the florist on Thursday afternoon if that's agreeable. My last exam is Thursday morning."

"Yes, I'd love to go with you. Have you decided on bridesmaids?"

"I have. John and I want a small wedding without the pomp and circumstance. As you've seen, he has a large family," I chuckled, "And we do not. We're scraping the bride's side, the groom's side tradition. I'm inviting a few of my astronomy club friends and Dr. Hammersmith. I want you to be my matron of honor. And I hope Astrid will be able to handle being my maid of honor."

My mother placed her hand over her heart, "Oh, Lenora, I feel so honored." She kissed me on the cheek.

"John's housemate, Dorian, will be his best man. Do you remember his Aunt Marie? Her son, James, will be across from you in the processional."

"Astie, Mother and I are taking you shopping tomorrow."

"What kind of shopping?"

"Dress shopping. Astrid, will you be a bridesmaid at my wedding?"

No response. Astrid was thinking; her index finger flipped her bottom lip up and down. Her long, reddish-blond hair covered her face, her black Maryjane shoes tapped on the wooden floor. I waited for a response.

Her shrill voice questioned, "Will I be your maid? You said, bride's maid?"

"No, Astie, a bridesmaid stands next to the bride. It's a place of honor. You are my best friend. Will you please be my maid of honor?"

"I don't know. People will say, there goes the weird girl. I'm the weird girl, Lee." Her eyes bugged out, "I'm weird."

"I don't care what people think, Astie. You're talented and smart. I don't think you're weird! John wants you by my side."

Mother interjected, "I'm going to stand next to you. I'm the Matron of Honor."

"Oh, well, okay, I guess."

"You can try on beautiful dresses on Saturday."

She asked, "What color?"

"Any color you like, except orange, yellow, or green."

"Okay!"

I knew Astrid's mood could flip on a dime; I'd do a lot of praying.

We reminded Astrid on Saturday that today was dress day, as she called it. Bouncing around the kitchen, Astrid was giddy.

"I've got a secret," she sang out. Mother and I shot a glance at each other.

Mother asked, "Astrid is this a secret to share?"

Twirling like a whirling dervish, she made me dizzy. "It must be a good secret. You're going to run into something." I took her hand to slow her down.

"Dr. Dryer said I could tell on Saturday. Today is Saturday, isn't it?"

Mother and I said *yes*, simultaneously.

"Okay." Astrid took the calendar off the wall flipping it to August. There was a big red circle on Saturday the fifth of May.

"See this day? I'm playing piano with the orchestra. And I have a musical surprise, too. I can't tell you. But you'll see!"

"It's months away, Astie," I gently said.

"I know! I have a lot of days of rehearsals, rehearsal," she began to count on her fingers, "rehearsals!" She switched her demeanor then blurted out, "Can we buy dresses now?"

Mother and I sat stunned. This was the first time Mother heard this news. A phone call to Albert could wait until we returned.

I held Astrid's hand. It always helped to calm her. She talked to herself on the bus. People often stared; I'd smile at them as Astrid prattled on. Turning to an older gentleman, she said rather matter of fact, "I'm seventeen. Today's my birthday." The gentleman got off at the next stop.

"No, Astie, your twenty-one. May sixteenth is your birthday." I'd stopped being embarrassed by this behavior. Today she was good. Spring was always kind to Astrid.

Wilson's Fine Clothiers read the sign on the glass doors. Mannequins displayed in the windows wore pastel party dresses, evening gowns, and elegant bridal gowns.

Astrid stopped abruptly; her mouth gaped open. The expression on her face was priceless, "Are those dresses for us?"

"Let's go inside," Mother escorted her.

The older white-haired woman with a bun greeted us. "Miss Lenora McConnell?"

"Yes."

"We've been expecting you and your bridesmaids." She winked at my mother.

"And you are Astrid Innis. John Hopper told me how gifted you are."

Astrid's wrinkled forehead stood as a sign of uncertainty.

"She knows you play the piano, dear," Mother explained.

"Okay." Astrid's head was on a swivel, moving up and down, right and left.

The woman was Elizabeth Wilson, the boutique owner. Off to the left, the door opened to a private showing room. "I've picked out several dresses for your viewing pleasure, but if you don't find anything you like, we have many more."

She left us. Three mirrors gave us a full view of dresses we'd try. There were four racks of different bridesmaid dresses and two bridal gown racks.

"Take your time; when you're ready to try a dress, just press the buzzer by the door. Astrid sat on the settee, overwhelmed, still oddly moving her head with her eyes closed. The voice in my head said she was overwhelmed. I said something to Mother.

She touched Astrid's hand and sat with her. "There are a lot of beautiful dresses; open your eyes, and let's look together."

"No yellow, orange, or green. Lee doesn't like those colors."

"You are right, Astrid. The dresses are in other colors."

Lost a world of taffeta, silk, and crystal buttons, I took a deep breath. My wedding was going to happen; I was getting married. Lost, I stared at endless racks of gowns. I thought I knew what I wanted, but I heard a gentle voice say, "You'll never find the right one if you don't look."

Two hands rested on my shoulders. My mother's cheek pressed against mine; in the aroma of her Chanel No. Five, I found comfort, realizing how much I loved her. She kissed my cheek and said, "Go on, find your perfect dress."

I watched her tend to Astrid; it took a remarkable woman to care for Astrid and put up with my shenanigans. A measure of my mother's patience and love, I longed to be like her.

Settling on three dresses, I tried on each one. In front of the three-way mirror, I stepped onto a wooden box wearing the first. Mother said the bodice fit well, and the lace sleeves were pretty. Astrid said nothing. Her knees crossed, elbow on knee, her chin resting on hand, Astrid had no reaction to the elegant gown. Mrs. Wilson placed the veil on my head. I scowled at my reflection in the three-sided mirror; it made my butt look as big as a horse. Dress number two, a satin gown with a V-neck and long sleeves, the shoulder-length veil of lace, looked very sophisticated. Again, no reaction from Astrid. Mother sat up straight, asking me to do a quarter turn, like a show pony. Her hand rested on her chin. "Let's see the last one. Then, if we still don't like it, we'll try another one."

I love how she said, "we." Finding the right dress wasn't about her; it would be my decision. Trying on these enormous bundles of lace and tulle made me wilt. If this one didn't do, I could be through for the day. Mrs. Wilson laced the corseted bodice, three feet of lace trailing behind. The sleeves were a sheer mesh, the satin cuffs buttoned with pearls surrounded by tiny crystals. The heart-shaped, lace-trimmed neckline made it perfect for showing off Lady Hopper's pearl necklace and a little bit of cleavage.

I loved this dress; a lacy touch of Victorian meeting the sophistication of Dior. Then Mrs. Wilson brought me a tiara with three rows of crystal beads attached to a waist-length cascade of matching lace. Bubbling with excitement, I could barely wait to model this gown for my mother. I thought perhaps this dress would get Astrid's reaction, who kept untying and tying her shoelaces.

Walking out onto the box, Astrid jumped up and shouted, "A princess! You're a princess!"

Mother broke out into a big grin, and she sniffled, "Oh, Lenora, this is the one." Goosebumps ran all over me. Mrs. Wilson helped me stand on the box so she could measure the hem. She and my mother discussed the details. Tall and lanky, Astrid approached the box; finally, we were eye-to-eye. Cupping her hand around my ear, she whispered, "You are a bright full moon today."

I whispered to her, "Astrid, my shining star, will stand by the moon on her wedding day."

Glum face to the floor, Astrid concerned me. "Astie, did you and Mrs. Mary pick out a dress?" Mother overheard my question.

"Come, Astrid, it's our turn to stand on the box."

I waited for the handclapping to start; it didn't. Instead, Astrid walked flat-footed to the dressing room. I changed into my street clothes and waited to see what Astrid picked out. I overheard resistance from Astrid; Mother's voice of patience and calm prevailed.

"Come on, let's show Lenora what you've chosen. Hold your head up, Astrid."

Astrid appeared in an A-line, elbow-sleeved, red rose chiffon, floor-length gown. The wide, pink satin belt around her waist and the heart-shaped neckline perfectly complimented my dress. For a moment, she stood tall; her eyes danced with delight, a big smile graced the extraordinarily beautiful face. For a moment, she seemed like everyone else.

I felt goosebumps. Taken back by her beauty, I said, "Oh, Astie, you're perfectly elegant. The color is perfect. Will you wear this beautiful dress and carry a bouquet of pink and white roses?"

Holding her head up, she said in a clipped staccato, "Yes, please!" Before me stood a different Astrid, a fashion model, but her mood changed when Mrs. Wilson tried to mark the hem. Her legs started to bounce rhythmically. Poor Mrs. Wilson, with pins in her mouth, didn't know what to do. Mother failed to calm her. Jumping up, I took Astrid's hands.

"Astie, look at my eyes. I'm going to hold both your hands; I need you to stand still for just two minutes so Mrs. Wilson can fix the hem of this beautiful dress. Remember how she fixed mine?"

"Uh-huh."

"I won't let go, okay?"

She closed her eyes, and her palms were sweaty. She began to count the seconds out loud while Mrs. Wilson worked feverishly and finished before Astrid's patience ran out. In stereo, Mother and I sighed with relief.

"Miss Astrid," Mrs. Wilson patiently said, "be mindful of the pins."

"Yes, ma'am." Mother followed her to the dressing room.

| 18 |

The Best Laid Plans

"Oh, God, no!" were the first words out of my mouth. Two weeks before our wedding, Lady Hopper passed away. John kept apologizing for his grandmother's death.

"Stop it, John! We can postpone the wedding. Your grandmother's funeral should take precedence. We can talk about it later." I furiously wrote down the details. Mother came to my side; tears fell like rain.

"I am so sorry, Lenora. She was a gracious lady. When is the service? I still have my mourning clothes."

"Mother, you kept your mourning clothes from grandfather's burial?"

She pressed my head to her shoulder, "No, from your father's funeral."

My head spun around as I pulled away from her. My forehead wrinkled so hard it hurt, "Why did you do that?"

"I knew I might need them again, Lenora. I don't expect you to understand."

"Good, because I don't. Right now, I don't want to! Poor Lady Hopper." I caught my breath, "I feel guilty for feeling sorry for myself. But all our plans have to change."

"Yes, darling, I will help with writing the regrets. I'll pay for the new invitations. Astrid can help too."

"The chapel, the florist, catering, our rehearsal dinner, the music," I felt faint. Mother poured a glass of wine for me.

"This will settle your nerves."

Footsteps hurried downstairs. On the floor, Astrid sat in front of my chair. "Why are you sad, Lee?"

"Do you remember John's grandmother?"

"Uh-huh. The old lady queen, she liked my music."

"Yes, my sweet love. She passed away last night. Tomorrow we must go to John's house. Before noon we'll catch the train."

"Where did she pass to?"

"She died, Astrid. I'll pack a lunch for the train," said Mother.

"Can I play a song for her so she will have music to lead her soul to heaven? Then she won't have to go to purgatory."

It was the most extended set of sentences I'd ever heard from Astrid. I smoothed her hair, "The music from heaven's brightest star will lead her way." She sat in the chair with me, as close as peas in a pod. Astrid threw her arms around me, kissed my forehead, and said, "Don't worry, Lee, everything will be just fine. Can we wear our princess dresses?"

I tipped my head back to see her bright green eyes, "We'll save them for another day, Astie."

"Okay."

On the train, Astrid was in rare form with all kinds of inappropriate questions. "Will she be sleeping? I heard people go to eternal slumber."

Mother patiently answered, "No, dear, 'eternal slumber' means they are dead. It's just a nice way to say someone's died."

Later, she said, "Do dead people wear their clothes to heaven? They're supposed to wear white clothes, you know."

"Astrid, your question can wait until later, after the funeral."

"Okay."

Birds sang sweet songs, and a breeze blew through our hair. John held my left hand, and Astrid held my right hand. I tried to keep myself together. Astrid saw the piano and organ; she was a bit too excited for a funeral.

"I can play both, you know," stated Astrid.

"Yes, Astrid." In a calm voice, Mother said, "but let's play the piano today. Lady Hopper liked the *Moonlight Sonata*; it sounds so much better on the piano." Mother led her to the piano and sat next to the piano. Astrid played while the pallbearers entered. At the end of the service, she played *It Is Well with My Soul*.

We returned to the Hopper house; Astrid exclaimed, "It was a beautiful day for Lady Hopper's burying." Her head bobbed up and down with a joyful smile. John dropped my hand and hugged Astrid, saying she made the day even better.

An oh-so-serious Astrid said, "You know, John Hopper, she flew right past purgatory. I played songs a sending her spirit straight to heaven."

"You played beautifully at the church, my sweet Astrid," he said. "After dinner, will you play another piece?"

"Yes! I will everyone cheer up." The word *up* was an octave higher.

"I know you will," John spoke to her as a father speaks to a child; on this sad day, Astrid shined brightly.

Flapping her hands, she raised her voice, "Yes, yes, yes! I will."

Later, after everyone turned in, John and I sat in the window seat. The full moon eerily lit the room.

"I'm sorry, Lee, our wedding plans are now waylaid. What should we do? The only time I can claim days off is in September. I'm so sorry for dashing your vision of a spring wedding, my darling." He sat staring out the window while holding my hand.

I exhaled slowly. "John, it wasn't like your grandmother chose to die. If we must wait until September, then we will. My birthday and a wedding in the same month; you'll be guaranteed not to forget the dates. Truthfully, we are only out the cost of the invitations."

I thought for a moment. "The chapel isn't available in September. Why not get married here? I'm sure the only resistance will be from your mother."

"Oh, Lee, you have no idea." My heart sped up; I knew how to approach her.

"John, we can make this her idea. Since the only people invited were mostly family, no one would need to travel far. We could give her the job of coordinating the event."

"God knows she loves to oversee everything." He took my hands and kissed me, "Lenora McConnell, you are beautiful and smart."

Catherine Hopper was in her element, delighted to plan the festivities. And so it was: I'd have a September wedding at the Hopper Estate. Mother sighed, "I hope you'll have some say in all of this."

"Me, too. The bright side is this; we don't have to pay for the catering or a wedding planner. We have our dresses. We only need new invitations printed and flowers rearranged. That's all."

On the train home, Mother asked if I was terribly disappointed.

"Of course I'm disappointed," I told Mother. "But life doesn't come with an expiration date."

The evening train ride became an endless discussion; cards with regrets, the printing of new invitations, we'd need a florist. I watched the landscapes and streetlights whiz by the windows, wondering about the future.

Astrid fell asleep with her head in my lap. A wave of melancholy washed over me, and guilt played tricks with my mind. In the window's reflection, a girl, chin resting on her hand, void of a smile; the girl was me. I found myself stuck between guilt and anxiety.

I showed a sympathetic face on the outside, but my heart was devastated. I knew my friends from the university would be gone, traveling to their new beginnings. And there was the matter of not having a father to escort me down the aisle. A tear rolled down my cheek. Mother's head rested on a pillow against the arm of the seat. I didn't want her to see me cry. Instead, I held more tears inside.

| 19 |

Shambles

After the graduation ceremony, Mother said, "Lenora, your grandfather is smiling from heaven." Mother's voice broke, "And your father, I'm sure, is elated."

Mother dabbed her eyes with a handkerchief. Pulling me to her chest, the sound of her beating heart echoed in my ear.

"Save a hug for me," Astrid bellowed. The three of us embraced in a group hug.

"Excuse me," called a voice from behind; John said, "Can I get a hug too and maybe a kiss?"

My mortarboard sat askew; John kissed me to a flurry of "gross, stop it, yuck" from Astrid.

"Cut it out, Astie; he's allowed."

"My little astronomer," pronounced John.

"And the newly appointed educational liaison to the Observatory," I added. John gripped my hand a little too tightly.

With a forced smile, he said, "And that too."

Everyone milled around in the Commons; over the loudspeakers came the Beatles song, *With a Little Help from my Friends*. Singing and laughter filled the air; Astrid put her hands over her ears. I removed my cap and gown then we took a pleasant walk to a local restaurant near campus.

"Mind your manners, Astrid," said my mother. "You will have to choose something besides spaghetti. Is that clear?"

In her sing-songy voice, she said, "Yes, Mrs. Mary, no spaghetti. Bangers and mash, bangers and mash, Astrid wants some bangers and mash."

When we arrived, John sat by me. Astrid behaved in rare silence. Becoming quieter and less animated, I could tell she was worried.

In my mother's garden, John and I sat in silence. My beloved and I, side by side, watched the chimney swallows fill the sky at sunset. So many changes happened in such a short time. Then, I heard him inhale and exhale a sigh.

With the touch of his hand on my hand, I knew everything was moving in the right direction. He'd take his saved vacation days for our wedding; a honeymoon wasn't possible.

"Lee, I know you dreamt of a holiday in Paris," disappointment in his voice was unmistakable. "I promise I'll make it up to you next year."

"Oh, John, Paris will always be there." My hand caressed his face full of woe. "We can spend nights in front of the fire."

"Speaking of which, I got a chance to reserve appointments at a few apartments. Could you accompany me on Saturday? I have a couple of places to visit. One is a three-story townhouse with a second-floor balcony on a very respectable street."

"Hmmm, I think I can pencil you in. I start my full-time position a week from Monday. I have my own office with my name on the door. Oh my, I'll have to tell my supervisor to change the name back to McConnell."

"Wow, your name on the door of your own office." His tone, I could tell this bothered him.

"As soon as we're married, it will say, *Lenora Hopper, Education Coordinator of The Royal Observatory*," I said in my defense.

He stood up and buttoned his jacket. Oh, God, it bothered him. I'd have my own office; he worked in a room with two other people. I couldn't turn down this opportunity. His ego would struggle with my salary; I could never tell John my income would be more than his until he became fully vested. The chill I felt wasn't just from the night air. I walked out to the front stoop. Without a word, he kissed me.

"Call me tomorrow," I said.

He refused to look me in the eye, "I will."

Hurrying to his car, John never turned back. Suddenly, an uneasiness came upon me. Closing the door, Mother sensed a problem, asking if I was alright. I assured her everything was fine. My mother gave me one of her *you're-not-being-truthful* looks but chose not to interfere.

When we arrived home, I felt conflicted, a melting pot of emotions brewing inside me. The stairs to the third floor took every ounce of energy I could collect. Astrid's room was dark. I opened the door to my room and flipped on the light.

"Astie!" She was in my bed! "What are you doing in my bed? You scared the pants off me."

"Look out the window." She pointed to the sky. I turned off the light. We lay together as an eerie sky loomed overhead, bright without the moon. Cotton candy clouds moved by. I saw one bright star.

"Are you sad, Lee?"

"Why do you ask?"

"Up there, see only one star. The moon is somewhere, but my star is alone. The moon is sad and hiding. Are you sad, too?"

We laid on top of the covers like two wooden soldiers. There were things in my life Astrid could never understand. I needed her shoulder to cry on this one time, but she couldn't relate to how I needed her.

"Sometimes, there are questions I need to find answers for, but I can't find them. Eventually, the answer will come when I least expect it. I just get a bit impatient."

"I get impatient, too, Lee." She snuggled up to me. "Do you want me to sleep here tonight with you?"

How sweet her concern! "Yes, please." Tonight, I needed the comfort of her innocence.

The House

"Are you sure we can afford this place? I love it, but neither of us makes enough money."

"Do you really like it?"

"Certainly. What's not to like? I do want to see the second and third floors."

The townhouse stood between two houses from the corner. Each looked the same: stand-alone, white-washed brick, three stories high, every floor with three white, shuttered windows and covered entrance. We stood in the living room discussing what we couldn't afford. Then, the truth came out.

"Honestly, Lee! My grandmother left me a large sum of money."

"So, our earnings won't allow such a luxury. Your grandmother's money will pay our mortgage?" A palpable tension filled the room. I wanted us to be independent, not living off his family's largesse. My arms crossed tightly across my body, and my foot tapped hard on the wooden floor.

"What about furniture, heat, electricity?" My impatience was unmistakable, and John's face was turning red.

"We have the means to take care of all those things. We don't and won't need to worry. Besides, Grandmother wouldn't have it any other way." He pointed his finger at me and barked, "And you know it! You are so headstrong, Lenora." *Lenora,* he called me in his aggravation.

His true colors were on full display as he paced the floor, hat in hand. Finally, reluctantly, I gave in. John strolled into the dining room to meet with the property manager.

Lace curtains hung in the living room. Maybe a flashback from my youth made me hesitant. I'd sat in the window every day waiting for my father. He wasn't there anymore.

"Lenora," John called after me breaking my trance, "I've signed the agreements. Now, we can shop for furnishings, wallpaper, whatever it takes to make it our home."

I never toured the whole apartment; he made the decision. I remained left out of the decision. Typically, I—a woman—had no say in the matter.

The dining room was across from the living room. Crimson and gold striped wallpaper covered the walls; from the chair rails down to the floor, mahogany in need of a shine. A dining room table for ten could fit comfortably with room for a sideboard or buffet table. The front room was once a parlor.

"Look at this kitchen! You can cook dinners for us," John said with exuberance.

The comment sat on the wrong side of me, but again, I kept my mouth shut. I liked the black and white checkered floor; the cabinets needed a good cleaning, as did the six-burner stove. The back door opened to the overgrown garden. As per every kitchen in England, there were ceiling fans.

John took my hand and pulled me up the first flight of stairs. On the landing, there was a window seat with a view of the lawn. A grey stone wall separated us from other houses behind and to the side of us.

The primary bedroom came complete with a lavatory. The wallpaper peeled at the corners or large pieces hung by a thread in every room. Some rooms smelled of old cigars. Fanning myself, I blurted out, "Oh, God, it smells horrible in here. It has the odor of an old man's smoking club."

John fired back, "With new wallpaper, it won't be a problem, I believe." He sounded aggravated.

"The whole lavatory has to be replaced." I put my foot down on this matter.

John turned to me, "All of it?"

Wrinkles on my forehead hurt; I gritted my teeth, "Have a gander." I pointed to the door, "This is what I get for not scrutinizing this place before you bought it. You didn't go in here, did you?"

A gray bathtub, a brown-stained toilet, and urine-stained floor tiles were even more disgusting.

John's face scrunched up so grotesquely it could stop a clock. "Oh, see." I turned away, but I heard his gagging sound.

"The rest of this house better not be the same, John Hopper!"

Across the hall stood a fully furnished lady's bedroom, reminiscent of Mrs. Havisham's house in Dickens' *Great Expectations*. A torn canopy, dusty bed, a woman's three-mirrored vanity with a silver comb and brush set, and dry-rotted curtains hung in the window of this room.

"John!" I saw his blank expression. "Now I see why I was a fool to take you at your word." There were fresh footprints in the dust. "You were in here! You knew what condition this was in? I've been hoodwinked!"

John was a boy waiting to be spanked. "I thought it only needed cleaning." But, to save face, he said, "This could be a bedroom for Astrid," he paused, "when it's cleaned up."

By this time, my blood was boiling. I needed to find a priest to confess the sin of premeditated murder, and me not even a Catholic! I took a deep breath of the dusty, noxious odor and sneezed.

John stood on the landing, a whipped puppy staring at the ground. I'd bruised his ego. Shame rippled through me. "I'm sorry for not seeing the potential here. Forgive me."

He glanced up at me. "It's a big house, Lee. A place to grow a family. Come upstairs. I promise it's better."

An oversized bedroom was empty and dusty; not been lived in for a while. From the heat, the wallpaper disappeared into crumbled pieces on the floor.

"I've heard of an air conditioner that fits in a window," John said.

"You should check it out. It certainly would be helpful," I smiled, "especially if this is to be a nursery."

John scooped me up and turned in circles, laughing.

"Put me down, John Hopper, before you hurt yourself!"

He put me down on my feet, "Miss Lenora McConnell, I will make this dusty, smelly place a beautiful home for the soon-to-be Mrs. John Hopper."

I gave a resounding *yes*, but this project remained overwhelming; many things needed fixing. We would have to make many changes. Perhaps, by September, everything could be remodeled. I made it abundantly clear I must have a say in wallpaper and paint.

| 20 |

Number Seven Mayfair Place

Renovations began on the red brick house at Seven Mayfair Place, our soon-to-be home. At times, my new job and picking out wallpaper and tiles left me suffocating under the weight of change.

As much as I disliked John's mother, Catherine became my ally with wedding arrangements. There appeared little time to properly put things in order—new floral décor for the wedding, new invitations, and a different minister; it was daunting. Mother and Catherine talked about a large white tent, big enough for the reception and ceremony, close to the back garden; there would be no need to worry about rain. Catherine and I discussed a color scheme to match the dresses we'd purchased. An appointment with a local florist, hand-picked by Catherine, was set for the following weekend.

Lazy ceiling fans turned above our heads in the dimly lit cafe. Across the table, John, awash in the candlelight, made my heart skip a beat. His eyes, a much bluer than I ever noticed before, his long eyelashes; my John. His stoic face dissolved into a playful smile. I reached across the table for his hand.

"I am the luckiest woman on earth. Me; you chose me above all others. And wow, a promotion in less than a year! Oh, John, I am so proud of you. Your strong work ethic is rare in today's world."

"You are so patient with me, Lenora. You said anything worth having is worth the work. You understood the long hours I worked; we have our dreams. Anyone else could have left me in the dust." The gentleman brought out a bottle of champagne, prearranged by John. The pop of the cork echoed through the room.

He raised his glass, "Here's to the future of Mr. and Mrs. John Hopper of Number Seven Mayfair Place." Dinner was lovely. John talked of his ambitions. He even asked about my work, although briefly, as our dinner arrived.

John hailed a taxi with a stomach full of champagne and handmade ravioli. We sat on the front stoop when the cab pulled up to the house. A late summer moon cast long shadows over the street, and the song *Moon River* lilted from an open window. Nothing else mattered in that beautiful, romantic moment. Tender kisses, a caress of his cheek. "Could this night be any more perfect?" I asked.

"Well, you know, Lee, this could be a preview of the many evenings we spend on our very own stoop." John's muscular arm rested around my shoulder; he pulled me close. John put the moon to shame with his chiseled jaw and broad shoulders.

"It's…" he pushed his sleeve up, "Good God," he whispered. "It's three a.m. I really should go. Will you call me a taxi?"

I stood and smiled, "You're a taxi."

He rejected my lame attempt at humor with a squint and grin. Careful not to wake Mother, I turned the key in the lock; John stepped inside. Then, quiet as a church mouse, I phoned for a taxi.

Mother's voice scared me half to death, "That better be you, Lenora McConnell! It's three-fifteen."

First and last name; I knew she wasn't happy, "Yes, it's me. I'm calling a taxi for John. Go back to sleep, Mother; everything is fine."

He cracked the door open; a quick kiss.

"We'll talk in the morning," she thundered. I rolled my eyes; John snickered.

"I'm almost twenty-one, Mother. Could you have been any ruder? It was an embarrassment."

Mother got up, tying her robe, "You still live under my roof, Lenora. Staying out this late without a call is inconsiderate. You'll understand a mother's worry someday. So, remember this night when your child doesn't come home at a decent hour!"

She put me in my place. "I'm sorry. I should have called."

"Good night, Lenora. Now lock the door and go to bed."

I tiptoed upstairs, not wanting to wake Astrid. I lay in bed with thoughts of having a family as I drifted off to sleep.

Number Seven Mayfair Place, with three remodeled bathrooms, fresh wallpaper, and paint stood ready for furnishings. Catherine Hopper donated six oriental carpets large enough for the dining room and living room. and four more for two bedrooms. John's office sat on the main floor just off the living room. Upstairs was our bedroom with a newly sanded hardwood floor and remodeled bathroom and across the hall, Astrid's room for overnight stays. We decided to leave one room on the third floor unfurnished for a nursery; the other smaller room stood designated for a nanny. I knew John wanted a family right away; I did not.

When John proposed, I'd visited a women's clinic to learn about contraception. He wouldn't ever try the pull-out method; diaphragms were uncomfortable and didn't account for spontaneity. There was a new form of birth control called The Pill. It came on the market, but I heard rumors that the health risk was too significant; indeed, John would disapprove.

For me, the time wasn't right to start a family. I needed a more discreet method—an IUD, an intrauterine device. Implanted in my uterus, he'd never know. I decided on the IUD, but the clinic refused to implant a virgin or someone without children. I had to be married. The decision was a moral dilemma for me. Someone told me of a discreet clinic on the east side of London, but my hymen needed breaking, another joy to subject myself to. As soon as the deed happened, I could go to the gynecologist's office. My prayer was that I wouldn't get pregnant on my honeymoon.

Slowly furnishings began to trickle in from Lady Hopper's estate. The living room and bedroom suite arrived in July. A slightly worn dark leather couch, two leather chairs, and one rectangular table made the living room gloomy. I wanted a mirror over the mantle. John hung a scene from a fox hunt that I deplored.

To the right of the entryway, a room once used as a parlor sat empty. John requested the late Lady Hopper's Victorian leftovers. The trappings of a bygone era would have to do; two matching brocade settees, a small round marble-top table, pink velvet tufted chairs, and two maple side tables. I loved the matching lamps with stained-glass shades inscribed with the name "Tiffany." But, if I told the truth, I hated that room and felt it could be put to better use; an office for me. I didn't bother to make that wish known.

The bedroom suite belonged to Lady Hopper; an oval-shaped carved rosewood headboard was quite lovely. However, I insisted on a new mattress knowing that Lady Hopper had passed away in that bed. The bed faced the smaller windows with new green moire curtains; a chest of drawers to the right of the window; a gilded oval mirror hung above the dresser. I loved having the end house; more windows! Two Louis XV chairs in green with a rose motif sat side-by-side in front of the window, a circular walnut tea table between them. I chose a quilted, rose-colored bedspread with matching pillow shams trimmed in lace. They complimented the chairs. Lady Hopper's matching bedside tables left ample room to get to the closet and lavatory.

I was elated to find the lavatory sparkling with a new white tile floor, a pedestal basin, and a white porcelain clawfoot tub with a showerhead.

John bought a lady's writing desk for my birthday. We removed the window seat on the second-floor landing; it was a sunny spot all my own. I wanted the desk and chair placed there; I'd have a view of the garden. I added a file cabinet for storing my work papers.

After the wedding, John wanted us to host a dinner party for his associates in the law firm. I was dubious about the start of my hostessing career. Bah Humbug!

| 21 |

Pink Roses and Boyfriends

With the wedding approaching, I tried to spend more time with Astrid. Her turn as guest conductor debuted two weeks before the wedding; it worried me greatly. She wouldn't allow anyone else to conduct it. With Mr. Godfrey at her side, he kept other musicians from losing it over her perfection. Everyone in the orchestra knew of Astrid's gift; however, some couldn't take the displays of displeasure, which manifested as full-on tantrums. Mr. Godfrey removed her more than once to finish conducting himself. If she couldn't handle the task, he would step in, and she'd play the piano. As the concert drew closer, Astrid seemed in better humor. I always felt she was one breath away from disaster.

Daily she asked if I was coming to the concert. In her mind, Astrid worried John wouldn't let me hear her music. After being pestered to death, John promised her we were going; he even showed her the tickets. She couldn't understand John's role in her life. He became a villain, tearing us apart. When his back was turned, she'd sneer at him.

The month before, I kept her busy with the new wedding invitations. I addressed them; she put the stamps on the wet sponge and placed them correctly on the envelopes. Astrid accompanied me to run errands.

Mother, Astrid, and I traveled to a Gloucester florist recommended by John's mother. We ordered the bouquets and reception flowers. Unfortunately, we also had to meet her for tea after.

"The pink roses," Astrid insisted, "and white lilies."

I explained how white lilies were for funerals. Then, the florist appeared with a tall container bursting with a kaleidoscope of bright flowers.

"Catherine Hopper said you were coming. You are wise to have a September wedding. It's a time for cooler weather and colorful fall bouquets."

Mother chimed in, "We hoped for more spring-like bouquets."

"Nowadays flowers are shipped from many countries. I feel certain we can order almost anything."

Showing us a book of different style bouquets, I settled on a cascade, pink and white tea roses, fragrant deep pink lilies, baby's breath, and ivy trails.

"What's the pink lily's name?" asked Astrid peeking through her fringe. "They all have names, don't they? I know they do."

The florist smiled at Astrid's innocent question. "Yes, you're quite right, love. They're called Stargazers."

Astrid jerked her head around; she glared at me with bug eyes.

"Well," I chirped, "We certainly want those."

Astrid was full of glee with her hands flapping. Mother gently took her hands. I thought she might scold her. Instead, she said, "I know! It's exciting, isn't it?" Still holding Astrid's hands, "I think we both should take some deep breaths."

The nosegay bouquets for Astrid and Mother consisted of a Stargazer lily surrounded by white roses with bits of baby's breath and wrapped with pink ribbons. Remembering John's mother's words about carnations being a lower-class flower, Mother selected an arrangement for the long head table of white spider mums, pink roses, and ivy. We shared tea with Catherine before heading back to Cambridge. I felt she'd approve of our selection. She and Mother discussed the seating and the catering menu. Astrid fell asleep on my shoulder.

Catherine "secretly" worked on my mother to exclude Astrid from the wedding party. As we left the café, I overheard my mother say, "Darling, no Astrid, no wedding." She couldn't see the jubilant expression on my face. Mother put Catherine in her place; we didn't speak of Catherine's scheme on the train home.

Astrid's concert was a week away. She didn't appear nervous; in fact, she was confident. Yet, her preoccupation with hair and makeup was very unlike her.

"French braids, please. Put makeup on me, Leelee, frosty, pink lipstick. Okay?"

I found one pink lipstick in my makeup bag,

"Are you sure? It doesn't right with your hair. I have a very nice red."

"Pink!" she said. Pink it was. Looking at herself in the mirror, she took a fist full of tissues to wipe it off.

"No, Astrid! You're smearing it. God, you can be a pest!"

"I want to be beautiful like other girls who have boyfriends."

"Boyfriends?" Curious, I asked, "Do you have a boyfriend? Astrid, tell the truth. I won't be upset."

Waggling her head with a sheepish grin, she said, "Charles. He smiled at me during rehearsals."

Astonished, I placed my hand on my chest, "Really? Do you fancy him?"

Nodding her head, "He's a nice boy, very nice boy. After rehearsal yesterday, he told me I was smart and pretty."

This was uncharted territory. I'd speak with Mother later. I used tinted dark pink lip gloss and blusher on her porcelain skin and a touch of mascara. Constantly envious of her natural beauty, I handed her the mirror. Those long fingers pressed against her cheek, "I like it! Let's show Mrs. Mary! I like it!"

I couldn't wait to see Mother's reaction. Mother heard the scurry of our steps down the stairs. Breathless, we both stood in the living room. Mother looked up from her sewing. She did a double-take at Astrid, "What have we here?"

"Astrid has a boyfriend, of sorts, named Charles Joseph. He plays cello in the Symphony?"

Astrid stood with her hands behind her back, swaying from left to right. she stared at the floor.

Mother sat up straight. It was the first she'd heard of a boyfriend. Mother was as shocked as I. Astrid never showed an interest in boys. Now at age twenty-two, suddenly, she was interested.

"I believe this is something we should discuss," Mother cleared her throat. "How do you know he likes you?"

"He smiled at me and said I was pretty. He's a nice boy, Mrs. Mary. A very nice boy, Mrs. Mary."

I offered the brilliant idea of asking him for dinner. Astrid started to wave her hands, "No, no, not yet! After the concert!"

Her answer seemed enough to appease my mother. She wasn't keen on the idea of a boyfriend for Astrid. Later a call would be made to Mr. Godfrey. Upstairs, I was curious about these new feelings Astrid expressed. I needed to know more. When I asked her about having a boyfriend, she said she wanted to be like John and me. A little confounded; I didn't know what to say. She wanted to see if it was okay for her to hold hands with Joseph; if he asked, she cautioned.

"Have you held hands with him?"

"No, but I don't mind. I want to be like you and John."

Great, now I needed to explain what was inappropriate when on a date. It was a discussion I never thought I'd need to have with Astrid. I wasn't sure how I felt; I wanted her to be happy and not taken advantage of by anyone.

"If he asks you to go on a date, we can double date."

"I don't want two dates." She held her finger up in my face and said, "One! Only one."

"Okay, just one. We will cross that bridge when we get to it. I just want you to concentrate on the concert and not be distracted. After your big night, we'll talk about it then, okay?"

"Okay. Okay."

"Do you want me to take you to rehearsal tonight?"

"No!" Her response was so severe it scared me. Then she calmly said, "No, no, thank you. Dr. Dryer is picking me up. Besides, the Symphony is a big secret. It's a big surprise for you!"

"A surprise for me?"

On tiptoes, hands clasped behind her, Astrid rocked back and forth on her heels; the word *yes* came out of her like a slow leaking tire. Her sneaky little grin popped out. Her long index finger pointed at me. Astrid warned me not to snoop around the concert hall. She held up a crooked pinky finger. She remembered.

"Pinky swear," she said solemnly.

Two pinkies linked together, just as we pledged our lasting friendship while at St. Agnes. I promised not to ruin Astrid's surprise.

Astrid answered the knock on the door with a face full of make-up. Dr. Dryer came in. "Well, well, what have we here? You look marvelous." Astrid blushed. The four of us sat together, talking over tea before rehearsal.

"Do you know Charles, who plays the cello?" Mother asked.

"Charles Johnson, yes, nice young man. He's from Liverpool. Why?"

"Astrid is rather fond of him." Mother said with concern.

Albert reassured Mother he was different, a prodigy of Jacqueline Lapin.

"Ms. Lapin was a prodigy herself, but a medical condition keeps her from playing She is a great teacher. Right now, Mr. Johnson is her only pupil. Charles has a solo bridge in Astrid's …."

Astrid hollered, "Don't say the name!" Everyone was taken back by Astrid's outburst.

Rattled, Dr. Dryer peered over the top of his glasses, "As you wish. Is it all a secret?"

Her eyebrows were squeezed into a V between her eyes, "Oh, yes."

"Well, my dear, not a word. We should be going. We'll talk about Charles later, but I assure you, he is harmless." He turned to my mother; "I have no idea how long we're going to be. Tonight is a full rehearsal."

Astrid picked up her sweater as he ushered her into the foyer. Behind his back, we could see his fingers crossed. Mother leaned forward and a snicker escaped her.

"Just a minute!" She jumped up, handing a sack to Albert, "There are apples and sandwiches."

"Thank you, Mary, how kind of you."

Astrid turned stalwart and imitated Albert. "Yes, thank you, Mrs. Mary."

| 22 |

The Symphony

"The days of floor pacing and lecturing herself makes me all the more worried for her, John."

"As long as I have known you, Astrid doesn't sound to be any different now. You shouldn't worry so much about her and think more about us."

Over the last two weeks, John had displayed behavior like a spoiled child. With wedding plans and constantly reassuring Astrid, trying to keep my sanity had taken its toll on me. With Astrid conducting her original music, my nervous stomach twitched.

John's comment about "us" made me bristle; Astrid needed me. John tugged my arm hard as we approached the concert hall; he held my hand a little too tight. I could see Mother and Dr. Dryer standing in the foyer from the door. I wanted to hurry to them, but John's grip restrained me. My gait slowed to match his steps. Mother read my face like a subway map; she knew I was upset.

"How is she?" I asked. "Is she holding herself together?"

Before the concert, against my wishes, John hauled me to our house to show me every room completed. Powerless, I tolerated the apparent delay. By the time we arrived, I glanced at my watch; ten minutes until the concert.

Dr. Dryer excused himself to let Astrid know we had arrived. Mother answered my question, "She was a bit worried you might not make it in time."

"I spoke with her briefly yesterday. For the tenth time, I assured her." Then, out of earshot, I whispered to Mother, "John refused to hear of coming any earlier."

Mother said nothing. The three of us were seated. Dr. Dryer returned. I leaned forward. With a smile and a nod, he gave me a thumbs up. Mr. Godfrey guaranteed Astrid was happy and ready.

On the front cover of the program was a candid black and white photo of Astrid sitting at the piano. I read Astrid's bio in the program. Clear and to the point, basic information concerning schooling and experience. At the bottom of the page, a special section with Astrid's *thank you*'s. She mentioned my grandfather for the musical start of her career; John Michael McConnell was an extraordinary man. There was mention of Mother and me, too.

The house lights flickered, signaling people to be seated. I turned to see the concert hall was packed. I wondered if Astrid's parents secretly mixed in with the crowd. I wished they could see how Astrid has become an accomplished musician and composer. As the lights dimmed, my heart fluttered. My butterflies were probably worse than Astrid's.

From behind the heavy red velvet curtain came Mr. Godfrey. He stepped out of the shadows and into a spotlight.

"Tonight, you're going to experience music that transcends words. Astrid Innis is an exceptional musical talent. In the second half of the program, she has written a symphony; moreover, she is conducting it. She is a pianist and a true savant, lucky for me," he chuckled.

"I was given the privilege of working with her thanks to Dr. Albert Dryer. Without ado, let's welcome Astrid Innis to the stage."

The curtains parted. Mr. Godfrey took Astrid's hand, leading her to the piano bench. In her black, mid-length dress with the white satin sash and Victorian white lace collar, she could be Princess Astrid. I missed being the one who braided her reddish-blond hair. Mr. Godfrey whispered something, then she nodded.

Before she played, Mr. Godfrey asked to hold our applause until the intermission. A highly unusual request brought a few murmurs. Inside, I knew the noise could set her into a tailspin.

A soft straw-colored light bathed Astrid. Her hands, perfectly arched long fingers, floated down to rest on the keys of the black grand piano. Astrid closed her eyes, blocking out every distraction. I immediately recognized the first few notes, Beethoven's *Moonlight Sonata*, a favorite piece of music for her. Each song grew stronger in tone and difficulty. Mr. Godfrey introduced the next segment.

To showcase her ability to work with other soloists, she played Debussy's *Beau Soir* with cellist Charles Johnson. Mother and I now placed a face with the name, a freckle-faced redhead. Then, lastly, the challenging Chopin's *Fantaisie-Impromptu in C Minor*. Her fingers were flying over the keys so fast. It made me dizzy; Astrid's body became a part of the music. Her eyes were tightly closed to block out everything. Sweat beads broke out on her forehead.

I recognized part of the music as the modern-day song *I'm Always Chasing Rainbow*s. My mind drifted to our days sitting outside watching the clouds. We were so innocent, so happy. She'd taught me patience and given me the joy of unconditional love.

The thunderous applause joggled me back to the present. Everyone stood; shouts of *bravo!* filled the air. When the house lights came on, Mother was missing. I was entranced; I didn't see her leave. Then, Dr. Dryer told me my mother was helping Astrid change clothes.

John excused himself. In a moment of self-pity, I wished I could have been the one helping Astrid. I wasn't married yet, but I missed her terribly with work and the wedding.

Everyone took their seats. John barely made it back, crawling over people. I wasn't happy with him. The house lights dimmed to black. The second half of the concert was entitled "The Surprise Symphony" in four movements in the program. Not in my wildest imaginings could I have guessed what happened next.

Mother had let Astrid's strawberry blonde hair down; the sides were pulled back from her face with shiny black combs. She appeared from the wings in a red sleeveless evening gown that shimmered in the light. Mr. Godfrey walked with her as she stepped onto the conductor's box. He handed her the baton then took his place at the piano. The symphony turned their attention to Astrid.

A projection screen behind the symphony lit up with deep blue background with a full moon and a single bright star. Then, in white letters, the title appeared: *The Astra and Luna Symphony*. I gasped, overcome with emotion. My mother took my hand; eyes straight ahead, she smiled.

The title of the first movement on the screen, *A New Friend by the Sea*, was our beginning. Astrid raised her baton; it began with the rumble of kettle drums mimicking the ocean waves. Then other instruments joined with a jolt, loud and strong. The piece reminded me of the fight that sent us running into the woods, beginning our friendship. A picture flashed on the screen of twelve-year-old Astrid and me, sitting outside at sunset. I'd never seen it before. I shot a look at my mother; she just smiled. A different image of us was shown on the screen with every movement.

From there, the music became more lyrical; our summer nights under the stars—a cello solo, warm with a touch of melancholy; Grandfather's theme. Two melodies reappeared in the other movements. It was the musical equivalent of our lives together.

The Teenage Thing was a movement with the sound of a waltz; a waltz of all things! On the screen, we appeared in our wild, 1960s mod clothes. I watched Astrid sway to the three-quarter time as the baton cut through the air. It was the music of our growing up, waltzing through our teenage years, wishing for adulthood. Our theme was incorporated into the complicated piano piece with soft strings in the background. The music was flung from a star and caught by the moon.

I glanced at John; my heart sank. He yawned, seemingly bored to tears. The last movement awakened him. Astrid composed a rollicking rondo; fast, energetic. At first, I thought, how unlike her. I heard castanets, definitely her hand-clapping excitement. Her arms moved quickly; her whole body was thrown into the music, fast and full of life. I couldn't have loved her more. I could hear her feet tapping out the beat as she soaked up the energy from the audience. People were clapping to the beat. Then, in a rising crescendo, rolling back to the symphony's last loud note.

Thunderous applause filled the hall; everyone was on their feet yelling *bravo!* Mr. Godfrey sprung from the piano to Astrid. She stood modestly looking at the floor as applause roared through the crowd; all the string players tapped their bows.

She turned to take her bow. Mr. Godfrey whispered something; she turned to the musicians, raised her arms, they took a bow. The musicians taped their bows once more, a sign of respect. The shouts and applause continued. When Astrid turned back to the audience, I bolted to the side door. John hollered at me; I kept going. I needed to find her.

The stage manager still wore his headset.

"Where's Astrid?" I raised my voice.

Mr. Godfrey heard me; he took me by the arm, "She's in her dressing room. She's in tears thinking you'd be disappointed." He read my expression, "She'll be happy to see you. Please try to coax her from her dressing room. We have patrons."

Astrid had locked the door. "Oh, Astie, it's me; please open the door!"

With a jerk, she opened it, "Lock it!"

She threw herself onto the chaise lounge. I cradled her in my arms.

"Astie, baby, don't cry," I laughed. "I cried enough for both of us. You have given me the greatest gift ever. I'm so proud and grateful you are my friend. I love you more than words can say."

She latched on to me, "I love you with my music. I don't want you to leave me."

There was knocking at the door. "Astrid, you're needed! You're expected!"

"I can't!" she whispered.

"Show me your eyes." I cupped my hand under her chin, "you can. I will be with you. You will say politely, *thank you*, and put on a smile."

"Will you hold my hand? I don't want to shake hands. So many people..." Her voice trailed off.

"So many people who love your music, Astrid Innis." I powdered her nose and freshened her lipstick. "There are a lot of people out there, but I'll be at your side. Now, let's go,"

Out of the door, an unexpected flurry of flashbulbs exploded. Astrid's hand flew to her face. She squeezed the life out of my hand.

"Please! No more photos!" I pleaded. Mr. Godfrey stepped in, "No flashes."

The Symphony's Chairman of the Board, Dr. Lucas Erline, came to meet her. He wanted to speak with Astrid; he held out his hand. Not returning his handshake, I jumped in, "Astrid prefers not to shake hands, sir."

"I see, my shy butterfly. You are truly a genius, and what a debut! I can't remember a better concert, simply brilliant."

I squeezed Astrid's clammy hand. It was her cue; with a forced smile, she uttered, "Thank you."

"Will you be writing more music?" The question came from came a female board member. Astrid began to rock back and forth on her heels. Finally, I asked, "Will you write more songs?"

She answered, "I will someday."

Many others congratulated her. She was the show pony; I was her handler. Then, out of the corner of my eye, I saw John, arms folded and looking at his watch.

Dr. Dryer arranged a reception party for family and a few friends at a nearby hotel. The concert left Astrid emotionally and physically drained. The crowd dwindled; Mother came to me, "I'll take care of Astrid: you need to take care of your future husband."

I didn't want to, but I knew I must; it was my duty. As I made my way across the backstage area, I sensed his hostility.

"I suppose you want to attend the reception." There was no joy in his statement.

I put my foot down. "I am. This is a memorable night for…" He cut me off.

"Well, I'll be glad when we're married so I can have your undivided attention."

Selfish bastard! In the blink of an eye, he changed. I stood there, stunned by his remark. When John and I began dating, he gave the impression of love for Astrid. My relationship with Astrid was clear, but apparently, I was wrong. For a split second, I thought about why I'd consented to marry him.

"You don't have to go." I sounded bitter, and I wanted my words to burn him.

"Maybe I'll just leave," he fired back.

"And what excuse will I be making for you?"

"Dammit, Lee! Let's just go."

Whether he liked it or not, this was my Astrid's night. My shining star has taken the world by storm. Besides, knowing her, the night wouldn't last long.

Astrid saw us through the window and began waving. She ran up to hug John; he was unprepared for her greeting. Her arm was around his neck.

"Did you like my music, John?" She longed for his approval.

"I did, very much. Your Chopin was flawless."

"Thank you, John Hopper."

"You're very welcome, Astrid Innis." He said, removing her arm from his neck.

She melted his iron heart. *Good for her.* She wiggled in between us; taking our hands, she led us to the buffet.

"Chef said, eat up! No leftovers!" announced Astrid. "Look, my favorite." She held up a boiled shrimp.

"Astrid," I said in my motherly tone, "that's not good manners."

"Okay, Leelee." She shoved the whole thing in her mouth, then smiled. John rolled his eyes then set off to get some wine. After her crude display, she stuck to me like glue. I caught a whiff of alcohol on her breath, not wine but whisky.

I turned her head towards me, "What have you been drinking?"

"I don't know, but it was hot! The man over there said he thought I could use a drink. I was thirsty. After the second drink, it was better."

"Oh, geez, Astrid. He's a bartender. You've been drinking whisky!" No wonder she was so candid with John.

Astrid saw my face; her green eyes got big, "Did I do something wrong?"

Flustered, I said, "From now, only drink water."

Her voice dropped an octave, "Oh, couldn't I have a cola? I've been good."

"Only if I give it to you."

John observed our discussion. "Is anything the matter, Lee?"

By this time, Astrid was leaning against me with a rare smile. I whispered to him, "She's tipsy."

He thought it was the funniest thing he'd ever heard. The more he laughed, the madder I got. Through my teeth, I gritted, "It's not funny, John!" Astrid's head rested against my arm, oblivious to our argument.

"Why? Is she underage?"

"You know Astrid and I are the same age, biologically."

"So, lighten up! She's legally allowed to drink."

I glared at him, "You'd give a ten-year-old girl a shot of whisky?"

"Of course not," he said with anger.

"Barrister Hopper, I rest my case."

I'd overstepped my boundaries. My mother overheard the heated exchange and approached us

"Oh, poor meadowlark." She referred to Astrid, who was now drooling on my sleeve.

Mother's finger tapped her lips, "Hmm, John, will you be a dear and help me get Astrid to the car?" Mother made the appropriate apologies as Albert brought the car around.

John draped Astrid's arm around his shoulder; Mother took the other side. I ran ahead to open the door of the waiting car. After she was safely in, John said, "Go with them. I'm going to the house."

It wasn't a request; it was an order. God, he was still mad at me, but I didn't care. Observing our interaction, Mother asked if everything was alright.

"He thought it was funny Astrid was snockered. I didn't."

"Well, I suppose you should be angry with me. I let Astrid out of my sight. I caught her talking to the bartender, drinking her second whisky and coke. I told him never to give her alcohol again. By that time, it was too late. When I saw you and John come in, I returned to my conversation."

I heaved a sigh.

"I'm sorry, darling. Did you and John have a disagreement?"

I leaned my head against the window, staring out at the city lights, "You could say that. Oh, Mother, he was so bored tonight. I wanted him to be happy like us. But, before we came to the reception, he made some hurtful remarks."

"I'm sorry, Lenora. You will find it's the way marriage is sometimes. You'll want to go to the ballet; he'll want to go drink with his pals."

"Did my father act this way?"

"I don't want to shatter your memories of him, but yes, some Fridays and Saturdays, he took off with the boys and not to the symphony. It's what men do."

"Well, I don't like it."

In her wise voice, Mother said, "Lenora, you will have to accept it, or your marriage will collapse. And you have to loosen your grip on Astrid also."

Her words cut me like a knife through my heart. After we got Astrid up the stairs, I retired to my room. Still wearing my evening clothes, I lay on my bed, questioning my decision to marry John. Was this what I wanted? Society dictates a woman's role: make love to her husband, get pregnant, and raise a family. But did I want to give everything up? I loved my job at the Observatory. I worked some evenings. I knew John didn't want me to work. It was a quandary.

Four hours of sleep was not enough. My night came burdened with so many emotions, so many unanswered questions. I knew my mother's response already; I needn't ask. The wedding loomed before me like a giant ugly monster wrapped in taffeta.

My morning coffee came with a plethora of mixed emotions. My head was in the clouds; foreboding, dark clouds.

"Lenora?" I jumped when Mother called my name. "It's six o'clock. You're up early." She sat next to me, "Are you having wedding jitters?" Her hand wrapped around my hand, just like when I was a scared child.

"I don't know what's going on with me. Would I be terrible if I went away for a few days?" There was a lump in my throat, "Grandfather told me when my mind was troubled, I should go for a walk. I'd like to go to Brighton for a couple of days."

Mother's forehead wrinkled, disapproving. I knew what came next. The tenor of her voice changed, indignant and raw, "You're not getting cold feet, I hope. A lot of work has gone into this wedding!"

She tried to make me feel guilty with the list of things she rattled off as if they were more important matters than my feelings.

With contempt, I said, "What will you have me do, Mother? Would you want me to walk down a beautiful aisle with all the beautiful, expensive dresses and flowers and be trapped in a bad marriage? Do you wish me a life of dread?"

Mother sat in shock with no response. Then came her answer, "You must go through with the wedding, Lenora. Swallow your prideful, independent attitude."

"Your attitude is the exact reason why I need to find my own answers. You are of no help, stuck in your old-fashioned ways. We don't live in the nineteen forties anymore, Mother." My following words were deliberately slow, "The world is changing. And right now, I don't know what I want."

I left her at the table to pack my bag. A walk on the beach and fresh air always helped me clear my head.

I peeked into Astrid's room as she slept. The sun's bright light illuminated the room. On her back, she lay, an arm covering her face. It pained me to think about what might happen to Astrid when Mother was gone. She could never be a burden to me. I loved her differently now. The music gave us an unbreakable bond.

Quietly, I walked down the stairs.

"Where will you go?" Mother asked.

"Wherever the train takes me. I'm going to the coast for a couple of days, and I'll be back. Tell Astrid," I paused, "I don't know. Just tell her I love her."

| 23 |

The Escape

At the platform to Brighton, I saw teenagers and young adults dressed like what I described as hippies. I sat on a bench, awaiting my train. There were twenty or so of these young people laughing and hugging each other as they came in my direction. They were having a jolly good time. I envied them. As they got closer, I heard them say something about me. The word they used was "uptight." I couldn't argue; I was uptight.

I was approached by a tall, thin guy wearing bell-bottomed jeans and a pirate shirt. His hair was long, brown, and shiny. Behind his ear was a cigarette.

"What's you're deal, little bird? Running away from home?" His tone was surprisingly sympathetic.

He sat down next to me. I stared at him, "Yes, in a way, I guess I am." The thought never crossed my mind, but I was doing just that. Running away.

A girl with hoop earrings, bleach blond hair, a tie-dyed tank top, and paisley pants who looked around my age asked if I wanted to go with them to the Isle of Wight.

"What's at the Isle of Wight?"

"Only the biggest music festival in Great Britain, sweetheart!" an African girl declared.

They started naming off a lot of bands. I'd never heard of half of those names, only The Who, Bob Dylan, and Joe Cocker.

"It only costs two pounds fifty, for the whole weekend. Leave your troubles on the tracks, and come with us," said the pirate.

A very strikingly handsome guy with shaggy, light brown hair held out his hand, "You won't regret it, I promise."

The train pulled up with a hiss. I knew I shouldn't go, but I did. This group of vagabonds broke up into different cars. I ended with the six who introduced themselves: Frank, the pirate; Sandy, with blond hair; Diana, a beautiful African girl with hair like a dandelion; Seth, a quiet, average looking chap from Liverpool; Joy, with long, black hair, a short buckskin skirt, and boots. And then there was Dane; he enticed me to go with them. Although I didn't know what I might experience, I decided not to care.

Sandy sat next to me, smelling like patchouli, an oddly distinct aroma.

"How far is it from London?" I asked.

Dianna said it wasn't far to the ferry. Caught in the moment, I hadn't thought to ask about lodging before leaving. They laughed. I wondered what was funny.

Dane piped in, "Don't worry, little sister, Dane will take care of you." I should have been scared, but I wasn't.

Frank gave a narrative on last year's festival, "A lot of people came last year. We slept on the ground."

Sandy said, "We were a mess, but the music was groovy." *Groovy? What was "groovy?"*

"This year, I talked a sweet lady into letting us stay at her house. It's walking distance to the field of music."

Seth laughed, "It's why we hang with Dane."

With a serious face, Dianna said, "Sugar, we have to do somethin' about your clothes. You look like a doctor's wife." In my pink ruffle blouse and black polyester slacks, she was right.

Sandy put her hand on my knee, "I might have something for you in my knapsack."

We left the platform, walking toward the ferry.

"We'll make it in time for Dylan," said a joyous Frank. "You've heard of Bob Dylan, haven't you?

"Of course, he's a poet and songwriter. I'm not too square." They laughed, but I didn't know if it was with me or at me.

People milled around waiting for the next ferry. I stood there looking stupid with my overnight case. Dane came up behind me. A smell like old socks burning began to fill the air. A puff of smoke blew past my ear.

"Here, take a drag of this fag," he said.

I fanned my face, "What is it?"

Sandy laughed, "It's wacky-tobacky; it will make you feel fine."

"Drop your inhibitions at the dock, baby," Seth sounded poetic.

Dane coaxed me, "Suck it in and hold it."

I knew it was illegal; no one seemed phased.

"Virgin of the Weed, go on," Sandy prodded.

"Oh, what the heck," I'd broken the rules already.

I inhaled and thought, *I'm going to die*. I'd never coughed so much in my life! I doubled over, coughing as spittle drooled from my mouth, humiliated as they all laughed.

"The first time is the worst. Your second hit won't be as bad," smiled Dane, "I promise." It was my turn again. Oh geez. For me, this was a moral dilemma. Caught up in the moment, I took another drag.

"Hold it in," Sandy instructed me. My mouth barely opened, the cough came in spurts, smoke escaped between my lips. I laughed at myself. Dane put his arm around my shoulder. "It just gets better."

We worked our way to the edge of the dock as we finished off the "joint," as they called it. As the ferry docked, Dane grasped my hand. I felt relieved; crowds pushed and shoved me to get seats. Finally, Dane, Sandy, and I got seats together.

"I'm famished," I grumbled. My hippie friends assured me the lady of the house would have food.

"You've got the munchies," Dane said in my ear.

"What's a munchie?" I asked.

Sandy laughed, "So naïve."

I did feel a weight lifted off my shoulders and strangely attached to Dane. Not caring felt good. There were hundreds of young people filling the roads.

We walked forever before we found the house. I was expecting a little old lady in an English cottage. Sandy knocked on the door; gosh, was I wrong. A fifty-ish woman opened the door dressed in a multi-colored caftan, bare feet, and a scarf around her head.

"Well, well, well. What have we here?" the woman said, giving me the once over, "Dane, you didn't say you plucked a pretty flower."

"Tilly Sheridan, meet Lee McConnell."

"Do come in, children. Where are Frank and Seth?" Dianna arrived just before us.

"Lost in the crowd somewhere.'

Tilly fixed cheeses, fruit, and fresh-baked bread with butter. I was starved. Dianna told Tilly I wasn't as stodgy as I appeared.

She showed us the three bedrooms upstairs.

"Who's sleeping where?" I asked. Sandy and Dianna were sharing a room; Seth and Frank were in the other. That left Dane and me. I couldn't sleep in the same bed with him.

"Is there a couch?" I asked.

"Yes," said Tilly, "but you can sleep with me. I have a king bed downstairs."

What a relief! Tilly offered her clothes to help me fit in.

"You all should rest a while. The headliners don't start until nine with Bob Dylan."

I rummaged through Tilly's closet and found a pink, blue, and yellow, short-sleeved maxi dress. I tried it on, gazing at myself; I thought, who am I? Maybe I was still high, but my bra came off. It was a nice feeling.

"Come sit in the living room; I've got a bong!" Once again, I was in the dark. I waltzed into the living room to calls of approval.

Dane studied me with those dark, intense eyes, "Babe, you're one of us, now."

The first toke on the bong sent me to a place I'd never been before. The whole world was upside down. I'd been living another life. Floating along on the high, Tilly suggested a nap. In three hours, the concert started.

Lying on the bed, staring at the ceiling, I heard Tilly, "You have problems, little flower?" She climbed into the bed next to me.

"I'm supposed to get married in two weeks. My confidence is gone; John's become demanding, controlling. I have a great job I don't want to give up. And a friend who's different, brilliant, but she's been labeled a savant. Someday I'll have to care for her; I'm positive he doesn't get it."

"For now, enjoy yourself. It sounds like this may be your chance to discover who you are."

I closed my eyes and rolled over on my side. Tilly's hand was around my waist. She was kissing my neck! I quickly rolled over, "What are you doing?"

"Helping you relax, little flower."

"I don't think this is helping."

The next thing I knew, her hand was in my underpants. I went rigid.

"Have you ever masturbated?" She softly rubbed my vagina.

"No!" my response was breathless.

"This is the best way a woman can relax."

God, was I aroused? She found my clitoris and rubbed it in a curricular moment. I felt my hips rise as Tilly rubbed harder and faster. She kissed me; I was breathless. My back arched, and a gasp escaped me. Tilly rubbed harder and harder; the top of my head was about to explode. Then it happened, with a primal groan; I erupted. She stopped. I was exhausted.

"See, Lee? You don't need a man; you just need your hand. And you don't have to lose your virginity either."

"Oh my god. I didn't know." I enjoyed it. "Are you one of those women who," I hesitated, "you know, likes women?"

"No. think of me as a teacher. It was a one-time event, honey-bee. I've been married twice." In the bathroom, she washed her hands, "Come to the kitchen; I'll put on the kettle."

Tilly's eyes were full of wisdom. Something inside of me made me trust her. Maybe she'd give me a broader perspective on life, existing outside of my limited understanding. Tilly reached across the round oaken table and took my hand. "Is your mother or father living?"

What a strange question. "My father died when I was eight. I live with my mother and Astrid, the girl who's extraordinarily talented."

"I see. Your mother's dated values are old-fashioned to you. Don't fault her for those views, Lee. We're in a historical time; the world is in rebellion against the way things always were. Do you work?"

"Yes, I'm the educational liaison for The London Observatory. I know it's my calling."

"Your betrothed doesn't want you to work, right?"

I didn't know how to answer. John never directly said he didn't want me to work, but the implications were there.

"The innuendos are there. When John proposed, I clarified my goals and how Astrid would eventually come under my care. At the time, he indicated a compassionate understanding."

"How long have you been engaged?"

Dane and the others trickled down to the kitchen.

"We'll continue later," Tilly said, rising.

A big pot of vegetable soup and warmed bread were waiting.

"I know it's August, but you're going to need something hearty. Fill your bowls. Take an apple or a pear. There's cola in the fridge. The thermos full of cool water is in there, too. You know my two rules, right?"

Seth repeated, "Return quietly and don't drop acid."

"And," Sandy chimed, "we won't cack in the house."

"Well, that's very thoughtful. If you do, you'll clean it up," Tilly sounded like my mother.

I stayed in the living room, declining the invitation to join them, needing to continue talking with Tilly. The group tried every tactic to get me to go. Being in a sea of unwashed masses, listening to loud music just wasn't my thing. Tilly knew it, too. As soon as they left, we continued. Tilly married twice. Her first marriage sounded like my future. Being married to a successful accountant, beautiful home, wealth; she'd had it all.

"After three years of feeling isolated and depressed, I joined a book club. Eye-opening and informative, I concluded he was an alcoholic and had run off my close friends; his opinions were always the right ones."

She divorced him, receiving a large settlement. After the divorce, her ex made life hell.

"I ran away, meself, moved to this island and met a fisherman. We married, and I opened a little coffee shop. Life was good. We bought this perfect house, and he brought home his catch." She chuckled, "We ate a lot of fish."

Tilly lit up a joint, "One day, he was gone." Misty eyes, she sat lost in a memory. Afraid to ask what happened, I waited for her. She handed me the joint. She and I finished it off in silence. In the background, I heard the crowd's roar and loud music.

"A bad storm swept him out to sea."

My heart broke for Tilly. She still owned the coffee shop but boarded it up for the concert.

"Last year, it was sweltering. Someone broke into the shop at night. Anything not nailed was stolen. My friends helped nail up boards this year. We removed everything to a shelter outside of town."

"Weren't you angry?"

"Oh, yes! Brandon and I built the place. A piece of him was missing, but some of our friends helped me rebuild. It's a wee place, six tables now. Gertrude, down the street, bakes pastries. I get a big shipment of coffee from South America four times a year, and I roast it meself."

"Are you happy, Tilly?"

"Happiness is fleeting; it's contentment that matters, Lee. Talk to your guy. And don't compromise; if you can't be who you want to be, you will never be content, little flower."

I sat in a blurry-eyed stupor, but my answer was clear.

Tilly asked, "What does he do for a living?"

"He's a barrister, just starting to work his way to an office. When we got engaged, he was compassionate and loving. John is not the same person I fell in love with, Tilly." I thought for a moment. "It's not all on him. I've changed, too."

Her voice sounded far away, "It is my belief people shouldn't marry before age twenty-five. Your values aren't the same. Your political and spiritual views change. Couples begin to drift apart."

"My choice is easy; facing the consequences is difficult."

Tilly patted my leg, "Be strong, Lee. And be true to who you are meant to be."

With eyes of steely blue, Tilly saw my soul. "The first ferry comes at eight, little flower, then every hour on the hour. Oh, you can keep the dress. It looks better on you anyway."

I wrapped my arms around her, "Thanks, Tilly, for everything." I was grinning so hard my face hurt. Then, in the smoky haze, I fell asleep on the couch.

The noise of the others coming back didn't faze me. Instead, I woke up to the smell of coffee and wiped the crusty corners of my mouth.

"Morning, Lee. How was your night?" Tilly stood in her paisley caftan.

"Surprisingly well."

She poured me a coffee and a slice of the newly baked banana bread. Tilly touched my hand, "I guess you're leaving after breakfast." She paused, "I hope you find your answer, Lee. But just know, you're always welcome here."

Tilly was a kind and generous soul, one of the better people I ever met. I thanked her with a hug. Then, walking to the ferry in my new dress, I thought hard about the consequences of the decision I must make.

I caught the train from Portsmouth to Brighton; it was packed right like an old man's pipe.

"Brighton, next stop," echoed through the cars. A walk on the beach might air out the smell of marijuana. My first stop was Mrs. Glenn's

Bed, and Breakfast. I'd called earlier; it was a bank holiday. Mrs. Glenn gave me a warm welcome but was surprised I could wear such a dress; I explained it was on loan from a friend.

"How's your mum? Did she remarry?" she rattled off.

"Mother's fine. No, she never remarried, but she has a beau. He's one of Astrid's music instructors."

"Her prospects are much better around London. Music, hum?" She tapped her cheek, "Oh, yes, it's coming to me, the Innis girl."

"That's right, Astrid. She's a classical pianist and composer." My information about Astrid's extraordinary abilities shocked her

"Well, blimey! I didn't know she played anything."

When I told her about Astrid's competition at Paris's "Sorebarn," it made her howl. My room reminded me of my grandfather's house. Oh, how I missed him, my advisor in a dilemma. Yet, when I tried to imagine what he might say, I drew a blank.

I let Mrs. Glenn know I'd be going for a walk and getting supper in town. A wind whipped around me, blowing my wavy hair in every direction. The August beach was disappointingly full of families, frisbees, and dog walkers. Everything remained as I remembered. I sat on the big flat rock, the place where I'd tried to engage Astrid in conversation; now I know why she frustrated me. Children built sandcastles and hunted for shells like our younger selves.

A smile of remembrance came over me. Astrid kept that scallop shell we found. When we were close to twelve, I said it was her good luck charm. Our names were worn but still legible. Oh, those days seemed more straightforward. Astrid came into my life, and the world changed, but she couldn't change with it. She was still a silly, moody adolescent. We were like conjoined twins, forever attached.

I needed to be one hundred percent sure John understood it. Early in our relationship, he let on like he loved Astrid. For the life of me, I hadn't a clue what happened. But, if I was to marry him, I must know what changed in him.

| 24 |

He Would!

Around six pm, I returned home. Mother was displeased. I hoped for a warmer reception. Astrid's panicked voice called from upstairs, "Lee, is that you?" Before I could answer, trampling feet stomped down the stairs.

She kissed my cheek like a woodpecker on a tree.

"Whoa, you're going to break me!"

"You didn't run away! See, Mrs. Mary, she didn't run away! I knew she didn't run away!"

With a wrinkled forehead, upset, "Did you tell her I ran away from home?"

"Not exactly, Lenora." Her sing-song tone came out defensive.

"Mother, you have never lied to me."

Astrid butted in, "Mrs. Mary said you ran off to find your answers. I don't know what the question was, but I hope you got the answer. Did you find your answer, Leelee?"

I hugged her, "I did, mouse, I did."

She pulled away from me, "Is it a good answer?"

"I hope so."

My mother put her hands in her apron pockets; she couldn't resist, "I certainly hope they are the right answers, too."

"What you mean is, you hope the answer is the one you want to hear." I dragged my overnight bag upstairs and didn't come back.

I urgently needed to talk with John. We agreed to meet at the nearby park, a good place to talk. A public place, hopefully, would keep him from flying off. A bench near the fountain was vacant. I spoke first.

"I took some time to get away and collect my thoughts. There are some things I need to know. You must answer honestly. Don't say what you think I want to hear! Tell me the truth."

John nodded, "I will, I promise."

My words were well thought out and to the point. The first question I asked was about women with careers. While John said he was leaning toward the more traditional marriage, he didn't mind if I worked. And then came the caveat—if the household was in order.

Then I put the following question to him; it would decide everything.

"John, when my mother dies, are you willing to let Astrid live with us?"

"Aren't there homes for people like her? Institutions where people like her can live a happy life? Of course, she can visit at her leisure. "

Calmly I asked if he knew of a place. "Maybe it will help if we visit one of those places," I suggested. Again, I stayed low-key.

"I will see what I can do next month."

"No, sorry, it's not good enough, John. We need to go before Friday. I believe there is one outside of London. Why don't I set an appointment for Wednesday afternoon?"

"Fine! I have work to do." He stepped away, then turned to me, "Do you love me?" he asked.

"I do. I love you, and I love your family. Even your mother has come around to being pleasant."

With stooped shoulders, his hands in his trouser pockets, he walked away. I should have asked the same of him, but my answer would come soon enough.

"Lenora," Mother pleaded, "I don't like the fact we've become estranged. Talk to me about what you're thinking, please."

"When I try, you're quick to judge me against old-fashioned views; your views. The times we live in are not the status quo. Women no longer are chained to the ideas of housekeeping and popping out babies. I love my job, and I'm good at it! I met a woman on my quest last weekend. I believe what she said is true. We are in a time of substantial change. We are not our mothers."

Mother turned her back to me. Those words hurt her; the last thing I wanted was to hurt her. I continued,

"If something happened to you, Astrid becomes my responsibility. So, I asked John what we would do when the time came. Mother, he's talked about putting her in an institution."

Her jaw dropped as she turned, her eyes full of shock. "That's a bunch of malarkey, Lenora; you know he'd never put her away."

"I thought so, too. Wednesday, we're going to St. Marten's Asylum."

"What?" She sat at the table, shaking her head in disbelief.

With conviction, I said, "He seems hell-bent on putting her away. I want him to see firsthand the conditions of these institutions."

The door flew open; Astrid blew in, breathless.

"Where's Albert?" Mother asked.

"He's too slow. My happiness wanted to run." There was no sense in asking what happened; she ran upstairs. Dr. Dryer came puffing in with a red face. Mother and I looked like quizzical meerkats. I handed him a glass of water. He plopped down in one of the armchairs, exhausted.

"Well?" Mother glared at the poor man.

"Astrid has been invited to Princeton's piano competition."

"Well, it will be nice; she won't be leaving the country," said Mother.

"No, no, no! Princeton University in New Jersey!" Albert corrected her, "The United States!"

Mother almost fainted.

"It's not until the end of January, Mary, but there's a chance she may be playing with the New York Philharmonic." He held up his hands, waving them in the air, "Wait, wait, before you say anything, I haven't heard anything back from New York. However, the winner is usually invited to play with them."

"God, no wonder she flew in here all excited," I said.

After her prize at the Sorbonne and her composing debut, Astrid became the talk of the music community. Her presence was being requested all over the world. She might be happy now, but eight hours on a plane? I couldn't say. Mother and Albert continued talking. I heard Astrid talking; this wasn't her usual prayers or a one-sided conversation. It frightened me.

I knocked softly on her door, "It's me, Astrid. Can I come in?"

"Just a minute." I couldn't imagine what she was doing. When the door opened, an array of stuffed animals was all arranged carefully on the bed.

"What have we here?"

A childlike giggle escaped her, "My orchestra; they all have names. People send me lots. I picked out the ones I wanted, but Mrs. Mary said no more than ten. Ten, ten. The rest she sends to the orphans or sick children."

"I think it's wonderful!" I was relieved to no longer be alarmed by the voices.

"Some people write me letters and send other things, too. I don't read the letters, but Mrs. Mary, not Jesus's mother, helps me write thank you notes to other musicians. It's called eat-ta-cat. I'm not eating a cat! Ever! I wouldn't!"

"Oh, Astrid, you should know it's French for good manners."

"Oh," she took a breath, "Leelee, do you have to work tomorrow?"

"Yes, it's Tuesday. Why?"

"I want to eat pizza at the pizza place."

Our time together was reduced by events in my life. I missed being with her. We made a date.

"When I get home tomorrow, we can eat pizza at Angelo's."

Her hug wrapped around me like a boa constrictor. I pried her arm from me. "Let's go down for dinner."

She took my hand like a child, leading the way.

John drove us to St. Marten's Asylum. The administrator informed us visiting hours were from two pm until five. The large red brick building trimmed in white was ominous. The first thing I noticed was the bars on the windows. I had a knot in my stomach; it only got worse from there. John rang the bell; we waited. Finally, a man in a white lab coat met us at the door. Inside, the putrid smell of piss permeated the air. It was all I could do to not run for the exit. John looked straight ahead, unphased. The doctor explained the policies; four patients per room with a nurse on call twenty-four hours a day.

"Is there a piano?" I asked.

"Yes, an upright, but the patients aren't allowed to play. It's only for Christmas and mass." He grinned, "It's simply too much noise! I'm sure you understand. We have over a hundred patients here."

"How many staff?" I asked.

"Around thirty," he acted cavalier. John didn't say a word until now, "What's the cost for a female patient?"

"Five hundred pounds per month." His smile turned creepy.

"A bit steep, don't you think?" asked John.

"Understand, we have cleaning staff; then there's the medication, meals, and laundry service. We think five hundred is reasonable. I'll show you one of our rooms and the dining hall. Higher functioning patients work in the dining room."

In the rooms sat four black iron beds, and a metal nightstand for each patient. The floors were bare, no curtains hung in windows; I felt my stomach turn flip-flops. As we approached the dining room, an attendant yelled at a man with Down's syndrome. The director shooed them away as we approached the ding room.

"Why are there metal tables?" John asked.

"For cleanliness," the director replied, pleased with himself.

I couldn't believe what came from John. "What a good idea, sir."

Back at the office, the doctor asked questions. John told him how Astrid was great at music and no bother without mentioning her name. "We believe it's for the best to be around her own kind."

Anger bubbled up inside me when he said *we*. I knew my answer; it was all I could do to keep my composure. In his statement, John had the nerve to say *we will be in touch!* He acted as if he owned her. Astrid's life was none of his concern, now or ever!

In the car, I was fuming. This was the test.

"What did you think?" I asked pointedly.

"It's not horrible. Astrid will fit in there, Lee."

"Really? Take me home. I think we should talk with my mother. And you said *we* thought it best." Incensed, I gritted my teeth, "Don't ever use the word *we* again when talking about Astrid's welfare." For the twenty-minute ride home, he uttered not one word. I slammed the car door when we arrived.

Mother sat in the garden reading. John and I sat quietly on the garden stool.

"Hello," My mother eyed us. "Who died?"

"John has something to discuss with you."

His head whipped around, shocked, "Me?"

"This was your idea, so tell her."

"I just thought…" he began to stutter, "Well, I-I, just thought, in the future, we might, uh, find Astrid, you know, find a place when you're gone. Not now, I mean."

"For God's sake, John," my mother's patience was wearing thin, "I hope you don't argue a case anytime soon."

I interjected, "He wants to Astrid in an asylum after you die."

Appalled, Mother put her hand on her heart, "Is this true, John?"

He struggled, "It's not what you think. They have visitation!"

"It smelled like a public toilet!"

"John," my mother leaned forward, "do you see her as an embarrassment? You gave her a necklace. The worse deception comes when you pretend to love someone for the affection of someone else."

"Did you pretend to love her to win me over?" Disgusted, I said, "You aren't the same person I became engaged to."

Mother left us. He tried to explain his way out of the web of lies. He shouted at me, "The wedding is a week away! You can't walk away like this. We can work something out together. I bought you a house, for God's sake!"

"Firstly, you bought the place without my input. It was a wreck! I certainly never got to give my opinion because you guilted me into agreeing!"

His hands behind his back and began to pace, "If you call it off, what will I tell my mother?"

"Oh, there's your true colors, John. *What will I tell my mother?*" I mocked him. "Tell her the truth of your deception."

Defeated, he sat down.

"What kind of person could think of putting Astrid in any condition sure to kill her? I met a wise woman who said, 'Don't marry before age twenty-five; your view of your world will change.'" It stood out as the best piece of advice given to me by anyone.

I took the ring off my hand, "Here, come back when you're twenty-five; we can talk about marriage then."

Stunned, he put the ring in his pocket. We walked past my mother to the front door.

"I'll send your grandmother's pearls back, too."

"No," he spoke softly, "keep them. My grandmama wanted you to have them."

I kissed him on the cheek, "I'll see you when you turn twenty-five."

"The wedding is in a week! You're melodramatic, Lee. Haven't you crucified me enough? You're never going to find someone else to give you what I have to offer. You'll have a home, everything money can buy, and more. We can travel all over Europe. I can give you whatever you wish."

About to lose everything, John conceded defeat, "Astrid can stay with us, I promise." We were silent; I processed his words. He was right; I could have anything now.

"John, you've broken my trust. Trust is never easy to mend, if at all. Now, you will let Astrid stay with us. How do I know you won't send her away?"

"All I can give you is my word," he answered.

"No, you can give it to me in writing. I truly love you. You must understand I could never put Astrid in a place with metal tables and the smell of urine. It broke me to hear the attendant yelling at that poor man. I will never be the same after what I witnessed. I find it hard to believe you'd be so thoughtless."

"What do you mean by getting my promise in writing?" he asked.

"You should know about prenuptial agreements. I want one. You shouldn't have trouble getting one written. I want you to keep your word, a promise to help me take care of Astrid."

"What about after we have children? What then?"

"You told the doctor she was no bother. How could you, knowing how loving Astrid is? She helps me with the cleaning. She does chores now with my mother. It makes her feel useful."

"I don't want her caring for our children."

"I won't leave her alone with them. You have my promise."

"Who pays for her upkeep? Her presence will cost money and privacy."

"To set your mind at ease, my grandfather set up a trust for her; I've hardly touched it. Let me be clear: if putting her away ever comes up in conversation, I'll divorce you. There will be no second chance. This is your second chance. Are you satisfied?"

John conceded to signing the document or no wedding. My mother's legal counsel would draw it up.

I told John I'd never forgotten Tilly's advice about people not getting married before age twenty-five on the way to the door.

John's response was, "Let's prove them wrong," then he kissed me. All I could do was nod. He left.

"Well?" Mother paused, "Are you still having a wedding?"

"With conditions." She didn't understand.

"Celebrities and persons of wealth make a contract of sorts."

"What about the children?"

"If we have children, the courts will broker a settlement. In our agreement, I keep my account, and he keeps his."

"What did he say about Astrid's future?"

"She's the main reason I want a contract. If John ever suggests sending her away, the marriage is finished. And he will pay handsomely. We'll have our lawyer draw it up to make sure it's what I want."

When I went upstairs, I heard Astrid's muffled whimpering. I knocked.

"Go away!" She yelled at me. Stunned, I pleaded for her to open the door. Her eyes were red; she used her sleeve for a tissue. Sheets of music were strewn all over the place.

"Oh, Astrid, what's happened? I've never seen you like this."

She threw herself on the bed; an arm blocked her face; her breath came in heaves. Noticing a red mark around her neck, I put my hand on her leg,

"Where did you get the red mark on your neck?"

She moaned more, unable to talk. She pointed to the floor under her keyboard. I saw the reason for her tears. Peeking out from the sheets of music was the music note necklace snaked across the floor. I lay beside her, heartbroken; *oh, God, her window opens to a view of the garden.* Astrid overheard everything John and I discussed

"He doesn't like me. I did a bad thing, and now you don't have a wedding." Astrid moaned again. Then, catching her breath, "Do you still love me?"

"Now, why do you think I don't love you?"

"'Cause you don't have a boyfriend anymore. I messed up."

I sat up, "Astrid Innis, I don't want a boyfriend if they don't like you. They can all go to hell."

Astrid jumped up off the bed, pointing her finger at me, "Don't say the hell part again!"

Taken back by her reaction, "Yes, ma'am." I pulled a tissue from the box by the bed, "Blow."

"John was confused." I thought fast, "You didn't hear everything. You've been confused before, yes?"

Her arm moved away from her face, "Uh-huh."

"I still have a boyfriend, and we're still going to get married. And you can come live with us if Mrs. Mary gets sick. I won't leave you; I promised a long time ago. Do you understand?"

"But John wants to put me away!"

I hated making excuses for him, but there was no choice.

"John thought you might like to have friends who were more like you when we visited this god-awful place. It was dank and smelly. I will never let you go there, never, never, never! I made John promise never to mention it again. He promised and said he was sorry."

Her voice quivered, "What if he breaks his promise? People do, you know."

"If he breaks his promise, I'd choose you, Astrid. We could find our own home."

Then, there was a moment of quiet, "It will do." She dismissed me as if nothing had happened.

She laid down facing the wall so she could rest. I lay next to her. Then, she turned over and touched my face. I swept her fringe aside to see her green eyes; my poor Astrid.

"Astrid, we made a promise a long time ago?"

"Yes," she raised her arm, index finger pointing to the evening sky. "Astra," her other index finger shot up, touching the other one, "and Luna, forever together."

Never looking at me, she smiled.

Two days later, a courier delivered the prenuptial agreement. Mother took it straight away to our legal advisor, Robert Anderson. He knew what I wanted to be included.

After work, I came through the door. "Lee," Mother called for me, "Mr. Anderson is on his way."

"That was quick," I muttered.

I sat impatiently, waiting to hear what our lawyer thought. Then, finally, the doorbell rang, I jumped. Mother answered the door and showed him to the kitchen table. The briefcase held a folder labeled *McConnell-Hopper prenuptial agreement.*

"Well?" Patience was never my strong suit.

"Mary, Lenora, I've examined the agreement. Everything is in order," he paused, "But if you should divorce, for any reason, he will get the house."

"And Astrid?"

"When Mary is no longer able to care for her, Astrid will stay with you, and she must have her own room."

My hand rested on my chin, thinking over the condition. "I'd be willing to give up the house. Then, if the marriage came to divorce, I could move back here."

It was a question I had to ask, "Will you sell the house if …"

Mother responded in a flash, "Under those conditions, I won't entertain the thought of selling. You can keep it and rent it out if you wish. If something were to happen to both of us, Astrid could live here, with a suitable companion."

Mr. Anderson showed me where to sign. My mother witnessed the document. She asked him to draw up a new will for her as soon as possible. Her request concerned me.

"A will." I asked, "Is everything alright?"

"It's something I've meant to do for a while. I have a will, but I need to update it, that's all."

The next afternoon, a courier brought a copy of the agreement with John's signature, witnessed by another barrister. Though reluctant, Mother promptly set out for the bank to lock the document in our safety deposit box. This document meant a secure future for Astrid and me.

| 25 |

The Wedding

Astrid nearly drove me bonkers on the train traveling to the Hopper estate. Thank God we were in a private car. Mother and I practically tied her down. Every few minutes, she jumped up, clapping her hands and exclaiming, "We're going to a wedding!" repeatedly. Finally, I snapped, "Astrid! Sit down and shut up! You're driving me mad!"

Her bottom lip quivered, "I'm sorry, Lee." Her palms began hitting her head. "Stop hitting yourself!" Damn it, I'd hurt her feelings. Astrid buried her head in Mother's arm. "I don't mean to do it. Sometimes I can't make it stop."

"I'm sorry. I'm nervous; I need some quiet, just a little quiet," I reached across to touch Astrid; she flinched. Mother wasn't happy with me.

"Oh, Astrid, I know you're excited." I tried to soothe her, "I need a little quiet. Please?"

Sitting up, she blew her nose, "Okay."

As the landscape flew by, I kept wondering if marriage was a mistake, even with a prenup. Part of me felt anger, like a sexual conquest; he tried to control me. But, on the other hand, there were times when he was fun and romantic. Thinking those thoughts were better, I chose to concentrate on those moments.

When we arrived, we immediately unpacked. Astrid roamed away from us. In a panic, I searched for her.

"Come out, come out wherever you are." No answer. John's land was a mile in each direction of mostly woods. If she wandered off, it could take days to find her. I called her again.

"Where's Astrid?" asked Mother.

"I can't find her." Panic flooded my voice.

"Check the flower garden; I'll check the tent," she said.

I found her with a handful of flowers plucked from Catherine's Garden.

Astrid held the fistful of flowers, pointing them at me, "See! These are for you!"

I hoped to keep my voice down. If Catherine saw this, she'd surely be furious.

"Come here, Astrid." She knew there was trouble. You mustn't pick flowers from someone else's garden; it isn't polite. And you are not to go anywhere without permission, is that clear?"

As we walked to the guesthouse, Astrid said, "Pretty flowers are supposed to be picked, Leelee. It's not fair. They will die. Flowers wilt and die, you know."

"When you pick them, they will die too. You should look at these blooms, like paintings in a museum." I was getting nowhere. "Astrid, the bees will not make honey without the flowers."

"Oh, oh, do not pick flowers 'cause the bees will be unhappy. What if they're angry with me now? They'll sting me!" She dropped the bouquet and hung her head; I picked them up.

"You've already picked them, so let's look for a vase."

"Water, they need water! Water or they will die!"

Mother saw us talking. She shook her head in disgust. Even she had limits where Astrid took a toll on her nerves.

Catherine let us use the guesthouse to prepare for the wedding—a kind gesture from John's family. The tent was up; the weather was cooperating. Breaking from tradition, Astrid wanted to play Pachelbel's *Canon in D*, with a string quartet for the ceremony. She worried about not taking her keyboard, but John bought a keyboard approved by Mr. Godfrey. Mother whispered to Astrid for her cue. I couldn't have been prouder of her at the rehearsal as she played with a string quartet.

After the rehearsal dinner, John handed me an envelope; two tickets to Paris!

"I thought you couldn't get time off; why didn't you tell me earlier? I only have ten days off; I've used three."

"It's for six days at the Ritz, a honeymoon/birthday surprise," he said calmly, "We'll return Sunday afternoon."

"Oh, John!" I wrapped my arms around him and kissed him; momentarily, my doubts vanished.

After everyone settled for the night, I threw a cover over me, going outside to a crisp September evening. Gazing at the moon, I missed Grandfather's wise council.

Grandfather, how I miss you, "It's a waxing gibbous moon." Why do I feel I'm about to make the biggest mistake of my life? I wish you were here.

I watched clouds pass over the moon. Startled by the door latch opening, Astrid stood her nightgown and slippers; her face turned to the moon. I motioned for her to sit with me, wrapping her up the blanket as she stared at the sky. We sat in silence for the longest time. Still looking up at the moon, Astrid clutched my arm. "If he's mean to you, will you come home?"

"I will."

"I wish I could marry you, but girls don't marry girls." It was the comment of an innocent. I kissed her hair.

"Astrid, I will be a bus ride away. When we get home, we can ride the bus to the new house."

"It's okay, Lee." She pointed to the sky, "I am the star, and you are the moon. We will be together forever. I brought you this for good luck." She unwrapped her fingers from around our shell. I kissed her on the cheek and sent her off to bed. I drew my knees to my chest and lost control of my emotions, crying into the cover until there were no tears left. The watch's gold hands showed one-minute past midnight. It was the "something borrowed" from my mother. I read the inscription from my father, wondering what he might be like now. When I went inside, I washed my face; in bed, a cold cloth covered my eyes in the hope the evidence of my tears would disappear by morning.

One of Catherine Hopper's cooks fixed us crepes for breakfast to the utter delight of Astrid. I tied her hair back, keeping the sticky cherry syrup out of her hair.

"Mind your manners, missy." Astrid was licking the cherry syrup from her fingers. I barely ate a bite. Mother lectured me on not fainting from hunger. I managed to choke down a crepe. Two cups of coffee were my limit. The last thing I wanted was the urge to pee while saying my vows.

The wedding started at two pm, sharp. While Mother dressed, I braided Astrid's long hair, adorning it with tiny white fragrant flowers. Her side barrettes were little clusters of flowers. I helped her with her slip. Mother took over while I did my makeup.

My hands trembled; the eyeliner wasn't straight. Mother heard my frustration and came to my rescue. She made me do deep breathing to calm my nerves. It didn't last long. Finally, I slipped on a cold satin robe while a hairdresser wrapped my curls into an updo.

John made sure Mother, Astrid, and I had a heated tent of our own next to the venue, a perfect place for me to get dressed. My dress bought ages ago, was still an ideal fit. Mother pulled the corset strings tight. Astrid giggled. I almost forgot the sleeves were a sheer mesh, a little chilly for September. Mother buttoned the cuffs with pearls surrounded by tiny crystals. Lady Hopper's pearl necklace fit so well with the heart-shaped, lace-trimmed neckline. I purposefully tried not to look at the full-length mirror until I was fully dressed. Our bouquets were sitting in boxes on a long table. At one forty-five, Mother asked, "Astrid, are you ready?"

She sounded sad, "Yes, Mrs. Mary."

"Wait! I want to see the three of us together." We stood together, gazing at our reflection, our last time as a family. Mother hugged me, "You know your grandfather is watching from heaven."

"Please, don't make me cry," I said with a catch in my voice. Mother placed the tiara-style veil on my head then smoothed it. Astrid stared at me with her green puppy-dog eyes. A sliver of melancholy ran through me, knowing she would never be a bride.

A voice outside called for Mother, who took Astrid's hand. I laughed to myself when Mother told Astrid not to swing her bouquet. I stood alone as I awaited the fanfare announcing my arrival.

John's father had offered to walk me down the aisle; I politely declined. I imagined what it might be like if Father were here to walk with me. I knew he was walking with me. At the opening note of the wedding march, I took my first steps into the floral-decorated tent with an arch of roses and ivy. John appeared to have tears in his eyes. When I walked down the aisle into an alternate universe, my life changed forever.

| 26 |

My First Guests

Mother was right; John did get drunk on our wedding night. Truth be told, I got tipsy at the reception in the banquet hall. Albert came for Mother, which made me happy. Mr. Godfrey came for Astrid. I never paid much attention to Mr. Godfrey before; the black hair, graying temples, and brown eyes. Just this side of awkwardness. He was a prodigy at a young age. Like Astrid, he didn't care for loud music. Instead of pop music, we hired a string quartet. It was absolutely posh.

After traditional bridegroom dances, bride and father, I danced with John's father while John danced with his mother. Astrid wanted to "dance" She grabbed my hands, arms outstretched, we spun in circles, got dizzy, and were full of laughter. I paused to take a mental snapshot of Astrid, beautiful and full of unpretentious joy.

She sat next to me at the "big" table and stared off into space. When the crowd noise got loud, she put her elbows on the table and covered her ears. Mother gave me a look; Astrid needed to go to bed. Bless her; she was exhausted. She hugged John and told him not to be mean to me. Before Mother and Mr. Godfrey escorted her from the room, she hugged me tight; I told her I loved her, and I'd bring her a surprise from Paris on our short but sweet honeymoon.

John was still under the influence on our flight. The nighttime flight featured the lights of Paris, looking like stars on the ground. We checked into the Ritz. Our room overlooked the Seine and the Eiffel Tower; seeing it lit up was breathtaking. Champagne and caviar awaited us, along with two dozen white roses, plus a red one. How fitting; I was about to lose my virginity.

I stood at the windows; John came behind me to kiss my neck. I felt unexpected chills run down my spine. For the first time, I allowed myself the experience of overwhelming desire. He closed the drapes, turned me around, and unzipped my dress; it fell to the floor. Then, playfully, I unbuttoned his shirt. He was much more muscular than I'd imagined.

The sheets were silky against my skin. Hovering over me, John smiled and said something I never expected, "It's my first time, too."

I blushed, "Well if this doesn't work, we have a week to get it right."

We got right to it, the painful part of the first time. After that, our relations were better—not excellent, but better.

Paris was incredible; we shared more in common than I'd realized. Sitting at a cafe near the Arc de Triomphe, John commented on the various styles of architecture; I loved the multiple types myself. I wanted to go to the planetarium until I found out their system was outdated. We took a moonlight cruise on the Seine past Notre Dame, awash in golden light. Astrid might have lost her mind here. It gave me an idea for her gift.

The day before we left, John and I stopped at a perfumery. They put rose petals on the lard to absorb the rose oil! We smelled every fragrance before choosing gifts for our mothers. He also bought Astrid hand lotion. How sweet!

We made a stop at Notre Dame. I knew what I wanted for Astrid. I let the gift shop wrap it for me. We also bought her a tee-shirt printed with the rosette window. John insisted; I knew she'd never wear it but stayed quiet.

We boarded the plane to London. He held my hand. I convinced myself I'd made the right choice.

On Sunday evening when we arrived home, I called my mother. "He was so sweet; he carried me over the threshold when we got home! And Paris was fantastic! When can you and Astrid come to the house?"

"Slow down! You're making me tired. Astrid is preparing for the Princeton competition. But, Lenora, it's a true relief knowing you're happy."

I calmed down. "I want you to see the house now that John decided to allow it. He wanted it finished before company came. The workers finished everything except the top floor."

That week I put everything in order. This house was my home. My clothes hung in the closet across from John's suits. Our wedding present from John's lovely Aunt Marie was sixteen place setting of china with a beautiful wisteria design, now in the cupboards. I put Mother's gift of cookware to good use. There were still more unopened wedding gifts.

When the doorbell rang on Saturday afternoon, I was so happy to see my mother and Astrid I almost cried. There were hugs and a million questions. The room to the left resembled a Victorian parlor with Lady Hopper's furniture.

"I know all of this is very dated but in good condition." To the right was the living room; it was more John's room with leather furniture. "We're getting the windows replaced in the spring."

Mother commented on how she preferred the parlor with the brighter room, a settee, and matching muted light blue tufted chairs. They were fruitwood and elegantly placed on each side of the windows. "Those lace curtains remind me of our city home in Dublin. The oriental rug is new. Where did you buy it?"

"This one came from Catherine. We received six in different sizes. John's office was the room behind the living room. His father gave him a heavy oak desk.

Come with me to the kitchen. John paid to have the cabinets restored to their beautiful cherry. Thank you for the cookware, Mother. I used it last night. This morning I made John breakfast."

Astrid's only comment was that it smelled like bacon. Then, she started to get a scone.

"Not yet, Astrid. I want to show you the bedrooms upstairs. There's even a room for you."

She ran upstairs, "Which one is mine?"

After our argument, John had gotten a new canopy bed for Astrid's room, and the vanity sat refinished; I hoped to continue seeing this side of him.

"The door on the right, open it."

A gasp escaped her, "Ohhhh, it has a pink top!" The bed had a pink lace canopy bed with a green duvet. The vanity matched and there was a six-drawer dresser, all for her. Astrid flopped on the bed, staring up at the lacey canopy. "Is this really mine?"

"Yes, John picked this out for you all by himself."

Mother's eyes widened.

"I am just as surprised as you." I left Astrid on her bed, "Let me show you what we received from Lady Hopper's estate. We don't have anything new for ourselves."

Mother stood in the doorway, breathless, "Oh! It's rosewood. Your father and I owned a similar headboard, only rectangular with carved roses." I heard the sadness in her voice. I hoped she and Albert might see each other more.

"Your bathroom is beautiful. I love the black and white tiled floor." I showed them the writing desk on the landing, a perfect fit in the space left by the removed window seat. "Your sitting area at the window will be perfect for reading."

"I love overlooking the garden, but the view from my desk isn't the greatest; an abandoned house. It's been for sale for years, apparently."

Astrid yelled, "Can we go upstairs?" She peeked around the corner, "Can we, please?"

"I want to warn you; the rooms aren't finished. The wallpaper hasn't come in yet, and there's no furniture."

Mother asked what we were planning for the two rooms on our way up. I told her we decided to make a nursery and a room for a nanny in a single large room. She was thrilled, but Astrid stared broodingly at her shoes, rocking on her heels, rubbing her fingers.

"Don't worry, Astrid, you can play songs for the baby and push the pram in the park."

On Astrid's face, with squinty eyes and a scowl, "Where's the baby?"

"Oh, goodness! We won't have a baby for a long while."

In her matter-of-fact way, she gave an okay. I suggested we go downstairs for tea and scones.

Astrid turned to me, her intense green eyes scrutinizing me, "Are you having a baby? Where will my piano be?"

"Like I said upstairs, no, I'm not having a baby. You'll have a keyboard in your room just like at your house now."

"But I couldn't spend the night 'cause there's no keyboard here."

"I will talk to John. Now bring the scones and cakes to the table in the living. I'll get the tea."

Astrid sat with her plate on her lap. "Astrid," said my mother, "put the plate on the table when you eat. Lee doesn't want crumbs on the floor."

Astrid put her plate on the table with grumbling.

"Come to the living room, Mother."

I lit the fire, "I have a gift for you." Handing her the carefully wrapped box, I said, "It's called tea rose." Inside sat a small pink cut-glass bottle, "I hope you like it. We watched them make it at a perfumery."

Astrid's fingers moved on her knees, tapping out the music in her head, mesmerized by the dancing flames. I didn't want to interrupt. She pulled her chair closer to the fire again.

"Whoa," I cautioned, "you're getting too close. Pull the chair back, please. Now I have your attention; I have a gift for you."

Silent clapping, palms rhythmically hitting together was a new gesture for her and less attention-getting. "Presents, a present for me!" Under the side table were two boxes, one small and a bigger.

"Which one first? I don't know. Which one first? I have two?" I could see this wasn't working; she was confused.

"Here," I put the small box in her hand. "Go on, open it."

She acted like no one ever gave her a present. Methodically, she pulled the tape off and unfolded the paper; she opened the box. The firelight caught the crystal beads, making each one a prism of dancing rainbows. Astrid held them up; a medallion of the Blessed Mother held the strands of rosary beads anchored by a crucifix. It meant something special for Astrid.

Her eyes shined in disbelief. Then, rolling the aurora beads between her fingers, she kissed the medallion of St Mary. For her, this was a holy relic. Moreover, it came with a card blessed by Pope Paul.

She handed the card to my mother. She clutched them to her chest and began to say her Hail Mary verse.

Mother put her hand on Astrid's shoulder, "You can finish your Hail Mary later. Lee has something else."

I said, "Well, it won't compare to a rosary, but open it."

"It's a tee-shirt. Hippies wear these." She held it up. "It's pretty. Hippies wear these."

"Do you like it?"

She put it back in the box. I couldn't tell if she liked it. "It's a picture of a famous window in Notre Dame. Do you like it, Astrid?"

"Hippies wear these." She said again. New approach: I said, "You can wear it, too."

She shook her head. "It's pretty. You can wear it to bed, Lee."

I looked at Mother; we both rolled our eyes simultaneously, then snickered.

Still clutching the rosary, her monotone voice rolled the words, "I like the house. I like my room. Can we go now?" All I could do was shake my head.

"Tell Lenora thank you for your beads."

"Rosary beads," she corrected Mother, "Thank you for my rosary beads. You can keep the shirt. Hippies wear them."

Astrid turned around; I glanced at Mother and smacked the palm of my hand on my forehead.

"You know how she is," Mother whispered. I accepted defeat. I helped Astrid with her coat. John wasn't going to be happy that she rejected his gift. I whispered to Mother, handing her the tee-shirt, "Please, take it, you'll hurt John's feelings."

"Let's go. I want to go in the car, please," Astrid pleaded.

"Car?" I said in disbelief, "What car?"

"Albert helped me renew my license." Mother grinned.

"Well, bully for you!" I kissed her cheek," Be careful in this city; people drive carelessly. These are not the lazy roads of the countryside."

"I will; Astrid sits in the backseat," she winked. I waved goodbye and couldn't wait for John to come home to share Astrid's excitement.

| 27 |

The Challenges of Marriage

Everything settled into a sense of normalcy. John appeared to be busy under a pile of law books. It was nothing for him to work late; now he worked after hours at home in his study. Behind his study was a small room, a library of sorts, with a bed. When John burned the midnight oil, he slept there, not wanting to disturb me. It didn't happen very often; he liked having sex too much.

Before Christmas, John obligated me to throw a dinner party for four couples from the law firm. I hired a caterer and housemaid. John became upset with me. John argued that I should be doing this work in no uncertain terms. The disagreements began over a woman's place in the home. I couldn't work if I did the endless task of cleaning, cooking, and playing a gracious hostess. John disagreed. I didn't care. The money for the extra help came out of my bank account. I kept him ignorant of the balance of that account by putting half of what I earned away. I paid the housemaid and the caterers from our house account. The house sparkled; lamb chops with mint jelly were scrumptious. The ladies retired to the parlor, the men to the living room, and I hated the cigar smoke smell in the drapes. At ten, our guests left.

"You made me proud tonight, Lee. I will never argue about extra help again."

"Thank you; I hired the housemaid for permanent duty. She is spectacular and will take a huge burden off my shoulders."

Trying to stave off another argument, I said I'd pay her out of my salary.

"And that's the end of any disagreement, John. I simply need help keeping this house in order." He gave in, but not without a trip to the bedroom. It's the price I paid.

With Christmas around the corner, I found myself working late some days to get my last classes finished, preparing for the shutdown during the December holidays. John expressed his happiness when setting out to Christmas shop without Astrid in tow, a puzzling remark since he rarely saw her. When John worked late, I went to see her.

John's work took its toll on him. Some nights he'd come home frustrated and head straight for the bourbon. When we made love, it moved from tender to fast and furious. I read that some men needed sex to work out their frustrations; I accepted this theory.

Three days before Christmas, we journeyed to the Hopper Estate. Astrid needed the break as much as we did. Mother popped off a surprise the week before Christmas; she and Albert were engaged.

Albert asked Astrid permission to marry my mother to tamp down the chances of drama. In return, Astrid asked Albert if he would be her dad. The question caught him by surprise. Astrid shrugged her shoulders; she then stated he stayed at the house all the time anyway. She also questioned if Mr. Godfrey would still be her teacher. Albert convinced her nothing would change; Astrid said okay, then ran up the stairs. Two seconds later, Astrid ran back down and asked if they would make the wedding like mine.

Mother said no, they were getting married differently, but she could be a bridesmaid again. Astrid ran back to her room. She came down to ask if she could wear her princess dress.

Albert, tired of her questions, said they could talk about everything later.

It was a genuinely unremarkable Christmas at the Hoppers' estate; same food, same small talk. Astrid played Christmas songs, still displaying her awkward moments. For the first time, I noticed Astrid lost the look of a child. Next May, she would turn twenty-two. Mother and Albert were her protectors from predators. On more than one occasion, Mother shielded her from men making advances. She never went anywhere alone. The January trip to Princeton worried me. I wished I could go with her. Schools will be back in session by that point, which meant I'd be back to work.

Christmas night was quiet after dinner. Most of the older adults retired, leaving us and two male cousins—Phillip included—and Astrid. John poured brandy for us, except for Astrid, who was allowed a small glass of wine.

I overheard Philip tell John how he admired Astrid's beauty. John acknowledged his remarks but added how she was fragile.

"I'd be gentle with her." I found his implication to be crass and inappropriate.

Bristling, I said, "You'd be wise to leave her be."

He looked down his nose at me, "Oh, come now." Phillip took two steps toward the unassuming Astrid. John gripped his arm, "It's best to leave her alone if you know what I mean." He pulled away from John.

"I hear girls like her are easy."

I wanted to slap him across his face. John grabbed him, escorting him to the door; John grinned at me, "We're going outside for a minute."

I nodded my head with a half-smile, "Don't hurt yourself."

I join Astrid with her glass of wine. With a steady gaze into the fire, Astrid asked, "Do you think I'll get a boyfriend?"

"Do you want one?"

"I dunno." She continued to stare at the fire. "Sometimes, when I see people smiling together, I want someone to smile with me."

I wanted to ask about Charles but thought better of it. She was breaking my heart; I patted her hand, "Maybe someday we'll find a nice someone for you."

John returned, rubbing the knuckles on his right hand, his face red from the cold. "We'll have no more quarrels. I'm sure."

Seeing John's swollen knuckles, I said, "John Hopper, you're an honorable man." We escorted Astrid to the guesthouse, where Mother and Albert were still awake.

"I am returning precious cargo," said John.

Astrid gave him a funny look. I whispered, "You're precious to him." She put on her blank stare. On the way back, I let him know if Astrid knew, she'd be flattered by the protection of her honor. I appreciated what he did. The fact that it was Phillip was even better.

"My knuckles will appreciate the gesture. You can show me your appreciation in a few minutes."

I grinned, "I'll let you unwrap this Christmas present."

| 28 |

The Shift

"We have to go to your mother's tonight; it's urgent, Lee."

He never called me at work. Frantic; I asked, "What's happened to Mother?"

"Nothing, it's not bad. I promise. Just meet me there after work."

"Okay." Two hours to wait. My mouth dried, my mind was jumbled. What was so urgent? I spoke with Dr. Hammersmith about John's urgency. I asked to leave early. She gave me a sheepish grin, "I hope you're not leaving us."

I smiled, "I'll have your job when you retire." She thought it funny. Little did she know, I meant it. I was so beside myself, I hailed a taxi.

Opening the front door when I arrived, Mother called to me from the kitchen, "Do you have any idea what this is about?"

My eyes grew large, "I thought you knew."

"No, but I expect you to stay for dinner," she said, coming through the door.

"Of course. I'm hoping it's good news." Albert ruffled his newspaper like Grandfather used to do, "I hope so too."

"Me, too!" Astrid truly didn't understand what we were saying.

The bell rang at six-fifteen; Astrid ran to get it.

"It's John Hopper!" She sounded like a game show host, "And he brought flowers."

I ran to him in a panic. "Out with it!" I called.

"Sit, everyone. I haven't been candid. As you know, I've been working late many nights; I was working my tail off. I've been working with Barrister Samuels. They've offered me a full position in corporate affairs with an office of my own. I couldn't have accomplished this without your patience, darling. "

To the shouts of *hurrah*, John picked me up and swung me around. I kissed him.

With her hands flapping, Astrid shrieked, "Swing me around too!"

"No," intervened Mother, "no more swinging."

John took a bottle of champagne from the bag he brought, "I think a toast is in order." He poured us all a glass; even Astrid has some.

I spoke, "Here's to a bright future. I'm so proud to be your wife."

"And me, too. John Hopper!" Astrid shouted. John kissed her on the cheek; she wiped his kiss from her cheek with a *yuck*.

"Astrid, please set the table. On the menu tonight is shepherd's pie."

"One of my favorites," said John.

Over dinner, we discussed Astrid's upcoming competition in Princeton, New Jersey. I worried about her flying. Albert has been taking her to Heathrow Airport twice a week, coaching her on travel. Our family doctor prescribed a sedative.

"We're flying first-class," said Albert. "She'll have room to stretch. We recorded her playing all the pieces on cassette tape. It has headphones. It's a handy little device."

"When do you leave?" John inquired.

"We fly out on Tuesday," said Mother. "It will give us all time to get over the jet lag."

John elbowed Astrid, "Are you excited?"

Astrid did not act excited; she didn't answer.

"Astrid," I said, "answer John's question, please."

"I'm okay."

Everyone focused on her. "Is there a problem? If you want to go, you better lose the attitude. We paid for everything; it's expensive." Mother grumbled.

"I'm going." Astrid used her usual monotone, "May I be excused?" Astrid wasn't herself.

"Alright, rinse your dishes," Mother said.

Albert, clearly concerned, chimed in. "She hasn't been herself lately. Emotions like a yo-yo, up one minute, down the next. She threw the biggest temper tantrum I've ever seen. Poor Godfrey called me for help."

Shocked, I wanted to know if anything changed or if anyone else saw her. Albert pondered my question. A light bulb seemed to flash in his mind. Tapping his finger on his cheek, "I wonder if she overheard our conversation about brain research."

Stunned, I asked, "What brain research?"

"There are only a few research studies on an evolving mental disability called autism, a brain dysfunction," he explained. "In Astrid's case, few women are classified as savants. She has always been part of this study. The research institute wants to do something new, a brain scan. It maps the brain."

"Does Astrid know they want to do this to her?" I could feel the resentment rising within.

"We haven't decided to carry on with the study. To continue the study, we'd like to do a brain scan on Astrid."

"Does she know about this?" Mother turned to Albert, "We haven't discussed any of this with her or in front of her."

"I have a suspicion she knows." I turned to John, "Do you mind if I talk with her? I feel we've spoiled your evening, Barrister Hopper." I kissed him on the cheek.

He flicked his wrist, "Go on; it's alright."

I walked upstairs and peeked through the door. Astrid sat at her desk with headphones. Her eyes opened, I waved, "Can I come in?"

She took off the headphones. Astrid's face was stony, very unlike her. I sat on the bed and patted the mattress, beckoning her. She plopped down on the bed, holding her hands tightly together.

I put my arm around her shoulder, "What's wrong, mouse? You're not yourself?" I gave her time to answer, but she didn't say anything. She clutched her stomach.

My voice was just above a whisper, "I don't know how to help if you couldn't give me a clue."

"I can't talk about it," she said. I felt panicked; my mind wandered to a very dark place.

"Has someone hurt you? You must tell me, Astrid. We always keep each other's secrets. Haven't we?"

"Yes. I don't like people touching me. I hear things."

Oh, God, was her mental health going down the drain? "What kind of things do you hear? Are they bad voices?"

"The voices aren't angry. Instead, they whisper and say they want to put me in a tube with loud banging sounds. I'm scared if it's true; I'm scared I imagined it."

Now I knew she heard Mother and Albert.

"Astrid, you are an exceptional kind of person. Most people with your gift of music are boys. There are times when doing different tasks is hard for you. Dr. Dryer believes the more research people do, the more it will help others."

More fear than panic filtered through her voice, "Yes, but I don't want to go into a tunnel with loud noises. Or have needles in my head." The thought of needles in her head made my head hurt.

"Needles! Where did you hear that?" She didn't say anything. "I'm not going to say you should do these things, do you understand? Everyone is worried for you. We want you to be happy. I want you to play better than anyone in Princeton. Should we talk to Dr. Dryer?"

"You have needles in your head, Lee."

"No, I don't, Astrid. I got shots before, but no needles in my head."

She was silent until I held her hand, afraid the right words may not come out.

We came downstairs a while later. John leaned on the mantle by the fire, his head tilted pensively. Mother and Albert sat in separate chairs. We took our place on the sofa.

I asked Astrid if she wanted to talk first. Like a vice, her grip caused my fingers to smash together.

"Okay, I'll start. Astrid is scared. She heard something terrifying, not knowing if it's real or not."

Mother sat on the edge of her chair, pressing her lips together; Albert spoke up, "What is it, Astrid?"

"Don't want in the tube, or have needles in my head; bad things happen in the tube. Loud, scary noises."

Now they understood; she'd eavesdropped on their conversations. Albert explained the noise was loud from the machine. She could wear headphones to help with the noise. They wanted to see what makes a person like her different, gifted. It makes a map of the brain. He explained in more detail how people like her are helping doctors find better ways of treatment

"Treatment?" She looked at me, scared.

Dr. Dryer continued, "By treatment, I mean by doing this test, we can help people learn skills. You, my love, function higher than most savants. We want to know why you're so smart."

"I'm not smart; Lee is smart. I know I'm different. I have troubles; lots of troubles." She was on edge.

"Astrid," I said, "you can do many tasks the way others cannot. You're smarter than me in French. Besides, your abilities in music are something extraordinary."

Mother gave her a guarantee no harm would come to her. She said that Astrid was old enough to make her own decisions.

"For now, put all of this talk away. You," Mother said firmly, "have a suitcase to pack."

Astrid examined my face for confirmation, "Tell me you won't worry about all of this nonsense, and you will play your best in Princeton."

She hugged my neck; our foreheads touched. We both giggled; she promised to do her best.

On the way home, I expressed my concerns about Astrid. I also apologized for the interruption of his brilliant news.

He licked his lips, gave a sly side glance, "You can make it up to me at home."

"I will," I replied. Our sex life was improving. I'd shown John what Tilly taught me, bringing me to the brink of satisfaction, which made his urge stronger, explosive.

Dr. Hammersmith kindly gave me the day off to see Astrid off at the airport. I knew she felt scared. It was one time I was happy to be wrong or sort of wrong. Mother drugged her before we left. The ride to the airport took forty minutes. When we arrived, Astrid could barely walk.

"Are you okay?" I cupped her face between my hands. I wondered if she even heard me; a bit of drool slid from the corner of her mouth. She listed; I held her up, wiping the drool from her mouth with a tissue.

Incensed, I growled at Mother, "What have you done to her?"

"It's nothing. She'll be fine. It's a tranquilizer, nothing more." The way Mother dismissed my concern hurt.

I wasn't satisfied with her answer, "Really! I thought you might give something to sleep, not knock her out."

"Stop acting like a wet hen, Lee, for God's sake."

We got to the gate; I could go no further with Astrid. I hugged her rag doll form. "I love you, my shining star." I doubted if she knew what I said. What my mother did to her wasn't in Astrid's best interest; it was for herself. Mother took her by the hand; Albert joined them. It broke my heart to see her drugged and listless. It reminded me of the asylum; I hated it. They disappeared down the corridor.

| 29 |

Failure

John shuffled into the house, hanging up his raincoat; rain came down for fours day straight, matching his mood. He grumbled about a case he was working on. Sadness overtook me as I prepared supper.

I noticed his silhouette against the door frame; his arms crossed his chest. I sensed him staring as I moved through the motions of setting the table.

"What's wrong, Lee? You looked like you lost your best friend." Then, realizing what just came out of his mouth, he recoiled, "You didn't… is Astrid okay?"

I crumpled into the kitchen chair.

Fear filled his voice, "What happened?"

"She came in third."

"God!' His hand jolted to his chest, "I thought she died! Coming in third isn't a tragedy."

"It is to her. Mother and Albert are baffled. Her timing was off. Her joy is lost."

He grasped my hand, "I don't understand." I struggled with how to best describe what I meant.

"You've watched her play. Remember the way she appears when she plays. There's passion; she *becomes* the music."

"Yes, she is extremely passionate."

"Mother described how Astrid's passion dwindled as she played. Disappointed, Albert tried to get Astrid to talk about what transpired. She said nothing."

"Really?" John sat there as baffled as I.

"I asked to speak to her; she refused." I began to cry. "I talked; she didn't respond, John. I'm helpless to know what she needs. Astrid has always expressed her worries to me, even if to no one else."

"She's not speaking at all?" I shook my head.

"I've heard of a disorder called catatonia. It's a disconnect. Some people have strange movements like lying down but holding the neck inches off the pillow. I researched a case in law school; a normal factory worker became rigid, holding his arms out like a crucifix for no apparent reason. As a result, he lost the ability to communicate."

I sat on the edge of my chair, anxious to know his fate, "What happened to him?"

"They admitted him to a mental facility. It sounds horrible, but they shocked his brain a few times; he lost some long-term memories. After that, however, he never experienced another incidence."

I bolted up from my seat, "Oh, gosh. What if this is happening to Astrid?

"Maybe Astrid is in a state of confusion. Perhaps she doesn't know how to process losing."

It made perfect sense, a plausible theory. I chose to believe. Mother, Albert, and Astrid were coming home tomorrow.

After dinner, John asked me about my job; was I still happy there, was I bored, did I give thought to any alternatives? But, again, the hints were anything but subtle.

I let it all hang out, as they say, "We have been married less than six months. I hope you're not anticipating having a family yet because I'm positively not ready for motherhood."

"Well, I want you to be happy."

"Any time someone says they want me to be happy, there's a self-serving reason behind the statement."

"Don't get upset with me, please. When do you suppose we might be ready? You're not taking the pill, are you?"

Inside my head, I said, *answer his question but volunteer nothing*.

"No, I don't take the pill; it's dangerous."

"Good." He was fishing for an answer. "I didn't find a diaphragm in the drawer."

"There are other means of birth control, John."

"Any you might want to discuss? This should be a mutual discussion, don't you think?"

"You could wear a raincoat."

John took a swig of brandy, pointed his finger at me, "Oh, no, you don't! I'm not wearing one of those, my love."

"So, it's all on me. Okay, then you can withdraw. Or I can use a cervical sponge and spermicide."

"I'm not withdrawing. That part of me is too hard to control, sorry."

"Then the sponge."

"I've heard other men say spermicide can cause skin irritation. We'll let Mother Nature take her course."

"I will not let Mother Nature take her course. An implanted device lasts for seven years."

"Implanted device? That sounds dreadful. And seven years! Do you want to wait seven years? I forbid it!"

"You *forbid* it? What gives you the right to tell me what I can and cannot do to my body? I did not refer to us. I merely said it lasts seven years, not *I want* to wait seven years!"

"As your husband, I have a say in your birth control!"

"Well, here's a solution, Barrister Hopper." I ran upstairs, "It's called abstinence!

"How dare you take that tone with me, Lenora!"

I threw his pillow and blanket down the stairs. "Good night."

He hollered, "Rubbish, Lee. This is my house, too. I'm coming up."

He struggled up the stairs with a pillow under his arm, dragging the blanket. I sat exhausted on the bed; he was remorseful,

"I get it, Lee. What do you want to do?"

"The birth control pill had too many unknowns. I've opted for an intrauterine device with minimal side effects, John. I can have it removed anytime when we're ready to start a family. Not that I need your approval, but is this decision okay with you?"

Beaten, he conceded, giving his approval. I didn't tell him I already had one; he didn't need to know. With all that was happening with Astrid, that discussion should not have happened. I was upset enough.

The carpet beneath my feet stood threadbare from people like me anticipating an overseas flight to land. The wool coat came off, and my face felt flushed; my stomach churned with worry. Hopefully she'd talk to me.

Because of new security measures, I couldn't get closer to the gate. Their British Airways jet taxied to the gate. My heart didn't know whether to beat happy or upset. Over the intercom, a voice announced their arrival; I impatiently waited. Even standing on my toes, I couldn't see over the top of the incline where passengers arrived. People begin filtering down through the security checkpoint.

There they were; my mother and Albert flanked Astrid. Her eyes were glazed and lifeless; I thought she was probably still drugged. Mother smiled and waved. My concern was with Astrid; no cheery greeting from me.

I hurried to Astrid, hugging her, rocking her back and forth, telling her how much I loved her.

"Did you drug her again?" They couldn't miss my apparent displeasure.

"Pipe down," said Albert. I guess he didn't want the world to know how pissed I was. I took Astrid's hand; a short walk to the baggage claim, then Albert hailed a taxi. Mother informed me that Astrid had spit out the pills. I was as mad as a storm in a teacup; Astrid shuffled along.

Once home, I took Astrid to her room. We sat together on the edge of her bed. With her hand in mine, I said, "Astrid, we have no secrets. Tell me what happened. No one else has to know."

No response. I lifted her chin; "Show me your eyes, Astie. I want to talk to you. Are you in there somewhere?"

She blinked like someone coming from a deep sleep. The first words that alarmed me were, "She's gone, she left with all of her music."

"Where did she go? I want her back."

"Oh, Luna, I don't want to come back. I messed up. There's no music left in me."

"But you have to come back to me. I don't care about the music. I need you."

"It's gone; I couldn't play anymore. I don't hear the notes in my head anymore." Lost somewhere in a place, I could not go; I just couldn't lose her.

"I tried to remember the notes, Lee, but they kept drifting away like bubbles," her hands tried to catch imaginary bubbles, "so fast I couldn't catch them anymore."

"Lie down with me."

"No, go home to John. He'll be angry. He'll be upset with you and mad at me."

"No, he won't. John knows where I am." I struggled to get more insight, "I know, let's go to my room. The moon is full tonight."

Clomp, clomp, clomp, her heavy feet trudged up the stairs. The moonlight poured through the skylight illuminating the room with a bluish tint. On our backs, in my bed, we gazed at the stars. She took my hand.

"My heart is alone, Lee. No one will want me without my music."

"That is not true, Astrid."

"I have no music; no music in here," she pointed to her heart. "People only want my music."

"Not me. I want you to find your happiness again. It doesn't have to be music. You are my star; I'm all alone without you."

"I want to be up there. I want to be an Astra." Astrid pointed to the star-filled sky.

"Astrid, what do you mean?" My heart jumped into my throat. Did she want to die?

"I want to float among the stars." Her hand waved slowly from left to right, coming to rest over her heart.

"You don't mean to die, do you?" I waited for her answer.

"No, just float."

I breathed a sigh of relief, "Are you tired?"

She nodded yes. I suggested Astrid change into her nightgown; she resisted.

"Lee, can I sleep in your bed?"

"Of course you can. Take off your shoes, and I'll tuck you in."

Astrid kicked her shoes off. When I pulled the covers up, she latched onto my hand. "Don't tell Albert and Mary the music is gone, please, Lee. If you do, I'll run away, and you'll never find me. I'll run away."

They must know; I had no choice but to tell them. So, I lied to Astrid. "I won't, just rest. Things will be different tomorrow." My heart crumbled into a million tiny pieces.

I made my way downstairs. Mother sat on the edge of her seat, "How is she? Did she say anything?"

"Albert," in anger, I guffed, "You don't know if the drugs disturbed her mind, do you?"

"I can say with certainty they did not." His voice was full of resentment. With the new disorder, autism, I knew he couldn't be sure. Fighting with Dr. Dryer wasn't an option. We sat in silence, without a plan of how we'd deal with this situation. The phone rang, John's voice sounded harsh and controlling. He demanded I return home. I took the phone to Mother's bedroom to keep our conversation private. Unreasonable demands came from him. Anger seethed in me; I'd endured enough.

"John Hopper," I said with as much calm as I could mustard, "I'm needed here. I'm not coming home tonight."

"I'll come over and drag you home if I have to."

A flash of the schoolyard bullies tore through my mind, "You and whose army? I told you many times; I won't be bullied by you or anyone else. You're my husband; I expect more empathy from you."

"You never gave me a chance to tell you, but I'm going to court in Wales tomorrow. I'll be gone for a few days. I hope to find you home when I return. Goodbye, Lee."

His goodbye sounded final; I shouldn't have married him. My eyes were full of tears, angry tears. Mother called for me wanting to know if everything was alright. She thought I was upset with John until I explained his court appearance in Wales tomorrow morning to mask my anger.

"You should go home, dear. Astrid will be fine."

"No, I'm staying with her. John wanted me to stay." I'd lied to Astrid and now Mother. She didn't need the truth. She'd be on his side; I should be a good wife. I knew my mother didn't believe John wanted me to stay. The conversation stopped. My concerns were for Astrid.

"Astrid told me the music's left her. In her words, the notes were floating away; she couldn't catch them. Her fear is no one will want her anymore." The floodgates opened; these were tears I couldn't hold back. Mother's arm wrapped around me; I felt like a lost child. I was a lost child, helpless to comfort my only true friend. Regaining my composure, I left Mother and Albert to contemplate Astrid's fate. In my room, moonlight washed over Astrid. She frightened me. Arms crossed over her chest, eyes wide open, a blank stare; I thought she was dead. Panicked, I froze. I watched her chest rise and fall; she wasn't dead. Thank God!

Sitting on the side of the bed, I took her hand, "I'm spending the night with you, my Astra."

"Okay, my Luna."

The chest of drawers still held some of the clothes I left behind. I handed Astrid a pair of my flannel pajamas; she slipped the pants over her long legs. She stared at me, then at her feet. The pants were comically too short.

"They don't fit. These are not mine. The pants don't fit. I want mine."

"Sit, I'll go. Which drawer?"

The top is underclothes and socks. The second drawer is …."

She rattled off the inventory of each drawer: color, size, and texture.

"Third drawer, left-hand side, pink flannel nightgown."

"Is that what you want? The pink flannel nightgown?"

"Yes, the one with tiny red roses." With her finger making the tiniest opening, she whispered, "Tiny roses, tiny red roses."

"All right, the nightgown with tiny red roses, I'll get it,"

"Pink, Lee, pink."

Struggling to get the gown over her wiggly body, "Couldn't you do this? Who dresses you when I'm not here?" Astrid cringed and sat on the bed. "I'm sorry, Astie. It's been a long day for everyone. Scoot over." Her head rested on my chest as I stroked her long silky hair. In my heart, my marriage came to an end during that conversation. John needed a traditional, old-fashioned wife; I was not that person. He didn't need me, and I didn't need a husband.

"Luna?"

"Yes, Astra."

In a voice void of emotion, she recited, "I love you to the moon and back."

Surprised, I asked, "Where did you hear that?"

"On the telly."

My arms wrapped around Astrid. Her head rested on my chest; I knew Astrid would be my child, my only child.

PART II

Seven Years Later

| 30 |

The 1980s

Mother and Dr. Dryer parted ways years ago. Caught in a lie, Albert admitted Astrid was his experiment, as I always suspected. Mother expressed how she felt foolish for Albert's lies. Throughout the rest of her life, guilt plagued her. I believe the drugs altered Astrid's brain; she was more childlike.

Life with John was a battle I got tired of fighting. My marriage had gone into shambles. I did the unthinkable, divorcing John. Women like Mother never divorced. I was never like her. At times, Mother could get cheesed off at me. She leveled accusations; I shamed her. The divorce was always my fault, no matter what. According to my mother, I let Astrid ruin my marriage and made her feel incapable of taking care of Astrid. In my heart, I knew by marrying John, I fulfilled her wishes. John returned to his ballerina, who gave him three children, something I could never do. Having a baby never suited me; I could never imagine myself as the mother of an infant.

Tilly, from my island adventure, said it perfectly: don't marry before you turn twenty-five. Hindsight is always twenty/twenty. Sometimes, I wondered what happened to Tilly, my hippie mama. God, she was full of wisdom.

As time passed, my mother had terrible mood swings, making studying and working harder for me. She turned sullen, then sick. Astrid was so confused. It took a while before Mother disclosed her condition. Cancer, out of the blue, overtook her. Vainly, she refused treatment, not wanting to lose her hair. While I was working on my doctorate, Mother's illness took a sharp turn for the worse; she required my care and a visiting nurse. Mother declined a hospice stay, choosing to die at home.

Suffering was a concept Astrid couldn't process. We started therapy twice a week. Unlike my mother, I couldn't be so selfish. Her decision to die at home was cruel.

The Sad Return to Dublin

I assumed guardianship of Astrid. And before she died, Mother planned everything for the funeral, making me promise to bury her next to my father in Dublin. With Astrid's debilitating fear of flying, we took Mother's coffin by train, then ferried her to Dublin. The hearse met us at the dock.

"Is Mrs. Mary in there dead?"

"Yes, Astrid."

Astrid held my hand as I cried in the cemetery of St. Audoen's church.

"It's okay, Lee," she said in a quiet voice. "Mrs. Mary is in heaven with your daddy now."

"Yes, Luv, they are together again."

On that somber grey Irish day, Astrid laid a wreath of roses on the dirt and waved, "Goodbye, Mrs. Mary, I'll see you later, in the sky. Right, Lee? We'll see her in the sky."

With a knot in my throat, I smiled and nodded yes, still numb from it all. So many questions from Astrid, answers I didn't have. I did the best I could.

Dublin City had changed; I'd forgotten many things. Leaving as a traumatized eight-year-old, how couldn't I? One memory of the few I have from my father is crossing the Ha'penny Bridge. I walked with Astrid on the bridge.

"Why are there no cars, only people?" she said.

"The Ha'penny Bridge is only for people to cross the water," I told her. "A long time ago, it cost a halfpenny to cross." Then she asked if pennies were hay inside. Sometimes I forgot to be literal. "Pennies are not made from hay; they are just a half penny to spend."

"Okay."

The day couldn't have been drearier. A cold wind blew; Astrid held on to her hat. For years, no music came from her, not a note or a sound. That afternoon, she hummed. Afraid to say anything, I took pleasure in listening.

We found an Italian restaurant near our hotel. Astrid asked the slightly overweight waiter if his name was Angelo; I braced myself for embarrassment. He glanced at me like a scared rabbit; I nodded a "humor her" side glance. His answer made me chuckle. With a wink and a smile, he said, "No, I'm his brother, Antonio, but you can call me Tony." Astrid bought it, hook, line, and sinker, giving her order: pizza, extra pepperoni, extra cheese. When he asked for our drink order, Astrid announced her choice, "I'll have a beer, Tony!"

Flabbergasted, I said, "What did you say?"

"Beer, please."

Indignant, I answered, "You certainly will not." Tony got a chuckle. "We'll each have a cola. And please bring extra napkins."

On the way out the door, I overheard a conversation between two young punks laughing, saying Astrid was retarded. All I saw were two schoolyard bullies; those were fighting words. Astrid heard them. Before I could say a word, she flipped herself around, "I'm not a retard. You are because *I* live on the Isle of Genius." They were stupefied; I was stupefied. I winked at those bully boys and smirked, "No, she really does live there." We left.

I buttoned Astrid's coat against the chilly night air and held her hand on the way to the hotel. I couldn't stop smiling. Mother would be proud of her; she beat them with words, not fists. Grandfather must be smiling from heaven, too.

I woke up to Astrid pacing the hotel room floor, moaning. I sat up, "What's wrong with my bright star?"

In a voice of distress, Astrid moaned, "I don't want to, no, no, no. Don't make me, Lee!"

Hopefully, she could tell what bothered her. The fear of flying, she believed we were flying home.

"Oh, Astie," I cradled her. "We're not going on a plane; we took a boat. Listen to me; we took Mrs. Mary's coffin on the train, then do you remember what came next?"

"The boat, a big boat."

"That's right; not an airplane. Take your breaths, slowly in and out."

After a few breaths, Astrid's eyes popped open, "Can we eat breakfast now?" Bouncing on her heels, her hands flapping.

"Let's get dressed for the boat and have breakfast."

Mesmerized by the water, Astrid stood, both hands pressed against the ferry's window. As I watched her that day, I wondered what thoughts were in her head; the humming, the nightmarish memories. What secrets hide inside, Astrid Innis? Who holds the key to unlocking your mind? Right then, I wasn't sure what to do with her music. If I talked to her about music, I was afraid she'd rebel. If I didn't, would the music leave again?

| 31 |

Lyndon

Our world had changed; the whole world was in flux. Countries were racing to conquer the exploration of outer space. Women's rights were at the forefront of every conversation, whether for or against the issue. The war in Viet Nam ended badly. The televisions were in color. Our half-crown coins didn't exist as legal currency. For her twenty-seventh birthday, Astrid was given a portable cassette player with headphones. She never used it. Our half-crown coins didn't exist as legal currency. The Beatles broke up in the 70s. The London Underground was full of punk music. Much to my chagrin, cold-hearted goth teens in black were seen more often. They were cruel to Astrid.

I watched Astrid like a hawk. Our neighborhood was different; no cheery greetings, only silence from people passing by. Once fashionable apartments had become rental properties in disrepair. Our economy tumbled. The internet began creeping into homes by the late 1980s, answering our questions with lightning speed. Everyone owned a cordless phone.

The Space Race flourished during my time at Cambridge, leading to my master's degree in astrophysics. The subject that once belonged to dreamers was now a reality. The need to drop out of my doctoral program came with Astrid in my care. My life was difficult without

Mother. Dr. Lyndon Hammersmith, my mentor, hired me as a research assistant. When Dr. Hammersmith offered me a part-time job where Astrid could come with me, I jumped at the chance. I'd learned to use a computer for my research on asteroid paths. The clock ticked away as more rockets and a Space Station rushed to be built.

Research kept me busy. Technology provided more data than ever before. It allowed me to analyze photographs from telescopes worldwide.

Mother had taught Astrid to knit. I bought a bean bag chair for my small office after being told bean bag chairs were suitable for people with autism. They called it "cocooning." While I worked, I heard the clicking of her needles. It used to bother me, but not anymore.

The planetarium moved to the Observatory grounds; I took Astrid to the shows once a month. Astrid asked continually about Sunday Mass at St. Marten's Church. The last pew was our chosen spot; she became antsy and "whispered" during service, attracting unwanted attention.

No longer the diagnosis of profoundly mentally retard, the word now was autism. The research was on genetic science and not just a behavior disorder. Astrid's condition is formally known as an Autistic Savant. Routine was the key that kept Astrid on an even keel. While there are many drugs to stabilize her moods, I refused everything except sleeping medication. We went to therapy once a month now.

After one visit, Astrid sat by the fire. Eyebrows puckered, with a serious face, she asked, "Am I still a retard?"

"Astie, you were never retarded. You have a disorder called autism. It means you understand many things. You're very good at," I paused to wonder if I should even say music, "memorizing."

"I know about flags and dogs."

"Yes, you do. You're very smart."

The psychologist tried my patience with new, improved medication; I refused to have her drugged anymore, only allowing sleeping medication. Her fits came from frustration.

Dr. Davis stupidly believed Astrid could harm herself or me. Too late for that; I had the battle scars. It was nothing I couldn't handle. Any time he even suggested institutionalizing her, I'd explode. He even had the nerve to tell me I should consider an antidepressant! I wasn't depressed. This was the way my life was, that's all.

Then he came out with, "I know this isn't a pleasant subject, Ms. McConnell, but if you should die before Astrid, do you have a plan?"

"Of course I do! How insulting! I would never leave her alone." I grabbed an unsuspecting Astrid's hand and we left. Waiting for the city bus, Astrid asked, "Are you going to die, Lee? Because if you do, I'm going with you."

"The only place we're going is to Angelo's for pizza."

The hand flapping no longer bothered me. I overlooked the reaction of strangers. Astrid expressed happiness in odd ways; she brought me joy.

Astrid went right to sleep that night. I ruminated over Dr. Davis' words. He was correct; I needed help. I called Dr. Hammersmith, apologizing for calling after nine. I couldn't put this issue off anymore. For years, she'd suggested I bring in some help.

"Please don't say I told you so, Lyndon."

She listened to my plight and offered to make some calls.

"Why not come to lunch on Saturday?"

"Oh, what a nice idea, Lee. I'll come with bells on."

As I hung up, guilt washed over me; I'd involved Lyndon in my plight. With no new friends and old ones moving away, I had no one to turn to. When my role changed to Astrid's caregiver, I couldn't leave her by herself, even for an hour. It was simply out of the question. With a non-existing social life, I felt no other choice. My life revolved around Astrid; in many ways, it always had.

I helped Astrid dress for Dr. Hammersmith's visit. I shouldn't call Lyndon *doctor* around Astrid. Several times I reiterated Lyndon wasn't a medical doctor. Astrid couldn't comprehend; for her, all doctors were psychiatrists. At high noon, the bell rang. Lyndon arrived, met by Astrid, who took her hand and led her into the living room. Astrid stood there holding Lyndon's hand with a goofy smile plastered on her face. This wasn't her usual behavior, but she knew Lyndon.

"Astrid, Dr. Hammersmith can sit down now." I'd blown that one.

Dropping Lyndon's hand, Astrid's eyes narrowed, staring a hole in the ceiling. "Are you a real doctor?"

"Yes, but I'm a doctor of the stars."

"Okay," Astrid seemed satisfied with the explanation. "Can I go outside now?"

"What will you do outside, Astrid?" I asked.

"Listen to the birds."

"Yes, slip on your jacket." I always sat facing the back garden where I could see her. Lyndon lost her smile when Astrid left. "How are you, Lee? You take excellent care of her, but are you taking care of yourself?"

"I'm holding up. You know, good days and not-so-good days."

Her eyes shined wise, "Holding up isn't taking care of yourself. I have watched you diminish over the years, feeling helpless. When you called, I thought, now I can help. Or at least, try." Lyndon was probably ten years old than me, but a million times smarter.

"I put myself in your shoes thinking, what are the options for Astrid, other than an institution? There are private group homes with full-time caregivers. What do you think?"

Those were ideas tossed around previously. "I bucked against the idea of a group home, Lyndon. Those places are not regulated; believe me, I've checked. What do you mean by a caregiver?"

"Women out there who do more than keep house. When my mother's illness became too much to manage, I hired a living-in nurse. She became more of a companion for Mum. At that point, my mother could use a wheelchair. Julia took her to the art museum and shopping. She fixed meals for us: she was a saint, Lee."

"Did you say she lived with you?"

"Yes, I fixed my brother's bedroom for her. He'd moved to India. The room sat across the hall from Mum's; Julia knew when Mum needed her at night. With her there, it brought such comfort to me. It's something you should consider, Lee. You'd have live-in help freeing up time for yourself."

"I've been so blind to this option. Still, there are scores of what-ifs. And where would I find such a person who understands Astrid's needs?" I pleaded.

Lyndon spoke somberly, "You couldn't hold her hand forever, Lee. I've watched you sacrifice your adult life for her. I understand how you want to protect her. When is the last time you did something for yourself, alone?"

My eyes met the floor; I couldn't remember the last time I was alone.

Lyndon moved close to me; her arm rested over my shoulder. Out the window, in the garden, Astrid turned in circles. "Lyndon, she needs me. No one ever needed me the way she does."

Lyndon gave my shoulders a shake, "I'll help you find someone, Lee. If it takes a hundred interviews, we'll find the right person. Astrid would be well cared for if something were to happen to you. Okay?"

Sucking on my bottom lip, I nodded in affirmation. Astrid burst through the door heading straight to the refrigerator snatching her water bottle.

"Are you hungry, Astrid?" I asked.

She shook her mane, nodding *yes*. Astrid set the table for three, repeating *one, two, three, one, two, three*. Then something remarkable happened. Over ten years, she'd never talked about music; then she hollered, "I found a waltz!"

Chills ran down my spine; I grabbed Lyndon's hand, "She hasn't spoken a word of music for years. Astrid, you remembered the timing for a waltz?"

With the flip of her hair, she barked, "Of course, silly Lee. I play the piano. Can we eat now?" Astrid sat the water pitcher carefully on the table, "I'm not allowed to pour."

"May I pour, Astrid?" asked Lyndon.

Astrid sounded like a foghorn, "You have to ask the boss."

Lyndon didn't know if she should laugh; I didn't either. I asked Astrid where she learned to talk like that.

"On the telly."

"Merciful heavens, I let you watch far too much of the telly. Elbows off the table, missy." God, I'd turned into my mother. After lunch, Astrid went to her room; Lyndon told me of three reputable agencies. She'd give me a call later with names and phone numbers. Lyndon volunteered to screen candidates with me. At first, I balked, but Lyndon made a good point: two sets of eyes were better than one.

"I don't know how to thank you, Lyndon."

She smiled at me, "When we find a suitable companion for Astrid, you can take me to dinner."

"It would be my pleasure."

Lyndon gave me a squeeze, whispering, "I'm glad you thought to call me."

"So am I."

A few weeks later, I found a note taped to my computer, "Call me. I have some news. Lyndon." I'd call her from home, later. Astrid sat in the corner knitting away, but something was different. The typing stopped. I listened to Astrid humming; Beethoven's *Ode to Joy* I didn't know what to make of this. For now, I wouldn't say anything.

I never played the radio on the ride home in my mother's old 1965 MG Sports sedan. Astrid couldn't tolerate radio station advertising. My heart skipped when she began to hum the *Meadowlark* song. That night, Astrid was my music.

"Astrid, what song are you humming?"

"I dunno, just a song."

"Do you know where you could have heard it?"

She crossed her arms, "Nope, I made it up."

It was all I could do to restrain myself from saying more. Bedtime for Astrid came at nine o'clock, or the world was ending. After my goodnight cheek kiss and prayers, I called Lyndon.

Lyndon surpassed my expectations.

"Lee, I called three agencies, all highly recommended. One agency for special needs adults provided me with two names. Would you like for me to set up interviews, Lee?" I thought the question strange. I could do it myself.

"I'm sorry that probably sounded intrusive. You're certainly capable of doing this."

Guilt-ridden, I asked if she could be here for the interviews, "Someone said it couldn't hurt to have that extra set of eyes and ears. If you're interested, tell me when you're free."

Lyndon perked up, "Any Thursday or Friday afternoon, I don't have office hours at those times."

Lyndon conveyed the phone numbers. Since I didn't work the next day, I'd make some calls. She advised me to prepare Astrid. Her reactions to strangers were hardly pleasant.

The October winds whistled outside as I lit a fire. My nightly glass of chardonnay sat on the side table. After a couple of sips, I stared at the fire; my mind wandered back to a time since forgotten, the gala. Mother disapproving of my dress, meeting John and his now-wife, Emily. Lyndon was with Claudia: I wondered what happened to Claudia. No one said for sure if Claudia was her lover; people didn't talk of those things. I guess they still don't; caring for someone of the same sex was taboo.

| 32 |

Help

"Lyndon, will Thursday afternoon at three be okay? A1 Home Services has two candidates ready for interviews."

"Three is good. I'll put my scrutinizing cap on," Lyndon chuckled.

"Oh, Dr. Hammersmith, I know that cap," I laughed.

The most challenging class I ever took was astrophysics; Lyndon Hammersmith was the queen of scrutiny.

That evening, I sat down with Astrid to simplify what Thursday would bring. I prayed she'd understand. I heard the therapist's voice in my head, "Remember; she is only eleven. You're lucky; she understands more than most with her condition." Everything I said to her should be with the least number of words. I gave her the basics: Lyndon was coming, two ladies were coming, and I wanted to see if she could help me.

"Help you? Help you with what?"

Too much information; her forehead wrinkled for the longest time while she tried to process all I said. Then came a barrage of who and why questions. Why were ladies we didn't know coming to our house? Then things got tricky. I couldn't say, *Astrid, if I die, you'll need someone to take care of you.* I thought of every logical way to answer the eleven-year-old questions, but I rarely succeeded.

"Astrid, Luv, I need help around the house. If we have a nice lady to stay with us, she can do the laundry…" She interrupted me.

"And take out the stinky trash?"

"Yes, and take out the stinky trash."

"Who is she, where does she live, what's her name?"

"Whoa, slow down. I haven't met these ladies yet. That's why I need you to sit with me when they arrive. Can you do that?"

Astrid buried her face in the sofa pillow; a barely audible "okay" came out. From behind the pillow, I heard a question.

"Astrid, take the pillow from your face."

Still holding the pillow, she peeked over the top, "How many days?"

By now, I fully understood her half-questions. "They're coming on Thursday, one at three o'clock, the other at five. Thursday is two days away. Run upstairs and bring me your planner."

Dutifully, she fetched me her day planner, with doodles all over it.

"Red pencil, please."

"Ugh, why didn't you say that in the first place?" She stomped upstairs and ran back down, "Here!" She threw it in my lap and stood with her arms crossed.

"That is bad manners. Sit down, please." I circled the date in red, "Now you can remember. Lyndon is coming, too."

"Why?"

"So, the three of us can decide on who we like. That's why."

Astrid's head rested on my shoulder, "The clock says fifteen minutes until nine. I want to go to bed now, please and thank you."

"Yes, you may."

At nine-forty-five, the phone rang, scaring me half to death. Thank God Astrid took her pill earlier. Lyndon wanted to know if I'd spoken with Astrid. I replayed our conversation for her.

"It doesn't seem too terribly bad."

"No, but she threw a pencil at me later," I heard Lyndon gasp. "Honestly, it was almost comical."

"Now that she's older, is Astrid becoming harder to handle? Tell the truth, Lee, not what you think I should hear."

I didn't want to go there, but Lyndon would keep pressing me. "Yes, this is difficult." I paused. "My frustration comes from her inability to express her feelings. My inability to understand her frustrates both of us. When we were younger, I wrapped myself around keeping her from destroying everything in her path. Breathing techniques work sometimes. Other times, she hits her head on the wall. All I can do now is put a pillow between her head and the wall until she's exhausted."

"Oh, Lee."

"The only one who knows this is her psychiatrist. He wanted me to fit her with a helmet. Fat chance of that happening. Honestly, it doesn't happen that often." Lyndon asked a question I dreaded to answer: "Has she physically caused you harm?"

"Last year, during one of her fits," I sighed, "she broke two of my ribs. I drove to the hospital, praying they wouldn't admit me. While sitting in the emergency room, Astrid kept repeating, *I'm sorry.*"

"All the more reason you soon have help, Lee."

"I couldn't explain the truth of what happened. The authorities might have taken Astrid from me. I told the doctor I had fallen off the front steps. They wrapped me with an elastic bandage and told me not to laugh. If they knew how unfunny the comment was, they wouldn't have said it. I'm sorry; I've gone to the dogs." I wanted to cry.

"Pish-posh. After all, I did ask. I received exciting news. I wanted to wait, but I hope it will uplift your spirits. This morning my secretary laid an envelope on my desk from NASA. They studied our data collections, specifically your collection of asteroid trajectories, Lee. We are invited to a spring seminar at the Kennedy Space Center in Florida. It's on deep-space objects and flight safety. The Jet Propulsion Laboratory wants permission to use your data."

Floored, silent, I couldn't believe it. I immediately thought of Astrid.

"Lee?"

"I'm dumbfounded, Lyndon. I never thought my work was that important."

"Why? You have an advanced degree in astrophysics. You would have your doctorate if ... Sorry, Lee, I shouldn't have said that. Your intelligence is far greater than any student I've ever known."

"Should I cry or thank you? Or maybe both."

"It was careless of me to bring that up. I wish your life could be different. There's hope, you know. If the caregiver works out, you can have more time to finish your thesis. It's part of the reason I want to help you. If we find someone suitable, you can go with me," she paused, causing me concern. "I mean, you and four students of my choosing received invitations."

"I'm flattered, but we have to get through the first hurdle."

In bed, I laid awake, remembering a little girl sitting on her grandfather's lap as he pointed out the constellation of Virgo. "You gave me the gift of wonder. I love you, Grandfather."

Astrid came down for breakfast carrying her day planner, still in her robe and pink house shoes, "What is this red circle doing on my calendar?"

"The circle is a reminder; today, we have company. Lyndon is coming over this afternoon, and two ladies are coming to see if they can help us around the house."

"Okay. Now I want my scones, please and thank you. Oh, with tea and sugar and black currant jam."

Astrid's okays were her way of saying, *I halfway understand.* Over breakfast, I reminded her to sit with me when the ladies came.

"Chew with your mouth closed, please."

"Bad manners, bad manners, I know, I know."

I followed her up the stairs to approve her choice of clothes for today. Usually, I let her wear whatever she wishes unless we go out for dinner or an outing. Some days, she resembles a clown wearing a mishmash of stripes and plaids. But that day she chose a houndstooth skirt, a purple suede vest, a white blouse with long puffy sleeves, and her signature black leggings. Rocking side-to-side, arms crossed over her chest, she asked, "Did I do good, Lee? Did I?"

"Astrid, you've made a very sensible choice. I'm very proud of you." She flapped her hands, accompanied by bouncing up and down on her toes, with squeals of delight.

Astrid met Lyndon at the door. She accepted Lyndon as my friend. Astrid cleared the table, then sat in her armchair, her feet curled, kitting away. After lunch, we pored over the dossiers on the two women the agency chose. One of the candidates was older than me. I expressed my doubts about that one.

"I don't want her to die before me."

Astrid's radar tuned into our conversation, "Who's going die? Me?"

I shot her a look of contempt, "Turn your radar off. We're not talking about Astrid."

"Then who? You?"

Exasperated, I said, "Oh for God's sake, Astrid, no one is going to die."

"Mrs. Mary did."

"Okay, Astrid. Enough." I sighed, "This is what I deal with most days."

"It's precisely why you need help for her. How does she feel about having help?"

"She asked if the person would take out the stinky trash." There was no way I could keep a straight face; Lyndon couldn't either.

At precisely three o'clock, the doorbell rang; Astrid jumped up.

Lily

"I'll get it, Astrid," I called.

Lyndon stood up as I greeted the younger woman, "Astrid, come sit by me. Lyndon, can you sit next to this young lady?" Turning to look at our guest, I said, "I'm sorry. Lilith Michaels, this is my friend Lyndon Hammersmith, and this is Astrid." I took her coat.

Instead of sitting, Astrid stood behind the sofa, head down, hands behind her back, rocking up and down on her toes. I motioned for the young lady to sit by Lyndon.

"Come sit with me, Astrid. You can meet Lilith."

The young lady stood tall, of mixed race. Her skin was a beautiful copper brown, with loving brown eyes and a bright smile; she said, "You can call me Lily."

Eyes trained on the floor, Astrid blurted out, "I like that name; it's a flower name, Lilium Stargazer. And you're brown. She's brown, isn't she, Lee!"

With a pasted-on smile, I nodded at Astrid, "Yes, it is a pretty name." Astrid then decided to hide behind the sofa.

After reading Lily's experience, I knew the answers. My inquiry as to Lily's background was more for Astrid's benefit. Lily had finished nursing school and found working in the hospital didn't suit her. Instead, she opted for home care. She knew of Astrid's needs but knowing and seeing were two different pairs of shoes.

Halfway through the conversation, Astrid jumped up from behind the sofa, plopping down next to me, blurting out, "Do you take out stinky trash?"

Lily smiled, "Yes, I can take out stinky trash. But you have to show me the bin."

Astrid got up; I pulled her down next to me, "We don't need to show her just now."

She answered with an Eeyore-sounding *"Okay."*

Lily jumped back in, "Astrid, what do you like to do?"

Astrid stared at her lap, fiddling with her fingers., I said, "Please tell her something you like to do."

"Knit and eat pizza at Angelo's."

"Knit, how nice. I like pizza, too, Astrid," said Lily.

"Okay," said the unemotional Astrid.

"Do you want to show Lily something you made?" I prodded her.

She began to fidget, "No, can I go now?"

"Yes, you may."

"Where are you going?" asked Lyndon. Astrid pointed to her chair by the back window.

I turned to Lily. "She eavesdrops. We'll talk quietly. I didn't see any experience with special needs adults in the notes sent to me."

Lyndon asked, "What makes you qualified to handle a person with autism like Astrid?"

The smile on Lily's face changed to seriousness as she gathered her thoughts. After a minute, I said, "I expect an honest answer. While Astrid seems subdued today, she's given into occasional fits, sometimes in public. How could you handle a meltdown without experience?"

"I helped raise my brother. He was born with Down's syndrome. Because of that, people teased him heartlessly, and we are half African. Tad, my brother, was given to fits, also. The older he got, the harder it became for my mother. My father left when Tad turned three. At ten, she sent him to an institution even though I begged her to let him stay home. He died in St. Albans at age thirteen of pneumonia."

"Oh, Lily, I'm so very sorry. Astrid's needs are different," I said. "What do you know about autism?"

"I tried to research information before I came, but I didn't find much."

Lyndon chimed in, "That's understandable. You'd think by now, we should know more. Truthfully, it's like astronomy; we know space objects are out there, but not how and why. The operation of the brain is the same. We know it's there but how it operates is still a mystery."

Lily remarked, "In the description, I read she has a special gift, and her IQ is below average."

"Yes, Astrid and I met at age eleven. Astrid is childlike and still eleven in many ways, Lily. Classified as an autistic savant, she played the piano concertos of Beethoven and other composers by ear. Astrid defied the conventional definition of savant by composing music. One day, she stopped playing; no one can tell me why." I heard a catch in my voice; an unexpected tear came from the corner of my eyes.

Lyndon knew me too well, "You do realize this is a live-in position?"

"Yes, ma'am. I share a flat with two other people. So, truly I wouldn't mind."

Lyndon is a harsh realist, "You'll be responsible for taking her on outings, showers, and helping her during the monthlies."

Lily was a fish out of water.

I said, "We have a few others to interview. Thank you for your time, Lily. I'll be in touch. "Astrid," I called, "Could you get Lily's coat for her, please."

"Why?"

"She's going home, now."

"Is she coming back?"

"Are you going to get her coat?"

"No!"

"Very well." I helped with her coat and whispered, "This is mild compared to what you'd have to deal with if offered the position."

Pensive, she replied, "Oh, I see."

Astrid sat with her legs slung over the arm of the chair. "Astrid, you were rude to Lily."

A smart-mouth answer came out, "No, I wasn't! She could get her own coat."

I turned to Lyndon and shook my head in annoyance. An hour before the next woman came, I knelt in front of Astrid, who kept knitting, "I can see your bloomers, sit properly. I need you to listen. Please stop knitting and listen." In defiance, she dropped everything on the floor. I sighed. "How long have we been friends?"

"I dunno, a long time."

"I want you to use good manners as Mrs. Mary taught you. The other lady will be here soon, and I need you to sit by me. You can ask her a question if you like, but I'll tell you when to get up. Understood?"

"Okay."

I returned to the sofa. Lyndon suggested a drink after all this was finished. I did keep a bottle of whisky in the cabinet for a special occasion; this was certainly one.

"What did you think of Lily?" inquired Lyndon.

"She seemed nice enough, but her story of her brother, I don't know why, but an odd feeling came over me. She's only twenty-five. I thought she'd bolt for the door when you explained the terms. Do you think I'm wrong to be suspicious?"

"While I don't share your suspicion, I believe I understand the reason. I saw you wipe that tear away."

I recognized what she implied. "Lyndon, it's so hard to hand Astrid's care to someone else."

She handed me a tissue and hugged me, "It's about caring for yourself, too, Lee."

Fifteen minutes before the doorbell rang again, I pulled myself together.

Mildred

Fifty-year-old Mildred Evans came ten minutes late, explaining her son was ill. She still cared for her son; a red flag shot up.

"Please sit. I'm Lee, and this is my friend Dr. Lyndon Hammersmith. Astrid," I called, "Come sit with me, please."

"No, thank you."

"Blimey, she's a shy one," Mildred laughed. Her condescending tone I found off-putting.

I asked, "To be blunt, did you read the description of our needs?"

Mrs. Evans squirmed, and replied with a thick Cockney accent, "Well, not all of it, Misses."

With my forehead wrinkled, my eyes narrowed, I cocked my head, "Tell me what you know, please."

"Well, you need a housekeeper and someone to stay with the retard girl."

Astrid sat up and shouted, "I'm not retarded! I'm not! I'm not!"

Lyndon glared at the woman, "Shall I show her the door, Lee?"

About to blow a gasket I stormed, "Definitely!"

"She's a mean lady, Lee." Astrid grabbed my arm, "A mean lady, I don't like her."

"Me, neither. That woman will never come back here."

Lyndon and I were flabbergasted. How could they send someone like that? With a vice grip on my arm, Astrid fell to pieces, repeatedly saying how she was not a retard.

"Isn't there anyone out there?" I felt defeated. Astrid put her hands on my cheeks, turning my face at hers.

"Lee, I like the Lily lady." She let go of my face.

Lydon asked Astrid, "What if Lily stayed with you for a week to see if you like her?" Lyndon always knew what to say. Astrid wanted to know where the cocoa lady might sleep. I told her Lily could stay in Mrs. Mary's room; Astrid made her serious face.

"Where will you sleep? With me? Cause my bed is too small."

"I can sleep in my own bed." I needed a diversion. "Shall we go to Angelo's for pizza?"

Hands clapping, Astrid jumped up and down in excitement.

Astrid was a bit too excited. I sat with her in the backseat. I understood her overzealousness; that was why she sat in the back with her seat belt on. On the way, Astrid repeated, "Good manners," at least ten times.

"She's trying to remember," uttered a sympathetic Lyndon.

"Yes, she tries very hard."

Angelo's staff knew Astrid by name; Angelo always waited on us. I truly appreciated his kindness. I took Astrid to the loo before we sat down. After an overly excited accident a few months ago, this had become a necessary ritual

She slid into the booth, looked at Lyndon, then announced loudly with her half-smile, "I peed!" Something typical for Astrid caught Lyndon off-guard. Unable to help myself, I rolled my eyes, "Astrid, everyone in the restaurant didn't need to know you went to the loo."

When Lyndon and I ordered a glass of wine, Astrid asked for a glass, too. Angelo was aware of Astrid's tricks. When he brought the wine, Astrid received her wine glass full of sparkling grape juice. It appeased her to think she was drinking an adult beverage.

Astrid finished her bedtime routine with a kiss on the cheek. Referring to Lyndon, Astrid asked, "Are you spending the night?"

Lyndon smiled, "No, I'm going home soon."

"Okay." She took her pill and ran upstairs.

I kept a bottle of Russian cognac left over from my grandfather hidden on the top shelf. I held the bottle up. "It's never been opened;

I can't guarantee how this might taste. It belonged to my grandfather; he's been dead for over fifteen years. Would you chance a shot?"

"Why not?"

I didn't have any shot glasses; juice glasses would suffice. I remembered Grandfather saying a two-finger shot was proper. I sat next to Lyndon, "It's been a long day. I'm grateful you chose to help me; it means a lot."

"Cheers. To new beginnings."

I took a sip, "Wow! It's warm going down."

Surprised, Lyndon asked, "You never drank cognac before?" I shook my head. "I've tasted Irish whisky. I didn't want to start on the hard stuff. One glass of wine each night settles my nerves."

"Do you ever hear from John?"

"Oh, heavens, no." On the second sip, I felt no pain. "I shouldn't have ever married him, Lyndon. I never understood why he threw Emily Thurston over for me. He put on a good show making me think he cared about Astrid. Firstly, he was amazed by her talent, but with the flip of a switch, he wanted to institutionalize her. He's certainly a good barrister; he can lie through his teeth and never blink."

"I can understand why you left John, but you've given up so much for Astrid."

"Not really; that gawky eleven-year-old has always been my first love." I'd never acknowledged these feelings before. Backtracking, I said, "I'm sorry, I shouldn't have said it that way. Besides, I didn't mean romantically."

"It's alright, Lee." She didn't finish her drink, "I think I should go."

"You must think I'm terrible."

"No, Lee; you're human.

"When's the cocoa lady coming?"

"She couldn't come, Astrid," I held my breath; the whys were coming.

"How come? She didn't like us?"

"No, Astie, she got another job." It's my belief Astrid seemed more challenging than she thought. Astrid was even on her best behavior.

In her Eeyore voice, Astrid said, "Okay." She didn't understand. We were back to square one. When Lyndon heard the news, she hatched a new plan: an advanced Special Education student. Special needs children suffered so very much and were often institutionalized. The government now moved them to age-appropriate group homes, but the lack of services became apparent upon my investigation.

The sound of a special education prospect gave me hope. The next weekend the university's new Special Education Department would hold its second annual seminar. Lyndon would go scouting for us. I sometimes wondered why she bothered. I hoped Lyndon didn't view me as a charity case.

A Visit from Mr. Godfrey

The phone rang, scaring me half to death. I rarely got calls in the afternoon.

"Ms. McConnell, this is Franklin Godfrey. I hope I'm not disturbing you."

Since Astrid's breakdown, we'd never heard a peep from anyone in the Symphony. What could they say? *Our deepest sympathy?* Astrid wanted nothing to do with music; Dr. Godfrey felt like an unwilling accomplice.

The purpose of his call was to inform me of Dr. Dryer's death. I expressed my condolences, but my heart remained bitter.

"I wanted to check on Astrid several times, but she must still hate me," his voice was broken and sad.

"I'm not sure she even remembers, Mr. Godfrey. Astrid stopped listening to classical music; her keyboard sits in the closet. Last month though, she hummed a tune for the first time in years, which astonished me. I knew the music, Beethoven's *Ode to Joy*. When asked, she knew it by name."

"It breaks my heart, Ms. McConnell. Astrid filled me with such joy. I miss teaching her." With a sad little laugh, he said, "I think she taught more than I taught her."

"Mr. Godfrey, I have an idea. Granted, I have no idea how Astrid will take this, but would you consider visiting us?"

With caution, he said, "I can. I'll leave if I upset Astrid."

"I can't suggest attending a concert anymore. She throws a fit, so I stopped asking. I want to believe seeing you will awaken the music. Yes, I realize Astrid may never play again. But, if Astrid sees you, it might bring her love of music back." We set a visit for that Saturday, hoping for a good outcome. Mr. Godfrey sounded lost.

At two o'clock Saturday afternoon, the doorbell rang.

"Astrid, could you answer the door, please?" She lumbered to the door, head down, looking at her feet.

Opening it, wide-eyed, she turned and hollered, "It's Mr. Godfrey!"

"Well, invite him in."

She took his hand, leading him to the sofa. Her mouth gaped open as she sized him up. We held our collective breaths, waiting for a response.

"Come sit with me," I said to Astrid, "Do you mind that he came for a visit?"

Her eyes narrowed, a wary expression came over her face, "Why'd you come here?"

Mr. Godfrey sat on thin ice; he smiled, "I miss you, Astrid."

She jumped up and hugged him tight, "I missed you too." I breathed a sigh of relief.

He knew the answer but asked anyway, "Are you still playing your keyboard?"

Her eyes drifted to the ceiling, "No." The question made her uncomfortable. Astrid moved away from him to rejoin me.

"May I ask why?"

"Albert is a bad man. A bad, bad man. Albert took my music away with bad pills." Neither one of us said a word for the longest time.

Then Mr. Godfrey said, mild as a lamb, "Astrid, Albert died last week. You don't have to worry over him anymore."

Astrid jerked her head around, eyes squinting at me. I lowered my voice, "He's telling the truth, Astrid."

"Okay." To break the stillness, I offered Mr. Godfrey a cup of tea.

Astrid sat very still, "I'm no good anymore, no music, no Astrid."

"What do you mean, Astrid?" he asked.

"Can I go to my room now?"

"You don't want tea and biscuits?"

She quietly shook her strawberry-blond hair from side to side. Defeated, I said, "Alright, go on, but tell Mr. Godfrey goodbye. He came all this way to see you."

She meandered up the stairs, "Goodbye."

He shrugged his shoulders, crushed. "Don't give up yet, Mr. Godfrey. It's a lot for her to process; seeing you, the death of Albert. Give her time; we'll stay optimistic, right?"

"Yes. Do you mind if I go?"

"Tell me you'll come back again," I begged. "Perhaps, I'll hear some music coming from Astrid's room."

"We can hope. Just give me a bell."

"Certainly. Astrid was glad to see you, you know."

His lips pursed with a forced smile, "Yes."

Partial good news came a few days later. Lyndon called with information on a grad student, Hannah Johnson. Her undergrad degree was in nursing; she would soon graduate with a master's degree specializing in brain disorders. Evidently, Hannah became orphaned at age eighteen. At twelve, her mother jumped off the London Bridge. Before Hannah turned eighteen, her father was driven into madness, later dying of brain cancer. Lyndon relayed that the estate brought in enough money to see her through college. Last year, she sold her childhood home in Liverpool and now lived with two other grad school students who didn't share her enthusiasm for her studies.

"I spoke with her advisor, who told me Hannah confided in him that they drank too much and were often late in their share of rent payments. Hannah has trouble studying with all the noise. It upsets Hannah when her flatmates make fun of her desire to work with 'retards.' I spoke with her about Astrid; she seems interested, Lee. I think Astrid should meet her. I've cautioned Hannah not to mention her family. We don't want to upset Astrid."

Saturday morning, after breakfast, Lyndon arrived with Hannah. Close to Astrid's height, Hannah Johnson possessed the look of someone from the Far East. Her shoulder-length hair, the color of ebony, her skin bronze. Astrid held my hand, hiding behind me.

"She's new, she's new, very new," Astrid repeated at least three times.

"Lyndon's not new. We know Lyndon. It's okay, Astrid, let's sit down."

Astrid said, "Not next to me; she's a stranger."

"I'm Hannah, Astrid. How old are you?"

Still behind me, "I dunno, I dunno. How old I am, Lee?"

"You're thirty-one, Astrid."

"Okay." Peeking over my shoulder, Astrid whispered, "She has black hair."

"Yes, I do, Astrid."

Referring to Mr. Godfrey, Astrid said, "People with black hair are nice, really nice."

"That is a nice compliment," said Hannah. "I have green eyes, too, but not as bright as yours."

Astrid squinted at me, "Lee, are my eyes bright like the light bulbs?"

"Not quite that bright; green like lollipops."

Slowly Astrid moved from behind me, inspecting Hannah's face. "You are a different color. Why are you a different color?"

"My mother was from India, my father was British."

"Okay." Then Astrid said something that shocked me to the point of wanting to cry.

With a timid smile, gazing up at the ceiling, Astrid announced, "I play the piano." Lyndon and I stared at each other with open mouths. Poor Hannah didn't understand our expressions of astonishment. The explanation for Hannah would come later. For the moment, she took it in stride.

"Astrid, what else do you like to do?" asked Hannah.

With her arm tightly wrapped around mine, she said, "I do knitting; Mrs. Mary taught me. I knit scarves for sick people."

"Mrs. Mary was my mother," I clarified.

"Mrs. Mary is in heaven now. Isn't that right, Lee?"

I patted her hand, "That's right."

"She's not coming back, never, never coming back. She's in the sky."

"I see," a neutral answer from Hannah. "Do you like the park?"

"Which park? Which park?"

"We like to go for walks, Astrid," I reminded her.

"I like walking; Lee says it calms my nerves. She doesn't like my nerves. Do you, Lee?"

I kept silent.

"Would you take a walk with me someday, Astrid?"

Astrid stared at the ceiling; her eyes scanned left and right as we awaited an answer.

"Okay." Later, I informed Hannah of the meaning of Astrid's okay. Astrid never admitted to her uncertainty; okay was her response.

"Do you think you and I could be friends?"

An echo from the past came from Astrid. Distorted words came out as if someone slowly pulled Taffy from her, "Okay. I don't know how to be a friend."

I hugged her, "Sure you do. We've been friends for over twenty years."

In her monotone, she leaned into me, and repeated our mantra, "You are the moon; I am the star. Astra and Luna, forever together." With her chin held high, she squeezed me, "I love you, Lee. I love pizza, too." I came close to laughing out loud.

"I love you, too, Astie."

Hannah observed our interaction with eyes full of compassion, but it didn't mean acceptance.

"Astrid," said Lyndon, "Do you want to come with me to Angelo's? Can we get a pizza to bring home?"

"Okay." Lyndon helped her with her coat. Astrid suddenly dropped to the floor, pounding her hands in her lap, "No, no, no, I couldn't go! I couldn't go without Lee!" She came just short of calling Lyndon an idiot. She'd never gone anywhere without me. Lyndon understood, knowing not to touch Astrid. She'd become a hurricane.

"What if I go and bring pizza back?" Lyndon asked.

Astrid threw her coat in the corner, "Okay. Extra pepperoni, extra cheese, extra pepperoni, extra cheese, Lee says, cut it in squares."

"Yes, yes, I will tell them," Lyndon asked us what we wanted. I asked for the house ravioli.

"I'll have what Astrid likes, pizza with extra pepperoni, extra cheese."

"In squares," exclaimed Astrid. Lyndon left.

"Pick up your coat, Astrid." Her head jerked up, ignoring me. I repeated my request; she ignored me again. With my command voice, I said "Time out." Dutifully, she brought the egg timer.

"How long this time?"

"Until Lyndon gets back. Put the timer back. When you hear the door open, you may come down. No running, Astrid."

"Okay."

As she trudged upstairs, I turned to Hannah. "Her mood swings have gotten worse with age, Hannah. Astrid just shocked us by saying she played the piano. Astrid was, at one time, a brilliant concert pianist and composer, defying what the experts believed about autistic savants. A savant in music plays like a tape recorder. You are familiar with the term 'savant'?" I asked.

"Yes, they hear the music and play it back. I read a paper, a study of a young man, blind from birth, who is a musical savant."

"I'm impressed. Astrid's awards could fill the floor-to-ceiling bookshelf." I took a deep breath, "One day, she quit. Something in her brain short-circuited: there's been speculation but no concrete explanation. A few minutes ago, when she declared she played, was the first time she's said that in years. I didn't ever expect to hear those words again, Hannah."

"I understand, Ms. McConnell. My father's brain went haywire, too. For the longest time, no one knew why. That's when, after his death, the autopsy showed a large tumor pressing on his skull. An operation couldn't have saved him. He's the reason I chose neuropsychology as my master's program."

"You do understand the employment arrangement? It's a live-in job, hardly meant for academic life."

"I do. Don't think me wrong but keeping a record of Astrid's behavior and interactions could help with research." She quickly added, "I don't mean she'd be a guinea pig. It would be only observation, nothing else. I graduate in December and want to forward my observations to the research department, with your consent."

"Who might receive this data?" Unfortunately, I felt hesitant.

"The new Autism Research Centre at Cambridge. We've just begun trying to unlock the mind of persons with different forms of autism. I can work from home; Dr. Hammersmith said I could have a computer to use here if I get the job. I won't put her through any kind of testing; you have my word."

The bell rang and Astrid came flying down the stairs.

"Walk!" Astrid's shoulders slumped. "Get the door for Lyndon, please."

Ladened with pizza boxes, Lyndon sat them on the table. The hand flapping began, then Lyndon asked for plates; Astrid's hand flapping stopped, but the squeals were ear piercing.

"Take some breaths, Astrid. Calm yourself," I said.

I watched Astrid put four squares on a plate then hand it to Hannah, "You can have some of mine." This signaled acceptance of Hannah, which threw me for a loop. I hoped Hannah could be part of our household if she wanted the position.

I spoke with Astrid in the evening, "Do you like Hannah?"

"I dunno. Can I watch the telly? Five minutes until *This is Your Life*! With Eamonn Andrews." Her expression mimicked the announcer. "Every Saturday night. It's Saturday night."

"Alright, but we need to talk about Hannah before bedtime."

"Okay."

While Astrid watched the telly, I wrote some questions for Astrid. *Okay,* answers wouldn't do. I also wrote some questions for Hannah. After seeing a short interaction with Astrid, I hoped for the best. A phone call to Hannah could wait until I hear what my star might say.

"Show's over. Turn the telly off. Come sit by me," I waited until Astrid plopped down. "I want you to answer some questions."

"Like the doctor's office?"

"No, not those questions. Did you like Hannah?"

"She has black hair and green eyes."

"Yes, she does, but do you like her?"

With a hand stroking her chin like Grandfather used to do, she contemplated the question and was not quick to answer.

"Could she live with us? Sleep here? Sleep here all night?"

"Yes, live with us. And she could have Mrs. Mary's old room."

I slept in Mother's bedroom to hear when Astrid got up in the middle of the night. Her pacing came and went. I kept an ear out in that bedroom as Mother did years ago.

"Will she sleep with you?"

"Of course not, silly. I'd go back upstairs."

Then came her okay.

I rarely lost my temper. But at that, I lost my temper. "No *okay* answers, Astrid. Could you go for walks or to the library with Hannah?"

"And you?"

"No. She can be a new friend, but you'll still be my best friend." Astrid never tolerated change very well; I wanted her input. "Lyndon and I are friends, but you're my best friend. Right?"

"Okay."

My patience disappeared and I lost my temper again. "No, Astrid! No *okays*! I need to know if Hannah can live with us!"

In a fever pitch, "I made you mad; you're mad. You're angry." Both her fists flew up, pounding her head. I tried to contain her; Astrid kicked my shins, covering them in bruises; my forearms were pinched. Running behind the sofa, I grabbed both hands, pinning them to her sides. I cried, begging forgiveness, telling her this was my fault. "Please, don't hurt yourself. I love you; I upset you."

"Let me go, let me go, Lee!"

I whispered, "Deep breaths. I need to breathe, too." She calmed down; I sat next to her on the floor. An exhausted Astrid lay in my lap; I stroked her hair.

"Better now?"

"Uh-huh."

"Could Hannah spend a week with us?" I waited for an okay.

"Yes, Lee. I promise to be good; I promise."

"I am the moon," I whispered.

"I am your star."

"That's right, Astrid."

| 33 |

Hannah with the Green Eyes

After speaking with Hannah, she agreed to a trial run. During that week, I hoped she could earn Astrid's trust. Never knowing Astrid's reaction to change, I broke the news carefully after lunch. It was Tuesday. On Tuesdays, if the weather was good, we went for a drive to Milton Country Park north of Cambridge. Fall colors painted the trees; the paths were perfect for a stroll. At the small café, we ate the day's special: tomato soup and toasted cheese, Astrid's favorite. Not many people were in the park. As I scanned the room, we weren't alone. The time to talk about Hannah could wait. On our walk to the car park, Astrid picked up leaves of red and yellow, stopping to examine each one.

"Looky, Lee! This one has yellow with red edges. Can I keep this one for the pressing book?"

"Yes, the leaves will be a nice addition."

"Violets, tulip and rose petals, fronds of fern, pressed between the pages. Yes, these will be a nice addition; a yellow one and a red one!"

"We can't take the forest home with us, silly. Choose one of each color." The clouds of golden hues began to show themselves, "Astrid, we must go now. The sun setting." I hated driving in the dark.

Once home, Astrid ran up the front stoop, shivering with her hand full of fall leaves, "Hurry, Lee. I'm cold." Her cheeks were rosy, red, and her strawberry-blond hair shined in the porch light.

"I'll light a fire. Hot chocolate?"

"Five marshmallows, five marshmallows, Astrid wants five marshmallows!"

There were always five marshmallows. The glow of dancing flames was mesmerizing, but I wanted Astrid's attention.

"Astie, did you like Hannah?"

"Black hair and green eyes, green like mine."

"Yes. Did you like Hannah?"

Squinting eyes meant she was thinking; I held my breath.

"Hannah with the green eyes, yes, Hannah with the green eyes, yes, yes."

I breathed a sigh of relief, "Could we ask her to visit us?"

"Hannah with the green eyes, yes," she paused. "Hannah with the green eyes can sleep in my bed."

"But where will you sleep?" I asked.

"In your bed, silly," she said, "Where we look at the stars."

"Maybe Hannah can sleep in where I sleep now. in Mrs. Mary's bed."

"Where will you sleep? In my bed?"

"No, silly goose, I'll sleep in my old room."

"Then where will I sleep!"

I understood her confusion. "Calm down, let's think, if Hannah sleeps in Mrs. Mary's room, I sleep in my old room, where will Astrid sleep?"

"In Astrid's bed."

"Correct. What time is it?" Fifteen minutes until nine, Astrid's get-ready-for-bedtime time. After the nightly ritual, she came downstairs before her goodnight kiss; she asked when Hannah might come.

"I'll call her tomorrow afternoon; now go up to bed." I felt good about Hannah with the green eyes.

Every Monday and Wednesday, Astrid was glued to the telly to watch "her show." Wednesday at seven-thirty in the evening, *Coronation Street* came on. Astrid sat fully engrossed. I phoned Hannah. As soon as I said hello, Astrid jerked her head around, "You're too loud."

Hannah twittered in the background after hearing Astrid. Throughout our conversation, I hinted at Astrid's quirks, including how she eavesdrops. It made Hannah laugh. We set up the next week as a trial run. I very much wanted everything to work out. The test would be if she can handle Astrid's fits.

"Who were you talking to?"

"Hannah. She is coming on Saturday and staying a week with us."

"Hannah with the green eyes?"

"Yes."

I was caught off guard by unpredictable hand-flapping and squeals of joy; normally Astrid hated change. Why was Hannah different?

"Okay, miss, time for bed. Check your watch."

"Eight-forty-five, it's eight-forty-five, Lee. Bedtime, nine o'clock," muttered, making her way upstairs. Within five minutes, she ran down the stairs, pajama pants in hand, "Is Hannah with the green eyes coming tomorrow?"

"No, Astrid. She comes on Saturday."

"Why couldn't she come tomorrow? Hannah with the green eyes."

I had learned that patience is a virtue over the years, or *I* would be institutionalized. Soon Astrid would be in bed, and I'd have time to relax.

| 34 |

Literal, please

Astrid practiced how to show Hannah the house when she arrived. When the bell rang promptly at ten a.m., Astrid waited at the door.

"Hello, Hannah with green eyes," said Astrid, rocking side to side.

"Hello, Astrid. It's nice to see you."

Giggles from Astrid? Before I could say anything, Astrid grabbed Hannah's suitcase with one hand and Hannah's hand with the other, "This is your place to sleep. It was Mrs. Mary's room until she died. They buried her in the ground, but she's really in the sky. Right, Lee?" I nodded; she continued, "Lee sleeps here, but she's going all the way upstairs."

Undoubtedly, it was the most animated Astrid I'd seen in years. "Astrid, you can show her the rest of the house later? Let Hannah take her coat off by herself, please."

A gasp escaped from Astrid; a hand covered her mouth.

"You've done nothing wrong, but let Hannah settle in a bit. Okay? Could you set out the scones and napkins?"

"Okay, Lee, scones and napkins, scones and napkins."

Over tea, we discussed Astrid's morning and evening routines. Hannah asked Astrid a few questions. I had to prompt answers from her.

"What's your favorite thing to do?"

No answer. I rephrased the question, showing Hannah the need to be more direct.

"Astrid, do you like to go walking?"

"Yes, we walk in the park with ducks and ice cream."

"What is the name of the park?"

"Milton Country Park, lots of pretty leaves, the Milton Country Park, with ducks and ice cream." She started fidgeting, rocking in her chair. I laid my hand on her shoulder, "It's okay, Astrid."

"I have to go to the loo. No accidents."

"Go on."

When Astrid stomped upstairs, I told Hannah everything she talks about with Astrid must be literal, black and white—recalling John's remark about Astrid's strawberry-blond hair and Astrid's response of strawberries not being stuck in her hair. Hannah laughed.

"Many issues are trial-by-fire with Astrid."

Clomping down the stairs, Astrid made her usual announcement, "I peed!"

"I tell her every time; there's no need to tell everyone. Does she remember?"

Talking to herself, Astrid mumbled, "I peed, but I didn't poop."

"Okay, I understand." I paused. "Did you need to poop?"

"No, I just peed."

"Well, this issue is settled. Are you okay with showing Hannah the upstairs bedrooms?"

"Okay, Hannah with the green eyes." Astrid took Hannah by the hand. "I have a toilet in my room."

Hannah wanted to laugh but thought better of it. I'd kept all of Astrid's diagnosis, medication, triggers, and miscellaneous information in a folder for Hannah. Instead of sending it, I decided she should arrive with no expectations.

The fireplace required attention as I waited. I heard giggling on the way downstairs.

"Hannah with green eyes likes your telescope."

"I told her stars twinkle, planets don't."

Amazed, she caught me off guard, "You remembered."

"I remember lots of things."

"I know you do." Then she came out with the BBC nightly television schedule rattled off like a machine.

"Perfect, Astrid, but that's enough."

"*Coronation Street*, every Monday and Wednesday at seven-thirty."

"Oh! You like *Coronation Street*! So do I."

"I watch *Coronation Street* every Monday and Wednesday at seven-thirty."

Jerking her head around, slapping herself in the face with her braid ponytail, she declared, "It's Saturday! *This is Your Life*! With Eamonn Andrews."

"Yes, and Hannah can watch it with you."

Astrid whipped her around to Hannah and squinted, "Do you watch the telly, too?" Hannah began to understand how Astrid's mind worked or, in this case, didn't work.

"Yes, we have a date to watch *Coronation Street*, remember?"

"I don't go on dates. I don't like boys. Boys are mean. I don't go on dates."

Seeing Hannah's scared expression, I repeated, "Literal." She began to understand.

"No dates. Tonight, we can watch *This Is Your Life* together. Is that okay?"

"Yes, Hannah with green eyes."

Astrid fell asleep, sitting in her knitting chair. "This is when she's on her best behavior," I winked at Hannah. Hannah flashed a smile.

"Do you feel exhausted?" I asked.

"No, I find Astrid to be interesting. And yes, quirky, but I feel a connection with her. I don't exactly know why, but I do." Those comments meant the world to me. While Astrid slept, Hannah unpacked.

Hannah joined me at the kitchen table for tea. An open floor plan allowed me to keep an eye on Astrid from the kitchen. Now I had to explain to Hannah the many parts of Astrid's behavior.

"Astrid's quirks are many. Disrupting her routine brings fits of rage, as you witnessed before. I keep a record of her triggers; here's a manual I made weeks ago based on records I keep for the doctor. Turn to the page on triggers, the word Dr. Davis taught me. He said it was like pulling a trigger on a gun. She explodes."

After reading over the page, Hannah remarked, "Researchers are on the forefront of autism, Lee. Many items on your list are subjects I've studied. Emotions are challenging to express. Astrid, most likely, is unable to tell you what she feels. There's a disconnect behind what the brain is saying. The words of expression can't come out. Words feel caught in her throat."

I paused, reflecting on Hannah's grasp of autism. There were words of passion. "In five minutes, Hannah, you gave me more understanding of why these behaviors happen. No doctor has ever explained this to me in the way you did just now." I stood there, blown away. "Even if you decide not to stay, I value any insight you can give me."

On Hannah's face came a hint of a smile, "I want to be upfront with you. A tumor pressed on my father's brain; I had no idea what was happening to him. Guilt and shame followed me after Mum's suicide, and then my father's strange behavior left me baffled. I worried insanity might be hereditary, which made me wonder how the mind functions. For a time, being Catholic and parentless, I thought deeply of becoming a nun."

She studied neuropsychology to find answers. "I became fascinated with autism and cutting-edge research. My final exams are on December tenth, but my thirst for knowledge will never end. I couldn't hope to understand everything, but Astrid will give me a sense of purpose. A few minutes ago, while unpacking, I hope you can understand, the Holy Spirit spoke to me." A nervous chirp escaped her, "It might make you think twice about hiring me. Like a nun dedicated to a vocation, Astrid will be my vocation in life. Have you read the biography of Helen Keller, Ms. McConnell?"

I nodded my head, "Yes, I have. Please call me Lee."

"I know why I'm here, Lee."

"You can't make her like you, you know."

Elbow on the table, Hannah's hand propped under her chin, "I know."

Groggy from her nap, Astrid asked if dinner was ready.

"Where's your watch?"

"On my wrist."

"What time is it?"

"Four-thirty, one and a half hours before dinner. Six o'clock dinner, one and a half hours."

Astrid stared in her lap, "Did Hannah with the green eyes, go home?"

"No, she's in the bedroom."

Astrid darted to the bedroom; she flung open the door, "Are you in here, Hannah with the green eyes?"

Waiting for an answer, I heard a chuckle, "Yes, Astrid, I'm here for a while."

The patter of feet ran upstairs, "What's she doing?" Hannah asked.

I threw my hands up, "Who knows?"

With her day planner thrown on the kitchen table and her red pencil in hand, she studied it.

"How many days?" she asked. Hannah approached her. Hannah nodded at me. She sat down next to Astrid, who immediately cowered, scooting away from her.

"Astrid, may I point to the days?" Seeing all the circles and Astrid's meticulous notes, "You can circle them. Okay?"

Putting her finger on today's date, with her head down, Astrid read what she wrote, "Saturday, November twelfth, Hannah comes here."

Hannah pointed to Sunday, "Sunday, Mass at St Marten's," Astrid repeated.

"Astie," I said, "Hannah is Catholic like you."

Astie's eyes grew big with disbelief, then she spoke with the sound of a tommy gun, "Hannah with the green eyes is Catholic, like me? Are you Catholic, Hannah? Hannah with the green eyes?"

"I am," she smiled, "Shall I recite the Hail Mary, Astrid?"

Dumbfounded, Astrid put both elbows on the table, holding her head. I'd never seen her so astonished. I lowered my eyes to meet hers, "Are you alright?"

She made eye contact with me; I held my breath. Then, poof, Astrid came back to earth asking how many days. When she finished, Hannah asked, "What else is written there for Saturday?"

In the voice of an announcer, Astrid said, "'*This Is Your Life* with host Eamonn Andrews' at seven-thirty." Holding her watch at eye level, "Three hours and forty-five minutes." Hannah glanced at me.

"She's excellent at timekeeping. For me, a blessing." I mouthed, "and a curse."

After dinner, Hannah wanted to help with the dishes. I asked her to observe. When it came to silverware, forks followed spoons, and lastly, butter knives. "Be careful with knives," Astrid muttered a reminder, "and Lee will put them away. Lee will put them away."

I took care of sharp knives and pots and pans. Hannah asked if she might put everything in the cabinets; the answer came out as an emphatic no. That is my job.

"Maybe tomorrow Hannah can help?"

"No, Hannah with the green eyes is a stranger."

"Well, maybe on Wednesday."

Astrid rattled off, "Wednesday, seven-thirty a.m., breakfast then office at nine o'clock, lunch at twelve-thirty, knitting, at four o'clock pack up knitting, come home, dinner then dishes, *Coronation Street* at seven-thirty, fruit-Wednesday fruit, no cookie, eight-forty-five brush teeth, nine o'clock p.m. bed."

Leaning on the chair, I said to Hannah, "Well, there you have it. Wednesday's schedule."

"Go up and show Hannah your books."

Later, I could check over my note for Monday's office work while Astrid watched her show. I took advantage of every quiet moment, which never lasted long.

Astrid ran down the stairs leaving Hannah behind. Checking her watch, Astrid announced, "*This Is Your Life* with Eamonn Andrews in ten minutes!" The small black and white television rested on the shelf next to the fireplace. Before supper, I made sure the fire died down.

Astrid turned on the telly, fluffed two small pillows placed in the sofa's corner, and positioned herself to watch her show. Hannah asked if she might watch with her.

Pointing to the loveseat, she barked, "You have to sit there."

Hannah did as told. If Hannah commented, Astrid countered with, "No talking!"

Five minutes before the program ended, I gathered my paper to clean off the table. Astrid marched herself to the table every night; milk and a cookie waited.

"May I sit with you?"

"No, you stay over there." Astrid relegated Hannah to the wingback chair in the living room. Astrid shielded her eyes so Hannah couldn't see her face. Periodically, Astrid checked to make sure Hannah stayed put.

Astrid asked, "Is she spending the night?"

"Yes. Do you remember our sleepovers?"

"Uh-huh, you are the moon. I am the star to the left of the moon."

"That's right."

"Hannah couldn't be our star or moon. Stars twinkle, planets don't."

"Correct. Let me think. What could Hannah be?"

Astrid blurted out, "A black hole!" Hannah snickered.

"Let's think of something nicer. What about a nova or a comet?"

In a bust of words, with a flurry of claps, "A comet! The Hannah Comet."

"Oh," she surprised me.

"Hannah with the green eyes is a comet with a long tail."

I shifted my eyes to Hannah. "What do you think, Hannah?"

Her eyes lit up, "I like that very much. Thank you, Astrid."

Suddenly embarrassed, Astrid covered her face. Green eyes peeked from under her hand, "Okay. Is it bedtime?"

"Yes."

Astrid never walked upstairs; she ran. "Despite how many times I ask her to slow down, she still darts up and down the stairs."

"It could be a sensory thing for her, the sound and vibration."

That blew my mind; this sensory idea was a new concept. In her nightgown, Astrid gave me a goodnight peck on the cheek. Whirling around to Hannah, "No kiss for you." Hannah smiled.

"Is she sleeping here?" Astrid asked again.

"Yes."

"Okay." She ran upstairs.

A sigh of relief escaped from me, "So far, so good. Care for a glass of wine?"

"I don't drink, Lee. It's a religious thing, plus I don't like the feeling of being out of control. Given into peer pressure, I drank at a college party. A guy tried to grope me. I ran out the door, stumbling to my dorm; I vowed never to drink again."

"I hope you won't mind if I do. What's your opinion of today?"

Hannah made several observations after a moment of reflection, especially Astrid's recollections of schedules and short-term memory problems. "The inability to remember the answer to questions asked after minutes or hours is typical of an autistic individual."

Baffled, I told her of Astrid's decline since her early twenties.

"Why do you think that happened, Hannah? Powerless, I've watched her go downhill." These are concerns never directly answered by Dr. Davis.

"Yes, you've had a long-term relationship with her, Lee. She hasn't regressed. Mentally you've gotten older; she has not. Her world never expanded, but the world around her did. Hence her inability to cope as well."

I wiped a tear away, then chuckled, "If you don't stay, I'll need to make a weekly appointment with you."

"With time, I believe she'll come around to trust me. It's a God thing."

I desperately wanted to believe it to be true. Hannah set off to bed to pray and sleep. Mass was the next morning.

The first question from Astrid, referring to Hannah's presence at the breakfast table, was, "What's she doing here?"

Oh, boy, here we go, "Hannah spent the night in Mrs. Mary's old room. She's going to Mass with us."

Questioning everything like a three-year-old, Hannah stepped in, "Lee is the moon, you are the star, and I am a comet. Do you remember?"

Her eyebrows made a V; she thought hard about the question.

An answer was on the way; she threw her head back, and checked out the ceiling, "Yes, a comet with a long tail."

Astrid gave me a stern glare, "Yes, Astie, you made Hannah a comet."

"Okay, Hannah with the green eyes is a comet. It's okay. Lee, braid my hair for Mass."

With my hands folded, I ignored her.

"Please, Lee, will you braid my hair?" She scooted to the edge of her chair, "Please and thank you."

"Alright, get dressed and bring me your brush."

Mass at St. Marten's

"Normally, we walk to Mass; with the rain, I'll drive."

"In the new car," Astrid said gleefully. I sold Mother's 1965 GM sports sedan to buy a used BMW, nothing flashy. The neighborhood street parking wasn't conducive to a new car.

"Put your Mac and wellies on, Astrid." Astrid contorted her face.

"Why do they call boots 'wellies'?"

"I don't know."

With an umbrella in hand, Hannah emerged from the bedroom.

Astrid began to howl. Not understanding, Hannah froze.

"It's the umbrella, Hannah. She's terrified of them."

An about-face, the umbrella disappeared.

"It's gone, Astrid." I held her shoulders to face me, "Hannah didn't know. Deep breaths. We're going to Mass. We'll be there in fifteen minutes; let's go."

In her black robe and oversized white collar and hood, Sister Mary Francis, in her sixties, stood at the door every Sunday waiting for us. In her high-pitched, happy voice, she said, "My, my Astrid, you've brought a friend. How nice. Can you tell me her name?"

In her monotone with eyes on the floor, she said, "Hannah with the green eyes."

Sister Mary Francis, with her jovial laugh, "Oh! She does have green eyes, how nice. We welcome you to St. Marten's Church. Are you a Catholic, dear?"

"Yes, Sister."

"Wonderful! We're still working on Lee." She laughed; so did Hannah.

"Lee is not Catholic," Astrid mumbled.

The back pew close to the exit was reserved for us. Only once did Astrid misbehave. An Italian tenor with a booming voice set her off during an eleven o'clock service. The nine o'clock Mass was more reserved. Today, she kept staring at Hannah, then squinted at her and loudly whispered, "Are you sure you're a Catholic?"

To keep from laughing, I covered my mouth. At the time of the Eucharist, Astrid stood up and snatched Hannah's hand, practically dragging her to the front of the church. She was testing Hannah! Astrid made Hannah go first. Father Joseph smiled and winked at Hannah as she held out her hands to receive the host. Astrid refused to touch the wafer. Like a baby bird, her head tilted back, her mouth opened wide, the priest tossed the host in her mouth like it throwing a penny in a fountain. The first time she took communion, Astrid refused to drink from the communal cup; she had a special cup from then on. Astrid never took her eyes off Hannah. I studied their interaction. Could Hannah be right? Did God send her to us?

We were always the last to leave. Father Joseph, a good-natured man, was allowed to hug Astrid. It started with a handshake. Two years ago, out of the blue, she hugged him, calling him God's father. I called him the following Monday to say that hug was a milestone. And hopefully, fingers crossed, another milestone with Hannah.

Later that evening, I sat with Hannah. "You're the first person she has taken an interest in since Mr. Godfrey."

Puzzled, she asked, "Who's Mr. Godfrey?"

As I recounted Astrid's relationship, vivid scenes of concerts, laughing, and struggles flashed through my mind. Even if she rejected him now, Franklin Godfrey would always be her mentor.

"He came for a visit last month after ten years. At first, Astrid seemed happy to see him. He missed her and hoped to spark interest in playing again. It didn't last long; a disconnect; she stomped upstairs. I felt sorry for him; dejected, he left. The will to play left her. False hope is all I have left." The story of Dr. Dryer's involvement with Astrid upset Hannah. She offered an insight.

"Ideas conceived become etched in our minds. Even with a neuronormal person like us, it happens. Negative associations are challenging."

Because of my personal history, I realized she was spot on. My skepticism came from my negative experiences in my life. I wanted to believe this experience with Hannah would be favorable.

Monday, during breakfast, Astrid kept wiggling in her seat.

"Astie, what's wrong?"

On the verge of panic, "Where's Hannah with the green eyes? Was I bad? Did she leave?"

From the back of her chair, I put my arms around her, speaking softly in her ear, "You were wonderful. She likes you." I pulled a chair next to her, holding her hands. "Hannah is still in school; she'll be home later."

"Later, when later? Monday evening, seven-thirty, *Coronation Street*. Hannah likes my show."

"I know she'll watch it with you. I gave her a key to the house."

"Why can't I have a key?"

"Because," I had to think fast, "because I only have two."

"Okay."

In the office, the phone rang. Lyndon wanted a progress report on Hannah Johnson. Our conversation was cryptic. Lyndon asked questions and I gave answers like, "I think that will work; the gravitational pull is strong." Lyndon chuckled. I asked Astrid's permission for Lyndon to join us for dinner that night. Immediately came questions about the dinner menu.

"How about Angelo's?" I promised we'd be back in time for her show. Astrid's approval brought a flurry of squeals and hand clapping. Lyndon would meet us at six. On the business side of our conversation, Lyndon asked me to finish my lecture notes for the NASA seminar. Butterflies fluttered in my stomach from anxiety and nerves. The fact that NASA was interested in my work continued to baffle me. With all the volume of their data, why was my work so interesting?

Astrid burst through the front door, "Where's Hannah with the green eyes?"

"I'm in the bedroom, Astrid. I'll be out soon."

"Are you in the loo?"

"Astrid, you shouldn't ask that," I scolded.

"I'm studying, Luv. My big paper is due, and I'm to give a presentation next week." Hannah emerged from the bedroom.

"Presentation, what's that? Like a Christmas present, Hannah with green eyes?"

"Um. It's like a concert without music. I stand in front of people instead of playing an instrument, I use words."

"Staccato or pianissimo?"

Now, Hannah tilted her head and paused. I was amazed.

Warily, I said, "Astrid, tell Hannah what staccato means." I waited.

In a voice matching the short quickness of plucking strings, she punctuated the words with fingers tapping out the rhythm, "Short, quick notes, duh, duh, duh!" My heart skipped a beat.

Astrid hunched over, fingers poised over imaginary keys. "Pianissimo," she whispered, "softly. Mr. Godfrey says, make the piano whisper."

My hand covered my heart. The music still existed in Astie, dormant but still inside.

"A little of both," answered Hannah. I decided to call Mr. Godfrey the next day.

Lyndon met us for supper at Angelo's. Astrid was floating in space somewhere. Then Lyndon asked for onions on her pizza. Astrid hollered, "Oh, stinky breath!" We snickered; Astrid didn't think it was at all funny. Lyndon promised to brush her teeth later.

In the middle of our conversation, Astrid looked at her watch, "*Coronation Steet*, in forty-five minutes, hurry, eat fast." The ride home took less than five minutes. I promised we'd be on time.

While Hannah and Astrid watched their show, Lyndon and I sat at the table talking about Sunday Mass. "On Saturday, Astrid assigned Hannah a chair for telly watching. Their interaction is better than I expected, although Astrid keeps her distance occasionally. In the morning, if we're up before Hannah, she'll ask if Hannah is still there. There's a bit of irritation in her tone. Saturday was rough, yet it seems every day is better. Hannah's knowledge of autism is mind-blowing."

My report on the recent events delighted Lyndon. But she wondered if leaving her in March could be a problem. Nothing was certain with Astrid.

"Why is NASA interested in me anyway? Don't they have anyone doing these studies?"

"They do, but your findings on the elliptical paths of the asteroids headed to the sun is of value to their work. It's your analysis of large asteroid trajectories, Lee. Your calculations are of great value."

"Oh, stop, Lyndon. You, above all people, should understand the complexity of my circumstances."

Lydon reached for my hand, "But, I do, Lee. You recall bringing in help was my idea. That's why I'm praying for a good outcome."

I noted her intention, nodding my head, quietly saying, "Yes, I remember."

Astrid jumped up, "Shows over, milk and a chocolate chip cookie, then bedtime!"

Lyndon said, "I should go; classes tomorrow require sleep. This group of students is quite precocious." I hugged Lyndon, "See you Wednesday."

The whereabouts of Hannah was becoming a part of our morning ritual. "When you finish your breakfast, go upstairs and bring me your day planner."

"And red pencil?"

"Yes."

"And get dressed first?"

"Yes, please."

Inward, I chuckled at Astrid's striped blouse and plaid pants outfit. We marked the days until Hannah's graduation with her planner in hand.

"Ten circles. When did I graduate, Lee?" Astrid didn't graduate after her breakdown; school ended for her. I recounted her spellbinding recitals and certificate of completion to keep the peace. Those times were her graduation.

"Okay, but did I get a paper?"

"Yes, and you received medals and trophies."

One eye narrowed, and an eyebrow raised, "Okay." I dodged a bullet.

| 35 |

"Is Hannah Coming Back?"

Tuesdays were park days. The weather had soured, turning cold and wet. Astrid could not discern appropriate clothing for the season. Since mid-September, we had picked out clothing together. Many days this became a battle of frustration. Even when prompted, her selection was hit or miss. I began putting summer clothes away, little by little, hoping she didn't notice. Astrid wore black leggings despite the season, even in summer. Her psychiatrist told me to pick my battles, words echoed from my mother. Today, her choices were sensible. Astrid chose a green cable knit sweater; she reminded me my mother had made it for her years ago. Black tights, wool trousers, heavy socks. Our macs and wellies were essential this afternoon.

That morning we took a bus to the British Museum, one of Astrid's favorites, especially the Egyptian exhibit. Inside, she examined each mummy sarcophagus display. The benches in the room were a blessing, as she could spend half an hour surveying the colors and patterns. The glass enclosures were, too. I constantly reminded her of hands in pockets as she rocked side to side, moving at a snail's pace, looking at each one.

"Is Hannah coming back to our house? Will Hannah take me here?"

"I believe Hannah is coming, and I'm sure she will bring you here. You can show her the mummies."

After lunch at the Montague Café, we headed to Hokusai's rare brush drawings of life in nineteenth-century Japan. Astrid hid behind me at the site of "scary drawings" of a caterpillar with a person's head and Japanese warriors with scary faces. Our favorite and most famous was *Under the Wave off Kanagawa* and the woodblock section. No trip was complete without a stop at the gift shop. That day, she asked politely for a sixteen by twenty-inch framed print. Typically, it was a pen or stickers, but not today. Hokusai's *Cloud Ladder to the Moon*, a black and sepia-toned drawing of a robed figure with outstretched hands holding up the moon, fascinated her.

She wrapped her arm around mine, fascinated. "Please, Lee, may I take this one home?" Such politeness, I couldn't resist. Besides, I liked it too. The sales clerk wrapped it tightly and we took a taxi home.

"Be careful with my picture, Lee. Don't drop it!"

"Yes, Astie." All the way home, those words repeated through the taxi. The annoyed driver closed the partition.

Once we got home, the decision came of where to hang her picture. At every suggestion, a chorus of *no, no, no* rang out as she threw herself on the sofa, arm draped over her head. I sat in the chair, exhausted.

"Astrid, why did you want this picture?"

"You are the moon; someone is holding you up. I see the moon, but it's not nighttime. There, put it on there!" Astrid pointed to the mirror over the mantel, "There, put it there for everyone, Lee. You are the moon."

I sat the print on the mantel; Astrid couldn't take her eyes off the image. The lock clicked; Astrid covered her head with the sofa pillow.

"Hello, everyone," called Hannah. Astrid peeked over the top of the sofa.

Her tone was unfriendly, "Why are you here?"

Poor Hannah. I stepped in, "Astrid, Hannah is staying with us for a few more days. Think about this morning, your day planner; what did you do in the day planner?"

"Red circles."

"Why you make red circles, do you recall?"

Like a marble statue, Hannah stood frozen. Astrid put the pillow down.

"For Hannah with the green eyes?" I nodded yes. Hannah relaxed.

"How are you?"

"Frazzled and tired. Writing and researching, then more researching and writing. Oh, the picture on the mantel is new! I like it."

"It's from the museum. It's Lee. The moon is Lee."

"Put your briefcase up. We'll have a spot of tea."

Astrid set the milk and sugar on the table as usual. One, two, three; spoons and three napkins waltzed to their places.

Astrid educated me, "It's a waltz, Lee, in three-quarter time."

"It is," my mouth turned up at the corners. Hannah joined us; I got the teacups from the cupboard. Astrid finished setting the table. Steam rose from the cups.

Astrid said, "Don't touch, hot, very, very hot." Hannah agreed. The steam mesmerized Astrid, waiting for permission to sip.

"Tell me about the new picture, Astrid."

"It's a Japanese moon, like Lee. Only she's not Japanese. She Irish English."

"I see," Hannah didn't understand.

"I was born in Ireland but moved to England after my father died," I changed the subject. "I hope you like salmon, Hannah."

"Look! I'm a fish!" Astrid sucked her cheeks and wiggled the back of her hands against her cheeks. Hannah giggled; I rolled my eyes.

"You're so silly," I said.

"Oh, no!" cried Astrid, "No scones!"

"Calm down, calm down. The basket's on the countertop. Hannah, could you reach them, please."

"No! That's my job!" Astrid jumped up, sloshing the tea from our cups. I said, "Stop," but she kept going. The basket she grabbed from Hannah's hand tumbled onto the floor. Astrid threw herself on the floor, head in hand, saying, "Oh, Astrid, you did it this time. No scones for you." She covered her ears, waggling her head.

To comfort her, Hannah bent down, and I let her.

Hannah sat eye level with her, "Look, Astrid, some are still in the basket. All is not lost." Gently, she moved Astrid's hand from her ears, "It's all right, Astrid. Nothing's broken. See here, three scones are still in here." Astrid turned away. Hannah took the basket to the table. She extended her hand to Astrid: I awaited a response.

Astrid stopped Hannah's hand, "No hugs."

"No hugs," said Hannah as she helped Astrid to her feet.

Hands in her lap, eyes cast down, "I did a bad thing, Lee."

"Yes, you did." I'd learned not to baby her. "How are you going to fix what you did?"

"I dunno."

"Oh, I think you should try."

Hannah's mouth opened, my hand went up and I shook my head. In this situation, Astrid had to make right her wrong.

"This type of impulsive behavior must be corrected." God, I hated sounding like my mother.

"Astrid, what should you have done?"

"Waited, be patient, Astrid. Lee says, be patient."

"Apologies?"

"I'm sorry."

"To whom?"

"I'm sorry to Lee and Hannah with the green eyes, I'm sorry." The cups were sitting in saucers, half full of lukewarm tea.

She sulked, "Time out?"

I didn't respond. The egg timer sat on the kitchen window ledge. The chair scooted across the floor, "Five minutes, Lee?" The egg timer clicked as she set it.

"Yes, five minutes."

Clomp, clomp, clomp, quickly up the stairs. For Hannah, this became a teachable moment. There were countless moments where Astrid didn't understand the world around her; this wasn't one.

"It's my fault. I should…"

I cut Hannah off. "There's no 'poor Astrid' in this house. There are but a few rules outside of safety. Astrid is not allowed to leave the table under any circumstances without permission. You may think me harsh, but it's a safety issue. Her only concept of time comes from routine, her watch, and her day planner. And, yes, the egg timer."

My explanation came out clear. Hannah must know I couldn't let Astrid run amok. "A hurricane builds up speed the longer it moves, a snowball rolls aimlessly down a mountain turning into an avalanche; so it is with Astrid. Damage happens when the brakes aren't applied; damage to everything. You're knowledgeable, and I respect you for all the wisdom imparted. However, Astrid is a constant work in progress. I will not lie to you; it's exhausting. I'm reminded every time I look in the mirror. Do not indulge her because she's different. There is a fine line to walk here. I stopped you from helping her, not to be mean-spirited, but to give you a teachable moment. I hope you understand." I gave an apology for the lecture.

Hannah placed her hand on mine, "You're right, Lee. Books aren't the same as experience. Thank you. I'll watch more and practice restraint the rest of the week. At least, I'll try."

We cleared the table and waited for the clunky sound of footsteps. I put on a fresh kettle as Hannah rinsed the teacups. "Is she able to help with cooking?"

A short blast of laughter burst from me, "Sorry, Hannah, that was a perfectly logical question. Hand whisking in a large deep bowl, scrambling eggs, and tearing salad greens are solo tasks. We bake together on Thursday mornings. She chooses the type of cookies for the week, and we follow the recipes. She reads on a fourth-grade level, mostly."

The ding from the timer sent Astrid flying downstairs; abruptly, she stopped.

"Come, I made a fresh pot, and there's still a scone for you."

Astrid lumbered to her chair and sat, head down.

"Tell Hannah what we did today?" The brightness of my voice forgave all her antics.

Eyes to the ceiling, she said, "British Museum to see the mummies and the Japanese man's paintings."

Astrid flipped her glance at me, "Where's my painting?"

"It's sitting on the mantel, silly. Finish your scone. Chew, you're not a vacuum cleaner." I discussed the rainy-day places of choice. She loved art. I relayed the story of our youth when Astrid's knowledge of art and artists threw me for a loop. At twelve, she knew more about paintings than I ever imagined.

"Back then, I was very jealous of her. When I asked where she learned about art in my twelve-year-old haughty tone, she put me in my place. The church, she told me as if I were an idiot."

"I don't say idiot to you, Lee. Lee is not an idiot. Lee is smart."

"Thank you, Astrid. You don't call me an idiot. Put dishes in the sink."

Astrid led Hannah to the mantel, "Hokusai's *Cloud Ladder to the Moon*," Astrid said correctly. "I bought the big one." She grinned. It took up most of the mantle.

"Tell me about this picture, please."

Hannah held Astrid's hand, fingers interlaced as they stood before the fireplace. Astrid said I was her moon, and somebody was helping me stay in the sky. Part of me wanted to cry. I was the one with a problem, the problem of accepting help.

"Can we hang it up? Can we hang up there, please?"

Hannah and I carefully removed the mirror under the supervision of Astrid's chorus of *Be Careful's*.

| 36 |

NASA?

Astrid's acceptance of Hannah grew each day, but not without minor meltdowns. I tried very hard to let Hannah defuse these episodes without my help. A major test came a few days later when I planned to go to Lyndon's to debrief. With Hannah at home, I was taking a big step for myself, cutting the cord with Astrid for the first time since Mother's death over five years before. At lunch, Hannah and I explained the plan to Astrid. At five o'clock, I'd leave to meet Lyndon to talk business. Astrid and Hannah would eat dinner together, watch her show, have a cookie, then bed.

"When are you coming home? Are you coming back?" I heard the panic in her voice.

With my arm around her shoulders, I softly said, "I will be home shortly after nine. You may stay up with Hannah or go on to bed. I am coming home to my shiny star. No worries. Okay? I wrote everything out by the hour. Can you read it to me?"

Her finger pointed to each word as she read. Hannah stuck it to the refrigerator with a magnet.

The laundry room located in the basement was off-limits to Astrid. The door under the stairwell was always locked inside and out to keep Astrid from falling. Saturday morning, Astrid would bring her laundry bag, and I would wash and dry it. Together we folded clothes and put them away upstairs. Astrid's task that day was to show Hannah where to put things. As they went upstairs, I channeled my eavesdropping skills. Astrid's wardrobe was divided into three sections: the left side held drawers, the center for hanging clothes and shoes; and the right-side compartment was closed. It held her keyboard, draped in plastic. I heard Hannah ask what was behind the door.

Astrid replied, "Bad dreams, don't open it." She dropped the issue. Hannah fully understood what transpired, killing the music in Astrid. The fact she described the compartment as bad dreams was a new revelation.

At four, I began to get ready for my dinner with Lyndon. Just like days gone by, Astrid sat on the bed watching me put on make-up. The wrinkles on my face made me appear older than my thirty-two years. Hidden in my hair were depressing strands of grey.

"Are you going out with John?" There was a surprise question.

"No, Astrid, John is married to someone else. I'm going to see Lyndon tonight."

"On a date with Lyndon to Angelo's?"

I turned to her, "No, Astrid, she's my friend. I'm visiting her at her house."

"She doesn't like me anymore."

"That's not true. Lyndon likes you very much. Why do you think that way?"

"She's not eating dinner with us."

I explained her flawed logic in third-grade terms the best way I could without upsetting her more. Downstairs together, before I left, I took her by the shoulders, looking up at her, "Astie, are you my best friend?"

She said yes in her standard pose, slumped shoulders, eyes on the ceiling.

"Then you know I love you first. It's not like going out with John. Do you understand?"

"Yes. You're coming back, and I can stay up if I want to."

"Yes, you can get ready for bed and stay up with Hannah. Maybe she can read you a story."

"Okay."

Hannah was in the kitchen, stirring a pot of vegetable soup; I glanced at her. She flashed an okay sign at me.

"Give me a hug." Arms outstretched, never wrapping her arms around me, Astrid squeezed me like a pair of tongs.

"Have fun with Hannah, Astrid."

Pointing her finger at me, Astrid said, "Use good manners, Lee."

"Yes, ma'am. Should I tell Lyndon hello from you?"

"No."

"Okay, then. See you later. Thank you, Hannah."

New Found Feelings

The car found its way to Lyndon's, my mind unquieted.

"How's everything, Lee?" Lyndon asked. "You're wringing your hands. Relax!"

"I'm sorry, Lyndon. It's difficult."

When she asked about Hannah, I gave no complaints. I just prayed the phone might stay silent. After four days, everything proceeded smoothly despite two minor meltdowns. Lyndon poured the wine, "I think she'll work?"

"Trust is always an issue with Astrid. It's only been four days."

"You've said that twice in two minutes, and it's difficult. It's more complicated for you, isn't it?"

Hesitating, I answered her. "Yes. I hate to admit it, but yes. Astrid has always been a sizeable part of my life."

"It's time you have a life of your own. You're intelligent and attractive, Lee. How did Astrid take it leaving her with Hannah tonight?"

"Astrid sits behind me every time I put on makeup. She asked if I was going out with John. I was amused by the question. When I said I was going to Lyndon's house, Astrid didn't understand why we were going on a date."

"Obviously, it's been a while since you've been out," she chuckled. On an empty stomach, the wine made me lightheaded. The aroma of garlic and butter wafted through the house.

"Come in the kitchen. If memory serves me well, you like shrimp."

"Shrimp Scampi, wow, you went all out."

"It's a special night for you, Lee. The first night in a long time, and hopefully the start of many more." It sounded a bit suggestive, yet I wasn't offended. The wine helped, I'm sure. The plates were China; Lyndon arranged the food like a fine restaurant. Candles were lit, a toast in my honor; I suddenly thought about Claudia and got slightly nervous.

"You cook like a chef in a five-star establishment. Everything is perfect."

"Do I make you nervous? You seem fidgety."

"I'm sorry, Lyndon. I keep waiting for the phone to ring."

"Oh, God, Lee. Relax. What's the worst that could happen? She throws a fit. Trust Hannah, for God's sake."

"I'm ruining the night. I'm so sorry." She poured me another glass of wine.

"I'll take care of the dishes later. Come to the living room." While she stoked the fire, it was indeed the wine speaking when I asked about Claudia. Lyndon looked puzzled.

"I'm sorry, it's none of my business." The glow of the fire gave her skin a beautiful radiance. Salt and pepper hair made her look distinguished. She sat next to me.

"Why do you ask, Lee?"

"Honestly, I don't know. The wine, I suppose." I think I insulted her.

"Well, you know what they say, a drunk man's words are a sober man's dreams; or in this case, a woman's. Claudia went her way; I stayed put. My mother was ill. Claudia was stealing my time away from what was more important."

"After Mother passed away, I threw myself into my work. Mum died two years ago. I haven't seen anyone socially in a while. Now you understand why I jumped at the chance to help you and Astrid. I feel needed again," she took a sip of wine. "Why did you call, Lee."

"You are someone I respect, the only one who understands what I've been going through. You let me flex my schedule. You encouraged me to enroll in the doctoral program; you are my mentor and most trusted friend, Lyndon Hammersmith."

"Maybe once Hannah settles in, you'll come back to the program. You always said you wanted my job." My hand rested on my cheek; I gazed into her eyes full of wisdom and compassion for a minute.

"Lyndon, maybe I should go. I promised to be home by nine."

"I'll drive your car and take a taxi home. You're tipsy, Darling."

"Oh, Lyndon, I can take a taxi. You don't have to drive me. You've been drinking too."

"I've had one glass to your three. I'll drive."

With a sigh of surrender, I handed her the keys. Yes, I was tipsy and couldn't correctly button my coat. She reached for the top button; my eyes met hers. The feeling was foreign but not off-putting.

"Let's go," she said. In silence, I wondered how she interpreted my actions.

At the house, she walked me up the stoop, "Should I come in?"

"Of course, I'm not leaving you out there to freeze."

The key turned in the lock; I expected Astrid to come running at me. The house was quiet. Hannah tip-toed down the stairs.

"She's asleep; I gave her the pill. Five minutes later, she was out. When it got so quiet, I checked on her."

"How did it go?" I expected some wild tale.

"I stuck to the routine. At dinner, Astrid asked where you were. I told her. Twice she asked when you were coming home. I said nine-thirty, in case you might be later than nine."

"Smart girl," Lyndon said to Hannah. Hannah excused herself from the room to study.

"Lyndon, I know what you're going to say, so don't."

The remark tickled her, "I won't. So, it's your turn. You said if Hannah worked out, you'd buy me dinner."

I felt my mouth turn up in a grin, "Yes, I do owe you dinner."

"Next Friday? Hannah's only staying for a week."

'I ... I'm… it might be too soon." Lyndon's face lost the smile.

"I'll ask Hannah to come back next Friday. Who knows? She may never leave."

Before she left, I caught her sleeve, "Lyndon, thank you. For everything. It was a lovely time. I enjoyed every minute."

"Me, too, Lee."

| 37 |

"Is She Staying?"

Emotions were complicated for Astrid. She sulked all of Wednesday. The day was full of *okay*s, and *I dunno*'s. Hopefully, today would be better. She never mentioned a word about the night I went to Lyndon's.

"It's Tuesday, cookie day." She sounded like a weather reporter.

"What cookies are we making today?"

"Chocolate chip. Hannah likes chocolate chip."

"Oh, how nice. You both like the same kind."

"Hannah likes chocolate chips. Chocolate chips for Hannah."

There was a connection between them. I could feel it. Astrid sat at the table, "Is Hannah leaving?" She almost sounded sad.

"I don't know. We'll ask Hannah tonight at supper. Okay?"

"Okay." Astrid concentrated as she rolled the dough into ping pong-sized balls. "I don't want Hannah with the green eyes to go home. Can she stay, Lee? I promise to be good. "

"I know you will. I don't want Hannah to go home either, Astrid, but it's Hannah's decision. I can't tell her what to do."

"I can." She pointed to Hannah's chair, "Hannah! You stay here. Don't go home!"

"You sound mean, Astrid. How can you say that so it's not mean?"

Astrid licked the cookie dough from her fingers.

"Astrid, if you're going to speak to Hannah, how should you talk?"

"Stay here, Hannah, please. I don't want you to go, please."

"That is much better. But remember, Hannah gets to choose."

Astrid turned in for a late nap. At four, Hannah returned. A finger moved to my lips, "Shhh, she's asleep. We have a few minutes to talk. We were baking cookies, and she asked me if you were going to stay. Before supper, I wanted to ask you if … Will you be staying with us, Hannah?"

Elbows on the table, hand in prayerful pause, she spoke, "I've given this situation a lot of thought."

I wanted to shout, *"Out with it!"*

"And prayers, Lee. I sometimes visit my brother and cousins in Wales."

Shocked, I said, "I didn't know you had a brother."

"When my mother died and my father got sick, I couldn't watch after him. There was trouble; he fell in with some hooligans. Our aunt and uncle, my father's brother, took him in. Teddy stays out of trouble now and wants to be a fireman. We're not close, Lee."

"I see. So does that mean you're staying?"

The upstairs door slammed, and Astrid ran down, stopping immediately at the bottom, "Hannah's back, Lee. See, Hannah's back!"

"Yes, I can see that."

Running to my side, Astrid whispered in my ear, "Can I ask her?"

"Get the milk and sugar; we can talk over tea."

With great care, Astrid set the milk on the table. Astrid measured the placement of the sugar bowl exactly two fingers away from the milk.

"Hannah likes chocolate chip cookies, Lee." She rocked rhythmically, side to side. It was her way to ask if we could have cookies. I set two bread plates on the table and put the cookie jar next to them. Astrid pointed to the cat-shaped cookie jar.

Her eyes fixated on the jar; hand tucked under her arms. "I don't… I don't like to take kitty's head off."

I lifted the black and white cat's ceramic head off. "Wash your hands first, then you may have two cookies each."

Astrid gracefully laid two cookies on each plate, "Lee doesn't like chocolate chip cookies. Hannah likes chocolate chip cookies."

I wanted to think Hannah would stay, so I daringly told Astrid to politely ask her question, with an emphasis on *politely*.

Astrid held her head back, "Hannah, with the green eyes, will you stay with me?"

I shook my head and smiled; it sounded like a wedding proposal. "I informed her, come what may, it's your decision. Say what you think, not what you think we want to hear."

Hannah sucked in her bottom lip. My heart stopped; Astrid pushed herself halfway up from the table.

Then Hannah said, "I didn't want to be stuck in a research lab. What I desired the most was a purpose, a reason to get up in the morning, to be helpful. If I had become a nun, I'm sure I wouldn't have found life very challenging." Hannah took Astrid's hand; with love, she said, "I found what I desired, is here."

I was in tears; Astrid was absolutely confused.

"Literal, Hannah."

"Astrid, I'm staying with you."

"Don't jump!"

Her hands were flapping, feet stomping, and a cross between a wail and laugh came from her. "She's staying, Lee! Hannah, with the green eyes, is staying, Yippee!" Astrid stopped abruptly, "Why are you crying, Lee?"

"Because I'm happy."

"Happy doesn't cry, Lee. Happy does this," Astrid ran around the table. With a finger on each side of my mouth, she pushed the corners up.

"Happy does this."

"Yes, Astrid. No more crying. Only smiling. Let's go to Angelo's for supper." As Astrid jumped around the kitchen, I asked Hannah if she was positive.

"Yes, I'm positive."

"You read everything in Astrid's folder? The soiled sheets, embarrassing public behavior, the bruises you'll sustain?"

"Yes, Lee, I've read it all. I have accepted all of it."

"You'll get your vacation and a day or two off every week. Is the salary sufficient?"

"It's more than generous, Lee. I'll sign the contract whenever you want."

"I'll have Mr. Roberts come by the house Monday evening. Get through your studies, Hannah. If you need time off, just say so. Oh, gosh, I forgot. Franklin Godfrey is coming for tea on Sunday. I haven't told Astrid yet."

Astrid had her coat on.

"Astrid, take your coat off and sit down. We'll leave at five-thirty. What time is it?"

"Four-forty-five. Forty-five minutes. I gotta pee."

"Go."

My hand touched my forehead, "Are you sure, Hannah?"

She chuckled, "I'm sure, Lee."

After dinner and when the excitement died down, Astrid went to bed. Hannah and I discussed moving details before she turned in for the evening. I dialed up Lyndon.

"Hello, you. Want to talk?"

"Lee? You don't sound like yourself. Are you all right?"

"Never better."

"She's staying!"

"Yes, and I owe you dinner. Friday, 6:30, I'll pick you up, and I promise to stay sober."

"Well, that's no fun! Seriously, I'm truly happy for you. And, yes, 6:30 is fine."

"Sorry to call so late, Lyndon. I couldn't wait to tell you. If I waited until tomorrow, I'd burst."

"You're fine. Should I dress up for Friday?"

"Absolutely, a dress." I have no idea what I was doing, but it felt like fun. I caught her off guard.

"I don't think I have one."

"Buy one; you can afford it." Silence. "Are you still there?"

"Uh, yes."

"Friday, 6:30. *Ciao, Bella!*"

I sat in the dark, watching the fire's last embers flicker. Something inside me felt different; it was freeing. My mind ran through a field of flowers and along sandy beaches. As the Beatles sang, this bird had flown. 1981 was ending, Astrid had Hannah, and I could breathe.

I started my presentation for NASA at work that week, gathering data and photographs. I checked my email; Lyndon replied to an email I sent with a memo attached. NASA was collecting our data for input into a new supercomputer. Their focus on deep-space objects was expanding. The conference in the spring would bring several countries with similar data together to share our findings. It was a big deal.

After Christmas would be an excellent time to start dropping hints of my departure to Astrid. In the meantime, I needed to tell Astrid about Mr. Godfrey.

Oh Friday, I calmly told Astrid, "Sunday, Mr. Godfrey is coming for tea."

She made an ugly, scrunched-up face, "Why?"

The suspicion of Mr. Godfrey lingered. I assured Astrid his motives were admirable.

"Hannah hasn't met Mr. Godfrey. I thought she might like to meet your teacher."

"He's not my teacher. I don't have a teacher!" I was startled by her outburst. Astrid shouted at me, "No teachers!"

I pointed to the floral armchair, "Sit there and calm yourself. There's no reason to shout." Astrid drew deep breaths, slowly blowing them out. Counting after each breath, ten in all.

"Better?" She nodded yes. "Good. Mr. Godfrey isn't your teacher anymore. He's a good friend. And Mr. Godfrey was never mean to you. He's a gentleman. Isn't he?"

"I dunno."

"Well, I'm telling you he is a good man. I expect politeness from you. No running upstairs when he comes. Clear?"

Astrid's head hung low, "Okay."

"Hannah will be home soon. I'll make some tea."

Over tea, I discussed Mr. Godfrey's visit with Hannah in front of Astrid, emphasizing the *former* teacher.

Shifty-eyed, she mumbled, "He's not my teacher."

When Astrid left the table, I informed Hannah of the earlier meltdown. I wanted to remind Astrid I was going out tonight, but she fell asleep on the sofa.

"Should I wake her?"

I shook my head. Astrid needed a nap, and the quiet was welcome.

"How's your paper coming along?"

"I'm finished. My dissertation is Tuesday," she twittered, nervously.

"Oh, I remember the day I gave mine. Three grumpy old men sat on the board. I was shaking in my shoes. One of the stodgy old men yawned and cleared his throat; I knew I'd failed miserably."

Hannah sat with bated breath, "What happened?"

"I passed and was told to apply for my doctorate. Those men found my research intriguing."

"Why didn't you go on?"

I sighed, "My mother became gravely ill. Advanced colon cancer. She refused chemotherapy. It left me to care for Astrid."

Hannah expressed her regrets.

"Don't pity me, Hannah, please. I have few regrets. Besides, I like research; it gives me purpose. Lyndon is a godsend, finding an office for Astrid and me. There could be no other way for me to work and care for Astrid. That's why I'm taking her to dinner."

Astrid bolted up from the sofa, "Who's going to dinner? Me?"

I smiled at Hannah, my eyebrows arched, "I told you she has radar. Astrid, I am taking Lyndon to dinner tonight."

"Lyndon? Why?"

"Yes, my friend Lyndon. She helped us find Hannah."

"Was Hannah lost?"

I took a deep breath, "No, Hannah wasn't lost. Lyndon helped me." Geez, explaining everything in literal terms could be taxing.

Hannah replied, "Lyndon gave me your address, Astrid, so I could find you."

"Okay. Am I going, too?"

"Not this time."

"Next time? Am I going next time?"

"Yes, next time you can go. You can help Hannah with dinner. She's fixing dinner: salmon patties, mash, and steamed carrots."

Astrid followed me upstairs. The twilight sky began turning darker. Astrid lay on my bed staring up through the skylight as I dressed.

I saw her reflection in the vanity mirror, "Astrid, do you remember our first sleepover?" I asked.

"You are the moon; I am the bright star."

"What else?"

"I dunno."

"Forever together," I said,

In a moment of rare reflection, Astrid spoke, "Will we be together forever? Some people die, you know. They die and go up in the clouds. If they are bad Catholics, we must pray them out of purgatory. We don't go to purgatory, Lee." Astrid crossed her hands over her hand. "Will we die, Lee?"

"We all die, Astrid. All living things die, Luv. Don't worry; we're not dying anytime soon. Okay?"

"I see the moon. It sees me."

I held out my hand, "Come on, star bright, let's go downstairs. I smell something good."

"Fish! It's Friday! Fish day. The fish day, every Friday."

I slipped on my coat; she gave me a kiss on the cheek. "Hannah, the number to the restaurant is by the phone. And…"

She smiled, "And I know Lyndon's number by heart. No worries."

"When are you coming home? Bedtime at nine o'clock."

"Later. Behave for Hannah. Should I tell Lyndon hello from you?"

"No."

I glanced at Hannah and shrugged my shoulders. Hannah reassured me they would be fine.

The Date

The door opened to Lyndon in a dress, "Close your mouth and sit down."

"Yes, ma'am."

"Lee, I'm puzzled by your request. This newfound freedom is bringing out a side of you I've never seen before. I don't know whether to be happy or worried."

"I just want to have fun, Lyndon. I've been cooped up in a cage for years. Dressing up and going out for dinner is exhilarating for me. And you always wear pantsuits. You look smashing in that Christmassy red."

Lyndon's elbow rested on the arm of her chair, hand tucked under her chin. She bit her bottom lip, "I need to know your intentions."

After a moment, I carefully said, "Lyndon, I admire you greatly. You've always been in my corner with compassion and support. I find myself caring about you." I smiled at her, "And you're incredible company. I hate small talk; we have a lot in common."

"I'm ten years older than you. Are you attracted to me, Lee? I need to know." She didn't ask out of desperation but out of need.

I found myself biting my fingernail, "I don't know what I am. I'm trying to figure myself out, Lyndon. But yes, I find you attractive."

Lyndon turned away from me. I felt ashamed, thinking I'd ruined my only friendship. There was nothing else I could say.

Lyndon chuckled, "A nervous Lenora McConnell walked into my office with a wet shirt. Bright, curious, and full of life, this young woman. I watched her as she grew with a thirst for knowledge. Then I watched her get married to a barrister who would try to stick her in a cookie-cutter marriage. I used to pray that wouldn't happen to you," she breathed, "And it didn't."

With my hands in my lap, I leaned forward, "I shouldn't have gotten married. I saw the writing on the wall but, I did what was expected of me. Astrid's breakdown was my breakout. Then you caught me before

I hit the ground." I moved beside her, "Can you help me find out who I am?"

The back of her hand brushed my cheek, "I don't want either of us to get hurt, Lee."

"I know, but I want you to kiss me. I want to know how it feels."

"What if you don't like it? What then?"

"If it makes me uncomfortable, we'll still be friends. Right?"

"Yes, but let's go to dinner. I know of a special place. They have good food and a great atmosphere. Give me your keys."

We navigated the back streets, parking in Cambridge's downtown. We walked two blocks in the biting cold down an alleyway. Lyndon knocked on the heavy wooden door, a small window opened, and she showed a card. It was a private club with an exclusive clientele.

We were met by a voluptuous young African woman in a daring blue sweater dress. She knew Lyndon and led us to a dimly lit booth. The room was extensive, with a long-mirrored bar of walnut, and maybe twenty booths. A disc jockey played pop music. There was even a small dance floor. Lyndon introduced me to Sheba; she took our drink orders. I checked out the room to find all women.

"Surprised?" Lyndon asked.

"Pleasantly."

She invited me to sit next to her, where I could fully view the dance floor. Lyndon ordered a seafood platter for two.

"I didn't know places like this existed. All women."

"You've led a sheltered life, Lee, but it's the 1980s. This lifestyle is more tolerated now. We still must be careful, thus the membership. How do you feel about the place?"

"Comfortable. I don't worry about some man hitting on me," I chuckled.

"With your dazzling hazel eyes, you might have to worry about a woman hitting on you."

Her remark made me laugh; my cheeks flushed. I watched the dance floor, entranced by all the different kinds of women. Some were masculine in appearance; short hair, tucked-in Oxford shirts, wide belted pants with a wallet in their back pocket. Others were soft, pretty with long hair and short skirts. Lyndon educated me on the terms: butch and femme.

Lyndon asked, "What do you think I am?"

"Neither and both. Just because your hair is shorter doesn't mean you're a butch. You wear make-up, and that red dress is very flattering. You have a feminine side."

Lyndon stared ahead and grinned. After dinner, Lyndon led me to the dance floor. Someone said they hadn't seen her in a while, and she looked fantastic. The music was slow; she pulled me to her. Chanel No. Five. I took a deep breath, laid my head on her shoulder, and kissed her neck, "You smell wonderful."

She whispered in my ear, "Thank you." Her voice, her breath in my ear, was arousing. I liked the feeling.

Later, in the booth, she turned my face to her. "Do you still want me to kiss you?"

"Please." Her eyes were the blue of an ocean. Warm lips caressed my lips; I indulged her. Catching my breath, I wanted more. This time I kissed her, nibbling on her bottom lip.

"Slow down, Lee," whispered.

She drove us to her house and invited me in.

"Do you have to be home by nine?"

"No, not this time." She made a fire to warm the room. I took notice of her body in the sweater dress, wondering what it looked like underneath.

"Are you undressing with your eyes, Lenora McConnell?"

"Dr. Hammersmith, I'm desperately trying not to."

Lyndon laid down the rules. "Well, let's not move so fast, Lee. Discretion. If we pursue a relationship, we must be careful. No one—and I mean no one—can know. I could lose my job and be disgraced in the academic world."

Her words sent terror through my veins. "Oh, God, Lyndon. I'm selfish. I had no idea what might happen to you. I don't want anything to be noticeable. For me, I now realize the authorities could take Astrid away. Maybe I should leave."

As I stood up, Lyndon caught my elbow, "It doesn't mean we couldn't see each other, Lee. We just need to use caution. I find you desirable, intellectually and physically. I always have."

Her arm encircled me; a kiss of passion engulfed my lips. Automatically my arms circled her neck. I loved feeling these emotions, but I couldn't bear the thought of ruining her life. I pushed away from her. There was so much at stake if I allowed this to continue.

"You've given me things to think about, Lyndon."

"Does that mean we won't be seeing each other like this again?"

"Don't rule anything out, please. I care for you deeply." I took my coat from the rack.

She buttoned the front of my coat, "And now you know how it feels. I've given myself away."

Lyndon opened the door.

I pivoted to her, "Thank you for wearing the dress. It suits you."

| 38 |

Hannah and the Snowman

"You seem to have a lot on your mind lately," wondered Hannah. I blew off her concern about the seminar preparation. The subject changed to Christmas shopping with Astrid.

"On Tuesday, I'm taking Astrid to Harrod's. She'll want to buy you a gift. Any suggestions?"

Hannah couldn't think of anything. I warned her that potentially, Astrid's purchase could be a stuffed animal. Whatever she chose comes with an Astrid scarf. Astrid's scarves were meticulously knitted. If she missed a stitch, she started over without frustration. When mother taught her, it was with stalwart patience. Astrid learned that mistakes happen to everyone. We planned to go by the yarn store Tuesday also.

"Today is cleaning day."

Astrid's job was to vacuum the living room and sweep her bedroom. I let Hannah know the caveat; she tended to vacuum the exact same spot for five minutes. It was also linen day. She could strip her sheets but needed help putting on the fresh ones.

"That's where you could help. I keep fresh sheets and towels in a cabinet in the linen closet. I bring them up for Astrid to make the bed. I have a key to the basement door for you. Tuesday evenings, I wash our clothes. Astrid leaned to keep light colors in one pile, darks in the other. You can do yours anytime, but keep the door locked, please or towels will be everywhere."

I collected her linens. Astrid came flying downstairs. All the running up and down was an accident waiting to happen. I wasn't in the mood for an emergency room visit with Astrid.

When she came in the room, Oh, gosh. Astrid's shirt was on backward, and her pants unzipped. I nicely asked her to check her clothes and tell me what was wrong. Her body bent halfway to see her pants. She lifted her head with an oops, then zipped up her pants. The long-sleeved navy shirt had her initials embroidered in yellow on the front.

"Where's your name?" I asked.

She ran her hands down the front and nonchalantly answered, "It's gone."

"Are you sure? Where's the tag?"

Pulling her shirt away from her chest, she exclaimed, "It's here!"

"Where should it be?"

She proceeded to pull her arms from the sleeves, turn the shirt around, point to her name, and with great surprise, "It's here! Looky, Lee, it's here."

Astrid forgot something. Running back up, she came down with her signature black leggings and began taking her pants off in the living room. Thank God Astrid wore underwear. Never could she put on her leggings by herself. It was necessary to roll them up and get her feet in, or there'd be a meltdown of frustration.

The snow was falling in big fluffy flakes. Hannah finished the breakfast dishes while I built a fire.

"Psst," Hannah pointed at the back door. With hands plastered to the window, Astrid fixated on the falling snow. Then I heard a humming; *Silent Night*. Hannah stopped to listen. Hearing her hum gave me chills.

I gently put my hand on her shoulder, "It's beautiful. After your chores, should you and Hannah make a snowman?"

No flapping, no stomping. "Yes, please."

"Go up and change your bed. Hannah will help."

Typically, after her housework finished, she took a supervised shower. Her shower days were Tuesday, Thursday, and Saturday. Not being in the area while she showered meant soap stayed in her hair, or she'd forget to wash certain areas. I usually rattled off the checklist of body parts to be washed. Today, however, I'd let her play in the snow, monitoring the time or frostbite could set in. People with autism seem to have trouble distinguishing the temperature flux within themselves. Astrid could be shivering but stay too long outside.

The Snowman

Upstairs, Astrid's happy squeals filled the stairwell, followed by Hannah asking her to slow down. Coming to an abrupt stop, Astrid said, "Hannah wants to play in the snow, too! Can we go play? Please. Hannah wants to play!" Astrid fidgeted, awaiting my answer.

"Yes, you may. However, when I tell you to come inside, you must. Clear?" Astrid nodded.

"Let Hannah in pin your braid up to fit under your hat to keep your hair dry."

Hesitant, Astrid turned to Hannah, then to me, "No. You put my hair up, not Hannah. You, you pin my hair up."

"Fine, go upstairs, bring me the pins. Your mittens and hat are on the top shelf of the wardrobe." Astrid pushed Hannah out of the way. Hannah shrugged her shoulders.

"I wanted to gauge her reaction. I got what I expected."

"Give her time. She'll come around," said Hannah.

The snow slowed to a light flurry as I watched their interaction. Instinctively, Hannah knew when to give Astrid space to try and fail until she asked for Hannah's help. I couldn't be more pleased. Hannah's statement about her presence here was that it was a calling. I believed wholeheartedly. After only ten days, her progress with Astrid was astounding.

"Hot cocoa is waiting for two young ladies. Astrid, sit by the door and remove your snow boots. Hannah, grab the coats and hang them in your bathroom on the shower rod."

"Did you see him?"

"I did, indeed."

Astrid hovered over her snowman mug, "Five marshmallows, Lee. Where are my marshmallows, Lee?"

I handed her the bag, "Sit down." The marshmallows were in a perfect line behind the mug. Hannah watched as Astrid counted them three times. Always three times. One by one, she dropped them in the hot liquid to watch them melt. Studying my face, she waited for permission to drink.

"Blow on it; use your spoon to test it."

The spoon touched her lips, "Too hot! I'll wait, too hot. Astrid, you'll burn your tongue. Cookies, please, Lee."

A plate of cookie Christmas trees sat on the table, iced white with colorful sprinkles. Astrid handed the plate to Hannah, "Take one, only one, Hannah. Now, you give it to me, Hannah."

She never ceased to amaze me. This behavior was new.

"Lee, we need raisins and a carrot!" General Innis commanded. My eyebrows raised, "Oh?"

"I don't want to eat them, Lee," she said with contempt as her eyes widened, "They are for Mr. Snowman. He doesn't have eyes or a nose."

"I see."

With her eyes bugging out, "No! He couldn't see, Lee."

"I understand. Hannah can run out and fix him when we finish."

"Okay."

Raisins for his mouth, a carrot for his nose, and I found two large buttons in the button box for the snowman's eyes. Hannah received applause from Astrid. They stood by the fire, warming their hands.

"Will he melt?" she asked Hannah. Reassuring Astrid, Hannah said he'd stay for a few days. The answer satisfied her.

"Shower time, Astrid. It will warm you," I said.

"Five more minutes," hold up five fingers, "Five more minutes, Lee."

"No, go upstairs. Hannah will help you." Astrid slinked up the stairs.

"Hannah, be warned; she doesn't know what modesty is. And make sure the shampoo is out of her hair, please."

"Oh. I will." I'm not sure Hannah was ready for this part of the job.

Later, Hannah and I talked seriously about her future. Did she grasp the responsibilities of her employment with us? It encompassed many details. Astrid was high maintenance. The bathing, Astrid's menstrual cycle, cleaning up accidents, keeping her safe, wrangling her in public, the staring and ugly remarks; could she handle all these things?

"You truly haven't seen her at her worst. The meltdowns you've seen are average for her, but" I pulled my pants leg up, showing her my shin, bruised from the kicking, "There's this. And she bit me on the forearm once. My spontaneous reaction will forever haunt me; I snapped, smacking her in the face. Naturally, it stunned us both. She said, 'Lee, you hit me; hitting is bad, Lee.' I showed her the bloody bite mark, telling her never to bite me again."

Hand on her cheek, Hannah sighed. With that horror story, she was bound to leave.

"Lee, I'm twenty-four. My practicum happened to be in the city-run mental hospital. A patient nearly choked the life out of me; there was no choice other than to fight back." The hospital staff taught her the release and resistance tactics for self-defense. She learned the holds to keep a patient under control without harming them.

"I expect some bruising and aggression from Astrid. It comes with the job, Lee. As much as I've studied, there are no surprises. I am fully aware of the challenges, but I'm also aware of the joys. It's my desire to stay here and accept everything that comes with caring for Astrid."

"You are a godsend, Hannah. I feel you have meaningful insight that's taught me aspects of Astrid's affliction I never understood. My home is your home."

Under her contract, when I died, Hannah would receive everything for Astrid's care. The house was fully paid; my grandfather entrusted our financial future to the best advisors. Robert Baron, the son of Grandfather's fund's manager, paid our taxes; I received a statement of expenditures and all receipts each month. Astrid's medical records and guardianship papers were kept in a file in my bedroom upstairs. All these instructions and documents were held there.

"Astrid's medications are her 'vitamins.' Astrid is on birth control pills to keep her cycle regular. At night she is given a sleeping pill. They stay locked in my writing desk drawer; the key is underneath the mantel clock."

I suggested Tuesdays and Thursdays should be her days off. Hannah balked at days off, but I insisted, knowing what lie ahead. She'd need a day to herself. In the new year, I wanted to wean Astrid from my Friday office hours. The group going to Florida would be meeting every Friday starting in February.

"Oh my, it's eleven o'clock. I need to go to bed. One more thing: what would you like to do for your graduation? I insist on a celebration."

Pleasantly surprised, Hannah said, "I'm not sure. My undergraduate degree finished without fanfare; I'll have to think of something."

After Mass that Sunday, we stopped at the bakery to buy fresh blueberry scones and bread.

"Blueberry scones!"

"Astrid, we have a visitor for tea today." I hadn't reminded her Mr. Godfrey was coming.

Her forehead wrinkled, "Who? Who's coming? Lyndon? Lyndon's coming for tea?"

"Let's go inside. Take your coat off. I made a pot roast for lunch."

She banged her fist on the table, "Who's coming?"

Hannah surprised her by saying she was using bad manners. Astrid hadn't expected that; neither did I.

Hannah took over, "Astrid, Lee told me about someone who used to be your teacher. Mr. Godfrey."

"Oh, no," she whined.

"I want to meet him, Astrid. I heard him play with the London Symphony."

That got her attention, "You did? Was I there?"

"Sadly, no. I wish you were. I'd love to hear you play."

"I don't have music anymore," she shook her head. "It blew away like bubbles. It floated away."

I cleared my throat, remembering that awful day, "Ladies, please set the table."

"Could your music come back so I can hear you play?" Hannah asked. Placing the silverware, Astrid was deaf to the question. Hannah didn't ask again.

With the precision of a German train, the doorbell rang at four o'clock.

I told Astrid that she'd agreed not to leave the room. "Please, sit up straight."

After introductions were exchanged, Hannah told us of the concert.

"I saw you play in June, Mr. Godfrey," Hannah gazed at her teacup, "You were amazing." We sat at the table while Astrid *hmph*ed and guffed from the sofa. Mr. Godfrey paid her no mind, which I found odd. Hannah asked the name of the piano concerto.

"It was Beethoven's *Piano Sonata Number Fourteen in C Minor.*"

Astrid jumped up, "That's not right! It's the *Piano Sonata Fourteen in C-Sharp*! Not Minor!" Poor Mr. Godfrey; he'd experienced her wrath. We held our collective breath. Astrid sat at the table, fingers poised over the imaginary keys, "Da, da, da, Da, da, da. Like that, Beethoven's *Piano Sonata Number Fourteen in C-Sharp*, not C-Minor!"

Mr. Godfrey smiled, "You're right, Astrid. It is C-Sharp, I'm sorry. I made a mistake."

She patted his shoulder, "It's okay, Mr. Godfrey, we all make mistakes sometimes."

Then I realized he'd said it on purpose to spark her memory. Her reply, was a memory of music once played.

"Will you play for me again sometime, Astrid?" Mr. Godfrey asked. I watched Astrid's face for a clue into her thoughts; her eyes went to the ceiling. We waited.

Fingers fluttered toward the ceiling, "The music's gone. It floated away."

Mr. Godfrey asked, "Who told you that, Astrid?" His hand rested on his chin as he waited.

Staring up, she said, "Nobody."

"Then how do you know that's true, Astrid?"

"I dunno."

"Maybe we should try," he encouraged.

She shut down, "No. No music."

The tension broke with my direction, "Please, get the basket of scones from the counter. I'll get the tea."

"I don't want any," she said as she sat the basket on the table.

Astrid pulled at her sweater sleeve, twisting it out of shape. I knew the talk of music bothered her by her glum expression. While small talk carried on, I watched Astrid. One hand shaded her eyes; the other held the scone. When finished, she asked to be excused. Permission granted, she returned to her room.

Mr. Godfrey clasped his hands together, "I guess I did it this time."

"No, what you did was clever." I wanted to jump for joy. "No matter how brief, the glimmer of hope showed through. She corrected you, Mr. Godfrey. Your intentional mistake bothered her." I calmed myself, "Don't you see? The music is still there," I laughed, "Would anyone like a cognac?"

There was laughter until I heard a commotion upstairs; something hit the floor. My joy turned to panic.

"Astrid?" The three of us ran up the stairs. Astrid froze. She was wrestling her keyboard out of the closet. In shock, I stood there, speechless.

Me. Godfrey grinned, "Do you need some help?" Her head bobbed up and down with a yes. He waved us off; there was no resistance from me. Mr. Godfrey knew how to handle Astrid, always with kid gloves.

Bewildered, Hannah sat on the sofa beside me. I requested prayer. She crossed herself.

My words were from a dream. "Music was her world. It was a place of peace, of normalcy. She became the music." I drew a deep breath, "To think she could do it again is something I've dreamt, yet never thought it possible, Hannah. This is my Christmas miracle."

Mr. Godfrey came down, "I helped her set up the keyboard. Don't expect her to play anytime soon. She's fine but thinks you're upset with her, Lee."

"Oh, but I'm not. I'll talk with her. Help yourselves to tea or cognac or whatever." I turned my attention upstairs. "Astie, I'm coming up."

I heard her throw herself on the bed. The covers were pulled over her as she lay on her side. "I'm not upset about the keyboard." I pulled the covers down, laying on the bed with her, "I love you, my shiny star. I am very pleased with you. You set up your music again. Are you okay, Astrid?"

Astrid turned her head towards me, "You're not upset with me? I dropped it on the floor."

"I know, I'm not upset. Mr. Godfrey helped you fix it, right?"

"He fixed it. It's not broken."

"It's fine, Astie."

We lay facing each other. It felt as it did twenty-one years ago. Two young girls sleeping in the same bed. I brushed her hair from her eyes, those lollipop green eyes. "Will you come downstairs with me?"

"Is he still here?"

"Does that bother you?" She gave no response. I stood, offering her my hand. She took my hand and walked behind me. Mr. Godfrey held out the basket. Sweetly he said, "I saved you a blueberry scone, Astrid."

I coaxed her to the table. She sat with her hands in her lap. Mr. Godfrey put a scone on her plate.

"She's not mad at me. Lee's not mad at me."

"I told you she wouldn't be upset. Right?"

"Okay."

Hannah helped Astrid understand there is no pressure for her to play. Mr. Godfrey echoed the same sentiment. She peeked up at me through her fringe.

"Mr. Godfrey..." He interrupted me.

"How long have we known each other? Twelve years? Please, call me Franklin. I think I like that much better. It's not so formal."

In a moment of wonder, Astrid didn't disappoint, "I thought your name was Mister. Your name isn't Mister?"

A chuckle passed his lips, trying not to burst out laughing. "Your name is Astrid Innis; my name is Franklin Godfrey."

She jerked her head around, pointing at him, "Lee! His name is not Mister; it's Franklin! Isn't that nice? His name is Franklin."

I grinned, "Yes, it's very nice."

| 39 |

A Hole in the Hat

"What day is it, Astrid?" I asked.

"It's Tuesday, December the fifth, eight-forty-one in the morning."

"Do you remember what we're going to do today?"

With her head tipped back, she thought, "I dunno."

My voice filled with excitement, "Christmas shopping!" Astrid loved seeing the animated window holiday displays at Harrod's. She hated the "real" Santa in the store. One year she pointed her long finger at him and shouted, "You're not real!" I covered my eyes and pulled her to the elevator, leaving crying children and appalled parents in her wake. Now, we went in a side entrance, straight to the elevator.

Since Mother died, Astrid and I brought gifts for each other. I let her pick something for me. Every year I received a pair of socks or a piece of costume jewelry. Astrid wrote a wish list of three things. Astrid usually got one of three requests. When she asked for a bicycle, I crossed that off. Once, Astrid wished for an elephant to keep in the backyard. I asked if she would clean up poop; that was the end of the conversation. Last Christmas, Astrid broke my heart: she wished Grandfather could come from heaven to visit her.

Christmas was a little different this year; we were getting a gift for Hannah. On the way to the store, I asked Astrid what Hannah might like for Christmas.

"A llama in pajamas?" Hannah read her a book by that title.

"It's a nice idea, but I doubt if we'll find one at the store."

Astrid crossed her arms, "Humph. Books! Books, so Hannah can read to me." I explained how books were more of a gift for her. She thoughts some more.

Nearly scaring me to death, she yelled, "A hat! There's a hole in her head!"

"She has a hole in her head?" I asked.

"Yes, Hannah has a hole in her hat," Astrid stretched her arms out, and with bug-eyes, she exclaimed, "A big hole! Hannah needs a new hat."

"Well, that settles it. Hannah will have a hat for Christmas."

I parked the car, "Before we get out, Astrid, don't holler about Santa Claus."

"He's not real, just a man in a red suit. Santa's not real." Her head wobbled; she was obstinate.

"You know that, and I know, too. But little children believe he's real. We don't want to spoil Christmas for them. Do we?"

She mumbled, "He's not real. He's a man in a red suit."

"Please, Astrid, we can't shop for Hannah's hat if you yell. They will make us leave. Again. Promise me you won't yell."

"I won't yell, Lee. I promise I won't yell. He is just a man in a red suit. He's not Santa."

I smacked my forehead and hoped for the best. Straightaway, we headed for the elevator. It was crowded with shoppers. Astrid tried to push all the buttons; I grabbed her hand firmly with a "no." I politely smiled.

"Where's the elevator man who tells us what's on each floor?" she asked. To keep a barrage of questions at bay, I said he retired.

"Okay," she paused cocking her head to listen, "*Silver Bells. Silver bells, it's Christmas time in the city.* Did you know *Silver Bells*, Lee?"

"Why yes, I do. It's a pretty song. Where did you hear it?"

"On the BBC radio in my room." There was a radio in her room, but I'd never heard her turn it on.

"I know lots of Christmas songs. I played Christmas songs in the big house." She referred to John's family home.

"I remember." If Astrid wanted to say more, I wouldn't coax her.

The Shopping Meltdown

The elevator door opened to an extensive array of hats. Astrid's voice broke with panic, "Hat, hats, hats, so many hats! Oh, no! Too many hats."

I grabbed both her hands. "Astrid, look at me. There are many hats. We'll find a winter hat for Hannah. Let's think of a color and only find that color."

"Okay, Lee. Hold my hand. Too many hats."

"Choose a color." I knew what she wanted.

"Red, a red hat for Hannah. One with ear flaps to keep her ears warm. A red one."

A section of knit caps in a Norwegian style suited Astrid. "Reindeers and snowflakes, rabbits and holly, snowmen and snowflakes, which should we choose?"

"No green!"

We were down to two hats with ear flaps, "Which one?"

"Red and white, Hannah likes snowmen. Red and white reindeers, Hannah likes reindeers, red and white."

"Which one do you like?"

Her body swayed. Aggregation set in, "I dunno, I dunno!"

"What if we get both? Will you make a happy face if we get both?" I tried my best to stave off a public meltdown from an adult woman. Astrid covered her ears. I pulled her along to the register.

A nervous cashier asked if everything was okay. I asked her to hurry; obviously, things were not okay. We couldn't wait for the elevator and headed to the stairwell instead. I prayed she wouldn't yell; everyone might think I was murdering her. Astrid sat hard on a step, shaking her head violently, "Noise, noise, stop the noise!"

Noise? I wondered what noise. I couldn't stop her, nor did I try. With these meltdowns, she needed to quit on her own. We were out of the public eye, thank God, and she wasn't yelling. I waited. The door to the floor below us opened. Great, just what I needed, company. The concerned security guard stood on the landing,

"Is everything alright, Ma'am?" I hated the question. She continued shaking her head.

"Sir, she's autistic. These things happen. We'll be fine."

"A customer thought you might need help. I…"

I put my hand up, "We're fine. It will pass. Don't worry, we'll leave as soon as we can." He said he felt sorry for her. She didn't need his pity. I understood his concern and thanked him.

Astrid finally exhausted herself. Disheveled, we walked down four flights of stairs. It took forever stopping on each landing until we reached the bottom; a nearby exit opened to the street.

"Do you want to see the windows?"

"No, I want to go home."

"I need to stop at the butcher shop, Astrid."

"No, I want to go home." At the risk of another meltdown, we went home.

Graduation Day

For a winter's day, the sun miraculously came out in time for Hannah's graduation. As usual, we sat in the back of the auditorium. To my surprise, Franklin came to sit with us. When Hannah's name sounded, Astrid proceeded to jump up and down. Franklin grabbed her left hand; I took her right as she yelled, "Hi Hannah!" Sweetly, Hannah waved at her.

"Hannah's wearing a funny hat, a very weird hat." The word *weird* came out like a deflating tire. People turned around, peering at us.

"Shush, Astrid, pipe down."

"Okay, but Hannah's wearing a funny hat," she whispered to Franklin. He told Astrid it was a special hat only worn once. Astrid began to quiz him with *whys* and *how come*. He took her to the hallway, garnering less attention. I was glad he came, but I didn't remember inviting him. The old Mr. Godfrey seemed more reserved and a little on the awkward side. Not anymore; now more self-assured, I felt certain Dr. Dryer's death changed him, for the better. Franklin and Astrid returned in time for the ending processional. After graduating, the only request from Hannah was dinner at Angelo's. Trying to suggest a more upscale restaurant, she resisted.

Franklin came along; he sat beside Astrid and directly in front of Hannah. I saw the way he looked at her. This was scary.

Franklin knew something was amiss, "Are you alright, Lee?'

"Quite, yes, quite alright. Are you coming to the house?"

"No, I have a private lesson at three; in fact, I should be going." Astrid latched onto his arm, "Are you coming back then?"

"I'll come on another day; I promise."

"Okay."

Franklin smiled at Hannah, "Thanks for inviting me, and congratulations."

Now I knew without a doubt why he came. Astrid busied herself by licking her fingers. I turned to Hannah, "Do you fancy him?"

"Oh, no. Not like that, he's nice. Franklin is fond of Astrid. I don't mean…" She fumbled on her words.

Kindly, I replied, "I understand what you mean, Hannah." She breathed a sigh of relief.

"Shall we go home to decorate the Christmas tree?" I asked.

Excited, Astrid started putting her coat on. "See!" she pointed at Hannah's hat, "There's a big hole!"

It made Hannah self-conscious. I shot Astrid my mean face. Her head hung in shame; she knew it was wrong. Astrid didn't know why, but she hurt Hannah's feelings. She stroked Hannah's arm, "It will be okay, Hannah. Don't be sad. It's okay if you have a hole in your hat."

To hide her smile, Hannah covered her mouth, "Thank you, Astrid."

Busy with Christmas decorations, Astrid froze, "What time is it?" she bellowed. I pointed to my watch, and she said, "That's Mrs. Mary's watch, not yours!"

"She left it to me."

"Left it? Why didn't she take it with her?"

"People don't need watches in heaven," I could see where this conversation was going.

"Come finish hanging the ornaments," Hannah rescued me "*This is Your Life* comes on in ten minutes."

Saved by the telly!

The telephone rang while Hannah supervised Astrid's shower. Lyndon was on the other end.

"You didn't have much to say at the meeting Friday. Are you okay?"

"I'm fine, just a bit preoccupied with life in general. I've been mulling over our encounter. My mind is conflicted, Lyndon." I paused, thinking how to explain myself, "I am attracted to you, without a doubt."

"There's always a caveat to a statement like that one. What is it? You won't hurt my feelings, Lee."

"My eyes will betray me. The way I see you now is different. People will surely take notice. I know it's the 1980s; regardless, you had better hide your lifestyle. I absolutely do not want to jeopardize your position, Lyndon. I couldn't. God knows I want to. I want to experience what it feels like to be skin-to-skin with you, just once. Having said that, I'm afraid."

"Afraid of what, Lee?"

"That I'll only want you more."

An awkward pause overshadowed the conversation until Lyndon spoke, "Can it be just once? If it could be only once, could you live with it? You have no idea how much I want to be with you right now. What I feel is not just physical, Lee. You're smart, easy-going, and your unique hazel eyes; it's everything about you I desire. I worry about giving myself away, too, Lee."

"Then maybe we shouldn't see each other socially. It could be a passing fancy. If we try to put it out of our minds, maybe it will go away."

"That will be extremely difficult, but for both of our sakes, I will try. Perhaps you're right, Lee. What is enticing is usually a bad idea. Ha, just ask Eve; forbidden fruit is always tempting, and the consequences are rarely worth the price."

I hung up the phone with a heavy heart. Hannah came down. I could tell she wanted to ask why I was upset but didn't. With her hands behind her, she examined the print hanging above the fireplace, the Hokusai print. I welcomed the chance to tell her the story of the first night Astrid spent with me.

"Astrid's bewilderment, her innocence shown through that night. What our future held scared us both. When Astrid felt frightened, I told her to look at the night sky. She was the shiny star next to the moon—Astra and Luna. We'd always be together. I had no idea our lives would be so entwined."

"What a beautiful story."

My wine glass was empty when Hannah asked, "May I invite Franklin to Christmas dinner? His family moved to the States years ago. I feel bad for him. He told me of Dr. Dryer's treatment. After Astrid, Franklin stopped teaching, and a bout of depression sent him to therapy, Lee. His desire to help Astrid is his mission now ..."

"I'd love for him to come. I hope he doesn't steal you from us," I chuckled. But truly, I was serious. Hannah assured me that here, with Astrid, was her home.

Christmas Day

On Christmas Day, the tree was fully decorated with twinkly lights and cherished ornaments, topped with Astrid's tree topper, a giant blinking star. Our special China with winter scenes was laid out on the table. Hannah arranged the mantel with red tapers in my mother's silver candle holders, red-berried holly, and the garland of fragrant evergreens wafted through the house. I brought the neatly wrapped gifts from my bedroom. It was Astrid's job to put them under the tree. With each present, she asked who the gift belonged to.

"We have more presents this year, don't we, Lee?"

"Yes, one for you, one for me, one for Hannah, and one for Franklin."

"Franklin? Why does Franklin get a present? He doesn't live here."

"No, but he doesn't have a family in England. Hannah thought it would be nice to invite him."

"Oh, four/four time, like music. Four plates."

"Yes, that's why I asked for four place settings."

"Okay."

As I removed the beef Wellington from the oven, the bell rang. "Astrid, please answer the door."

"It better not be Santa Claus. Santa isn't real. It's a man in a red suit."

"Just answer the door."

In walked Franklin laden with presents. Astrid squealed and clapped her hands.

"Looky, Lee, more presents! Can I put them under the tree too?"

Franklin handed Astrid three presents. She waltzed through the living room to the tree.

"I smelled the beef all the way up the stoop! It's been a while since I celebrated a real Christmas." Franklin spoke from the heart, "Thank you for having me."

"When Hannah asked, I gave a resounding *yes*. I'm delighted you're here."

Hannah poured the wine (and grape juice for Astrid). The beef, gravy, roasted potatoes, steamed carrots, and pigs in a blanket all waited to be devoured. A Christmas cracker tied with ribbons lay across each plate. Before Astrid sat, I reminded her to use good manners. Hannah and Astrid said a prayer, and Franklin toasted to new beginnings. Astrid eyed the cracker. Her hands stayed in her lap, using self-restraint, waiting for my cue.

Through her shaggy fringe, she peeped at me. "Alright, let's pop!" Astrid counted to three, then a shower of confetti rained down. We put our paper hats on, and Astrid inspected everyone's trinkets. Hannah and I had plastic bracelets, Franklin had a blue plastic cat, and Astrid made pig sounds while showing us her pink pig.

Franklin, seated next to her chortled, "I hope you're not going to eat like a pig!"

"Good manners, Lee said good manners. Good manners or no presents."

Shocked, "I never said that, Astrid."

"I did. Good manners, Astrid, or timeout," she said to herself.

It was my turn to say "okay." After the dinner plates were cleared, I announced, "Hannah made a special dessert for us." The dome-shaped dark pudding with dripping white icing was straight out of a gourmet magazine.

"Is that plum pudding?" asked Franklin. Unsure of his reaction, Hannah asked if he liked plum pudding. He said his grandmother made it every Christmas.

Astrid squirmed; her patience wore thin.

"Eat your pudding, then presents. And no big bites. Use your small spoon," I instructed.

Oh, she made a face sour at me, her forehead wrinkled, and shoulders slumped. I said nothing.

We all went to the living room for presents. Astrid opened her gift from Hannah first; a charm bracelet with one charm.

"It's a bracelet, Lee!" Hannah helped her with the clasp, "Looky, it's got a tiny sparkly star and a moon!" She thrust her hands in my face. I recoiled, "Not so close. I see it. It's lovely."

"Astrid," Hannah said, "Sit by me. I want to show you something." Under the sleeve of her sweater, a bracelet jangled, "This is my charm bracelet." Hannah removed it, showing Astrid the different meanings of each charm. Hannah's mother started it for her when she was six years old. A small book represented her first day at school, a birthday candle, a cat, and a small crucifix, all for milestones in her life. Astrid sat mesmerized by the charms and Hannah's stories.

"I'm starting this bracelet for you. You are the star, and Lee is the moon. On birthdays and holidays, we'll add more charms."

Astrid gently handed the bracelet to Hannah, "Where's your mother?" It was the question of innocence.

"I suppose she's with Mrs. Mary, Grandfather, Lee's dad, and my dad, too."

"In heaven, in the sky, right, Lee? Past the clouds."

"Yes, Astrid. Shall we have more presents?"

When Hannah opened her gift from Astrid, she understood the remark about the hole in her hat. She loved the snowman, which brought flurries of hand flapping and garbled giggles.

Franklin spoke, "This little gift has your name on it, Hannah. You both have the same little boxes."

Franklin cleared his throat, "I was with Hannah when she bought Astrid's gift."

Hannah's box held another charm, a graduation cap with the date.

"If your mother was here, she could have gotten this for you," said Franklin. Hannah choked back tears, not wanting to upset Astrid, who probably didn't notice.

"It's so very thoughtful of you, Franklin. I shall cherish it."

Busy tearing the wrapping paper off, Astrid held up a tiny piano, "Is this teeny tiny piano for my bracelet?"

Afraid she didn't like it, a tentative "yes" came from Franklin.

"I don't know how to put it on," she whined. I searched the junk drawer in the kitchen.

"Aha! I found the needle-nose pliers. Meltdown averted." Franklin took the bracelet, Astrid watched him attach the piano charm to the link.

With the bracelet on Astrid's wrist, the flapping and jumping came to a halt. "It jingles!" Shaking her wrist again, she smiled, "It jingles!" But her joy turned into a sad expression.

"What'd the matter, Astrid?" I asked.

Her index finger pointed at Franklin, "I don't have a present for him."

"Yes, there's one for him. Look under the tree."

Indignant, she said, "I didn't buy this."

"When I found out Mr. Godfrey was coming, I purchased a gift for him."

The present was still in her hand, "His name's not Mister, it's Franklin. What is it?" she asked.

"Give Franklin the gift, please, then you can see."

The long slender box held a tie. Franklin held it up for Astrid to see.

"Music notes! A blue tie with golden notes! Do you like the tie, Franklin?" she asked. "It's a pretty tie."

Franklin was so pleased; he immediately replaced his old tie. Hannah whispered sometime in Astrid's ear. She bounced on the sofa, "You tell Lee." She tried to whisper. Hannah eyed Franklin.

While Astrid pulled at her sweater, Hannah announced Astrid's gift to me didn't fit in a box. Whatever it was, I was being pulled upstairs by a squealing Astrid.

At the door to her room, she barked, "Stay there! It's not ready yet." The three of them filed into Astrid's room.

After a minute, Franklin asked me to come in. My jaw dropped; light-headed, I sat on the bed. With great concentration, Astrid began to play, *Oh, Holy Night.* My folded hand covered my mouth as I watched her. Overcome with emotion, I wept. I stood with my arms open on the last note, praying she would let me hug her.

Confused, Astrid said, "Why are you crying? Hannah said you were going to be happy."

"Oh, Astrid, these are tears of joy! I am beyond happy. May I have a hug? I really need one." Her arms stuck straight out; there was never a genuine embrace. Then she squeezed my cheeks intensely, in her monotone, "I did it. The music is back in my brain."

"Don't expect too much, Lee," uttered Franklin.

"Oh, no, I'll be happy with whatever she's capable of doing."

"I played your favorite song, Lee. Did you like your song? I found my music up here." She pointed to her head.

"Oh, Astrid, I wish you could understand how my heart is full of joy." I hadn't a clue this had happened.

"Come downstairs; you still have a present to open." I prayed she liked this gift.

Between Hannah and Franklin, Astrid sat twisting her stretched-out sweater sleeve.

"Hold out both hands."

She interrupted me, distressed, "Do I need to close my eyes? I don't want to close my eyes, Lee."

"No, silly girl." The gift wrapped in gold paper lay in her hands.

"It's a book!" Astrid loved books.

"It's a special book. Go on open it."

A red leather notebook embossed with her name in gold lay in her lap, her finger traced the letters, puzzled; she muttered, "I didn't write this book. Why is my name on it? I didn't write this book."

"The book is for you. A gentleman made it, especially for you. Open the first page."

"It's blank music."

"That's right. I don't care if you don't play anywhere except here. I hope someday you will write more music."

Astrid stared at the book. Had I pushed her too far? The book went under her arm, she ran up the stairs. I waited to hear the book drop into her trash bin.

"That was a disaster; what was I thinking?" Hannah made tea. No one knew what to say. What could they say? With head in hand, I screwed up Christmas.

"You wanted the same thing we wanted, Lee," Franklin sympathized.

"Should I go check on her?" asked Hannah. She was best left alone for a while. Checking on her might set her off. The three of us sat down for tea. Hannah took my hand with a good intention speech. Hannah cut Franklin another slice of pudding. I declined.

Astrid, running downstairs, hand behind her back, I reminded her to use the handrail. Astrid stood beside me. I watched her stare at the ceiling, rocking back and forth.

"Sit beside me."

"Here," she said. The red leather notebook came close to hitting my face. It wasn't an act of aggression. Astrid still inspected the ceiling. Disappointment ran all over me, she returned it.

"Open it," said the emotionless voice.

On the first page, black x's cover each line, at the bottom three o's. I didn't understand. On top of the next page was written in pencil, *The*

I'm Sorry Song. Twenty minutes in her room, she'd composed a song. She sat by me, never looking down.

"Will you play it for me?" I asked timidly.

"No. Not today. I'm not playing today. I already played. *Rudolph, the Red-Nose Reindeer* is on the telly in ten minutes," Holding her watch to her face, "In ten minutes. Rudolph comes on at Christmas, and I couldn't miss him."

Hannah turned on the telly, and Astrid parked herself on her spot on the sofa. Hannah sat in her assigned chair.

"Three minutes!" Astrid called out like the town crier every minute. When the music started, she yelled, "Showtime!"

Franklin reached for the book, "May I?"

Baffled by everything, I asked, "What does this mean, Franklin? This day is all topsy-turvy."

As he read the music, his fingers tapped out time, a waltz. I shared the way Astrid set the table, counting out three-quarter time. It made perfect sense; the first song should be a waltz.

Franklin studied the composition with intense concentration, an elbow on the table, hand resting on his cheek. With a crisp nod of his head, "It's true to everything she's written before, Lee. In my heart, I know she will never perform publicly again. Astrid isn't the same as before." We agreed. Astrid wasn't the same; she had regressed.

"When did you have the time to work with her on the carol?" I asked.

"It was Hannah's idea. You were shopping when she phoned me. I came over to do a little coaxing. Surprisingly enough, I received no discord. All I did was to ask if she remembered your favorite Christmas song. She sprung straight to the keyboard and played like a master, as usual." He couldn't help but smile.

My fingers were crossed, "Let's hope it lasts. You're right; we shouldn't get our hopes up. I asked Astrid's psychologist once if he thought she could regain her sense of music. The answer was, there was no answer. So little is known about what the psychiatric community calls savant syndrome."

I relayed to Franklin what Dr. Davis told me about a man in the United States who memorized over 6,000 books and postal codes for every area there. He said many musical savants are visually impaired; Astrid's vision was perfect, as far as I could tell.

"No one can explain how Astrid, with an IQ of fifty-two, can be so gifted. I sat down with Dr. Davis, another neuroscientist, and two colleagues, showing them Astrid's sheet music. I could have knocked them over with a feather. Astrid broke every rule in the diagnostic manuals!"

"Shhhhh! I'm watching Rudolph. Shhhh!"

Franklin and I both covered our mouths, hiding our smiles.

"If only we could possess one-tenth of her innocence, the world would be a much nicer place," he sighed.

I agreed with Franklin. Then I saw a light go on behind his eyes.

"What is it?" I asked.

"Just an idea, far ahead," he whispered. Now I had to know what he thought.

"There's a studio I know of. It probably won't happen; who knows? Somewhere in the future, Astrid might record an album." He stuck his palms up, waving, "I know, I know, it's a pipedream."

I winked, "Oh, now that's an idea. One can hope."

| 40 |

In a Dither

After the new year, I began to wean Astrid from my workday. I was sure of one thing: God did send Hannah to us. I was the one with separation anxiety; no clicking needles made my little office feel lonely. At Friday's staff meetings we were given a tutorial on using a new computer program from NASA. It seemed so confusing. The carousel slide projectors were being replaced with the PC DOS computer program.

In February, Lyndon gave us a personal computer for the house. Astrid's curiosity led me to set it up in my bedroom, where I could lock the door. When Lyndon came over to hook up everything, she hugged me tightly, "I never got a chance to thank you for my gift. Christmas felt empty this year. Your thoughtfulness was appreciated." she smirked. "Flannel pajamas aren't the most romantic gift." I must have seemed a bit disappointed.

"Truly, Lee, I love them. They keep me warm on cold nights. Just like I know you would if you could." A sense of profound sadness filled her voice. She reclined on my bed. My fingers stroked her salt and pepper hair, I wanted to kiss her, so I did.

"Have you assigned rooms for the trip yet?" I asked.

"I thought you might not want to be in the same room as me."

"Please don't put me with that dull Teresa girl or Jackie the jabberer."

Lyndon laughed, "Well, that just leaves me, Darling."

With eyebrows arched and a sheepish grin, "I know."

Lyndon raised an eyebrow, "We better go downstairs."

I invited Hannah to use the computer if she wished; she declined. She'd use her handwritten journals.

After Astrid finished her shower, Hannah blow-dried her hair. The blow dryer was a whole new concept. If the air wasn't too hot, everything was okay; otherwise, she hollered. Astrid still refused to get her waist-length hair cut. She said it hurt her hair. After my mother died, a battle arose when I tried to trim her fringe. Her fringe came out looking like sharks' teeth; since that day, she'd cooperated. Astrid's long hair was always braided before bed, or we'd have a rat's nest the next morning.

I still saw Astrid's eleven-year-old self on rare occasions. In the mirror, I saw myself aging not so gracefully. My mother held on to her grace and beauty even when she got very sick. What might she say of me now? That night, as I lay in bed looking up at the skylight, a million stars filled the sky. I felt so tired. Thank God for Hannah; her energy and positivity were rare assets.

March Jitters

When March rolled around, my trip to Cape Kennedy, Florida, was two weeks away. Every day Astrid asked the same questions—when was I leaving? when was I coming back?—even though it was on her planner.

"She's worried, you know," said Hannah.

"Yes, I know. I'm worried too. I've never flown before, and it's eight hours of traveling. Astrid must have felt this way when she flew to the States."

"Even after her medicine, she's pacing at night, Lee."

"While she's pacing, I'm tossing and turning."

We came up with a plan. For every day I was gone, Astrid could call me at twelve-thirty in the afternoon. It would be seven-thirty a.m. in Florida.

"The seminars start at nine; I can talk with her briefly, for five minutes or so. You'll have to set the timer. Come to think of it, she's never really spoken on the phone."

Astrid occupied her time upstairs with picture books; I sat down with Hannah for a frank conversation. I presented her with a temporary power of attorney in case of the unthinkable. The folder also contained the name of our barrister and our financial advisor.

"As stated in your contract, if anything happens to me, you will be the sole proprietor of this house, in the total care of Astrid. Hannah, I trust you with her life." My voice broke, "I know you love her. And in her own strange way; she loves you, too."

With a long exhale and a smile, Hannah said, "Yes, I know. Lee, I care for her as if she were my child, too. I may not have the history with her as you do, but someday I will."

"I don't know what I'd do without you, Hannah. Well, yes, I do. I could never work alone or travel without being joined to her at the hip," I chuckled. "When I return, you can have as many days off as you wish, as long as you come back."

Amused, Hannah shook her head emphatically, "Where else could I go? This is home."

The next day was Hannah's day off, so Astrid and I had the whole day to spend together. At the breakfast table, out of the blue, Astrid proudly stated, "I know dogs."

Surprised, I said, "You do? What kind of dogs do you know?"

"All of them. Encyclopedia D for dogs. I know all of them."

The statement stood as my invitation to quiz her. Not knowing how to ask for it, I understood Astrid's code.

"Very well, finish your breakfast, slowly," I emphasized, "then bring me your book."

"The D is big. Lots of D stuff; dinosaurs, dictatorship, dingo, dolphins, donkey, deer…"

"Astrid, let's talk about dogs. Okay?"

"Okay."

The illustrations were all in a row. Covering up the names with her bookmark, I'd point, and she answered. Dr. Davis once said typically autistic persons often memorize things in a particular order. Astrid's not typical. To keep her sharp, I could switch the order.

However, in her daily routine, I dared not switch. Her toothbrush always faced left, towels must be white, the bed made a certain way with my mother's crocheted Afghan folded in a perfect rectangle at the foot.

Astrid correctly identified forty-eight breeds. She knew the world's flags—all two hundred and forty-six; she even kept up with the new flags of colonies winning independence. All her memorization skills began to show after the music died. Astrid received an invitation to be on a German television show called *Did You Know?* I declined the offer; she wasn't a show pony. Applause and loud laughter were the ingredients for a disastrous meltdown.

"You got them right. I'm very proud of you, my shiny star."

"Okay." She started for the stairs.

"Where are you going?" I asked.

Without turning around, she huffed, "To my room!"

"Sorry, that was a dumb question." I listened for the tapping of her keyboard. I couldn't hear the music she played; she wore headphones. Yet I didn't think she'd played a note since Christmas. I'd ask Hannah if she heard anything.

On my way upstairs to my room, I looked in on her. I heard something through the door crack, a repetition of Paris landmarks. In French, she remembered the competition at the Sorbonne—what she wore, who traveled with her, the schedule of events, the name of the pieces she played, even the train ride in detail. I was flabbergasted. I knew she'd memorized current information like the television schedule or Angelo's menu, but nothing like this. The next appointment with Dr. Davis was Thursday, and I meant to bring it up.

"Astrid, do you mind if Hannah goes to your appointment today?"

We all sat at the table, waiting for an answer. Head tilted back, tapping fingers on her chin, she replied, "Okay, Dr. Anthony Davis, two o'clock, Thursday, January twentieth. Today. Leaving at one o'clock, car ride forty minutes." Looking intently at her watch, she announced, "Forty-seven minutes until departure. I got to go pee. No accidents."

Nodding my head, "Go."

Hannah kicked me under the table to keep me from laughing.

"I have something remarkable to discuss with the doctor today. Have you ever heard her speak French?"

Baffled, Hannah answered, "No, why?"

Recounting our days at St. Agnes and again at Cambridge, how Astrid became proficient in French and algebra, I explained that written language was out of the question. Her reading comprehension stayed on the sixth level, never progressing. Although she never graduated, Astrid received certificates of completion.

"I haven't heard her utter a word in French for eons. I'm glad you're coming along. She doesn't like to go. I bribe her with ice cream or dinner at Angelo's."

"I bet she loves those treats."

"We have twenty minutes until departure." Astrid sounded like a train conductor.

"Come down and let me see what you're wearing, please."

Clomp, clomp, clomp! She turned in circles wearing a long batik cotton dress with a pullover sweater and boots.

"Will you be warm enough? The dress is rather thin, don't you think?"

"I have on tights and a sweater, see!" Astrid raised her skirt up to her stomach, showing her the tights.

"Pull your dress down. You're fine. Come here, please." I reached up to smooth her fringe; she fidgeted. "Get your coat, hat, and gloves, please."

"Okay." Then Astrid repeated, "Hannah, get your coat, hat, and gloves, please."

"Mockingbird," I whispered as I rolled my eyes at Hannah.

"Astrid, who is your friend?" Dr. Davis asked.

Hesitant to answer, she wiggled in her chair, head cast down. Shy, softly she spoke, "Hannah Johnson."

"How do you know Hannah?" He tried to pry answers from her.

"She takes me to the park and builds a snowman with me."

"Astrid," I prompted, "Tell Dr. Davis where Hannah lives."

"In our house, Hannah lives in our house with me." Then out of the blue, Astrid said, "Lee is leaving, going far away. She's leaving next week on Tuesday, on an airplane. I hate airplanes."

Dr. Davis studied her face, "Where is Lee going?"

"Cape Kennedy, in Florida. It's far away, I couldn't go with her. Hannah isn't going either. She lives with me."

"Are you worried, Astrid?"

Astrid wadded up her knit hat, holding it to her face, rocking in her chair, "Yes. I'm worried Lee won't come back. Airplanes crash, you know. Airplanes aren't safe."

This exchange marked the first time Astrid showed genuine emotion in Dr. Davis's presence.

"Astie," I called her by her childhood nickname, "I'll be fine. We can talk on the phone every day. I'll know you are alright, and you can hear I'm alright. I promise I'll be home."

"Ten days, your gone ten days. Planes crash, you know. You can't promise."

Dr. Davis talked with her, "What you said is true, planes do crash. But," he pointed his finger gently at her, "the odds of that happening to Lee is highly unlikely. Do you understand?" She nodded. "I can give you another vitamin to keep your worries away if you like. It's up to you."

"What color is it?" she asked.

As long as it wasn't green, we were okay, I hoped. Dr. Davis typed something in the computer and up came a diamond-shaped light blue pill. Astrid's vitamin came in the form of an anti-seizure drug that could stabilize her mood. I needed more information.

"Do you like the blue one?" he asked.

"Yes, it's pretty."

"Good. I'll write the instructions for Lee to get filled."

I asked Hannah to take Astrid to the bathroom while talking to Dr. Davis. Voicing my concerns about the drug's off-label use, he assured me the dose was low with minor side effects, no worse than a sleeping pill. He knew how I hated drugging her.

"Isn't there something just for anxiety?"

"There's Valium, a low dose sedative. In layman's terms, it calms the brain."

"What color is it?"

"Not green or yellow. And Astrid must take it in the morning. It may make her a bit drowsy."

"I understand, and I'll tell her they ran out of the blue." Dr. Davis found my remark amusing.

Astrid began her dose of Valium a week before I left. After a few days, the anxiety didn't seem as intense. The day before I left, Astrid began asking questions. Over her shoulder, Hannah stood helping Astrid as she circled the days in the day planner. Repeatedly, she expressed her hatred of airplanes.

The afternoon before my departure, I sat with her. With an arm covering her face, she refused to look at me.

"Astie, I will come back. Remember, I will come back. As planned, you can talk to me every day. Hannah can dial the number for you. And I'll bring back a surprise for you."

That got her attention; she jumped out of bed, "What kind of surprise? No tee shirts. I don't want a tee shirt."

"Fine, Astie, no tee shirt."

"A pin, I'd like a pin for my jacket, please, and thank you."

Last Christmas, I bought her a denim jacket with various cartoon character pins and buttons. The rainbow button she loved, telling me it was God's promise not to drown us. A colorful peace sign and a Mickey Mouse were favorites; she loved Mickey Mouse. Astrid bought a miniature Van Gogh pin depicting boats on the beach at the art museum. It reminded Astrid of Brighton Beach, she said. On occasion, she came down from bed wearing her jacket. I wouldn't let Astrid wear it to bed, telling her the pins might stick her at night.

| 41 |

The Heat in Florida

When my departure date came, I hid the suitcase in Hannah's room, trying to stave off a meltdown. The early spring brought a sunny Tuesday morning, a perfect day for the park. After breakfast, I informed Astrid that today I'd leave. Waiting for a fit, she surprised me. "I know, silly. Hannah wrote in my book."

"And you're okay with my leaving?"

"Uh-huh, because you're coming back. Hannah said, you're coming back, isn't that right, Hannah?" She took Hannah's hand.

"Yes, Lee will be back next Thursday."

"Can we go to the zoo today, Lee? Can Hannah take me to the zoo?"

Shocked by the lack of upset, I said, "Yes. You can go to the zoo."

Astrid grabbed her coat and pulled Hannah to the door.

With my hands on my hips, I said, "Hold on. Aren't you forgetting something?"

Astrid's finger tapped against her cheek, "No."

"Hey! Where's my hug? I won't be home when you get back."

"Oh, here," Astrid gave me a peek on the cheek, "Bye-bye, see you later."

My feelings were hurt. Hannah could tell, "Lee, you know there's no sense of reference for this experience." Hannah hugged me, "Have a great time. We'll call every morning starting Thursday." They left.

I heard a familiar car drive up. "Are you ready?" asked Lyndon as she came through the door

"Yes, surprisingly, Astrid couldn't wait to get to the zoo. My feelings were a bit hurt."

Lyndon gave a cocky smile, pulled me to her, and kissed me. I thought I'd faint.

Breathless, "Lyndon, don't do that again." That statement distressed her; she began to apologize.

I confessed, "I've thought about you for months and guilt crowded my mind every time I saw you." I couldn't look her in the eye. "Sex makes me uncomfortable. I'm sorry, Lyndon."

Lyndon pushed my hair behind my ear, with longing in her eyes, "I'm not insulted, but it doesn't change the way I feel. Let's go."

I purposely asked Lyndon not to sit with me on the plane. For months, I'd tried to put her out of my mind. The harder I tried, the more desirable she became. Lyndon's presence was indeed commanding because of her intelligence and beauty. Her thick eyelashes, her blue eyes, tall and slender, all business in the classroom; in contrast, warm and witty in private. Her hair, the color of salt and pepper, cut in a shag, her fringe swept to the right.

On take-off, Bryon Edgewood must have thought I would pass out. My head hit the back of the seat; I gripped the armrest.

"Are you alright, Lee?"

"I will be when we land." He thought it funny. I did not. Wouldn't you know, my first flight was seven hours, transatlantic. Then he said, "Don't worry. The law of physics is in our favor. You know, what goes up must come down." Then he paused, laughed, and said, "One way or another." Then the asshat clapped his hands together and made a crashing noise. I sat unamused. He thought too highly of himself.

"Gosh, Bryon, you're such a comfort." When the stewardess came by with the drink cart, I ordered a bourdon on the rocks. I examined the tiny bottle and immediately ordered another. A shocked Bryon asked if I liked getting smashed, to which I replied, "Only when I sit by you." He didn't say a word the rest of the flight.

I learned I couldn't stand the smell of sliced turkey or cod, our in-flight meal choices. The little plastic container of diced peaches and cheese and crackers were all I could stomach. The landing was far worse than the take-off. I fell forward, grabbing the armrest. Though kissing the ground might have been overkill, I never was so thankful to be back on the ground. After collecting the luggage, we were shuttled from the airport an hour's ride to the hotel in Titusville. Of course, Bryon called it "Tittieville," which brought a rebuke from Dr. Hammersmith.

After settling in, Lyndon and I were bushed but hungry. We were treated to a dinner buffet of southern foods at the Holiday Inn. The fried chicken, greasy though it was, tasted delicious. Lyndon reminded everyone to meet in the lobby at eight-thirty a.m. for the shuttle service. Lyndon and I shared a room with two double beds overlooking wetlands full of unusual birds. Far in the distance, I could see the rain coming. Reaching in front of me, Lyndon closed the curtains, turned me around, and kissed me.

Why didn't I stop her? What happened that night was incredible, fireworks at the touch of a woman's hand. Oh, Tilly taught me well; my mind danced in confusion, caught between elation and guilt. No light, only darkness, filled the room. Next to me, Lyndon lay, breasts uncovered.

Her words cut through the silence, "Are you all right with what just happened?"

Searching for an answer, I thought *am I all right?* "I let it happen."

"But are you... I mean, did you..." she took a deep breath, "like what we did? God, that sounded stupid."

"Lyndon, I'm not going to lie to you. Did I enjoy the sex? On a primal level, yes. You are amazing, but I'm still conflicted." My mind turned to mush as I sat up, pulling the sheet over me. "Don't get me wrong, I dreamt of us doing what we did."

Turning on the light, Lyndon sat up. God, her breasts were full, her nipples light brown. She turned me on.

"Was once enough, Lee? If you say yes, I'm good with that. The last thing I want to do is pressure you into doing something you don't want."

My eyes closed, I nodded. "I know Lyndon, if I asked you to stop, you would; however, I didn't. Your touch made me feel more like a woman than John ever did. Maybe I need more time to digest what just happened." She lay beside me, the back of my hand stroked her cheek, those ocean blue eyes, no one could hold a candle to her. I wanted to love her, but I didn't want to hurt her, either.

Propped up on her arm, with a steady gaze, Lyndon said, "I'll wait for as long as you need. And if one time remains enough, then I'm glad you chose me."

"Your patience with me is more than I deserve, Lyndon." I could have slept in the other bed, but I didn't.

I turned down the other bed the next morning, rumpling up the covers. The maids didn't need to know we slept in the same bed.

Lyndon finished her lipstick, seeing my reflection in the mirror. "You know you're acting paranoid, don't you?"

Exasperated, I said, "Yes. However, I refuse to be the cause of your firing. I'm going down to breakfast."

Lyndon called after me, "Save me a seat."

Before I closed the door, I spun around, "No."

I picked at my breakfast, sitting alone, reminding myself I wasn't here for a roll in the hay. The agenda given out yesterday filled with lectures, tours, and social events was rather overwhelming. On the second page I saw, *Astrophysicist Lenora McConnell, lecture hall three, two o'clock. Topic: The Importance of Tracking Near-Earth Objects.* Dear God, help me. Leaving breakfast, I saw a poster for a Meet and Greet, four until eight this evening, Main Ballroom.

Lyndon had meetings all morning. I carefully checked over my notes, falling asleep until she came back. My dreams were naughty; my subconscious knew what I wanted. Lying beside me when she came back to the room, Lyndon heard audible growls coming from my stomach.

"It's happy hour downstairs with cocktail sandwiches and plenty of finger foods." I let her nibble on my neck.

"Should I stop?" she asked.

"No, I believe I need to release some tension. Maybe you can help."

"Are you being serious, Lee?" I guided her hand between my legs.

"Oh god, Lyndon." She didn't stop until I cried out.

"Shhh, you'll get us both sacked," she said.

"You made me do it. Get dressed; I'm hungry," I commanded. While she finished dressing in the bathroom, I found myself pacing.

Coming out of the bathroom, she said, "Are you nervous, Lee?"

"A bit, yes."

"You go on then; I'll come later. Get something to eat."

Heading straight for the buffet, I took a couple of small sandwiches. Then I felt sick as I scanned the reception full of great scientific intellectuals. A hand touched my shoulder; Lyndon said, "Are you alright?"

"What am I doing here? Don't feed me a line of tripe, Lyndon."

Before she answered, an older gentleman approached, "Hello, Dr. Hammersmith. It's been a while."

A distinct French accent. Lyndon introduced Professor Doctor Jacques Badeaux, Claudia's father. Well, I wondered if Claudia hid somewhere. The whole time he spoke to me, I felt I was underwater. Lucky for me, Lyndon could speak.

I glanced up at Lyndon; her face tightened, "Are you alright, Lee?"

"What am I doing here, Lyndon?" I sighed.

"Come with me."

I followed her around the corner, out of sight of the others. With intensity, her hands were on my shoulders, "You have got to step out of your pity party, Lee. Take advantage of your surroundings. These are the most brilliant minds in every area of astrophysics and astronomy. Lee, you are not some insignificant speck of stardust. They respect your work; you are one of them. From now on, hold your head up and act as if you belong here."

Now I understood how Astrid must feel. I heard her voice telling me, I can do this. I lifted my chin with an air of self-confidence.

"Okay, I can do this," I muttered.

"You can; don't embarrass me." That was an order. Lyndon rubbed the back of her neck. She returned to the reception while I did some breathing. *If I pretend to be someone else, someone important, I'll make it through*, I thought. God knows I didn't want to disappoint Lyndon. With a pasted-on smile, I walked in like I belonged there.

I found a group mixed with young Black women and an Asian woman talking amongst themselves. I introduced myself to an attractive African American woman named Christine. Impressed by her courage to stand up to her superiors, Christine was responsible for the research leading to the quieting of the sonic boom.

"I used to hear those booms as a child. Older people were seen ducking and flinching when it happened, thinking the Germans were bombing England again. So, on behalf of my British elders, thank you."

Her eyes brightened, "You're quite welcome. I never realized my research could have such an impact. That's a new spin."

Here it came: she asked me what I did in England. Smiling, I tried to think of something clever to say. All that came out was, "I calculate flying rocks."

It was obvious; I now had two heads by how they chuckled among one another.

"Seriously, I've calculated the trajectories of asteroids in relationship to the Earth's orbit. While most large asteroids fly right by us, there are some that have and will come close. Some travel at speeds up to 21,000 miles per hour from the data I compiled. Without this type of data, asteroids may cause problems with launching rockets."

A collective hush came over the group; one woman asked if we were in danger of a collision.

"Some are small of no consequence, leftovers from asteroids colliding with one another. The asteroids I study are called NEO's:

Near-Earth Objects. When I used the term, *near*, don't fret; they're still over twenty-eight million miles away."

Suddenly, questions rushed at me. My hands flew up, "If you attend my presentation, most of your questions can be answered. Know that you can sleep comfortably; no NEOs will hit the Earth in this century." Hopefully, I didn't sound like an English snob. We dispersed cordially. Lyndon caught my eye, I pointed up. Jet lag and being engaging took their toll on me.

Hours later, the key clicked in the lock. Lyndon came in slightly inebriated and sprawled out on the bed, "Honey, I'm home."

"You are too much, my darling Lyndon. Regular life of the party, what?"

"Kiss me and undress me."

"I'll kiss you, but I'm not undressing you. You smell like a brewery. Go take a shower and sober yourself."

Toddling off to the bathroom, she called, "If I'm not back in five minutes, send a search party."

After her shower and stark naked, Lydon jumped in bed, scooting under the cover.

"Oh, no," I cried, "I don't want oral sex."

"In that case," her knee found my groin, "there are other ways."

At seven-thirty a.m., the phone rang. it was Hannah.

"Someone wishes to speak to you." Then I heard, "Lee? Is it you? Are you there?"

"Yes, Astie, it's me. I'm here."

"Where are you, Lee? I miss you, Lee."

"I'm here in sunny Florida, about to start my day. How are you?"

"It's not sunny; it's nighttime." I should have known Astrid's confusion was to be expected.

"Yes, it's nighttime where you are in England. I'm on the other side of the ocean. Hannah can show you on the globe in my room before you take your vitamin."

"Okay. When are you coming home?" Astrid whined.

"You can check your planner. I'll talk to you tomorrow. I love you, Astie, my shiny star." I heard the receiver drop.

Hannah picked up, "She's run upstairs. We're fine. Call you tomorrow."

"Alright, bye."

Standing with her fist under her chin, Lyndon asked how things were going back home. I rolled my eyes, "What can I say? The house hasn't burned down, Hannah seems to be handling everything, and Astrid is, well, Astrid. All's well on Castle Street."

A hug was in order, and Lyndon didn't disappoint.

The Presentation

Friday's schedule included a tour of the Jet Propulsion Lab and my slide presentation at two o'clock. Before the tour started, Lyndon showed me the lecture hall where I would be speaking, a two-hundred-seat auditorium.

"Gosh, thanks for the heads-up. This place is massive!"

"You'll be fine. The slide carousel is set just as you left it. The clicker for the slides and your lecture notes are by the podium. I'll be sitting in the fifth row, center." She took her seat. "Talk as if we were alone, just like you and I practiced."

In a huff, I said, "Easy for you to say."

As we joined the group in the courtyard surrounded by massive rocket silos and maintenance hangars, Lyndon whispered, "That suit you're wearing is sophisticated and sexy."

I whispered back, "Stop it. You're making me blush." We boarded a tram riding through the land of giants. Solar-Max had just launched last February to send data from the sun's solar cycles. Everything was a buzz when we were allowed a glimpse of the Space Shuttle Columbia, due to launch in just weeks. Our tour concluded with a tour of Mission Control, a beehive of people in front of computer monitors.

Swallowing hard, I took a sip of water while being miked up. During my introduction from NASA board member Dr. McCartney, I heard him say my data helped plan the date and time of Solar-Max and the Space Shuttle launch. They applauded; flabbergasted, I noticed the room filled to capacity. Everything after that was a blur. Like a robot on autopilot, I completed my lecture; I remember very little. After the question-and-answer session, Lyndon told me what a great job I'd done. An introduction to the head of the JPL left me reeling.

"When Dr. Hammersmith began to send your research data two years ago," he stated, "our analysis showed how to avoid collision with asteroids on launch. When traveling at a high velocity, an asteroid the size of a football would be disastrous. The new technology we've developed needs the expertise of a brilliant mind with an eye for detail, Ms. McConnell. You fit the bill. NASA is prepared to offer you a job with the JPL."

Breathless, I responded, "While I am thrilled at the prospect and very flattered, I must respectfully decline, sir." I could tell by his countenance he usually got his way.

"I'm offering the chance of a lifetime; we'd pay all of your moving expenses and get you a handsome salary. Our equipment is far superior to what you're used to working with, Ms. McConnell."

Lyndon stood behind him with a pained face, knowing why I must decline his offer.

"Sir, I am humbled by your offer. Please understand I have obligations at home far too complicated to explain. It's extremely generous, don't get me wrong. Again, I must decline. I hope I will be able to continue my work in England."

He stuck his hands in his pockets, "Of course, you can continue. I'll see a new computer from NASA is sent to Cambridge, allowing the university to work in greater detail." He turned and walked away.

Lyndon and I stood alone in the emptiness of the dark auditorium. She embraced me, "I'm so sorry, Lee. I had no idea they were offering you a job. It would be such a great opportunity."

Inside I felt defeated in what should be a moment of triumph. Pushing Lyndon back, "Lyndon, you know I could never accept the offer for various reasons."

Bewildered, Lyndon asked for an explanation. Astrid wasn't the only concern; I needed a doctorate, and she knew it. "I'm going back to the room to lie down."

"I want to take you to dinner, Lee," she insisted, "someplace nice. What you've done is extraordinary."

If I impressed the NASA community, I didn't want to feel it. I only wanted to go home. In the room, I undressed, pulling the covers over my head. I cried.

Lyndon came in and sat beside me, pulling the covers from my head. Her stoic face telegraphed her concern. The back of her hand rested on my forehead, "You don't have a fever, but you're soaking wet. Have you been tested for diabetes, Lee?" she asked.

"I'm fine. I had a psychical six months ago, a regular check-up with nothing out of the ordinary except low iron. I'm just tired. I read crossing the international dateline can adversely affect some people. I must be one." Seeing that enduring face, "Lyndon, don't worry about me. Carry on with your duties. Have fun; I just want to sleep for now."

My phone calls with Astrid did not go well for the next two days. Hannah noticed more anxious behavior. Astrid paced the floor, praying the plane wouldn't crash. Stopping the calls was mutual. I'd be home soon. I managed to pull myself out of bed for a few other lectures. The last night was a black-tie affair thrown by the U.S. State Department. I dug out my black dress from twenty years ago. Not only did it fit, but it also wasn't that tight.

As I slipped on the most uncomfortable shoes in the world, Lyndon turned from the mirror, "Is that the dress from the gala?"

"It is. Surprisingly enough, it's not as tight."

"Don't take this wrong, Lee; you are gorgeous, but you've lost weight." Concern peppered her comment.

"And that's a bad thing? All my life, I've been pleasingly plump or adorable. Now I lose weight, and there's something wrong?"

From behind, wrapping her arms around my waist, Lyndon kissed my cheek, "You are smart and sexy. I'll have to keep an eye on the men tonight."

Before we left Florida, Lyndon and I had a heart-to-heart talk about events between us. In the whirlwind of that week, she stood as my rock; in my heart, I knew we couldn't carry on. I did promise to go to dinner with her now and again, but no more lovemaking. Though she tried to hide it, I knew I'd hurt her. Plus, I could never show her any affection in public; it didn't seem fair to her, and there was also my point of putting her in jeopardy. Truly, I cared for her, but my guilt could never cease to exist. If there's a heaven and people watch you, I was sure they were ashamed of my behavior.

Back Home

"Lee's home!" shouted Astrid. My eyes widened as I braced for her, a speeding train running at me. Her hug was different, a real arm-wrapped-around-me kind of hug. My arms were pinned to my side, squeezing me until my bones hurt.

Startled, I gasped, "Oh, my goodness, what a hug!" She left me breathless.

With a very serious face, Astrid said, "Are you staying home now?"

With my head cocked to the side, I grinned, "I am."

Astrid squealed, hands flapping like a little bird.

Sounding exhausted, Hannah spoke, "I'm glad you're back. Did everything turn out well for you?"

"Yes, we'll talk later."

Hannah frowned. I promised, nothing catastrophic happened. Digging in my pocketbook, I pulled out two small gift boxes.

"Let's sit on the sofa, Astie. I have something for you."

"For me, you have something for me?"

"Yes, I promised to bring you back a surprise."

Astrid twisted her hair, sucking on her bottom lip, then said, "What about Hannah? Did Hannah get a surprise too?"

I held the gift boxes, one in each hand, "I couldn't leave Hannah out. The one with the blue ribbon is Hannah's. You may hand it to her."

Doing as she was told, Astrid gave Hannah the box with instructions not to open it until I said to. I cracked a smile. "This one is for you." She stared at the ceiling. "Go on, open it."

"It's a little box, Lee."

"I know, go on."

With great care, Astrid opened it, "What are these?"

"Pins for your jacket. This is the Space Shuttle, a rocket. It's going up in space in two weeks."

Fingers carefully held up the pin as Astrid examined it, "It's very little. How is this going up to space?"

"Astrid," I drew a breath, "silly, the pin isn't going up in space; the real rocket is. The rocket is bigger than Big Ben."

"Okay. What's this, the blue one, N-A-S-A?"

I knew she wouldn't understand, but I explained what the letters meant. A simpler explanation followed, "It's a big place with tall buildings where rocket ships are built then sent up into the sky.

Grimacing, Astrid leaned back, "Is the rocket taking people to heaven?"

Here we go again. "No, Astie, it doesn't go quite that far. It circles the earth."

"Why? Will it come back down?"

I tried to figure out how to clear up my answers for a second.

"Two men in the rocket will take pictures of the earth to help understand the weather. The rocket is like a giant airplane. So, it will land like an airplane."

I knew this was coming. I got a lecture on airplane danger. I rubbed my forehead; Astrid was wearing me out.

"Yes, Astrid. But every precaution is being taken for the safety of everyone." I immediately changed the subject, "Hannah, why don't you open your gift?"

On the loveseat, Astrid plopped next to Hannah.

"Oh, how beautiful, is it coral?"

"What is it?" asked Astrid. Hannah held up the necklace of bits of coral and turquoise strung together in three strands.

Clutching it to her chest, she said, "Oh, Lee, I love it. Thank you for thinking of me."

"You're family. How could I not bring something for you?"

"Astrid, run up and get your denim jacket. We can add the pins."

In Astrid's absence, Hannah voiced concern over my appearance. "Don't take me wrong, Lee, but you don't look well. Seeing you every day, I don't think I noticed."

"I'm fine, Hannah, just tired from the trip. I have a week off to rest. And I'm sure you want a few days to yourself. I'm prepared to offer you a weekend stay at the Regency House. Please don't deny me; I know what a toll Astrid can take."

"It's a very generous offer, Lee, but…" Astrid ran down the stairs.

"We can talk later, Hannah."

Astrid pointed to spots for her new pins and, without haste, put them on, running to the mirror in Hannah's bathroom. She shouted, "Mickey Mouse likes rockets!"

Hannah and I snickered. Returning to the sofa, Astrid turned to me with her serious face, "I think I like rockets."

"Good. I like rockets, too."

"I like Chinese food, too."

That was news to me. "How do you know about Chinese food?"

Astrid immediately stared at the ceiling as if she'd done something bad. Hannah interjected, "Tell Lee where we went, Astrid."

Short and sharp, she said, "King Kung Pao Chinese Buffet with Franklin."

How did they get her anywhere except Angelo's? I admitted my shock, "Really? Did you like eating there?"

"Yes. Franklin likes moo gooey guy pans. I don't like that; it looks bad."

Inwardly, I laughed; curiously, I asked, "What did you eat?"

"No green stuff," she tentatively observed to Hannah.

Reading Astrid's uncertainty, Hannah said, "Remember, Astrid, the fried rice with chicken and…" she waited for a response.

"Egg rolls. I ate two egg rolls." She turned my head, squeezing my face between her hands, "Lee, they don't have eggs in them. Egg rolls with no eggs. Eggs are for breakfast. No eggs in egg rolls, Lee."

Removing her hands from my face, I thanked her for the clarification.

"Maybe you can take me there sometime."

On a dime, she began to wring her hands, "Do you think Angelo will be mad?"

"No, Astrid," said Hannah. "We'll still eat at Angelo's; he won't mind."

"Okay." Then, sounding like a television advertisement, Astrid announced, "We can eat Chinese at King Kung Pao Chinese Buffet."

"It would be fun to go together, just the two of us," I said with a chuckle. Once again, the serious face glared at me.

"Not without Franklin cause he's a monkey, and I'm a horse. Hannah is a cat."

Confused, I said, "Oh?"

"Chinese zodiac signs." Hannah clarified. "They have placemats."

"I see." Then Astrid informed me that I must go to find out if I was a rat. I asked her for the time.

"Eight-forty-one. Oh! Bedtime!" Right on cue, she ran up the stairs.

A Fine Romance

Hannah gave me the rundown for the week, including one meltdown when Hannah told Astrid to remove her winter coat. The weather was too warm for a wool coat. Hannah gave her an ultimatum. It worked. My curiosity over Franklin waited until Astrid went to bed. Yes, Hannah confirmed her relationship with Franklin! When did this happen, I wondered? She blushed.

"We liked each other because of our mutual love of Astrid. Things evolved from there. When you were gone, Franklin invited us to dinner. He wanted to broaden Astrid's horizons by trying new food. We both knew what might happen. One evening, Franklin brought some fortune cookies and a description of the restaurant to Astrid, using the drawing over the mantel to entice her. The restaurant is full of murals and ornate décor. I didn't take her to the buffet section for fear of overwhelming her. It was alright to take her?"

"Of course, I'm thrilled! You have the magic touch with Astrid. Now about the weekend, I want you to take time off. If not the Regency House, choose anywhere you wish."

"I know there's no changing your mind, so the Regency is fine."

"I'll make a reservation for tomorrow through Monday. I'm bushed. Sleeping in my own bed will be a pleasure. Tomorrow, we can talk about my trip before you leave."

On my way upstairs, I peeked in on Astrid. She slept in her jacket; I didn't have the heart or the energy to wake her.

In Hannah's absence, I desired for us to reconnect. Part of me sensed I was losing her. The first day brought out her anxiety over Hannah. Every few minutes, she stood at the window, wanting to know where Hannah went and if she was coming back. It took much reassurance before the two of us could go anywhere. When I suggested lunch at Angelo's, she asked if he'd be mad at her.

"I ate at the place with the red lanterns and the goldfish. They have egg rolls there. I like egg rolls. They don't have eggs in egg rolls. Will Angelo be mad at me?"

"No, Astie, Angelo won't be upset with you, but let's dress for the spring and not winter. I don't think we need wool trousers and boots today. What could be more suitable?"

A finger tapped against her cheek, her face tilted back, "I dunno."

"Let's have a look." I grasped her hand and we dashed up the steps. On the landing, she dropped my hand, puzzled. "Do you still love me?" she asked.

"I certainly do, Astie. Why do you ask?"

"If you die, will Hannah stay with me? If you die, can I go with you?" I sat on the bed with her.

"Firstly, I'm not going to die any time soon. But yes, Hannah will take care of you. And no, you couldn't go with me if I died. Why all of these questions?"

"Hannah says everyone dies. If you die and Hannah dies, I'll be alone. Who will watch me?"

"One of us will always be with you, Astie. You will never be without someone who loves you. Mrs. Mary taught me not to worry about what might happen; she said, 'think about what is happening now'." I held her hand, "This isn't worth worrying over, Astie. Let's pick out your clothes, then you can help me pick out my clothes."

Astrid stood with the wardrobe opened, hands folded to her chest, rocking from side to side. I knew she couldn't decide.

"It's a sunny day. What do you like to wear in sunny weather?" I prompted.

"Can I wear my jeans and jacket with the pins?"

"Good choice, what shirt?"

Astrid turned pointed her finger at me, "No tee shirts, Lee. No tee shirts."

"Yes, I know. After twenty-three years, I know, no tee shirts."

"Is my birthday soon, Lee?"

"May is six weeks away, Astie," anticipating her next question. "It's on your planner. You'll be thirty-three."

"I'm old. Thirty-three is old, Lee; when did I get old? I'm old, Lee."

"Astie, you are not old; thirty-three is not old. I'm turning thirty-three this year. I'm not old."

"Thirty-three is old."

"Okay, whatever you say. Get dressed and meet me downstairs."

I forgot how tiring she could be. Or maybe I was getting old.

"It's Monday!" Astrid yelled, running down the stairs.

"Astie, use your indoor voice, please."

Both her palms slammed down on the table's edge, "Where's Hannah? It's Monday. Where's Hannah?"

"Take a breath and sit down. Hannah will be coming back this afternoon."

"I want her to come back now," she whined.

"Do you want a time out before breakfast?"

Her head dropped, peeking from under her fringe, "No."

"Then stop whining; she's coming back. Do you know what we're doing at two o'clock?"

In a low groan came her answer, "Dr. Davis."

"Hannah is going with us. Now, eat your breakfast."

"Hannah likes me." She shook her head from shoulder to shoulder, "I don't kiss her good night. My good night cheek-kiss is for you. Girls shouldn't kiss on the lips. It's bad manners, Lee."

For a second, I got paranoid. "No, girls shouldn't kiss other girls on the lips."

Astrid licked her finger, picking up the crumbs from her scones, "Only boys, Lee. I don't want to kiss boys. Boys are mean and smell bad." She shook her head. "I don't want to kiss boys. Hannah kissed Franklin. I saw Hannah kiss Franklin on the lips."

Well, now! That's new. I asked Astrid what she thought about that.

"Franklin is her boyfriend, Lee. It's okay. It was a short goodbye kiss. Hannah said it was okay if they kissed a little. It was yucky. I don't want to kiss boys, and girls shouldn't kiss on the lips. Right, Lee?"

Now I really felt guilty about Lyndon. I answered, "That's right, Astrid."

Astrid sat in the chair knitting while I did my laundry in the basement with the door locked. Astrid pounded on the door, scaring me.

"Open the door, Lee! Hannah's home!"

"I'll be up in a minute." I heard Hannah tell Astrid not to squeeze her so hard. I walked upstairs and remarked on how rested she looked and inquired if she had eaten yet. "I thought we could have dinner at Angelo's later. Do you remember our appointment at two? Then perhaps a stroll at The Backs."

"Oh, yes," agreed Hannah, "the spring is a lovely time to go there the daffodils and tulips are in bloom. I'll bring my camera. Could we stop at the Photoshop before dinner? I want to pick up some prints I took while you were away."

"No problem."

The Appointment

After seeing Dr. Davis, I asked Hannah to wait in the hallway with Astrid so I could speak with him alone.

"I wanted to speak with you about Hannah. She and Astrid are pals now, which I find very comforting. I trust her, or I wouldn't have gone to Florida. My estate will go into a trust when I pass, allowing Hannah to take ownership of the house. She'll continue to be paid a reduced salary, inheriting everything else from me with conditions. She must continue to keep Astrid's appointments with you. You, in turn, will send a confirmation to my estate financial manager with confirmation. Please take note of her appearance, as well as behavior."

"Let me stop you, Lee. Is everything all right with you?"

"Of course, Doctor. A few months ago, you asked if I planned for Astrid's care. I'm telling you what has been planned, that's all. When I die, you will receive a detailed document from my lawyer outlining everything. I imagine you'll want a copy as part of her treatment plan?"

"Yes, that would be appreciated. Lee, are you sleeping well?" He questioned me the way my mother used to.

"Everyone seems concerned about me. Since the trip, fatigue has plagued me. I've only been back a few days; I'm sure it's jet lag."

"That's not what I asked. Are you sleeping well?"

"I suppose not. My sleep is unusually restless," I confessed.

"Are you in pain?"

Slow to answer, "I have muscle aches sometimes," quick to add, "It's rare."

"I suggest you get a check-up. I know how you hate pills, but I'm prescribing a sedative, a mild one, Lee. Try it for a week; if you don't like it, stop taking it."

A sigh escaped me as I gave in. Dr. Davis asked that I keep him posted. I said I would. Exiting the office, an impatient Astrid guffed, "Can we go now? Did you know ducks shouldn't eat bread, Hannah?"

"Is everything all right, Lee?" asked Hannah.

"Yes, you and Astrid go along. I need to run an errand. I'll meet you at Angelo's around five, and here's money for feed and a taxi. I'll see you at five, Astie," I said, hugging her as she concentrated on the watch face. I'd need to answer Hannah's questions later, a task I dreaded.

From across the street through Angelo's picture window, I stopped to watch the two musketeers talking in a booth facing the street, a lovely moment.

As soon as Astrid saw me, I was greeted with, "I peed! No accidents, Lee."

I complimented her on the achievement. Hannah buried her face in her arm to keep from laughing out loud.

"Three glasses of red wine, Leo, please." He winked at me. Over dinner, Hannah asked about my trip. I hit the highlights but left out the job offer. If Astrid heard about it, she'd, as the kids say, freak out.

"Astrid tells me you and Franklin are an item." Hannah blushed then, with her mouth full; Astrid butted in, "No, they're not an item, silly, they are boyfriend and girlfriend, Lee." She said it with wide eyes, sauce at the corners of her mouth, glaring with one of her *you're an idiot* expression. All I could do was roll my eyes.

"Um, yes, we're dating, I guess. I hope it's okay."

I whispered, "Just don't run away and get married."

Wrong choice of words for the ever-listening Astrid. A thousand reassurances were given to her; Hannah was not running away. Thank God it was time to leave when Astrid kept repeating the television schedule.

I promised as we walked home, "We'll make it home for *Coronation Street*." Hannah held her hand, walking ahead. They were like Astrid and me when we were young. In the back of my mind, I wished I'd never grown up.

After Astrid had gone to bed, I recounted my offer from NASA. Hannah sat flabbergasted, "I don't know what I would do, Lee. I mean, if I were you."

"Well, it's clear I could never take that job. Moving to the United States is simply out of the question. I didn't hesitate to say no. It caught me totally off guard; I felt flattered. But you know I couldn't leave England." Then I laughed, "Besides, the food is terrible there."

The mood changed; Hannah asked me whereabouts I'd gone while they were at the park. Shifting about, Hannah said, "I'm too nosy. I shouldn't have asked."

The jet lag, I alluded. "Dr. Davis prescribed a sleeping pill. It's mild. Take it for a few nights. I'll be back to work on Wednesday." I said my goodnight.

Until I uttered those words, I hadn't realized how much I didn't want to return to work. A breeze fluttered through my open window as I lay in my bed, the moon-illuminated clouds rolling by; I waited for the pill to kick in.

| 42 |

What Was and What Is

"I know, Lyndon, and I'm sorry. Another week off, and I'll be fine." Convincing her remained extremely difficult; she knew me too well.

Downstairs, Hannah brewed coffee, and the smell of bacon wafted through the air. The sound of cartoons and a giggly Astrid brought a smile.

"I thought you were going to work." Hannah noticed my attire wasn't my usual business dress.

Trying to sound upbeat, "My vacation days seem to multiply to over thirty. I'm taking another week off. Has Astrid mentioned her birthday lately?"

Hannah chuckled, "Yes, I doubt you'll want to get this particular item."

"It couldn't be worse than the elephant she wanted a few years ago. Out with it, what does she want?"

"A purple bicycle."

I dropped into my chair, "Really, a bicycle? What brought that on?"

Hannah described a trip to the park where children took a bicycle safety course. She said Astrid's expression was intense.

"Turning to me, Astrid asked if I knew how to ride a bike. I said yes. To wit, she asked if I could teach her. Astonished, I said yes."

The mental image of those two riding bikes did my heart good. Hannah opened new horizons to Astrid; this gave me renewed hope. "Do you think she can ride, Hannah? Be honest."

"It would be worth a try. I'd keep my hands on not letting her fall. Before you decide, there's a bike rental stand we could try."

"You are so very kind to her, Hannah. I love you for how you treat Astrid."

"Astrid gives me a sense of purpose and joy, Lee." Hannah took my hand, "You gave me my life back, Lee."

I cleared my throat from the lump inside. Hannah turned away from me to pour coffee.

Hard shoes on the wooden stairs, Astrid ran to make her grand entrance, "I'm hungry. Can I please have my scones now?"

"Yes, you may, Astie. Wash your hands."

Arms outstretched, palms close to my face, "See, no dirt. There's no dirt on my hands."

"Be nice and wash your hands, please and thank you."

She stomped into Hannah's bathroom, grumbling. The water was running; wise to her tricks, I said, "Show me your hands." With that guilty expression, head tilted up, she kept her hands behind her back.

Astrid started for the bedroom; I pointed to the kitchen sink, "With the hand soap, Astrid. You should know by now, no cheeky business with me." In silence, she washed her hands. Hannah handed her the towel.

"Coffee, Lee," asked Hannah. This morning, I passed on breakfast and went upstairs to dress. The ceiling fan whirled above my head; I had an errand to run. Before leaving, I suggested a trip to Milton Country Park. Astrid got excited and ran to Hannah's bathroom, then I heard an *oh no*. I cringed.

"I'll take care of her, Lee. Off with you; enjoy your day."

I wanted to visit the Royal Botanical Gardens for a deep reflection today. It gave peace of mind to my chaotic brain.

On my return, the house seemed awfully quiet. Then I heard, "Lee's home, tell her, tell her!"

Astrid stormed down the stairs with Hannah in tow.

"Astie, Hannah is not a rag doll. Stop pulling on her."

"Sorry!" Astrid pointed to her skinned-up knees with a smile on her face, "Tell her, Hannah, tell her."

A grin broke across Hannah's face, "Astrid had a mishap."

"Not that part, Hannah, the other part."

"Astrid rode a bicycle today, all by herself. It was a shaky start, but she rode in a circle and partway down the bike trail."

"So quickly! Oh, Astie, I'm so proud of you."

Swaying back and forth, the ceiling received a smile, "Hannah and I can ride in the park tomorrow if it doesn't rain. Isn't that right, Hannah? We can go tomorrow."

"If it's okay with Lee."

"Of course, it's okay. Astie, I want you to write a birthday wish list. Hannah can help you after dinner."

"Is it my birthday next week?"

"No, in two weeks."

"Am I three-three?" asked Astrid, holding up three fingers.

"Yes, you'll be thirty-three." My heart sighed. Twenty-two years yesterday we were walking on the beach and watching the stars.

The shepherd's pie sat in my dish staring at me; I had no appetite. Hannah warned Astrid to chew slowly before swallowing, just as I had a million times.

"You've barely touched your food, Lee" The concern in Hannah's voice was unmistakable.

I blew her off by telling her I ate a big lunch. "I'll be upstairs; I have some work to do. Astie, tell me goodnight."

Astrid did a double-take at her watch; indignant, she said, "It's not bedtime. I don't go to bed at seven o'clock. Seven o'clock is *Coronation Street*."

I smiled. "I know, your bedtime is nine, but I'm going upstairs to shower and work on some papers before bed."

"Okay."

"Cheek kiss?" Astrid ran at me, gripping the chair. I braced myself. A quick kiss, then back to the sofa for her show.

On my home from the bus stop, Lyndon's car sat in front of the house. No longer could I avoid her. Lyndon stepped out as I approached. She leaned against the car, stone-faced, arms crossed over her chest. Without making eye contact, she stared ahead, "It's been a week, and we need to talk. I need to know what's going on with you. No more cryptic messages, Lee. I mean it."

Robotically, I spoke, "Tomorrow is Astrid's birthday. I can't talk until Sunday, Lyndon. Can I come to your place?"

"I know something's wrong. I saw the bruises."

I stopped her, "No one's hurt. It's difficult; I promise to come over on Sunday at any rate. Now, please, don't ask me anything right now."

"Alright, I'll come by at eleven to get you. No excuses, Lee."

"No excuses, Lyndon."

Under cover of night, the delivery truck stopped in the alley. While Hannah supervised Astrid's shower, I opened the back gate. A lorry from the sporting goods store brought two bikes; I covered them with an old blanket. A helmet wrapped in purple gift paper was hidden in Hannah's closet. What Hannah didn't know was that next to Astrid's bike stood a dark blue bike for her. For two weeks, Hannah had rented bicycles for the two of them; now they'd have their own

Tomorrow was a big day for Astrid; concentrating on her special birthday pushed other concerns off my mind. After drying Astrid's hair, Hannah came down with the brush. "She will not let me braid her hair because it's your job tonight."

"All right. Hand me the brush."

I slowly trudged to Astrid's room where she waited on the bed.

"So, I have the honor of braiding the beautiful maiden's hair tonight." Astrid cocked her head to one side with a huh.

"I'm not a maiden; I'm a girl. Please braid French braids for my birthday. Is tomorrow my birthday?"

"Yes, silly, your birthday is tomorrow."

In the vanity mirror, a glum face reflected, "Am I old, Lee? I don't want to be old. When you're old, you die. I don't want to die."

"Oh, Astie, you're not old."

"I like to ride bikes with Hannah, Lee."

"Hold still, please. Yes, Luv, it's good exercise."

"Yes! Good exercise. Fat people don't ride bikes."

"Astrid, please, sit still. I'm almost to the end."

When I finished, Astrid got her vitamin and a glass of water; holding her pill between her fingers, she said, "This isn't a vitamin, Lee. It's a pill to calm everyone's nerves."

Shocked, I said, "Is it now? Who told you this?"

"Nobody, I just know it."

"Well, Astie, you're wrong. It's a pill to help you sleep. I take one, also."

Shock and disbelief were not in her repertoire of emotions until now when her eyes grew wide and her jaw dropped.

"It's true, Astie, I need help, too. So, take your pill, and say goodnight."

"Down the hatch!" she called, then jumped into bed.

On the edge of the bed, I sat, "Astie, don't ever forget how much I love you."

"Okay, Lee. I won't," she said, pulling her cover over her.

A purple, wrapped box sat on the kitchen table in the morning, waiting for Astrid. We heard her stirring upstairs. Hannah and I looked at each other, all smiles. Clomp, clomp, clomp, in her normal trot, still in her pajamas, she stopped, puzzled by the box.

Astrid examined the box, hand on her chin like Grandfather used to do. "Whose purple box is that?"

"Happy Birthday, Astie. Go on, open it."

Tediously, she pulled the tape off. It took her five minutes as we sat in anticipation. I wanted to say, *get on with it*, but sighed a deep sigh. Hannah glared at her.

Astrid's eyes narrowed as she glanced at Hannah. Agitated, she fired, "I couldn't tear the paper, Hannah." Every birthday, every holiday, not tearing the paper came from an impoverished childhood. I informed Hannah how Astrid grew up in a home where everything had to be reused. Some memories are imprinted in our brains.

"Is it a hat? It doesn't look like a hat." Astrid banged her knuckles on the hard surface. "It's hard."

Hannah played a guessing game with Astrid, asking if she had seen a helmet like this before.

Tapping that long index finger to her cheek, "I dunno. Am I supposed to wear it? I don't like it. It's not a nice present."

"Just a minute, Astie, someone else needs one like it." Astrid's forehead puckered, "It's not a nice present, Hannah. It's too hard."

I returned with another unwrapped box, a blue helmet.

"This is for Hannah."

In a mean voice, Astrid said, "You gave Hannah one of those."

"Calm down, Astie, give me your hand. I want to show you something. Hannah, too."

Hannah followed us to the back lawn.

"What are those, Lee, dirty covers?" Astrid pointed to the old covers thrown over the bikes.

"Pull the cover off, don't be shy," I urged. Tentative, Astrid uncovered the bike. Both her hands covered her mouth like a Japanese fan. Once before, I'd seen that expression, the first time she sat at my piano.

Astrid jerked her head around, "Is that for Hannah?"

"No, the purple one is yours. Hannah, the other one is for you."

Astrid pulled the cover off the blue one and grabbed Hannah's hand, jumping up and down and squealing with delight. Hannah handed me the camera. Capturing memories, the excitement of an eleven-year-old with a new bike.

Hands clapping, jumping around, Astrid begged to ride.

"Finish your breakfast, change into your pedal-pushers, and then you and Hannah can go down to the Cambridge paths. I have knee pads, Astrid. You'll wear your helmet and knee pads. Understood?"

"Yes, Lee, yes, yes, yes!"

"I'm very grateful. Thank you, Lee," Hannah said humbly.

I put my hand on top of hers, "She couldn't ride without you."

Astrid flew down the stairs, hands flapping with a high screeching laugh.

"Before you go, Astie, I want to be clear, no bike riding without Hannah, ever. Clear?" Astrid jumped around with ants in her pants. "Repeat what I just said, Astie."

"I want to go now," she whined. My hand gripped the backdoor handle; my eyes narrowed. I gave her a hard glare.

Giving in, she said, "No riding without Hannah. I already peed. Can we go now?" I opened the door, handing Hannah the bike locks. A tall, lanky sixth-grade Astrid Innis stood before me, bike helmet, and knee pads, in a state of excitement I hadn't witnessed for a very long time. A wild head shake caused the helmet to slip over her eyes. Pushing it back, she smiled at me, directly into my eyes. Her green lollipop eyes shined. For a moment, I saw into her heart, her golden heart. After twenty-two years, I understood how much she loved me. The feeling came and left quickly as Astrid and Hannah left.

At the table, I lay my head on my arms and wept. So many years of pent-up tears. They could only fall in silence where no one could see. Exhausted, I pulled on the handrail upstairs to the bed.

The backdoor shut to Astrid's primal moaning.

From my room, I called, "Is everything okay, Hannah?"

"Nothing that a shower and bandages won't fix."

Oh, God. I hurried down to find Astrid's elbow being tended to by Hannah. She made it home only to catch her arm on the gate. Whimpering, Astrid told me she didn't fall.

"Not even once, Lee," she said through her tears. I loosened the chin strap. Removing her helmet, Hannah said, "Franklin's meeting us at Angelo's at six, Astie. Why don't you take a shower and rest? Later we'll get ready for Angelo's."

She took Hannah's hand, "Okay. Come on, Hannah."

I watched them go upstairs. Alone in the living room, I stared at the print over the fireplace. I whispered, "Whose holding up the moon, Astrid? No one." Only the embers lit the room; I faced a great sadness.

Hannah helped Astrid dress in her favorite puffy-sleeved blouse and paisley print skirt.

"See," Astrid stuck her face in front of mine, "Hannah put make-up on me. I have on make-up."

"I see. You are very grown-up, Astie."

Astrid's honest assessment of me came out, an assessment I denied. "You look sick, Lee. Are you sick?"

"I'm fine, Astie. Let's go to Angelo's."

The food stared at me from the plate. I tried my darndest to eat half of my portion of ravioli. I failed. By now, Hannah knew something amiss. I saw Franklin's concern.

"Not now, Hannah," I said quietly. After cake and ice cream, Franklin drove us home. With birthday hugs and kisses, Hannah and Astrid disappeared upstairs.

"You're not well, Lee. I can see sickness in you. The bruises on." I cut him off. "It will pass, Franklin."

"And if it doesn't? Have you been to the doctor, Lee?"

In a firm voice, I stated, "I am under a doctor's care, Franklin. It will pass, and everything will be fine. Thank you for being concerned."

Hannah joined us. Smiling, she said, "As soon as her head hit the pillow, she was out." Seeing Franklin's face, her smile faded, "What's…?"

"I need to clarify matters of my health; I am seeing a physician. My appetite has waned from the medicine I've been given. The doctor says it will pass; that's all to be said for now. It's a lovely night; feel free to enjoy a glass of wine and sit outside. I'm going off to bed."

Promptly at eleven on Sunday, a car drove up and stopped. Lyndon waited for me.

"I'm off to Lyndon's. I will be back later, how late I don't know. Don't wait up. Astie, give me a hug."

Lyndon stood by the car when I walked out of the house. "I thought I might have to come in and get you."

"I'm here; let's go." My eyes focused on the road ahead, thinking about what to say. There was no one else to tell the truth to, only Lyndon.

Lyndon's house was whiter, the flowers brighter; why was everything so alive when I was crumbling inside?

| 43 |

The Truth

"You're shivering, Lee. Here's a blanket." Desperate for answers, Lyndon sat close, "I need to know, Lee. You're always fatigued and losing weight. When you started taking time off, it wasn't like you."

With a deep inhale and slow exhale, "I understand. I used the excuse it was just jet lag. My blood work came back with a gut punch right before our Florida trip. I refused to let it stop me then. When we returned, I felt worse, and I knew."

"During the day, I began to hurt just walking or sitting. I always felt sick to my stomach. Last week's check-up revealed a highly elevated white blood cell count. I knew what was coming. I was dying."

"There's chemotherapy, Lee." Lyndon bent forward, hands clasped in front of her, "Does it have a name?"

"Chronic lymphocytic leukemia."

Lyndon straightened up, "Leukemia is treatable. It's not a death sentence, Lee."

I couldn't look her in the eye. "It's too late for chemotherapy. I have less than six weeks tops."

In denial, Lyndon rattled off, "That's not possible, Lee. You must have more time. You can have more tests."

"Over the last two months, I've taken every test, all with the same results. Lymphocytic is the most aggressive type of leukemia, Lyndon. For months I was in denial. It's too late for treatment. A week ago, I told Hannah I was staying overnight in Brighton. Instead, it was making arrangements for end-stage life with hospice. I met my lawyer the next day to update my will."

Walking to the window, her eyes fixed on her beautiful garden.

"I'm going to die soon, Lyndon."

A heaving sigh came from my stalwart Lyndon. I had never seen her in pain before. Teary-eyed, she shook her head. "Why? Why is this happening to you of all people?" She paused to sit by me, pulling me to her chest, "I will not leave you to die alone."

Pushing her away, I countered, "No, I don't want you to watch this happen to me. I don't want anyone to stand at my deathbed."

Voicing worry, "What about Astrid? What will you say to her?"

"She has Hannah now. Hannah has Franklin. I'm at peace knowing they will take excellent care of Astrid. Hannah and Franklin know I'm ill but don't know to what extent."

"But, Astrid," Lyndon's fearfulness wasn't unwarranted.

"I have a room in hospice at The Cancer Center of London. I plan to tell my Astie soon. I can barely make it up the stairs now."

"How do you plan to tell her, Lee? You have to tell her, you know."

I snapped at her, "Don't you think I haven't thought about this, Lyndon?" My hand covered my face. I broke down.

Warm hands cradled my head as I wept. We both wept.

"I love her. She has been the only constant factor in my life." I blew my nose and regained some semblance of composure. I continued, "By divine providence, you pushed me to get help none too soon. The first month Hannah moved in turned out to be terribly difficult for me. I'd never found a reason to allow anyone to get close to Astrid. Relinquishing control to Hannah was worse than divorcing John and disappointing my mother."

"My poor Lee," muttered Lyndon.

Through tears, I chuckled. "Now those two are inseparable. Hannah taught Astrid to ride a bike, Lyndon, something I would have never done. And Astrid now likes Chinese food. No, I'm very comfortable knowing my Astie will be taken care of now. With Hannah being ten years younger than Astrid, she'll…" I couldn't say any more.

"Can I make you tea?"

"Yes, I'd like that." Puffy white clouds dotted the azure sky out of the living room window. Over tea, I related Astrid's vision of heaven, somewhere in the sky.

"Astrid and I have nicknames for one another. Both of us were misfits in the sixth grade," I laughed. "At age eleven, we knew we were different than the other children. Astrid's family lived in a poverty-stricken area. I lived near the sea in a big, lovely white house with a thatched roof with my mother and grandfather." I recounted our story. "Astra and Luna, forever together, no matter where we were. Now there'll be no moon in her sky." Once again, I started to blubber.

"Let it out, baby. There's no pretending to be strong in my house, Lee. And remember the moon is always there, even when we don't see it." I nodded. Those were the same words I spoke to Astrid once. "I made lamb stew. I'm guessing you can't eat right now."

"Maybe later."

"Do you want to lie on the sofa for a little while?"

Spent emotions took their toll on me; haggard, I said yes to her offer. Later, the sound of a crackling fire woke me. On the floor next to me, Lyndon stroked my hair. A melancholy smile sat upon her face. I took her hand and kissed it.

"A blessing bestowed on me came in the form of Lyndon Hammersmith. You're my rock, my lover and my friend. You can kiss me if you want to." She did.

"Like it or not, I'm not letting you die alone. The thought of you dying alone in a deserted room would haunt me for all eternity."

My hand touched her cheek as I gazed deep into her blue eyes. "I give in. I'll sit down with Hannah and Astrid tomorrow. I'll tell Astrid

I'm not well and will go away for a few days. Astrid has no sense of time; a few days are easily lost track of."

"Are you sure that's what you want her to know, nothing more?"

"For now, yes. The longer I live, the worse I'll become. I don't want Astrid to remember me in sickness, wasting away like a ghost." Before Lyndon could object, I added, "I should go home now."

The lamb stew Lyndon packed for Astrid and Hannah. She hoped I'd eat too. My sense of smell had left me, along with the pleasure of eating. Lyndon made me promise to let her take me to the cancer center when the time came.

The next morning, I sat down with my girls. It was time.

"Will you be gone a long time?" asked Astrid.

"Maybe a week or two," I smiled through my pain.

"You're sick, aren't you, Lee?" Astrid acted like a prosecuting barrister. "You're sick. I know you're sick, Lee. You lost the meat on your bones."

"Yes, Astie, I'm not well. I don't want you to worry about me. This spring weather is a beautiful time to ride your bicycle with Hannah."

"And feed the ducks! Don't feed ducks bread. It's bad for them, very, very bad."

"Hannah tells me you're going with Franklin to play piano in a special room."

She raised up off her chair. "Yes, it's called a…" her words came out like a taffy pull, "studio—with no people. Just Franklin and me, nobody else." Astrid's eyes widened, and like a baseball umpire making a safe call, her arms cut through the air, "No people!"

"I got it, just the two of you playing music. Are you playing your music or someone else's?" I asked.

Each word, punctuated by jerky movements, "Both. Beethoven and me."

With my permission, Franklin took Astrid to a recording studio in hopes of making an album. As long as Astrid couldn't see the sound engineers through the two-way glass, she was fine. Hannah let me know Franklin would come around ten.

Our barrister, Mr. Easterling, prepared a folder for Hannah and Lyndon with my wishes and legal papers. Signing the guardianship papers for Hannah was the hardest thing I'd ever done. Lyndon was coming to take me downtown.

Astrid stood in her long, flowery dress. Hannah made small braids, pulling Astrid's strawberry blond hair back from Astrid's face, tied with a pink ribbon in the back. Signs of aging alluded her childlike face. Always striking that day she could be on a magazine cover.

"Before Franklin comes, sit by me, Astie." She plopped down, sending shock waves through my weakened body. Thank God she didn't notice my grimace. "Astie, remember when we were children sitting under the stars?"

"Uh-huh, I am the star," she pointed to my heart, "and you are the moon."

In unison, we said, "Forever, together."

"I want to always remember those good days."

Hannah spoke, "Lee, Astrid has something for you."

"For me?"

Astrid wiggled her hand in her pocket, holding out her fist, those long fingers unfurled, revealing a white scallop shell with two names, *Astrid* and *Lenora*.

"It's for you, for good luck to get better, Lee." With what little strength I had, I stood to embrace her. Franklin rang the bell; Astrid turned with a smile, "I'll see you later, Luna."

"Play beautiful music, my Astra."

Crumpling onto the sofa, Hannah came to my aid with a handful of tissues, "When I helped her get ready, I noticed her stick something in her pocket," Hannah's eyes welled with tears. "'It's a present for Lee,' she said."

From tears, my vision blurred as I explained the significance of this shell, the first shell Astrid ever found, a shell hidden in the pocket of each dress she wore to her performances. Clutching it to my chest,

"Now, this shell will see me through to the other side. Hannah, when I... when I die, give it to Astrid. Tell her it brought me to the sky with Grandfather and Mrs. Mary. Tell her the shell is white like the moon. I'll still be with her in the night sky."

Wiping tears on her sleeve, she promised. "Lee, will we see you again? Will you tell Astrid the truth about where you're going?"

"Soon, I promise."

Hannah firmly voiced her concern. "She'll want to know where you are now, Lee."

"Alright, I'll write her a note to say I'm going to rest, and I'll see her soon. You'll reassure her I haven't died. Understand?"

"I don't like it, but I'll tell her."

| 44 |

Forever Together

Heated blankets covered me; I stayed cold even though it was almost summer. I lay down, waiting for the reaper. It wouldn't be long before I saw Mother again. Lyndon visited daily. I didn't want her to, yet she came. On that day, her serious side showed through.

"Hannah sent this letter, Lee." I read silently:

"Dearest Lee,

Astrid asks every day when you're coming home; I couldn't keep telling her, "Soon." Today she wanted to know if you were dying. Lee, Astrid knows. You owe it to her. Please, say goodbye, and she will have an easier time accepting your absence instead of your abandonment. Don't just leave her, Lee. It's cruel. If you don't say goodbye, it will kill her. Astrid already thinks you don't want her anymore.

Hannah

"Read this, Lyndon." As she read, her fingers touched her lips. Her posture straightened. In her professor's voice, she said, "She's right, you know. Astrid will forever think she did something to make you go away. Right now, she's rediscovered music again. If you leave her like this, she will most assuredly decline, Lee. You think you're protecting her; you're not. Hannah sent this, too."

"We watched my mother die in front of our eyes. Astrid withdrew into herself. I can't let that happen again."

Lyndon handed me a photo, "Hannah wanted you to have this."

A photograph of Astrid and I holding hands, walking in the park full of tulips and daffodils, a happy time. I didn't have the energy to cry.

"If she sees me now like this, it's what she'll remember. I don't want that, Lyndon. We watched my mother die. That image of her lying lifeless in the bed burns in my memory."

I gritted my teeth. My body ached, racked with pain. Lyndon sat on the bed, stroking my hair. "I cannot imagine the anguish and pain in your heart, my Luv. You don't want Astrid to see you like this. Having said that, ask yourself if it's better than being lifeless in a coffin."

Without so much as a whimper, the tears I fought came uncontrolled; they ran down my face. Lyndon kissed the top of my head. I laughed through my tears, "The water fountain incident, remember?"

"How could I forget, Lee? When you walked through the door with a wet blouse, seeing me? The expression on your face, Lee, was priceless." Lyndon choked up, "I wanted so many times to tell you."

The nurse came in with my morphine. Lyndon stopped talking. "You may want to wait outside, ma'am," she said to Lyndon. The rush of the morphine often made me retch.

The door pushed open after the nurse left, and Lyndon sat gently on the bed. I pushed my tender bones up, "What did you want me to know? Because you shouldn't have regrets, Lyndon."

"I loved you from that first day, Lee. Your laugh, the sense of wonder, your compassion. Florida memories are the best memories for me. I know you don't feel the same way. I've learned to accept it. And it's alright."

"Oh, but I do love you, Lyndon. I was afraid. If I hadn't been such a prude, who knows? Yet here we are." I kissed her hand and pressed it to my cheek, "You've come every day." Morphine began to have its way with me. "I want to write Hannah a letter. There's paper in the drawer."

"Why don't you tell me what to write? I'll write for you."

The pain medication overtook me. I tried to make sense; the words just weren't there.

A beam of warm morning sun lay over my covers.

"Good morning, Luv." It was Lyndon; she said she spent the night on the fold-out couch. Days and nights drifted in and out. The smell of coffee wafted in my nostrils. Normally, I loved that smell; today it was putrid. Lyndon raised the head of the bed so I could see her.

"Lee," with tension in her voice, she said, "I love you, but you will be cross with me." A gush of air blew from her nose, "Hannah's bringing Astrid up this afternoon."

"Up where?"

"Here, around two."

I wasn't angry, only defeated.

Lyndon sat at the foot of my bed, her words rushing out, "Lee, you have every right to be unhappy with me. I didn't honor your wish because it's unfair to Astrid and…"

Not letting her finish, I waved her off. My speech was labored. "Hand me my hat; I'm finished. You're right; it's selfish. Hannah is right." My breath caught in my throat; I stopped breathing after each sentence. "I don't want to die. It's this giant wave rolling in from the sea. Nothing can stop it; it's coming for me. And yes, I yearn to see my Astie, to tell her I love her, and she will be fine." In brief detail, I recalled my conversation with Astrid only a month ago when she talked about death. Lyndon's warm lips caressed my forehead, and I mustered a smile.

I can't recall what happened after that. I woke up with an oxygen tube blowing air up my nose. Lyndon noticed my panicked eyes as she held my hand, "You're fine now. For a minute, I thought I had lost you. Thank God, you only needed some air."

"Astrid?"

"It's a quarter past one. They'll be along soon."

As a crushing pain shot through me, my lips pushed tight against each other. I squeezed Lyndon's hand. I panted with an exhale, "I thought with all the morphine… I'm sorry, Lyndon."

"It's okay. Like you tell Astrid, just breathe deep."

She started to hug me then stopped, knowing even the slightest touch brought pain to this weak excuse of a body. My veined hands were loose flesh hanging from the bones. I thought of my mother and what she endured, lingering far longer than I would.

"I want to sit in the chair, not lie in bed before they come."

"Absolutely not, you're too weak," said a nurse who unhooked the morphine drip. "But we'll change your gown, sweetie." My arms and legs had stopped working; I was at their mercy. Again, they insisted I stay in bed. Lyndon raised the bed to gently brush my hair.

"I hope you and Hannah prepared Astrid for a skeleton."

"Lee, you don't look as bad as you think. You don't look like a skeleton."

She assured me they talked with Astrid for a few minutes every day. I heard Hannah outside my door giving Astrid last-minute instructions, then a knock.

"May we come in?" asked Hannah.

I motioned for Lyndon to open the door.

Subdued, Astie gently called, "Hi, Leelee. I brought you flowers to cheer you up." She held a bouquet of daisies and roses at me. Leelee was a name from ages ago. She called me that when she was afraid of losing me to John. Now she was losing me to the Grim Reaper.

"They're beautiful, just like you."

Timidly, Astrid said, "Can I sit on your bed?"

I smiled, giving her permission. No one knew what to say.

"I'd like to be with Astrid alone, please."

Astrid studied my face, asking why I had a tube on my face.

"Do you hurt?"

"Yes, but I have medicine." I patted the bed. She kicked off her shoes to lay beside me face-to-face, softly speaking. "They told me you were going to die, that you didn't look like yourself. You're skinny, but you are still my moon, Leelee. As you said, we'll be forever together. Isn't that right?"

"That's right, Astie. I'll soon be gone where you can't go right now, but I'll always be with you, right here." I touched her chest.

"I'm sad, Lee."

"It's okay to be sad sometimes, Astie."

"Are you sad, Lee?"

"Yes, but remember what Hannah told you? We will all die at some time. Some sooner than others."

"Like Grandfather and Mrs. Mary. You'll see them soon. Hannah told me. Will you tell Mrs. Mary I make pretty blankets? And tell Grandfather I'm playing the piano again?"

I managed a smile. "I'm sure they know, but I will tell them." Together, in the same bed, like children huddled under the covers. I pushed a strand of hair behind her ear. I asked if she felt scared.

"No," she whispered. "Hannah said she's staying with me until I go to heaven. Lyndon promised to take me to Angelo's; Franklin will come, too." With a nod, she said, "I want Franklin to marry Hannah."

With a grin on my face, "Maybe they will someday."

"Hannah takes me to church every morning. I light a candle for you and pray. When are you going to heaven, Lee?"

"Soon, Astie."

"You know an angel will come to get you; you don't have to go by yourself. Some angels don't have wings." Astie pointed to the window, "They float in the clouds of heaven. Are we taking you to Dublin by Mrs. Mary?"

"No. Do you remember when Grandfather died? We buried him in Brighton at the churchyard in the countryside. I want to be buried by him."

"So, you can be by him?"

"Yes."

"Can I be next to you when I die?"

"Of course you can." My words grew tired. I needed to say one more thing, "Sit up, Astie, I want to give you something." I drew my hand from under the cover, "I want you to promise me you'll keep playing the piano. I can hear music in heaven, you know."

Astrid's head bobbed up and down. My fingers unfolded, revealing the shell, our shell. Thanks to Lyndon, our names were lightly engraved on the inside. Astrid, who rarely cried, bawled tears of sorrow; her finger wrapped around the white shell. Her arm covered her eyes. My heart was breaking with my last tears.

The door opened a crack, and I saw Hannah leaning against the door. I caught my breath and whispered, "Astie, look at me." With her beautiful green lollipop eyes, she made eye contact. "Even though I'll be gone, I'll never stop loving you. But I want you to live a good life with Hannah. Together, you'll ride bikes, feed the ducks, in winter, and make a snowman. She's going to take good care of you, Astie."

Astrid sniffled, blew her nose, and wiped tears on her sleeve. "Okay, Lee."

Her hand carefully swept my hair from my forehead; Astie kissed my brow ever so gently. Then in a voice of clarity, mature and wise, Astrid sat up, "You aren't leaving me forever, you know." She pointed up, "I'll look up in the sky at night. You are Luna, and I am your Astra, forever together. Isn't that right, Lee?"

"Yes, Astra and Luna, forever together."

EPILOGUE

Franklin and Astrid worked on their first studio album. At age forty, she made her second album of original music in a full-stage recording studio with an orchestra. She was a worldwide success. Piles of letters and children's drawings flooded in every day. She loved getting pictures and drawing from people. The foreign stamps always caught her attention. Astrid gained recognition for her work on the album and won a Grammy award. Of course, she refused to fly. At her insistence, Franklin accepted the award on her behalf. We politely declined offers to play in person, she would never play in public. Astrid began work on another symphony and rode her bike with me.

Franklin and I were married a year later with no plans for children. We cared for Astrid. Astrid still talked to Lee every night before her prayers. Shortly before her forty-fifth birthday, Astrid went to bed and never woke up. She found her resting place in Brighton next to Lee. On an adjoining headstone, we had engraved, *Astra and Luna, forever together again*.

Hannah Johnson Godfrey

ABOUT THE AUTHOR

Wendy Eastman

By birth, an Indiana Hoosier but a Southern girl at heart, Wendy Eastman attended Wesleyan College in Macon, Georgia, earning a bachelor's degree in theatre production. After graduation, a desire to travel prompted her to do something unexpected. She joined the Army. She gained a global perspective on life as a photographer stationed in Frankfurt, Germany. This career allowed her to travel through Europe during an exciting time. She even chipped off a piece of the fallen Berlin wall in 1989.

Her love of writing started in high school, keeping her writing a secret. As she grew older, she hid a journal which helped her through some trying times. Elements of her own life are often woven into the characters she creates.

Wendy received the Dr. Tom Maddox Award, the highest honor for service to students in the Owensboro Kentucky Public Schools, for her work as a Global Classroom Instructor. The program connected kindergarten through fourth grade in collaborative classrooms from nine countries, including Australia, Botswana, India, Ireland, and Singapore. The State Department chose six educators from the United States to attend an international workshop at Columbia University in New York. Wendy became one of the six chosen.

She moved back to her home state of Indiana, where she began working in mental health. Wendy has further studies in psychology at the University of Southern Indiana, where she was inducted into Psi Chi, the National Honor Society for Psychology.

Wendy is a proud mother of adult children. Her son Kevin is an Afghanistan veteran living in Wisconsin with his wife; they enjoy camping and riding motorcycles with other veterans. Her daughter Lucy is a former champion of rhythmic gymnasts and is an award-winning choreographer. She lives in Kentucky with her husband and sons.

Wendy is also an award-winning artist. Now retired, she is a world traveler who enjoys music and NFL football. Her home is the town of Berea, Kentucky, an arts-oriented community.

www.ingramcontent.com/pod-product-compliance
Lightning Source LLC
LaVergne TN
LVHW011942060526
838201LV00061B/4179